THE POLITICS OF PRESIDENTIAL APPOINTMENTS

THE POLITICS OF
PRESIDENTIAL APPOINTMENTS

POLITICAL CONTROL AND
BUREAUCRATIC PERFORMANCE

David E. Lewis

PRINCETON UNIVERSITY PRESS   PRINCETON AND OXFORD

Library of Congress Cataloging-in-Publication Data

Lewis, David E., 1970–
The politics of presidential appointments : political control
and bureaucratic performance / David E. Lewis.
    p.   cm.
Includes bibliographical references and index.
ISBN 978-0-691-13342-3 (hardcover : alk. paper)
ISBN 978-0-691-13544-1 (pbk. : alk. paper)
1. United States—Officials and employees—Selection and appointment.
2. Government executives—Selection and appointment—United States.
3. Presidents—United States. 4. Patronage, Political—United States.
5. Administrative agencies—United States—Management. 6. United States—
Politics and government. I. Title.
JK731.L49 2008
352.6′5—dc22   2007038761

British Library Cataloging-in-Publication Data is available

This book has been composed in Baskerville Typeface

Printed on acid-free paper. ∞

press.princeton.edu

Printed in the United States of America

10   9   8   7   6   5   4   3   2   1

For Saskia

Contents

Illustrations _____

Figures

Tables

Acknowledgments

THIS PROJECT has been under construction since the fall of 2003. Early on in this process I reread Hugh Heclo's *A Government of Strangers*. I thought to myself, "If I ever write a book this good in my career, I will really have accomplished something." I am not sure I have ever met Heclo but my hat goes off to him.

The research was supported by resources provided Larry Bartels and the Center for the Study of Democratic Politics, the Woodrow Wilson School of Public and International Affairs, Princeton's Department of Politics, and the Princeton University Committee on Research in the Humanities and Social Sciences. The Office of Personnel Management, the Office of Management and Budget, and the Partnership for Public Service all generously provided data. British Morrison at OPM and Rachel Goldstein at the Partnership were particularly helpful. None of these people or organizations had to help me but all did, at their own expense. This book would not have been possible without their generosity.

A number of people working in the nation's service gave generously of their time and insights. Republicans and Democrats, I found them to be smart, capable, and generally good natured. Each took on average one hour from their busy schedules to help me understand personnel politics better. I came away from my conversations with them with a real appreciation for just how capable our government's executives are and I am grateful for their service to our country.

Throughout this project I have benefited from my interactions with a number of very bright Princeton undergraduates. Melissa Collins, Carra Glatt, and Michael Shapiro helped collect the data for the Federal Human Capital Survey analysis and helped me track down information for the book. Michael Reilly was instrumental in collecting the background materials necessary for me to write the case studies of the Office of Personnel Management and Federal Emergency Management Agency. Rob Schimmel and Matt Sullivan wrote two excellent senior theses on FEMA and the Department of Homeland Security. Conversations with these two bright undergraduates helped shape my thinking on what went wrong in FEMA. One of the great privileges of being a professor is to be able to work with these students. I look forward to seeing what wonderful things they will do in the future.

I am indebted to my wonderful colleagues at Princeton. Doug Arnold helped me understand the grant-writing process early on and read the

whole manuscript, about half of it twice. He has been a consistent source
of both inspiration and encouragement. Fred Greenstein read parts of
the manuscript, recommended useful sources, and helped polish and
refine its prose. He sought me out with the goal of being a help and
mentor and he has succeeded. Tom Romer helped polish my grant proposals and provided useful feedback on the manuscript. Charles Cam-
eron read the entire manuscript and gave me some tough, good-hu-
mored, and necessary feedback. Chris Achen, Larry Bartels, and Joshua
Clinton helped me make good practical decisions about the data analysis. Arnold, Bartels, Clinton, Greenstein, Romer, and Keith Whittington
spent all day late in the fall of 2006 at a conference convened around
the manuscript and their comments in the context of this event shaped
the book in important ways.

Friends at other universities also generously gave their time and encouragement. Jim Pfiffner has been a friend and supporter since I was a
graduate student. Some of my earliest conversations on the book were
with him and he has been consistently helpful and supportive throughout. Shigeo Hirano and Adam Meirowitz walked me through some of
the more technical parts of the book without making me feel stupid. The
former also should receive credit for the creation of the "breakfast club"
at Princeton, a forum for junior faculty at Princeton to present their half-
baked ideas to other junior faculty. A lot of this book was hashed out in
this venue with Shigeo, Adam, Josh Clinton, Markus Prior, Keena Lipstiz,
Jessica Trounstine, Kosuke Imai, and others providing feedback.

Dan Carpenter, Jeff Cohen, George Krause, Larry Rothenberg, Andy
Rudalevige, and Charles Shipan took time out of their very busy schedules to come to Princeton in late 2006 and provide feedback on an early
version of the manuscript. Their comments significantly improved it. In
addition, Andy Rudalevige has been a sounding board, cheerleader, and
provider of archival and historical materials. He is a great colleague and
a friend. In other forms Brandice Canes-Wrone, Tom Clark, Dennis Dresang, Laura Evans, Delores Everett, Shana Gadarian, John Gilmour,
Sandy Gordon, John Griffin, Henry Hogue, Will Howell, Greg Huber,
John Huber, Stuart Jordan, Herbert Kaufman, John Londregan, Terry
Moe, Becky Morton, Ezra Suleiman, Rick Waterman, and Greg Wilmoth
provided both encouragement and helpful feedback. Seminar audiences
at the University of South Carolina, Harvard University, the University of
Notre Dame, Columbia University, the College of William & Mary, Virginia Tech University, Dartmouth College, Yale University, New York University, the National Academy of Public Administration, and the University of Washington provided great comments and suggestions.

A few friends deserve special mention for carrying me through the
process of researching and writing this book. Joshua Clinton has been

an important source of encouragement, advice, and common sense. In our daily coffee runs Josh has helped me see what is important and helped me through the hard times. I am grateful to him. Nolan McCarty has been a friend and mentor since we met back when I was a graduate student. He has been a source of encouragement and support. He has given me good ideas, explained things to me that I did not understand, and modeled for me how to do good political science. I owe a large portion of whatever career success I have to him. Jennifer Seidel read the whole manuscript and helped shine the prose and did so in a gentle, loving fashion. She and her husband, Kevin, have been unwaveringly supportive and dear friends. Stefan Bernhard came to Princeton at the same time I did in but in Chemistry. He has been a good friend and neighbor during our time here. I am persuaded his prayers on my behalf have made a difference. Jamie Rankin and I have run or lifted weights together most every day for the last few years. He has read draft chapters, proofread, suggested better ways of saying things, and tried to stop me from "stacking" (unsuccessfully). His willingness to listen, probe, pray, and encourage has been a constant reminder of God's goodness. I am grateful for him.

My thanks go to Chuck Myers and Princeton University Press who patiently brought this book to press and provided very helpful feedback and encouragement. Diane Price, Michele Epstein, and Helene Wood also deserve special thanks. Diane was the first person I interacted with at Princeton and was a guiding light during my early years at Princeton. She is a smart, kind, attentive soul. Michele ran my book conference with incredible efficiency, sensitivity, and good humor. She is also great fun. Helene has kept me on the straight and narrow, done my dirty work, tracked down sources, and kept me in good spirits. Importantly, she has encouraged me to "focus like a laser" on this book for three years now. She is a real joy.

Finally, I thank my family. They have been my biggest cheerleaders. In some ways, their believing I could accomplish what I set out to do made it possible. I thank my in-laws—Jan, Ineke, Craig, Andrea. I also thank the West Coast Lewises and Dad and Barbara. Thanks to G-ma, Mom, Johnnye, Jen, Mark, and Maya. My kids give me great joy and make me the luckiest father around. I am grateful for their patience, love, and good humor. Sometimes an impromptu dance party, wrestling, or a few chapters of Hardy Boys was just what I needed. They were happy to comply. They have sacrificed a lot to see this book completed. I hope I make them proud and look forward to making it up to them. Finally, this book is dedicated to my wife, Saskia, who literally birthed this book with me. She is evidence every day that God is good and he is loving and I love her desperately.

THE POLITICS OF PRESIDENTIAL APPOINTMENTS

1

Politicization in Theory and Practice

WHEN Hurricane Katrina ripped into the Gulf Coast on August 29, 2005, it left 90,000 square miles of devastation in its wake: 1,500 persons dead, hundreds of thousands forced from their homes, 1.6 million persons seeking disaster aid, and more than $80 billion in property damage.[1] In retrospect, the crisis it spawned was almost inevitable. A storm of such severity was sure to cause massive destruction, particularly since it struck an impoverished urban area and affected a region with limited local and state emergency-services capacity. One could only hope that it would not be too severe or widespread, and that response and recovery operations would be put in place quickly and effectively. But this was not the case. Response and recovery efforts were agonizingly slow, poorly coordinated, and frequently ineffective. While multiple factors contributed to these circumstances, Congress, the press, and public singled out the Federal Emergency Management Agency (FEMA), the federal government agency designed to respond to catastrophes like Katrina, for special blame.[2] FEMA's weak response cost hundreds of lives and contributed to incalculable pain and suffering.[3]

In the aftermath of the storm, major national newspapers, congressional investigations, and scholarly accounts questioned whether the large number of political appointees in FEMA contributed to the poor handling of this natural disaster.[4] By almost any estimate, the agency has a large percentage of appointees for its size and critics have argued that FEMA's appointee-heavy management structure created numerous administrative problems that contributed directly to the lax Katrina response. Among the problems identified was limited emergency-management experience among appointees. This was epitomized by the well-publicized fact that director Michael Brown's most significant prior work experience was with the International Arabian Horse Association.

This example raises two important questions about the American political system. First, why do some agencies have many appointees and others few? Second, how do political appointments influence management? This study seeks to answer these questions. It investigates the reasons for differences in the number and location of appointees across agencies in different presidential administrations and provides some of the first systematic analysis of the relationship between appointees and agency performance. The study examines how presidents use appointees to both influence public policy and satisfy patronage demands and how these practices influence performance.

State of Knowledge

There are several major studies that touch on this topic, but before reviewing them it would be worthwhile to clarify a few terms. People commonly refer to the act of increasing the number and penetration of appointees as "politicization."[5] Politicized agencies, then, are those that have the largest percentage and deepest penetration of appointees. The concept can be visualized in a conventional bureaucratic triangle as the dividing point between political appointees and civil servants (figure 1.1) Appointees are generally drawn from the political or private sector (that is, outside the civil service) and hold the jobs with the highest pay and greatest authority. Civil servants enter the system at positions of lower pay and responsibility, work their way up, and make a career of government work. They are hired, promoted, and fired on the basis of merit criteria. Where the line is drawn between these two classes of government workers and its impact on the performance of government agencies is the topic of this study.

Real personnel systems deviate from the ideal type depicted in figure 1.1, particularly in the United States, where there is an unusually large number of appointees, the civil service is relatively permeable, and rules

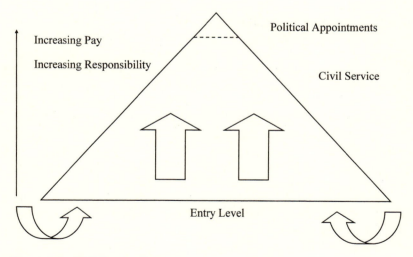

Figure 1.1. Civil Service Systems

and processes vary across agencies. After a presidential election a new president in the United States has close to 3,000 political appointments to make. In other countries such as France, Britain, and Germany, however, the number is closer to between 100 and 200 positions.[6]

The works bearing on this topic, whether academic papers, textbooks, and/or media reports, can be loosely categorized on the basis of three oft-repeated claims that appear therein: 1) politicization is increasing; 2) the increase is driven largely by Republican or conservative presidents; and 3) politicization has damaged bureaucratic competence, significantly contributing to a "quiet crisis" in the public service.[7] Paul Light, for example, describes an increase in management layers in the federal government (what he calls "thickening") and assesses both the causes and consequences of this phenomenon. He argues that some of this thickening is due to the increasing number of political appointees added to the government by the president and Congress.[8] The National Commission on the Public Service comes to the same conclusion. The commission (known as the "Volcker Commission" after its chairman, Paul A. Volcker) was formed in 1987 after a joint symposium on the public service held by the Brookings Institution and the American Enterprise Institute identified a "quiet crisis" in government. The commission issued a report on the problem in 1989.[9] Notable among the findings was a dramatic expansion in the number of political appointments. The commission connected the proliferation of appointees to increasing difficulties in recruiting the best and brightest to public service and an erosion of both morale and quality in the top levels of administration. When the commission reconvened in 2003, they concluded that the increase in political appointees they had documented in 1989 had continued into the Clinton administration with the same deleterious consequences for performance.[10]

Some works argue that increased pressure on modern presidents to control the bureaucracy causes the appointee increase. Terry Moe, for example, contends that presidents are held accountable for the performance of the whole government and respond by centralizing decision-making authority in the White House and politicizing the bureaucracy.[11] Others suggest that partisan or ideological motivations drive politicization. Richard Nathan identified politicization as a strategy emerging in the Nixon presidency and politicization efforts by presidents Nixon and Reagan receive significant attention in the political science literature.[12] Taken together, the latter set of studies gives the impression that partisanship or ideology drives the increase in appointees.

A more recent formulation of the view that ideology drives politicization is that executives who adhere to what is referred to as the "New Public Management" (NPM)—a general package of beliefs about government reform built on the concepts of entrepreneurism, customer orientation, flatter hierarchies, and alternative forms of implementation, such as privatization—increase the number of appointees.[13] The NPM has been adopted by many Republicans and moderate Democrats in the United States and influenced executives cross-nationally. In the United States the NPM was best embodied in President Clinton's "Reinventing Government" initiative.

Whether increasing steadily across administrations or primarily during conservative presidencies, most scholars see this as a worrisome trend because of the consequences of appointee proliferation for performance.[14] Reminiscent of the FEMA case, these works suggest that appointees are often ill-suited for the jobs to which they are being appointed. They also stay for short tenures, impeding efforts to plan and making intra- and interagency teamwork difficult. Appointed managers have a hard time committing to long-term plans or policy reforms and career professionals are slow to respond and grow cynical after multiple experiences with these "birds of passage."[15] For many scholars, increases in appointees have predictable consequences. Hugh Heclo, for example, decries the adverse consequences of "a government of strangers" created by the increase in appointees.[16] More recently, Ezra Suleiman has argued that increasing numbers of appointees delegitimize the bureaucracy and impair its ability to deliver important goods and services.[17]

The contribution of the present study is that it uses new data and analysis to not only revisit *why* and *when* politicization occurs, but also expose *where* politicization occurs, and to *what* effect. It uses a variety of methods including historical analysis, case studies, elite interviewing, and quantitative analysis of previously untapped data. By joining quantitative analysis with new qualitative research, the study puts the two questions that animate this effort in a very new light. It provides new answers to the questions first raised in the works of previous scholars and, by doing so, significantly advances our understanding of politicization and its role in the American political process.

Why Studying Politicization Is Important

From what has preceded, it is clear that this is an important topic of study. Nonetheless, it is useful to explain why it is important in further detail. A study of politicization provides insight into a fundamental tension in American politics and democracy between political control and government competence. It also sheds light on an important presidential tool for controlling the bureaucracy and a useful resource for political bargaining.

Bureaucracy and American Democracy

Studying how politicians make decisions about the number and location of appointees illustrates a fundamental tension in democratic governance. For democratic government and its elected officials to be responsive to citizens, the government apparatus must be effective. To be effective the modern administrative state needs a corps of professional, continuing personnel who are competent at what they do. Building a competent bureaucracy is usually accomplished through the enactment of civil service reforms that protect government agencies from the political selection, promotion, and activity of government workers. Protecting bureaucrats from political pressure helps ensure competence (since hiring and promotion occur on the basis of merit rather than partisanship) but, by definition, makes government workers less responsive to democratically elected officials.

The difficulty of controlling a professional bureaucracy was highlighted as long ago as 1919 by Max Weber, who noted the difficulties faced by generalist politicians relative to expert bureaucrats.[18] Bureaucratic officials develop expertise and have access to information that politicians and the public do not. This information is crucial for effective governance but can also be used to influence democratic officials to make decisions they would not otherwise make if they were fully informed. Bureaucratic officials also wield power delegated to them by democratically elected officials. They regulate, promote, and distribute (as well as redistribute) resources. Their choices have political ramifications since regulating, promoting, distributing, and redistributing creates winners and losers. Bureaucratic officials can also use delegated authority to cultivate independent political power, making them even harder to control.[19]

The extent to which politicians will need the bureaucracy to be insular and professional will vary depending upon the difficulty and scope of the federal government's tasks, the availability of competent personnel, and a host of other factors. It was the increased volume and complexity of government work that led Woodrow Wilson, for example, to call for a continuing and professional civil service to improve government administration. Wilson, like Alexis de Tocqueville and Max Weber before him, argued that the all-appointee personnel system (that is, the so-called spoils system) in the United States hindered performance and prevented the development and practice of a "science of administration" in the United States.[20] Wilson believed that administrative practice in the United States lagged behind that in other countries and the incompetence of the federal service was hurting democratic government itself. Government was not responsive to urban bankers, brokers, and merchants that had to deal with corrupt and inefficient customhouses and postal offices. It was also not responsive to citizens demanding government action to deal with new and complicated problems arising from massive immigration, industrialization, technological change, monopolistic practices, and dramatic economic cycles of boom and bust.

To Wilson's mind, the remedy was the creation of a professional civil service governed by merit criteria in hiring, firing, and promotion. For Wilson, as for Weber, the balance between control and competence should be reflected in a stark line between politics and administration.[21] Wilson stated, "Most important to be observed is the truth already so much and so fortunately insisted upon by our civil service reformers; namely, that administration lies outside the proper sphere of politics. Administrative questions are not political questions. Although politics sets the tasks for administration, it should not be suffered to manipulate its offices."[22] Thus, politicians should make policy and professional administrators should dutifully carry it out. The idea that there should be a line between politics and administration, reflected in the division between political appointees and civil servants, has strong normative appeal. It is the primary way politicians try to resolve the tension between securing control and yet preserving the competence necessary for government to be responsive.

Political Control of the Bureaucracy

A second reason why studying politicization is important is that it is a vital tool for controlling the bureaucracy. Despite the intuitive appeal of the idea that a line can be drawn between politics and administration, scholars after Wilson and Weber have pointed out that drawing such a line is impossible.[23] Beginning with the first congresses, bureaucrats have been given substantial authority to make policy decisions.[24] The amount of authority delegated to bureaucratic officials has only grown over time. Congress and the president must increasingly rely on the expertise and capacity of government workers, particularly in areas where elected officials lack experience or knowledge. As Frederick Mosher explained, "the great bulk of decisions and actions taken by governments are determined or heavily influenced by administrative officials."[25]

It follows, then, that whoever controls the bureaucracy controls a key part of the policy process. In order to understand how politicians control the bureaucracy it is imperative to understand the mechanisms of political control. Congress has numerous means at its disposal for controlling the bureaucracy: it writes specific statutes, mandates deadlines and consequences for poor performance, forces agencies to use the rulemaking process for policy changes, cuts or increases budgets, conducts investigations, and holds oversight hearings. Considerable effort has been devoted to explaining how and when Congress can control the bureaucracy through *ex ante* precautions and *ex post* oversight.[26]

Similarly, presidents use a variety of means to influence agency policy, including unilateral action (for example, executive orders, signing statements, presidential directives) and budgets.[27] Presidents, like Congress, also use agency reorganizations or terminations to influence policy.[28] Of course, the president's most important source of bureaucratic control is via personnel. Whether those in important administrative posts are responsive to the president, a patron in Congress, agency clients, or their own interests greatly affects policy outcomes.

Within agencies, political appointees can provide an important means by which presidents control the bureaucracy and influence policy. Appointees interpret the vague and sometimes conflicting laws enacted by Congress and translate them into policy. Since agencies have multiple responsibilities, appointee decisions about budget requests to Congress, rulemaking, personnel, and the allocation of resources inside the agency can significantly influence policy. More generally, appointees monitor bureaucratic activity and communicate the president's vision to the press and agency employees, clients, and stakeholders. Increasing or decreasing their number can have direct effects on agency policies and practices.

Understanding the means by which politicians fill administrative posts is central to a realistic understanding of the policy process. The work that studies political control of the bureaucracy, while highlighting the influence personnel can have on outcomes, rarely discusses how the president and Congress decide about the number and location of appointees.[29] The process by which presidents exercise their staffing power is often opaque, particularly when it comes to details about where presidents can make appointments, why some agencies have more appointed positions than others, and how new positions get created. A study of politicization augments our understanding of the means by which elected officials control the policymaking that occurs after legislation is enacted.

Presidential Political Power

Studying the causes and consequences of politicization also illuminates an underappreciated source of political power. The ways that presidents use appointees to influence public policy gets most of the attention in the recent political science literature.[30] No accounting of politicization, however, is complete without accounting for modern patronage processes. The president's control over personnel is also an important source of political capital.

Since presidents have meager formal powers in the Constitution, they have had to rely on informal powers such as bargaining, public appeals, and moral leadership to accomplish their political goals.[31] An additional resource is appointed jobs, and modern presidents have used the 3,000-plus appointed jobs at their disposal upon assuming office, as well as the power to create and eliminate others, as a source of political power. The leverage of these jobs often lies in their perceived potential, since the possibility of a government job induces many people to work on campaigns and provides presidents a credible means of assuring interest groups that their views will be represented in the administration. Such promises help presidents secure interest-group endorsements, manpower, and resources. The shrewd distribution of patronage provides presidents a means of governing more effectively by holding diverse party factions together. The giving and withholding of jobs is used to maintain party discipline or as a bargaining chip to help presidents get their way in Congress. In short, jobs represent a crucial political resource for presidents. Studying politicization illuminates how presidents generate and spend these resources.

Plan of the Book

In the following chapters I proceed to provide answers to the questions posed at the beginning of the chapter—*Why do some agencies have many appointees and others few? What are the consequences of appointees for performance?* My answers to these questions come primarily from an analysis of the United States since the end of World War II. The post-1946 period provides a long enough window to allow history to inform our understanding of modern practice but a period short enough to make generalizations across time possible. By the middle of the century, the dramatic shift in government responsibilities inaugurated by the New Deal was well under way. The modern roles of the president and Congress were also established in the management of the executive branch.[32] For example, both branches were heavily involved in restructuring government after the New Deal and World War II to rationalize the administrative structure that had grown up haphazardly in the hurry to counter the Depression and mobilize for the war in the Pacific, Europe, and Africa.[33]

Chapter 2 describes the nature and history of the modern personnel system in order to set up the discussion of politicization to come. The chapter reviews the history of the federal personnel system from the period before a merit-based civil service system to the modern system. It provides an overview of the modern personnel system with special attention paid to the different types of political appointees. The chapter then describes how pressures to fill existing positions and satisfy demands for patronage shape the presidential personnel operation. It also examines the most common politicization techniques and the tools Congress has used to rein them in. It concludes with a case study of the reorganization of the Civil Service Commission to illustrate the different politicization techniques and the influence politicization can have on public policy.

Chapter 3 explains when presidents politicize, analyzing both politicization motivated by concerns for policy and to satisfy demands for patronage. On the policy side, the chapter starts with four simple assumptions about presidential behavior and agency characteristics and deduces some interesting—and not entirely intuitive—predictions about when presidents politicize. It also looks at why Congress is less enthusiastic about politicization than is the Executive, and then expands to explore patronage appointments. The arguments of the chapter are summarized in a set of four testable propositions.

Chapter 4 uses previously untapped data from the Plum Book, a quadrennial congressional publication listing all policy and supporting positions in the government, to provide a quantitative overview of politicization. The chapter first describes which agencies have the highest percentages of appointees, which have been politicized most since 1960, and which gained and lost appointees between 2000 and 2004. It then uses these data to evaluate two of the propositions from chapter 3 and competing views about when politicization occurs. It supplements the quantitative analysis with a brief examination of two of the most publicized cases of politicization during George W. Bush's first term, those involving the Central Intelligence Agency and the Office of Special Counsel.

Chapter 5 uses data from the Office of Personnel Management for a closer quantitative analysis of politicization. It includes an analysis of politicization activity in different bureaus and agencies during the presidencies of George H. W. Bush, Bill Clinton, and George W. Bush. The chapter estimates econometric models for a more precise and comprehensive test of the theoretical predictions from chapter 3 and other common views about politicization.

Chapter 6 takes up the relationship between appointees and performance. It reviews competing claims about whether appointees or careerists are better for management. The chapter then explains the different causal pathways by which appointee management can influence performance. It focuses on both the differences in the backgrounds and experience of people selected to run federal programs and agencies and the hidden costs of politicization on the quality of *careerist* management in agency. The chapter evaluates the relationship between appointees and performance through an in-depth case study of FEMA from its creation through Hurricane Katrina in 2005.

Chapter 7 evaluates the influence of appointee management on federal program performance more broadly. It explains why large-scale studies of the relationship between appointees and performance have been difficult to execute and presents two new measures of agency performance that avoid previous difficulties. The chapter compares the performance of appointees to career managers and disentangles what differences among the two types of managers influence performance the most. The chapter concludes with the implications of the findings for the larger argument of the book, modern presidential staffing practices, and policy debates surrounding how to improve federal management performance.

Chapter 8 concludes by drawing out the implications of the study for our understanding of bureaucracy in American democracy, political control of the bureaucracy, and the modern presidency. It then takes a broader view of the topic, first by discussing the implications of the findings for our understanding of politicization in other countries, and then by looking at practices closely related to politicization, such as recruiting appointees only on the basis of party loyalty and making appointment and promotion decisions in the civil service on the basis of political attitudes. The chapter concludes with a discussion of the merits of recent policy proposals to cut the number of appointees, attach background requirements to certain appointed positions, and increase personnel flexibilities more generally.

Conclusion

The publicity surrounding Hurricane Katrina ignited a brief debate about cronyism. This debate served the useful purpose of focusing the public's attention, albeit for a limited time, on political appointees, where they are, how many there are, and whether they are qualified to do the jobs for which they have been nominated or appointed. To focus too much on FEMA would be to miss the prevalence of this strategy and its importance. Politicization efforts were not limited to FEMA in the George W. Bush administration. From the Department of Education to the Central Intelligence Agency to the Office of Special Counsel, executive attempts to assert control through increases in appointments were well publicized.[34] If we want to understand these episodes, as well as those that are less publicized, it is necessary to study causes and consequences of politicization across the modern presidency. These cases also illustrate what is at stake in these efforts—the quality of disaster response, education policy, the War on Terror, and the protection of whistleblowers.

2

The Nature and History
of the Modern Personnel System

FEW PEOPLE have heard of Schedule C appointments to the federal service. If queried most would connect a discussion of "Schedule C" to Internal Revenue Service tax forms, but in 1953 the creation of the Schedule C by President Eisenhower was a watershed event in the history of federal personnel management. Eisenhower created this new category of appointments after his inauguration not only in response to pressure from Republican partisans to create more jobs for party members, but also to help rein in the sprawling New Deal bureaucracy created and staffed by presidents Roosevelt and Truman for the previous twenty years. The creation of this new category of federal personnel gave the administration the authority to add over one thousand new appointees to the executive branch and immediately gain substantial influence in important public-policy areas like conservation and the environment.

Prior to Eisenhower's order, important bureaucratic jobs—like director and assistant director of the U.S. Fish and Wildlife Service, director of the National Park Service, and chief and deputy chief of the Soil Conservation Service—had to be filled by career employees who had worked their way up through the agency according to nonpolitical criteria.[1] After Eisenhower's order, these jobs could and were filled by political appointees reviewed by the Republican National Committee and named by the White House.[2] Future presidential administrations expanded the number of jobs included in Schedule C, both managerial positions and other confidential positions like staff, counsel, and special assistant positions.

It is hard to understand the details or importance of President Eisenhower's order without an understanding of the history and details of the civil service system in the United States. Very important and practical choices about the number and location of appointees occur in the context of a unique history and sometimes complex set of civil service laws and rules.

This chapter describes the nature and history of the modern personnel system in preparation for the discussion of politicization to come in subsequent chapters. It begins with a brief history of the federal personnel system. It then describes the contours of the modern personnel system, including an explanation of the different types of appointed positions and how they get created. The chapter then describes the presidential personnel operation and how it responds to pressures to fill existing positions and satisfy demands for patronage. The next section describes the most common politicization techniques and the tools Congress has used to rein them in. The chapter concludes with a case study of the reorganization of the Civil Service Commission to illustrate the different politicization techniques and demonstrate how politicization is used to change public policy.

A Brief History of the Federal Personnel System

One of the unique features of the Constitution is that it makes virtually no mention of the bureaucracy; its few limited references to departments or officers give virtually no detail apart from the fact that principal officers are to be nominated by the president and confirmed by the Senate.[3] Congress is empowered to determine the means of appointing inferior officers, and the president is granted the ability to request information from principal officers in writing. Apart from these few details the Constitution is silent about the design, function, and administration of the bureaucratic state.

The Constitution's silence leaves responsibility for the creation, nurturing, and maintenance of the continuing government to elected officials, who are divided by different constituencies, institutional responsibilities, and political temperaments. It is the decisions of these persons in the context of a shifting electoral, partisan, and historical landscape that shapes the nature and history of the modern personnel system.

The Personnel System before Merit

The personnel system that presided from 1789 to 1829 was selected and populated by and with persons from the same social class, who were defined by enfranchisement, property, common upbringing, and shared values. They were drawn from what Leonard White calls "a broad class of gentlemen."[4] The selection of federal personnel was dictated in large part by "fitness for public office," but fitness for office was itself defined by standing, wealth, or public reputation rather than relevant experience, expertise, or demonstrated competence.[5]

Long tenure and expectations of continued service were the norm, reinforced by the long dominance of one party in power from 1800 to 1829, the absence of a national party system, and, apparently, the personal conviction of early presidents that persons should not be removed from office because of their political beliefs. Presidents did fill vacancies and newly created offices in the expanding federal government with their partisans, but outright removals of Federalists by Republicans were rare. Regular rotation only occurred at the level of department heads.

The increasingly permanent and class-based federal service did have its detractors. There was a growing sentiment, particularly with expanded franchise, that more positive action needed to be taken to democratize the public service itself. Of particular concern to many were instances where sons inherited the jobs of their fathers, accentuating fears that federal jobs were becoming a type of property or privilege. In 1820 Congress enacted the Tenure of Office Act, requiring the explicit reappointment of all federal officials every four years as a way of contravening the establishment of a professional class.

The old system was not overturned fully until the presidency of Andrew Jackson. Upon assuming office in 1829 Jackson said, "The duties of all public officers are, or at least admit of being made, so plain and simple that men of intelligence may readily qualify themselves for their performance; I can not but believe that more is lost by the long continuance of men in office than is generally to be gained by their experience."[6] Jackson believed that public office was not reserved for a particular class or incumbents in government. Rather, it should be opened to the broader public. The political benefits of such an action were not lost on Jackson.

While his actions to democratize the federal service only led to the turnover of 10 percent of the federal workforce, his actions set in motion a full-fledged patronage system in the United States. Undergirded by the development of national parties hungry for federal office as a way of securing funds and votes, the regular rotation of a large percentage of federal offices became the norm. The national parties, loose confederations of state and local parties, gave out offices and expected activity for the party and political assessments in return. Office holders would return 1 to 6 percent of their salaries to the party. While rotation normally occurred with party turnover, James Buchanan actually replaced Pierce Democrats with Buchanan Democrats in 1857. The two rivals had struggled for the Democratic nomination, but most believed that Pierce's appointments would stay on since they had presumably worked and voted for Buchanan against his Republican opponent, John C. Fremont.[7]

The vast majority of federal jobs were located outside of Washington, D.C. They were an important political resource and were viewed proprietarily by congressmen who sought to distribute patronage to local and state machines that brought them to power. Presidents were expected to consult with the senators and, to a lesser extent, representatives in the states where appointments were made. The power of this norm was reinforced by the practice of senatorial courtesy whereby the Senate would refuse to confirm a nomination if an objection was raised by the senator from the state where the appointment was being made. While some strong presidents, such as Jackson or Polk, resisted this norm in principle, all usually followed it in practice.[8]

The deleterious consequences of the spoils system for bureaucratic performance were somewhat mitigated by several factors. First, Andrew Jackson was partly right that many federal jobs did not require a tremendous amount of expertise or special training. Herbert Kaufman writes, "Thus, under the spoils system, Presidents were no less aware than their predecessors of the importance of procuring competent personnel. They did not worry too much about it because of their assumption that most government jobs were simple."[9] The nineteenth-century bureaucracy did not look like modern bureaucracy, which has a division of labor, specialized offices and jobs by function, discretion, and extensive hierarchy. Most of the work in the civil service was still clerical and very little authority or discretion was delegated to subcabinet officials. In addition, many of the persons turned out of office with electoral turnover would return once their party returned to power.

Second, jobs requiring more expertise were sometimes filled by persons who did not turn over with each administration. Certain auditors, comptrollers, clerks, and personnel in the scientific offices stayed from administration to administration to conduct the business of government. White says, "After 1829 this simple, single system bifurcated under the influence of the theory of rotation. It was not, however, destroyed. Old-time clerks remained at their desks; 'party' clerks came and went."[10] The practical needs of a functioning government limited the extent of the spoils system and rotation in office. Indeed, some employees of long tenure moved up to key positions because of their expertise. Their competence and expertise in public work outweighed party patronage considerations in their selection.

This dual personnel system persisted during a period when the size and activities of government were limited. As the federal government grew in size and complexity, however, the weaknesses of the spoils system became increasingly apparent. The quality of the federal service suffered. Rotation in office did lead to the dismissal of many qualified federal officials, such as those who kept the accounts and records, made it difficult to sustain reforms, and prevented the development of consistent, purposeful management practices. Rotation-induced instability prevented functional specialization and the development of managerial and policy-specific expertise.[11] These factors, coupled with low pay, decreased the prestige of federal jobs and their reliability as long-term careers. Day-to-day performance was also hindered by the low quality of patronage appointees who were only competent in their jobs by happy accident or the limited requirements of their occupations. Many appointees spent a portion of their time in other jobs, in work for the party, or in leisure.

The democratization of the administrative state, while important for access and control, made the state ill equipped to take on the new responsibilities that accompany broad societal changes. The challenges of the Civil War, economic and territorial expansion, periodic monetary crises, massive immigration, and technological change meant the federal government would need to take on new responsibilities and expand to fit its new roles; and public pressure for greater federal government involvement meant the administration of government would have to change. It would have to specialize, organize, and stabilize in order to provide the expertise and services demanded by agricultural interests, businesses, pensioners, consumers, and voters of all types through their elected officials. Congress and the president faced increasing pressure to build a professional bureaucracy by enacting civil service reforms.

The Creation and Extension of Merit

A number of different groups were involved in the nascent push for civil service reform.[12] Included among these groups were urban merchants, bankers, and brokers, often motivated by their own frustrating experience with corrupt and inefficient postal offices and customs houses. A larger class of professionals including lawyers, academics, journalists, and clergy were also supportive of reform, partly as a moral crusade against the corruptions of the spoils system but also as a means of confronting a political system not responsive enough to their interests. Agency officials were also supportive of reform as a means of improving the performance of offices they were supposed to manage.

Efforts to alter the system usually engendered hostility from the parties and their sympathizers in Congress. As public pressure to change the personnel system mounted, however, the national parties acquiesced reluctantly, fearful of giving up the patronage they held or hoped to gain in the next election. They became more supportive when they needed to cultivate reform-oriented voters. They were also more supportive when they were out of power or expected to lose power since civil service would limit the opposition party's control over spoils.[13]

At the same time that pressure was mounting for reform Congress had arguably reached the zenith of its power over personnel. During the administration of Andrew Johnson, Congress passed the Tenure of Office Act over the president's veto. The act required that presidents not only get the Senate's confirmation for nominations but also for removals. Congressional influence derived from the fact that senators could withhold approval of a removal until they approved of the successor nominated by the president.[14] It was President Johnson's disregard for this act that led to his eventual impeachment.

The first serious government-wide attempt at reform came in the 1870s during the Grant Administration. The reform was motivated more by a desire to heal divisions in the Republican Party than that for substantive reform. Republicans had experienced significant losses in the 1870 elections and a split emerged among reformers within the party and Grant-aligned machine elements, particularly in the Senate.[15] To appease reformers, Grant requested a law authorizing the president to issue regulations governing the admission of persons to the civil service, to hire employees to assess the fitness of persons for the civil service, and to establish regulations governing the conduct of civil servants appointed under the new regulations. In response, the Republican majority delegated to the president sweeping authority to create a civil service system with the hope of bridging the rift before the 1872 elections.

When the commission recommended its first set of rules in 1872, Republicans in Congress said little.[16] After the 1872 elections, however, their tone changed. When the first civil service examinations came on-line in the Treasury Department in 1873, members of Congress were openly hostile. They responded by refusing appropriations for the commission in 1874. Since Grant's primary interest in the commission was to hold together the different factions in the party, he did little to defend it. When Congress refused to appropriate funds again in 1875, Grant revoked the commission's rules and closed its offices.[17]

Rutherford B. Hayes pledged to support civil service reform during his candidacy in 1876.[18] When he assumed office in 1877 he requested appropriations from Congress to reactivate the Grant Civil Service Commission. Congress turned down his request, but Hayes took a number of other actions to further the cause of civil service. He appointed noted civil service reformer Carl Schurz as Secretary of the Interior, where Schurz installed a vigorous merit system.[19] Hayes also instituted competitive examinations in the New York City customhouse and post office after a public investigation of the customhouse and a bitter feud with Senator Conkling from New York over patronage.

Hayes's actions coincided with the formation of a number of civil service reform associations. These organizations appeared earliest in the northeast where Hayes's controversy over appointments to the New York customhouse drew the most attention.[20] By 1881 the number of groups had grown substantially and societies existed from San Francisco to New York.

The assassination of Hayes's successor, James Garfield, by a disappointed office seeker in the summer of 1881 galvanized popular support for a more concrete and permanent merit system. One month after Garfield's assassination, the local civil service reform associations that started during the Hayes administration coalesced into the National Civil Service Reform League. In December 1881, Democratic Senator George Pendleton introduced reform legislation drafted by the league. The bill was reported from committee in May 1882 but had little support in the Republican Congress. The league, however, pressured for the legislation with a poster campaign and the publication of lists of opponents to civil service reform. With Garfield's assassination reformers had their crystallizing event and leading journals and newspapers aided their efforts.

Enthusiasm for reform increased after the elections in the fall of 1882. Republicans fared poorly and reform was clearly an issue. President Chester Arthur expressed his support for the legislation, and debate on the Pendleton bill began as soon as Congress convened on December 12, 1882. Debate lasted through December 27 and on January 16, 1883, President Arthur signed the Pendleton Act into law. The law created—for the first time in the United States—a merit-based federal civil service.

The law provided for the creation of a three-person bipartisan Civil Service Commission (CSC) that would administer exams and promulgate rules under the act. Under the provisions of the Pendleton Act only 10.5 percent of all federal workers were included in the merit system, and these were primarily employees in large post offices or customs houses.[21] Some employees from the departmental service in Washington, D.C. were also included. At this time being under the merit system meant only that persons had to do well on competitive examinations to be appointed. There were no effective protections against adverse job actions or firing after appointment. Job tenure was only protected by the requirement that new persons appointed to the job had to have done well on the same competitive examination. Formal job tenure and protection from partisan dismissal were not established until the late 1890s.[22] Rigorous prohibition on political activity by civil servants was not enacted until Congress passed the Hatch Act in 1939.[23]

The Pendleton Act delegated to the president authority to add the remaining unclassified federal jobs into the merit system with the exception of positions requiring Senate confirmation and common laborers.[24] Presidents added significantly to the civil service through presidential action; 65 percent of the growth in civil service coverage between 1884 and 1903 was through executive order.[25] Once positions were added, it was difficult for Congress to remove them since they would presumably have to do so over the president's veto. They were unlikely to override a president's veto given that one party was sure to prefer to have these positions under civil service at any given time.

Members of Congress on the losing side of the president's orders vented their frustration at both the CSC and the president. Some portion of Congress was unhappy with the CSC for the duration of the nineteenth century and subjected it to repeated investigations and funding cuts.[26] Pressure on presidents to roll back the expansion of merit was strongest after elections in which the control shifted from one party to the other, and thus when the president's partisans looked for additional patronage to bolster party fortunes. The pressure was not as strong as it could have been, however, since the expansion in federal government employment during this period meant that the raw number of spoils positions continued to increase even as the percentage of federal employees outside the merit system decreased.

Presidents, with a few exceptions, resisted pressures to remove positions once they had been included in the merit system. Presidents were bolstered by the interests that had pushed for the enactment of civil service reform in the first place. Notably, civil service reform leagues continued to push for the preservation and expansion of the federal merit system while also pressuring states and localities to adopt reforms of their own. Efforts to roll back merit system gains were met with howls of protest. Historian Leonard White writes, "The civil service reformers drove them [presidents] hard, and watched for every evidence of backsliding while urging the extension of the system to new offices and agencies."[27]

Nascent government unions also pushed for the expansion of the merit system. The passage of the Pendleton Act provided an environment in which federal employees could organize more easily since the act weakened the ties of federal employees to political patrons.[28] Workers in several occupations, such as mail carriers and postal clerks, organized in the late 1880s and early 1890s.[29] Postal unions were particularly effective at lobbying for pay increases and tenure protections.[30] They most demonstrably exerted their growing political muscle in 1902, when they campaigned actively and successfully against incumbent congressman Eugene Loud (R-CA). Loud was chairman of the House Post Office Committee and opposed legislation to reclassify positions and raise postal salaries.[31]

These unions were instrumental in the passage of the Lloyd-Lafollette Act in 1912 that formally allowed the unionization of government workers (provided they joined unions that would not strike).[32] The act also prohibited dismissal for reasons other than efficiency, and gave employees the right to be notified of possible firing in writing and respond.

The Lloyd-Lafollette act spurred a period of more aggressive unionization and the National Federation of Federal Employees organized in 1917 under the auspices of the American Federation of Labor (AFL). This was followed by the American Federation of Government Employees (AFGE) in 1932 and the United Federal Workers of America (under the Congress of Industrial Organizations [CIO]) in 1937.[33] These unions, along with the occupation-specific unions like the postal unions, were instrumental in securing higher salaries and benefits for federal workers.[34] They helped secure the enactment of the Civil Service Retirement Act of 1920 and the Classification Acts of 1923 and 1949. The former provided retirement and survivor benefits as well as improved tenure protections for civil service workers. The latter two acts created a job classification and pay system on the principle of equal pay for equal work and outlined detailed grievance procedures that strengthened worker protections against adverse personnel actions.[35]

Importantly, federal employee unions also lobbied for the expansion of the merit system.[36] The CIO, in particular, was very outspoken in response to the decline in merit system percentages in the 1930s. They resorted to "picketing, demonstrations, and mass publicity campaigns" when the Democrats in Congress failed to defend the merit system.[37]

The merit system continued to expand as all nineteenth-century and most twentieth-century presidents through Franklin Delano Roosevelt used executive orders to include new classes of employees in the merit system. Presidents frequently blanketed positions into the civil service just prior to leaving office.[38] It was not unusual for Congress to allow new agencies to be created outside the merit system originally, only to add them into the system later. For example, many agencies created to mobilize for war or to combat the Great Depression were originally created outside the merit system. In some cases, the creation of new agencies and new programs provided patronage opportunities that excited either the president or Congress. In fact, in the 1930s Congress on occasion specifically prohibited the president from placing agencies in the merit system.[39] Once these agencies were populated according to the dictates of the politicians in power, they moved to blanket them in to the civil service system. This protected their partisans from removal and ensured a degree of long-term loyalty to the programmatic mission of the agencies or to the patrons themselves.[40]

The percentage of federal jobs in the traditional merit system has varied substantially over time (figure 2.1). By 1897, the advent of the McKinley presidency, close to 50 percent of the federal civilian workforce was under the merit system, and by 1932 close to 80 percent of federal workers held merit positions,[41] a proportion that dipped during the New Deal but reached its peak of almost 88 percent in 1951.[42] This figure underestimates the actual extension of the merit system because many employees not covered by the traditional merit system were employed under other agency-specific personnel systems, like the Tennessee Valley Authority (TVA) or the Foreign Service, which included merit-like provisions. In

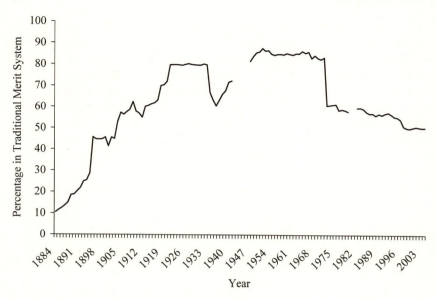

Figure 2.1. Percentage of Federal Civilian Jobs in the Traditional Merit System, 1883–2004

addition, many of the excluded employees were employed overseas and were unlikely to be consequential for patronage.

While the percentage of jobs included in the merit system peaked at midcentury, it is now decreasing as the federal government shifts its strategy away from a one-size-fits-all personnel system to an agency-specific model.[43] This trend has accelerated at the start of the twenty-first century, since Congress enacted legislation providing both the Department of Homeland Security and the Department of Defense with authority to create their own personnel systems. If these new systems are implemented effectively, the number of federal employees under the traditional merit system will dip below 30 percent of the federal civilian workforce.[44]

The Modern Personnel System

Today the federal government employs 2.5 million civilians in full-time positions (and 1.4 million uniformed military personnel).[45] Each civilian job is defined by a pay category and an appointment authority. To ensure equal pay for equal work, an elaborate pay system, including three primary classification schemes for blue-collar, white-collar, and top-level management positions, has been developed. The Federal Wage System (FWS) covers trade, craft, skilled, and unskilled laborers.[46] The General

Schedule (GS) defines the pay rates for administrative, technical, and professional jobs, while the Senior Level and Scientific and Professional (SL/ST) system does the same for high-level, but nonmanagerial, positions. Top-level management and professional jobs are covered under the Senior Executive Service (SES) pay schedule or the Executive Schedule (EX). The EX, with a few exceptions, is reserved for positions requiring presidential nomination and Senate confirmation. In each pay system there is a series of numerical pay categories that in the GS system are called *grades*. There are currently fifteen grades in the GS system. These pay categories define a pay range for jobs with equivalent levels of responsibility, qualifications, or experience. Each pay category allows for some flexibility in differentiating between employees who hold similar positions but have different levels of experience or backgrounds. In the GS system these are called *steps*.

The pay system ought not be confused with appointment authority. These two aspects of any federal job are distinct but often correlated. Top-level positions, for example, are filled outside the merit system (defined by competitive examinations) and receive the highest salaries, but some positions filled by political appointment receive relatively low salaries (for example, confidential assistants or chauffeurs of top officials).

Of the 2.5 million full-time civilian employees, about 1.32 million are included in the traditional merit system.[47] At the heart of the civil service system is a series of rules and regulations governing how people can obtain federal jobs and what their rights are with regard to promotion, removal, and other personnel actions. Merit system principles demand that persons be hired, promoted, and fired only on the basis of merit rather than on other factors, such as party membership, gender, or race. Persons initially establish their merit through competitive examination or, in some cases, appropriate background qualifications. Once a person's qualifications have been established, a determination is made about his or her eligibility for both position and pay grade. Persons employed under the merit system have a series of rights formerly defined in the *Federal Personnel Manual*, most notably rights to notification and appeal in cases of adverse personnel actions such as demotion or removal.[48] These rights are now defined in the *Code of Federal Regulations* and various Office of Personnel Management (OPM) handbooks.

Excepted Positions

As suggested above, more than half of all federal jobs are now "excepted" from the traditional merit system described above (figure 2.2). The excepted service is a residual category, catching all jobs that are not subject to the appointment provisions of Title 5 of the United States Code. There

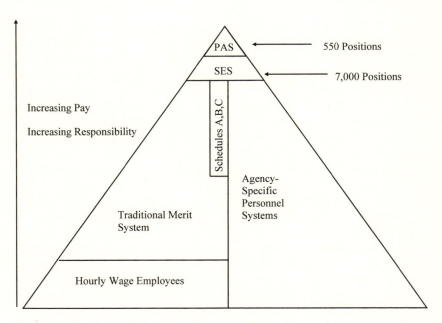

Figure 2.2. Federal Civilian Personnel System Appointment Authorities

Note: Excludes job-specific excepted positions. PAS excludes part-time, advisory, U.S. Attorneys, U.S. Marshals, and ambassadorial positions. The "excepted service" includes PAS, SES, Schedules A, B, C, and personnel in agency-specific personnel systems.

are four categories of excepted jobs: positions requiring presidential nomination and Senate confirmation (PAS); jobs filled by persons in the SES; positions in what are known as Schedules A, B, and C; and positions in agency-specific personnel systems.[49]

The most visible positions outside the traditional merit system are those that require presidential nomination and Senate confirmation. These positions are at the top of the federal personnel hierarchy. The United States Constitution (Article II, sec. 2, cl. 2) requires that all "ambassadors, other public ministers and consuls, judges of the Supreme Court, and all other officers of the United States" be appointed in this manner. The manner of appointing "inferior" officers is up to Congress (and the president) as the result of legislative determinations. Where one draws the line between "principal" and "inferior" officers, however, is unclear.[50] In 2004 there were 1,137 PAS positions in the executive branch, about 945 of which were policymaking positions.[51] The remainder is comprised of appointments to minor advisory or committee-supervisory roles often requiring only part-time employment, paid on a per diem basis. Of the 945 positions, about 186 were U.S. attorneys or U.S. marshals and 154 were ambassadors, leaving 550–600 key executive PAS positions in the cabinet departments and major independent agencies. The average cabinet department dealing with domestic affairs has fifteen to thirty PAS positions, including a secretary, a deputy secretary, a handful of under- and assistant secretaries, an inspector general, and a chief financial officer.[52]

Between PAS positions and the competitive civil service in the federal hierarchy is a space filled by a mixture of career employees from the Senior Executive Service (SES) and political appointees who will be designated noncareer members of this service.[53] The SES was created by the Civil Service Reform Act of 1978 and is comprised of a cadre of approximately 7,000 senior management officials. The OPM, based on its own assessment and the requests of agencies, allocates a certain number of SES positions to each department or agency, and the administration chooses which of the jobs in the agency will be SES jobs.[54] Presidents or their subordinates can choose either an existing member of the SES (a career civil servant who applied to be a part of the SES) or a political appointee from outside who will fill an SES job.[55] By law political appointees cannot exceed 10 percent of the entire SES or 25 percent of the allocated SES positions in a specific agency. In 2004 there were 6,811 persons in the SES, 674 of whom were appointees.[56] Some examples of appointed SES positions include Chief of Staff at the U.S Agency for International Development, Director of Intergovernmental Affairs for the Department of Defense, Deputy Assistant Secretary for Special Education and Rehabilitative Services, and Deputy General Counsel in the Department of Health and Human Services.[57]

A key motivation in creating the SES was to give presidents more flexibility in controlling policy and programmatic positions pivotal for implementing the administration's program. One way in which it did this was to provide more appointees at this level; another was to increase the ease with which presidents could reassign career senior management officials.[58] Under the law the president can reassign a career SES executive to any other position, provided the president and the new agency head have been in office for at least 120 days and the executive has been given 15 days notice (60 if the reassignment includes a geographical change).

Since the creation of the merit system it has been clear that there are some positions for which it is not feasible to hold exams, even in agencies where the merit system is otherwise entirely appropriate. There are three classes of such positions, designated as Schedules A, B, and C. There are no examinations at all for Schedule A positions, which historically have included lawyers, military chaplains, or positions in isolated localities.[59]

Schedule B positions have examinations attached to them but they establish a threshold level of acceptability and do not utilize comparisons among applicants. This schedule has included positions in new agencies or programs for which there are no established directions or guidelines, federal work-study positions, and positions set aside for those with certain types of disabilities.

The third schedule, Schedule C, is reserved for positions of a confidential or policy-determining nature. As the start of the chapter suggested, the schedule was created by President Eisenhower in 1953. Schedule C originally included both management positions below the PAS level and the assorted staff assigned to appointees (confidential assistants, drivers, and so forth). As such, the pay range for Schedule C appointees varied dramatically according to position. Top-level management positions in Schedule C were eventually converted to NEA positions in 1966 and SES positions in 1978. Lower-paying Schedule C positions remain (GS 15 and below). In 2004 there were 1,596 persons appointed to Schedule C positions in the federal government.

These constitute an important subtype of political appointment and, while technically selected by agency officials, presidents since Reagan have exercised substantial control over them. For example, one Clinton administration personnel official recounted that Clinton's nominees for cabinet posts were told, "These positions are Bill Clinton's and he appoints them—the Senate-confirmed positions, the noncareer SES positions, and the Schedule C positions—he selects them."[60] Typical Schedule C posts include special or confidential assistants to PAS appointees, directors of communications, press, or outreach offices, and officials in legislative liaison offices. Some current examples include the White House liaison in the Department of Interior, the confidential assistant to the Assistant Secretary of Education for Vocational and Adult Education, and the Director of Media Affairs in the Department of Labor.

The last, and by far the largest, set of positions are excepted because they are located in agencies that have authority to govern their own personnel systems (table 2.1).[61] They can be low- or high-paying jobs of varying levels of responsibility and character. Calling them "excepted" is something of a misnomer, however, since the rights of employees in these personnel systems are usually very similar to those in the Title 5 civil service system.[62] There has been a dramatic increase in the number of "excepted" jobs because recent congressional decisions give certain agencies authority to create their own personnel systems outside the merit system defined by Title 5. The most significant actions in this regard have been the reorganization in 1970 of the postal service into a government corporation, with its own personnel system in (800,000 employees); the creation of the Department of Homeland Security in 2002,

Table 2.1
Examples of Agencies with Broad Exceptions from the Traditional Merit
Personnel System

Department of Defense

Department of Homeland Security

Federal Aviation Agency

United States Postal Service

Postal Rates Commission

Central Intelligence Agency

National Security Agency

Tennessee Valley Authority

Federal Bureau of Investigation

General Accounting Office

Panama Canal Commission

Board of Governors, Federal Reserve System

Peace Corps

Railroad Retirement Board

Overseas Private Investment Corporation

Nuclear Regulatory Commission

Federal Election Commission

Source: U.S. General Accounting Office 1997a; U.S. Senate 2000.

with authority to create its own personnel system (170,000 civilian employees); and Congress's decision in 2003 to grant the Department of Defense authority to create its own personnel system (660,000 civilian employees).[63] Agencies, bolstered by outside critiques of the federal personnel system, have long clamored for more control over their own personnel systems, claiming that they need more flexibility in hiring, promoting, and firing in order to improve performance.[64] Flexible personnel systems allow them to respond more quickly to changes in the job market, agency personnel needs, and new programmatic responsibilities. Increased flexibility, however, can also lead to fewer protections against abuses in hiring, firing, and promotion, as well as inequities in pay, benefits, and treatment for comparable work.

In sum, politicization, when it does occur, is, at the top levels, defined both by pay and by appointment authority. It involves an increase in the number of PAS, SES, Schedule C, and similarly excepted agency-specific appointees.

The Mechanics of Adding Appointees

The three types of appointees get added in three different ways. Senate-confirmed positions must be created through legislation. Within this general requirement there is growing flexibility, however. Some statutes, rather than specifying the details of Senate-confirmed positions, authorize a fixed number of Senate-confirmed positions that presidents can allocate throughout a department at their discretion. For example, the law creating the Department of Homeland Security allows the president "not more than twelve (12)" assistant secretaries but does not specify where those assistant secretaries are to be placed within the organization chart of the department.[65]

Adding SES appointees can happen in two ways. First, a new job can be created. If the administration chooses this route, they must ensure that the agency has been allocated enough SES slots.[66] Provided there are enough slots, a position can be created and designated as an SES general position by the agency. The president can then fill this position with an appointee. In doing so, however, the percentage of appointees in the SES in that agency must not exceed 25 percent; the overall percentage of appointees in the SES must not exceed 10 percent. Once the appointee leaves, however, the appointee-nature of the position leaves with them. The new SES position just becomes another SES position to be filled by careerists or appointees. There are no SES jobs that must be filled by appointees.

Second, if a job is already designated as an SES general position it can be filled with an appointee. If the position is vacant, the appointment can happen without delay. If the position is occupied by an SES careerist, the reassignment of the careerist can not occur involuntarily until 120 days after inauguration of the new president or 120 days after a new agency head's appointment; a careerist may take a voluntary reassignment within the 120-day period. SES careerists must also be given 15–60 days' notice of a reassignment depending upon whether the reassignment involves a geographical move.

To add a Schedule C appointee, the agency must write up a job description that includes an explanation for the job's policy and confidential nature and include information about job responsibilities and appointee qualifications sufficient to justify the salary requested. OPM must approve these requests. In the modern personnel system, the authority for the Schedule C position is revoked once the appointee leaves, so in practice there is no such thing as a "vacant" Schedule C position.[67] If the administration wants to have an appointee in a role similar to that of the departing appointee, they must go through the process of creating a new Schedule C position.

The Modern Presidential Personnel Process

Given these different types of appointments, it is worth reviewing how presidents and their staffs go about filling PAS positions and determining where to place SES and Schedule C appointees. Both policy and patronage concerns shape modern personnel politics.[68] On the policy side, presidents are confronted with a need to fill hundreds of executive-level PAS positions across the government requiring specific skills, experience, and expertise. These jobs range from the Secretary of Defense to the Assistant Secretary of Labor for Occupational Safety and Health to the Under Secretary of Commerce for Intellectual Property. The success of the administration in controlling the bureaucracy depends upon their success in filling these slots. As Kennedy aide Larry O'Brien explained, "We approached this administration asking, 'How do you get control over this massive bureaucracy—control in the sense that it is directed in its activities to the president's interests?' If we can get control of the top 600 or 400 or 300 jobs, if we can only get this, get these people properly placed, then we will have some degree of control."[69]

There is almost uniform concern articulated voluntarily by persons involved in presidential personnel about how important it is to find loyal people with the right skills and background to fill these jobs. As Clay Johnson, George W. Bush's first director of presidential personnel, emphasized in a Bush administration personnel document, "This is not a beauty contest. The goal is pick the person who has the greatest chance of accomplishing what the principal wants done. . . . After the strongest candidate (s) has been identified, assess the political wisdom of the selection, and adjust accordingly."[70] Personnel is policy and White House officials recognize that in order to get control of policy, you need people who are loyal to the president and qualified for the job to which they have been appointed. In practice, evaluations of competence can be colored by ideology and the immediate need to fill literally thousands of jobs. Reagan aide Lyn Nofziger, for example, stated, "As far as I'm concerned, anyone who supported Reagan is competent."[71] That said, and importantly, most senior personnel officials define their job as finding the most competent people for senior administration posts.

Starting with President Nixon, many presidents have employed professional recruiters to help identify qualified persons for top executive posts. The most important personnel task at the start of each administration is that of identifying candidates to fill these positions. Each administration has produced lists of positions to be filled first. These include positions important for public safety but also usually positions that need to be filled early to advance the president's policy agenda. Transition advice to President Kennedy focused on the "pressure points" in government.[72] In the Reagan administration the transition focused first on the "Key 87" positions, which included executive posts necessary for implementation of Reagan's economic program.[73] These priority positions naturally receive the most attention throughout the president's term whenever vacancies occur. In some cases, the existing number of positions is sufficient to gain control and advance the president's agenda; in others, it is not.

On the patronage side, presidents and their personnel operations are besieged by office seekers who have a connection to the campaign, to the party, interest groups, or patrons in Congress important to the administration.[74] Recent administrations have received tens of thousands of resumes, and even more recommendations and communications dealing with specific candidates or jobs. One former Clinton personnel official estimated that they received 50,000 resumes in the first six weeks of the administration.[75] Overall, the Clinton administration received over 100,000 resumes.[76] Personnel officials describe the hectic and overwhelming process as akin to "standing at the intersection of four highways with Mack trucks bearing down," completely "chaotic," or characterized by the "insane pressure of every hour."[77] The pressure, the complexity, the emotional toll can be overwhelming, particularly when part of your job is explaining why aspirants have not been selected for the job of their choice. One personnel official even recounted being cornered in a restroom by a hopeful job seeker who thrust a resume into her hand![78] President George H. W. Bush's first director of presidential personnel, Chase Untermeyer, reflected, "Anyone who has done presidential personnel work never wants to do it again but can never stop talking about it."[79]

Dealing with requests for jobs involves evaluating the skills and backgrounds of priority job seekers and locating appropriate or defensible jobs in levels of pay and responsibility. In many cases, priority placements are young, inexperienced, or primarily qualified through political work. This makes them unqualified for top executive posts. The less background experience, the harder it is to find them jobs. Such applicants are usually given staff, liaison, advance, and public affairs jobs for which they are best qualified given their campaign experience. In other cases, people connected to the candidates either through personal relationships or contributions are too senior to take such jobs but are either not qualified for or not interested in top executive posts. Personnel officials often recommend these persons for ambassadorships, positions on commissions, or advisory posts.[80] These appointments provide a means for campaign supporters to feel involved in politics and get the psychic rewards that accompany service in the administration while working on a part-time basis.

Modern personnel operations have responded to the two sides of presidential personnel organizationally through an increasingly formal division between policy and patronage efforts. For example, one group of aides for President Kennedy headed by his brother was responsible for priority placement and patronage management. Another set, headed by Sargent Shriver, was charged with tapping "New Frontier Types" from their "egghead constituency" to direct the executive branch in a way responsive to Kennedy.[81] By the time of the first Clinton administration the demand-supply division was institutionalized in an office called the Office of Priority Placement. In the George W. Bush administration this job was handled by the Office of Political Affairs.[82]

This organizational division illustrates the different demands and tensions between the two operations. There is a disjuncture between the needs of those recruiting for executive positions and those handling requests from office seekers. What is demanded for the top executive slots is often not supplied through the priority-placement operation. The two streams in the personnel operation can run side by side and only intersect haphazardly since different people are involved in the two processes on a daily basis and the types of people the recruitment operation is searching for look different from the population that worked on the campaign or state party political apparatus. The number of people who want a job in the administration exceeds the number of jobs available, but this is not meant to imply that applicants are qualified for the specific jobs they are seeking. One director of presidential personnel described the job as one of traffic cop, there to ensure that the persons recommended for jobs had the competencies the position required.[83] The priority-placement operation will often recommend names of politically active people (for example, state directors, contributors, and the like) for open executive slots but these names are thrown into the mix with those uncovered in the recruitment process.

In practice, presidents and their subordinates in presidential personnel (PPO) determine the number and location of political appointees by starting with where their predecessor had appointees and then making incremental adjustments. Each administration learns what jobs were filled by appointees in the last administration through a variety of sources, including transition reports produced by teams sent to the different agencies in the executive branch prior to the inauguration, contacts with the previous administration, and government publications. Subsequent adjustments to the number and location of appointees are made based upon concerns about policy and the need to satisfy concerns for patronage.

The distinction drawn between policy and patronage activities in presidential personnel is not to suggest that policy-driven personnel practices have no patronage component or that efforts to reward campaign supporters cannot influence policy. On the contrary, patronage concerns invariably influence appointments, and appointees of all types can influence policy outputs. Rather, the point is that one process revolves primarily around filling *positions* and the other process revolves primarily around placing *persons*. These two fundamentally different goals are managed differently and have different effects on the number and penetration of political appointments in the bureaucracy.

Common Politicization Techniques

One factor that can influence the number and penetration of appointees in specific cases is the extent to which presidents and their appointees confront career personnel in management positions that do not share their ideology or priorities. Conflict between the president and agencies can emerge for a number of reasons. Sometimes the disagreement stems from what agencies do. Some agencies are designed with a specific policy goal in mind. For example, the Office of Economic Opportunity was the hallmark of Lyndon Johnson's Great Society. It was anathema to Richard Nixon, and he set about politicizing (and dismantling) it in the early 1970s.

In other cases the political biases of a particular agency have less to do with the mission of the agency embedded in law or executive decree than with issues of personnel. Career managers can be unresponsive because they are known to be partisans from the other party. For example, surveys of top executives from the Nixon and Ford administrations showed that many top managers, particularly executives in social service agencies, were unsympathetic to the policy goals of the Nixon administration.[84] More recent surveys confirm that top careerists in defense agencies are more likely to be Republican and conservative, whereas top careerists in social welfare agencies are likely to be Democrats and liberal.[85]

Career managers also often feel bound by legal, moral, or professional norms to certain courses of action and these courses of action may be at variance with the president's agenda.[86] Agencies act to implement policy directives spelled out in statutes, executive decrees, or informal directions from Congress. They are legally bound to implement the laws enacted, and the amount of discretion administrators possess to alter policy is not always clear. Differences of opinion arise about both managers' power and their responsibilities given this power. This is starkly illustrated in cases where career employees are asked to implement administrative policies they believe to be of questionable legality. For instance, career employees make administrative changes in the level and type of civil rights enforcement that might or might not include affirmative action as a remedy.[87] Directions from political appointees can also bump up against professional norms. The ranger in the Forest Service, the statistician in the Bureau of Labor Statistics, and the lawyer in the Justice Department has a point beyond which they cannot go and still maintain their professional integrity.[88]

In sum, there are a variety of reasons why career bureaucrats do not have the same perspective as their political superiors. As Herman Miles Somers writes, "The fact is that able men are rarely neutral in sentiment about important issues in which they share responsibility. Real neutrality would border on indifference and indifference soon becomes incompetence."[89] By virtue of their position, professional backgrounds, experience, and personal beliefs, career employees should and do have opinions about policy, but these opinions affect how presidents and political appointees perceive employee reliability and loyalty.

A number of different techniques for politicizing agencies address the perceived lack of responsiveness from career officials. These techniques are often used concurrently with other strategies for gaining control of the bureaucracy, such as budgeting, public statements, and administrative actions. To help visualize what this problem looks like, consider figure 2.3, an organizational chart from a hypothetical department in which the top three levels are filled by presidential appointments with Senate confirmation. Below this is a level of career managers who direct the operating programs and bureaus. Assume that one of these career man-

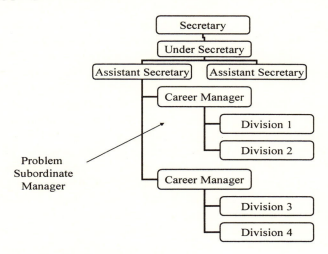

Figure 2.3. Hypothetical Agency Problem

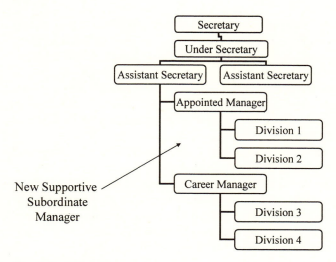

Figure 2.4. Replacement

agers is unresponsive or problematic to the administration in power for one of the reasons listed above.

Replacement

The first and most obvious solution to this dilemma is to remove the resistant career manager and replace this person with an appointee or more acceptable career person. If the position is a general SES position the president can replace the career SES manager with an appointee after a period of time, provided doing so will not put the agency over the statutory limit for the number of appointees in the SES or agency.

The president can also try to change the appointment authority of the position in question (figure 2.4). For example, a presidential administration could change a GS 15 career management position to a Schedule C position or a general SES position. Changes in appointment authority can sometimes be performed internally, as in the case of deciding which jobs are SES jobs. In other cases changes are performed with a request to the Office of Personnel Management (or earlier, the CSC). Most experienced personnel officers know how to use the appropriate terms of art to ensure their applications are approved.[90] The OPM director and many of her subordinates serve at the pleasure of the president, easing the way for the White House to get its way.

A good example of this type of replacement is seen in the Eisenhower administration's approach to getting control of the U.S. Fish and Wildlife Service (USFWS).[91] Prior to the Eisenhower administration the USFWS had been directed by a career employee of the Department of the Interior, as were most of the natural conservation agencies.[92] Upon assuming office, Eisenhower changed the director's position and two assistant director positions from career positions to Schedule C positions. He asked the existing director, Albert M. Day, to step down and become an assistant to the director. John L. Farley, a Seattle public relations official, was named director of the USFWS. Day's second in command, Dr. Clarence Cottam, resigned. Fifteen months after the shakeup the former director of the USFWS was fourth in command under an appointed director and two appointed assistant directors.[93]

The drawback of requesting that a position filled by career appointment be changed to an appointed position is that the career employee serving in this position at the time of its change often has tenure rights either in this job or a comparable job.[94] Requesting that a position be changed from a career position to an appointed position will solve the problem in the long run but perhaps not in the short run if the troublesome manager still works for the agency or has tenure rights to his job.

There are, however, three techniques well known in bureaucratic lore for getting unwanted employees to leave their current jobs.[95] The first and most obvious strategy for convincing a careerist to leave is the *frontal assault*. Political appointees meet privately with the career manager in question and tell the manager that her services are no longer needed. Career managers are offered help finding another job, a going-away party, and even a departmental award. The career manager is informed that if she refuses to leave, her employment record and references will suffer.

The career manager can also be *transferred* within the agency to a position she is unlikely to accept. The transfer offer is usually accompanied by a raise and perhaps a promotion to a newly created position. In such cases, appointees know ahead of time the types of jobs the career employee is likely or unlikely to accept. For example, the career manager known to have strong ties to the East Coast may be offered a job in Dallas or St. Louis. Appointees inform the career employee that if she does not want the new job, she can resign without prejudice from the agency and stay on in their current position for a limited amount of time until she finds another position.[96]

With a change in administration, careerists identified with the past administration's policies worry about being transferred to "turkey farms"—jobs with few responsibilities, limited staff, and no access to policymaking. For example, career SES employees in the George H. W. Bush administration who cut back disability benefits, tried to halt abortion counseling at clinics accepting federal funds, and implement U.S. policy toward the Sandinistas were at risk of transfer at the time of Bill Clinton's election.[97] As noted above, by law SES careerists cannot be removed without consent for 120 days by the new administration, but many waive these rights if the new administration requests it. If career employees do not waive this right, the new administration can transfer them after 120 days, provided they have been given appropriate written notice.[98]

A related strategy is the *new-activity* technique. Political appointees hatch plans for a new agency initiative, and the career employee in question is selected for the job ostensibly on the basis of his past performance and unique qualifications. The career manager is even promoted and given an increase in pay. The new initiative appears to be meaningful, but the real purpose behind it is to move the career manager out of his current position. In a less cynical way the administration can often accomplish two goals at one time, both by redirecting the energies of the career manager and by moving forward with a new initiative. Career managers who are a real obstacle to the administration in one job may not be as big a concern in another. For example, a competent but programmatically driven career manager in the Ballistic Missile Defense Organization may be moved to direct a new initiative in the Defense Advanced Research Projects Agency.

Of course, career employees have the advantage of both tenure protection and the knowledge that political appointees are birds of passage. Career employees can also forestall adverse personnel actions through connections to key interest groups or patrons in Congress. Career employees have the ability to leak information to the media or to press their case publicly. In fact, cases where career managers do not have connections leading to some media notice appear to be the exception. In 1977 President Carter removed the head of the U.S. Geological Service, Vincent E. McKelvey.[99] McKelvey was the first director ever to be removed by the president, and some suspected his removal resulted from the fact that his estimates of the amount of oil and natural gas in the ground were higher than that claimed by the White House. What was particularly noteworthy, according to accounts of his firing, however, was how little attention it attracted. "To hear those who asked for his resignation, McKelvey was fired in part because he had so few friends on Capitol Hill and in the White House that he did not know he was falling from favor."[100] Indeed, the article noted how few connections McKelvey had even on key committees in Congress.

Layering

Political appointees' difficulty in getting what they want through attempting to remove career employees and reclassifying their jobs often leads them to adopt other strategies. One of the most prominent is *layering*, the practice of adding politically appointed managers on top

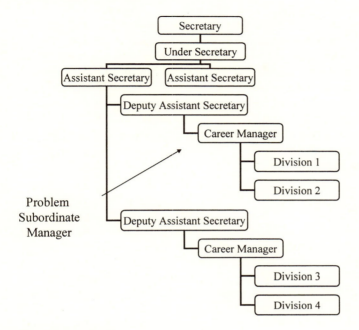

Figure 2.5. Layering

of career managers as a means of enhancing political control. For example, two deputy assistant secretaries are added between the Senate-confirmed assistant secretary and the career managers (figure 2.5). These new appointees can more carefully monitor the career managers and assume some of their policy-determining responsibilities through their influence in budget preparation, personnel decisions, and other administrative responsibilities.

A good example of the way layering can be used to enhance control is the reorganization of the Bureau of the Budget into the Office of Management and Budget (OMB) in 1970. In 1960 the Bureau of the Budget had fewer than ten political appointees: the director, the deputy director, three assistant directors, and a handful of personal staff.[101] The 1970 reorganization in the budget agency was supposed to focus increased attention on federal management, and the reorganization included a new appointee to head the management effort; however, it also brought in four new program associate directors.[102] These new appointees, the program associate directors (PADs), were put in below the existing appointed officials but above the permanent examining divisions. The examining divisions have always held a lot of power in federal budgeting: they review and control agency budget requests in the executive branch and are an important source of power and policy influence in government. Whereas previously the examining divisions were headed by career employees with access to the top of the agency, they were now subordinate to politically appointed directors. In total, the number of appointees in the budget agency increased from ten in 1960 to twenty in 1973. The increase was composed equally of positions with formal authority and ministerial staff for these positions. The Carter administration subsequently added more layers to the OMB.[103] In 1977, the Carter administration added two executive associate directors above the PADs added by Nixon. OMB also added six noncareer deputy associate directors below the PADs.

Add Appointed Ministerial Staff

A similar strategy is to *add appointed ministerial staff.* For instance, the Senate-confirmed assistant secretary adds two special assistants (figure 2.6). Titled positions like assistant secretaries often acquire title-riding appointees like chiefs of staff, special assistants, counsels, and public affairs personnel to help them perform their job.[104] The strategy of adding ministerial staff is different from layering in that the appointees added have little formal authority. While they have little formal authority, such appointees can acquire substantial informal authority as experts, gatekeepers, and public spokespeople.

Ministerial staff of this type usually comprises Schedule C appointees. Schedule C positions are created specifically for persons attached to the

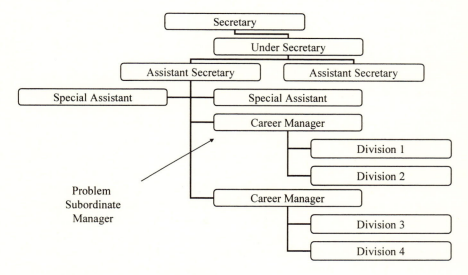

Figure 2.6. Increase Ministerial Staff

incoming appointees. Schedule C appointees gain power from being the primary advisors to higher-level appointees and from speaking with the implied authority of the appointee. In other contexts ministerial staff is given special projects, review budgets and legal documents, and help in personnel and administrative decisions. Schedule C positions can be training grounds for other appointed positions.[105] Persons working for higher-level appointees often gain valuable experience and exposure and move from these positions into managerial positions with more formal responsibility.

Reorganization

A fourth common politicization technique is *reorganization* (figure 2.7). Reorganization has been used strategically by managers to diminish the influence of problematic career managers and enhance political control. In the figure, the agency is reorganized so that the career manager is put in charge of a new division or project. This division can be entirely new, a nascent initiative, or it can simply be composed of preexisting personnel, responsibilities, and budgets put together in a new way. The nominal purpose of the reorganization can be to align organizational structure to better meet the bureau's stated goals or to increase efficiency but have the real or dual purpose of getting better control of the bureau. In large, modern agencies with complicated organizational structures, reorganizations can be subtle and effective means of getting political appointees in charge of important administrative responsibilities. In reorganizations, positions are created and disbanded, upgraded and downgraded, and these decisions are informed by the political needs of administration officials.

For example, in the 1980s enforcement activities within the Environmental Protection Agency (EPA) were reorganized at least three times.[106] In 1981 the Office of Enforcement was disbanded and the legal staff was parsed out to various other offices within the agency. EPA director Anne Burford assembled a new Office of Legal and Enforcement Counsel not long after, but key positions remained vacant into 1982. In 1983 a distinct Office of Enforcement Counsel was created under an assistant administrator. The effect of Burford's reorganizations, however, was to diminish the influence of inherited personnel partly through a decline in morale and high turnover among attorneys who had served in the old Office of Enforcement.

Reorganization can also be used to create parallel bureaucratic structures or processes to circumvent existing structures. This form of politicization takes two common forms. In the first, a new manager who is sympathetic to the goals of the administration is added to the management

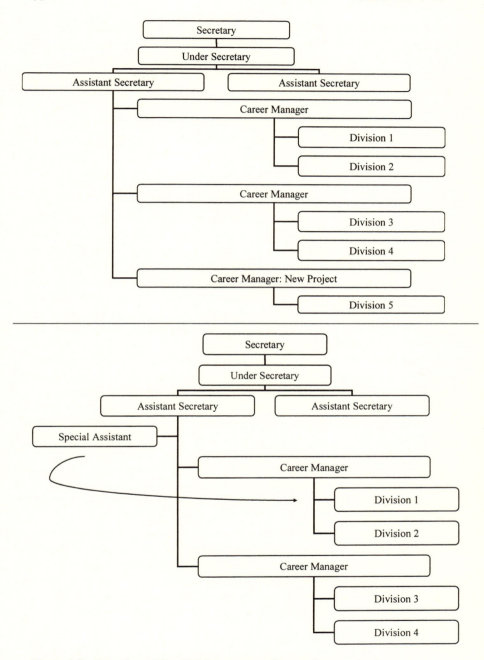

Figure 2.7. Generic and Parallel Structure or Process Reorganization

structure with staff and resources, as is illustrated in the top portion of figure 2.7. In this case, however, it is not the problematic career manager who is given this post; rather, it is the trusted, sympathetic manager with closer ties to the administration. This manager duplicates or explicitly assumes tasks performed by the division headed by the less-responsive career manager. The administration then cuts the disfavored manager out of decision making and downgrades the manager's division. A less costly way of building parallel processes is illustrated in the bottom portion of figure 2.7. Here, the administration trusts the work of the division but not the manager herself. In such cases, the administration can add ministerial staff to work around the career manager and get work directly from lower-level employees in the division.

Reductions-in-Force (RIF)

The final prominent technique for politicizing is the *reduction-in-force (RIF)*.[107] While RIFs are a normal part of organizational life in both the private and public sectors, they can also be used strategically to transform an unresponsive agency. Through RIFs federal officials cut employment as a way of getting control of the bureau. According to a general rule of "save grade, save pay," those career employees with the least experience lose their jobs first during RIFs, but those who stay with more seniority are bumped down in position and often assume tasks that are new or are different from what they were doing before. They often have to do more work for the same amount of pay, and the new tasks they assume are frequently jobs not performed by people in their pay scale. These ripple effects increase attrition beyond that caused by the initial RIF. For example, reducing the employment of Division 1 and Division 2 will lead to attrition in both divisions (figure 2.8). The career manager in charge of these divisions and her subordinates will have to do more work with fewer employees and manage through declining morale for an administration with whom they likely disagree ideologically.

The Reagan administration's treatment of the Council on Environmental Quality (CEQ) is a good example of this approach. In 1982 the CEQ's staff had been reduced from forty-nine, under President Carter, to fifteen.[108] The administration fired all of the immediate council staff, some of whom had served since the Nixon and Ford administrations.[109] Appointees from the campaign staff replaced those removed.

Informal Aids to Politicization

There are also a number of ways to augment politicization efforts informally. One common technique for politicizing administration is to leave

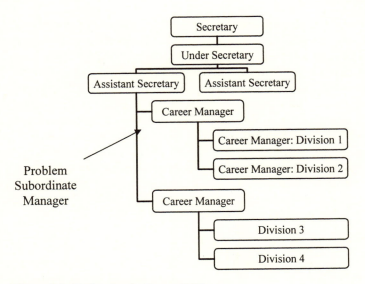

Figure 2.8. Reduction-in-Force (RIF)

Note: Career manager now takes on new and more routine responsibilities since subordinates have been removed or bumped down.

career positions vacant for significant periods of time and have appointees take over these responsibilities in an acting role. For example, during the second George W. Bush administration, when Sandra Bates, a career manager within the General Services Administration (GSA), decided to leave her position as Commissioner of the Federal Technology Service (FTS), Barbara Shelton was selected to fill that job in an acting role until a replacement was found.[110] Although career managers generally assume acting roles when appointees leave, Shelton was an appointee. She was the politically appointed regional administrator of the GSA's Mid-Atlantic region. No immediate plans were announced to select a permanent replacement in the agency. GSA was pursuing an internal reorganization wherein the FTS would be merged with the Federal Supply Service.

With lax oversight and informal norms, different presidential administrations have also been successful in influencing personnel choices inside the *civil service* without changing the appointment authority of the jobs themselves. Technically, personnel chosen for positions under the merit system are to be chosen outside the influence of politics. In reality, both Congress and the president can strongly influence the hiring of careerists at higher levels in the permanent federal service. The most formal and blatant attempt to do this was the Eisenhower administration's "Willis Directive."[111] Charles Willis, an assistant to Eisenhower chief-of-staff Sherman Adams, wrote and circulated an elaborate personnel plan for the new administration. The plan invited officials from the Republican National Committee (RNC), Republican congressmen, or other prominent state Republicans to recommend personnel for jobs both *inside* and outside the civil service. All jobs at GS 14 and above were called "controlled" positions. Federal agencies were to announce vacancies on forms supplied by the RNC and make regular reports to the RNC on how vacancies were filled. Both the spirit and contents of the plan violated Civil Service Rule 4, which state that career positions are to be filled "without regard to political or religious affiliation."[112]

President Johnson was known for his involvement in the selection of top-level careerists and for massaging them before they took their new jobs. Indeed, if appointees are making decisions about personnel in the career service, it is hard for them to divorce their political selves from their roles in the federal agency. Part of this direct interference in the selection of career employees is a natural response to the practice of *burrowing* that occurs regularly with presidential transitions. Administration officials and appointees seek to obtain career positions in the agencies where they work when a new administration is coming into office. Another source of creeping partisanship in the civil service, until it was repealed (effective December 1997), was the Ramspeck Act.[113] The act, passed in 1940, included a provision that was intended to help find jobs for congressional staff that lost legislative jobs after national elections. The justification for the act was that congressional staff had gained valuable experience, had served faithfully, and would perform competently in government service. Under the law, congressional employees could be appointed noncompetitively to the civil service at GS 15 or below if they had served three years in Congress and were appointed within one year of separation from congressional employment.[114] Congressional employees had to be qualified for the position for which they were being hired, but the agency was not required to consider other candidates. Between October 1984 and June 1994, agencies made 552 Ramspeck appointments, most in years after national elections. Of the 552 appointments, 28 percent were to GS 14 and GS 15 jobs, and 75 percent of the appointments were made to administration, program analysis, or public affairs jobs. The act was an important source of both partisan and congressional influence in administration.

In 1977 some career bureaucrats produced "hit lists" of political appointees from the Nixon and Ford administrations who had burrowed into career jobs. Less than four years later the Carter administration followed suit.[115] A GAO study reported that 30 percent of civil service hires made at the end of Carter's term were made improperly. A 1989 *New York*

Times article reported that 432 Reagan administration appointees joined the career service between January 1987 and September 1988.[116] In 1993 civil service unions gave the incoming Clinton administration what they called a "lizard list" of appointees and careerists who were alleged Republican collaborators.[117] Senator David Pryor (D-AR) also asked federal personnel to notify his office of cases where appointees were trying to obtain career positions. The incoming administration is usually informed by their own partisans who these former appointees are, and they take more or less active roles in trying to get them to leave. Should vacancies arise, they take an active role in ensuring that new people in these career positions are less partisan than their predecessors.

In total, the numbers and percentages of appointees vary from administration to administration because of replacement, layering, reorganization, and RIFs. These politicization techniques can be augmented by less-formal techniques, such as strategic vacancies, political influence in the hiring of careerists, and bending of the rules in administrative determinations and rulings.

Congressional Responses

Of course, politicization choices happen with an eye toward Congress since the legislative branch has both the means of learning about politicization and a variety of ways to respond—a topic I will revisit in the next chapter. Civil servants in the affected agencies complain to the press or friendly members of Congress. As one personnel official explained to me, "the *Washington Post* is their inspector general."[118] Others confirmed that the possibility that their actions might appear on the front page of the *Washington Post* constrained personnel actions. Personnel officials also suggested that members of Congress were attentive to appointee head-counts, and the existence of congressional reports including such counts confirms their claim.[119]

Personnel officials recognize that their missteps can lead to problems for the president and adjust their behavior accordingly. At minimum, an influential member of Congress can informally communicate his displeasure with the agency or the White House. Members can also publicize the president's action, creating an embarrassing situation for the White House. For example, in 1987 several Democratic members of Congress accused the Reagan administration of "packing" the top ranks of government with appointees to the detriment of the federal service. Backed by a GAO report tracking appointments, these members denounced an increase in appointees to the SES, particularly in the agencies that manage the government such as the OPM (personnel), the GSA (facilities), and the OMB (finances).[120] During the Clinton administration, Republicans publicly complained about the politicization of the Commerce Department, and they requested that the GAO investigate the burrowing of Democratic appointees and staff into civil service positions.[121] In the second George W. Bush administration, the Democratic minority used charges of cronyism coupled with data on appointee increases to score political points.[122]

More concretely, Congress can refuse presidential requests to create new Senate-confirmed positions or use their appropriations power to limit these and other types of appointed positions.[123] For example, efforts to elevate the EPA to a cabinet department in the George H. W. Bush administration were derailed partly due to Congress's refusal to accede to the president's requests for additional appointees.[124] Congress has also enacted limits on the number of positions that could be paid at appointee-level salaries as a means of limiting the number of appointees. They occasionally include specific language in appropriations bills mandating that none of the appropriations be used to pay the salaries of more than a set number of appointees. For example, the Department of Transportation and Related Agencies Appropriations Act, enacted in the late 1980s, includes the following language, "None of the funds in this Act shall be available for salaries and expenses of more than [insert number] political and Presidential appointees in the Department of Transportation." The number of appointees allowed has varied in other bills from a low of 88 to a high of 138.[125]

These instances are rare but this should not be taken as evidence that presidents can act with a free hand. On the contrary, White House officials anticipate the likely response of Congress and adjust their behavior accordingly. They are less likely to politicize if they expect Congress to overturn their action or impose serious political costs on the president.

Politicization in the Modern Personnel System: The Reorganization of the Civil Service Commission (CSC)

With the nature and history of the modern personnel system clarified, I turn to a case study of the Civil Service Commission (CSC) to illustrate how politicization happens in practice. The case illustrates how techniques such as reorganization, increases in ministerial staff, layering, replacement, and reductions-in-force can be used to change agency policy and, ultimately, public policy. They also illustrate, however, how such actions can influence agency competence.

The CSC, in existence since the passage of the Pendleton Act in 1883, performed the dual and competing roles of protecting the merit system and facilitating executive management. Historically, the former role took precedence over the latter.[126] The commission was characterized by an insular professionalism and a police-like reputation for pursuing merit system abuses.[127] As the 1970s progressed, however, dissatisfaction with the federal bureaucracy was growing. Public sentiment held that government workers were underworked, overpaid, and unresponsive.[128] A 1978 Roper Poll reported that only 18 percent of the public believed the civil service attracted the best possible people and less than 10 percent thought it was free of corruption.[129] The press retold stories of the twenty-one months it took one federal manager to fire a clerk-typist that was late for work every day or how one manager had to completely reorganize an entire division to get around one incompetent manager.[130] Several states initiated civil service reforms to increase bureaucratic responsiveness.[131]

During his 1976 campaign for the presidency, Jimmy Carter campaigned against the bureaucracy and pledged to reform and reorganize the civil service.[132] He followed up on this pledge when he proposed a major personnel system overhaul in his 1978 State of the Union Address.[133] Carter's efforts resulted in the passage of the Civil Service Reform Act (CSRA) of 1978. The act reorganized the CSC into the Office of Personnel Management and the Merit Systems Protection Board. The former assumed the bulk of CSC's staff, its physical plant, and its personnel-management functions. The latter assumed CSC appellate functions and was charged with conducting studies of the merit system. The act also created the Senior Executive Service, the Office of Special Counsel, and the Federal Labor Relations Authority.[134] The change from the CSC to the OPM was by all accounts intended to strengthen presidential and executive management of personnel.[135] This shift, however, did not end the OPM's role as one of the merit system's key defenders in government. The OPM partly determines which positions can be filled by appointment, and it audits and monitors other federal agencies to ensure compliance with civil service rules. Fundamentally, its job is to ensure the health of the federal civil service through activities intended to improve the recruitment, retention, and performance of federal employees.

Carter's change toward more executive control was not popular with career professionals in the CSC. Many careerists within CSC worried the new OPM would not aggressively protect the merit system, were alienated by the rhetoric accompanying the change, and resented the increase in political appointees caused by the reorganization. One careerist from the period explained, "When OPM was first established, some CSC people draped their offices in black believing that the political presence at OPM would serve to undermine the effort to assure adherence to the civil service merit system."[136] The reorganization came not long after CSC had uncovered serious merit system abuses that reached very high levels in the GSA, Small Business Administration (SBA), and Department of Housing and Urban Development (HUD). Career professionals worried that the change to OPM reflected a move away from merit and generally feared that "all hell [was] going to break loose."[137] The pain of the change was exacerbated by the bureaucracy-bashing that accompanied it. According to one long-serving CSC/OPM careerist, the "rhetoric Carter had to use . . . to get the political will to get changes in the law . . . had to be pretty strong." She continued, "Merit system stalwarts [in CSC] . . . felt the rhetoric driving the change very personally. . . . [They were] hurt, defensive, kind of 'how can you say these things about us?' "[138]

The change from the CSC to OPM increased the number of political appointees by six positions (figure 2.9). This increase does not reveal the full extent of the politicization, however, since the creation of the Senior Executive Service made transferring career managers easier and opened the door for appointees to replace careerists as heads of the major divisions in the future.[139] In the fall of 1976 the CSC had three Senate-confirmed commissioners, one noncareer executive, and two Schedule C appointees. Three of the six appointees ran relatively minor programs quite apart from the core functions of the agency.[140] In reality, there was no appointee presence in the agency below the level of the commissioners in 1976. By the end of the Carter administration, the agency had twelve appointees, including nine Schedule C appointees.[141] These additional appointees worked primarily in ministerial staff positions in the office of the director and deputy director. They worked as special assistants, policy advisors, and public and legislative affairs specialists. They replaced career professionals or were placed in newly created positions.

Turnover among career professionals in the agency was substantial. Some employees voluntarily left to take advantage of severance packages, while others departed, or were encouraged to do so, because of the reorganization.[142] One OPM aide explained, "I would say that anybody viewed as 'negative' about civil service reform, or who raised questions about the dangers of politicization that are very real and possible under reform, was marked as a 'mossback' by the new team."[143] Another said, "Obviously, the new OPM officials . . . have new and different ideas. . . . They would be comfortable with different people in some of the key jobs."[144] Among those who left the agency were the former executive director of the CSC, a long-time assistant to the CSC's three commissioners, and the top echelon of the retirement and insurance section.[145] Whatever the cause, the insular professional culture of the CSC oriented toward protecting the merit system was being opened up and reoriented with a new and expanded appointee team.

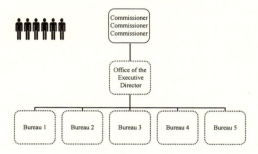

Civil Service Commission--1978

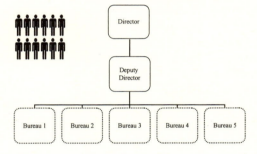

Office of Personnel Management--1980

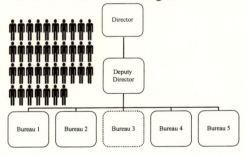

Office of Personnel Management--1984

Figure 2.9. Politicization of the Civil Service Commission and Office of Personnel Management, 1978–1984

Note: Solid outline signifies that the office is headed by a presidential appointee or inclydes an appointed deputy. A dotted outline signifies that the office is headed by careerist. The total number of appointees is reflected to the left of the organization charts.

The reorganization succeeded in changing federal personnel policy. In addition to the changes wrought directly by CSRA, the new OPM shifted its focus away from merit system protection to executive management. This is seen most clearly in a decline in the number of person-years allocated to merit system oversight and an OPM-approved increase of 800 Schedule C appointees government-wide. Outside reviews of the agency by the Merit Systems Protection Board and the National Academy of Public Administration between 1979 and 1981 noted insufficient attention and oversight of agency compliance with merit system principles.[146]

Reagan and a Return to "Bedrock Personnel Management"

The 1980 election brought a significantly more conservative administration into power and in early 1981 Ronald Reagan appointed Donald J. Devine to lead the newly reorganized agency. The Reagan administration and Devine shared the Carter administration's desire for more executive control but were significantly more conservative than both Carter and the career professionals that remained in the agency.[147] Devine sought cuts in federal employee health care benefits and an end to coverage of abortions for federal employees.[148] Within OPM itself he wanted to return to "bedrock personnel management," meaning he wanted the agency to do no more than the agency's statutes required.[149] As part of this effort Devine cut programs for which there was no clear statutory authority and sought to recentralize control over agency examining.[150] Devine also implemented a reduction-in-force and cut agency budgets. OPM's employment declined from 8,280 in 1980 to 5,929 by 1986.[151]

Government-wide, he sought to increase presidential control over agency activities. He met personally with the heads of cabinet departments and large independent agencies to encourage them to increase the number of appointees and make full use of their powers under civil service rules. Agencies had been nervous about increasing the number of appointed positions because OPM under Carter had begun clamping down.[152] Devine was credited with cutting employee pay and benefits and sought to implement rules to reward good performance. His efforts were estimated to have saved the government $6.4 billion in personnel costs.[153]

Devine enhanced his control of the agency by increasing the number of political appointments, reassigning career members of the SES, reducing the size of the career staff, and centralizing the decision making inside the director's office.[154] He more than doubled the number of politically appointed positions from twelve in the fall of 1980 to thirty-seven by 1984.[155] OPM employees from that period described Devine's appointees as "highly charged," "principled," or "determined."[156] Through layering or outright replacement, Devine placed appointees in program offices previously run by career professionals. While all five of the agency's associate directors (the heads of the agency's major divisions) were career professionals in 1980, by 1984 Devine had replaced two of the five with appointees (figure 2.9).[157] He also placed appointed deputies under two of the careerist associate directors. Among other new appointees were five Schedule C appointees to represent Devine in the agency's regions, referred to derisively by some OPM employees as Devine's "political commissars."[158] Their job was to serve as liaison between Devine and the ten careerist regional directors. They communicated the Reagan administration's policies to the regions, monitored their activities, and worked with regional offices of other federal agencies to coordinate and implement Reagan's vision across the government.[159] Devine also added three Schedule C appointees in the Office of the Director in staff roles.

In total, Devine's actions were successful in changing policy, particularly in the short run. Adding appointees helped Devine succeed in his efforts to secure control of OPM's decision-making processes, roll back OPM management to its bedrock statutory responsibilities, cut employee health benefits, and eliminate coverage of abortions. Through Devine, the Reagan administration decreased federal personnel costs, increased executive personnel control, and reduced the size of government.

The response of agency employees was predictable. Devine's policy changes and style made him unpopular with the federal workforce.[160] By the fall of 1981, the American Federation of Government Employees (AFGE) publicly asked for his resignation.[161] The combination of staff cuts and management style also hurt morale in OPM and led to the departure of a number of long-serving careerists. Devine's actions made it hard to replace those who had departed and to recruit new people to work at the agency. As one careerist explained, "You don't just replace these people with 20–25 years of experience. . . . Who wanted to come work for us? You couldn't replace [the departed people] with the same quality people. . . . [OPM] never recovered from that loss."[162] The departures hindered the agency's ability to perform both the bedrock functions required by statute as well as Devine's personal initiatives.[163]

The politicization of OPM had lasting consequences for agency performance in merit system monitoring, personnel policy research, and human resource management. In a ten-year review conducted in 1989, the GAO reported that the OPM had not provided the necessary leadership on human resource issues across the government.[164] The report was particularly critical of the OPM's leadership and noted that the starkly different policy views of the three directors, frequent reorganizations, and staff cuts had eroded the OPM's morale, communications, long-term planning, and, ultimately, capacity. The OPM had failed to identify and remedy key human resource problems in the federal government and had witnessed a decline in morale and human capital within the agency. The report also noted critically a "long-standing concern" with the OPM's oversight of the merit system. A survey of personnel officers showed that only 29 percent believed the OPM had been effective in monitoring agency personnel systems for abuses. Additionally, they were more negative than in 1980 about OPM's effectiveness.[165] Academics criticized the quality of the agency's research products and the erosion in staffing services.[166] Summary assessments of the OPM's first ten years concluded that it had neither protected the merit system nor provided effective executive management. It had lost credibility with the operating agencies and control of the governmental personnel agenda.[167]

Summary

The overall goal of both presidencies to enhance presidential control of the bureaucracy through personnel policy was successful due to the politicization of the CSC and OPM. It also helped both presidents change other aspects of federal personnel policy including executive training, health benefits, and experimental programs. It is noteworthy that the politicization occurred under both a Democrat and a Republican and that their shared goal was explicitly to enhance the control of presidents and their subordinates over personnel. It illustrates how the desire to control the bureaucracy crosses party lines.

The politicization came at a cost, however. Changing federal personnel management through the reorganization of the CSC into OPM and subsequent politicization through layering, replacement, increases in ministerial staff, and reductions-in-force had severe consequences for agency competence. Experienced career professionals left the agency and it was hard to replace them. It was also difficult to recruit bright young people to work in the agency. Morale declined, the agency had trouble conducting long-term planning, and by the early 1990s the agency was so poorly regarded that many feared it would be absorbed by the OMB.[168] While many credit Clinton OPM director James King with saving the agency, he did so at the cost of shedding agency activities and cutting employment almost in half.[169] Politicization helped change policy but at the expense of long-term agency capacity and reputation.

Conclusion

To understand politicization decisions from administration to administration one has to understand the context of both the history of the merit system and the details defining the different strategies and techniques employed. The professional merit-based civil service system was a late arrival in the United States. The United States federal government operated for almost one hundred years without a formal professional civil service, yet the importance of ensuring both loyalty and competence in the federal service was already evident. During the height of the spoils system, a dual personnel system existed with a continuing body of professionals working side by side with patronage appointees. The dual system presaged numerous attempts to institute merit systems in the period leading up to the formal creation of the merit system.

The 1883 reforms embodied in the Pendleton Act were focused on the task of eliminating spoils. Reformers sought to end assessments, political activity by public employees, and patronage hiring and firing through the expansion of merit protection and the merit system. The U.S. personnel system's narrow focus on spoils had a lasting effect on public personnel management. The United States was slow to focus on positive human resource management activities like recruitment, training, morale, and benefits. Instead, the personnel system was defined by rules designed to protect workers from the evil of spoils. Part of Congress's recent motivation for allowing individual agencies to develop personnel systems outside the traditional merit-based civil service system is to allow them to escape the cumbersome and antiquated federal personnel system. Isolated exceptions to Title 5 have now become a landslide, with less than one-half of all federal personnel under the traditional merit system. The Merit Systems Protection Board, the appellate body that hears employee complaints, is cutting its budget and closing regional offices.[170]

While the federal personnel system continues to change dramatically, the politicization calculus remains much the same. Political actors are making decisions about the numbers of Senate-confirmed, noncareer SES, and Schedule C appointees in an effort to make the bureaucracy responsive to them and satisfy demands for patronage. In the same way they feared turning over competent, long-tenured professionals in the Jacksonian era, so, too, they fear politicizing too much now. In the next chapter I explain how presidents balance these competing concerns in the context of their relationship with Congress and larger trends in executive governance.

3

Why, When, and Where Do Presidents Politicize the Bureaucracy?

IN 1999 the U.S. Department of Education was the subject of a scathing exposé by the *Los Angeles Times*.[1] The *Times* alleged that the department was poorly managed, partly because of the large number of political appointees in the agency. Since its creation in 1979 the Education Department has housed a large and increasing number of political appointments. In 1980 the department had 92 political appointees (compared to 7,321 total employees).[2] By the end of the Clinton administration, the pool of appointees had grown to 148 (compared to only 4,711 total employees). The *Times* report cited a number of cases where public officials friendly to the Clinton administration were given lucrative appointed posts in the department to perform a variety of activities, including work for the administration outside the department. This is not surprising, given that historically the department has been a holding ground for political appointees who have been awarded jobs because of their campaign support, political connections, or future considerations.[3] National education policy has also been the locus of fierce policy fights between Republicans and Democrats, leading each new administration to try to gain control of the department by increasing the number of appointees.

The Department of Education example illustrates important features of politicization that are highlighted in this chapter: namely, that both Democrats and Republicans alter the number and location of appointees and do so for reasons of policy and patronage. This chapter reviews the prevailing opinions about when politicization occurs and explains why these views are incomplete. It theorizes about *when* and *where* presidents will seek to change the number of appointees, focusing on the presidents' needs to control policy and satisfy demands for patronage. It does so, as well, in the context of Congress's key role in personnel decisions. The chapter concludes with a set of empirical predictions to be evaluated in the coming chapters.

Political Science Views of Politicization

The most prominent academic work on politicization in the United States was written in response to actions taken by presidents Nixon and

Reagan. President Nixon's administrative response to real and perceived abuses of the personnel system by the Kennedy and Johnson administrations was both vigorous and systematic and well documented in a number of sources.[4] Nixon's approach to the administrative state began unremarkably with the appointment of cabinet officials of generally high quality and independent national stature. Nixon publicly gave the secretaries the ability to make their own subcabinet appointments and tried to integrate appointees into the working of the White House through interagency vehicles like the Urban Affairs Council. Dissatisfied with what he saw as a disloyal bureaucracy tied too closely to patrons in Congress, agency clienteles, and interest groups, however, Nixon sought almost immediately to gain greater control of the executive branch. After his first attempts at gaining control through the expansion of the White House policy apparatus failed, Nixon began to employ other tools. He used impoundment, reorganization authority, and new rules to achieve policy ends administratively. Importantly, Nixon also shifted his personnel strategy. At the beginning of his second term he replaced existing appointees with loyalists, inserted additional political appointees deep into the departments and bureaus, and tried to accomplish informally what Congress would not allow formally in reorganization. An essential component of this personnel strategy was both the layering of appointees on top of existing structures and the replacement of unfriendly career officials with politically chosen executives.[5] In White House aide and OMB official Fred Malek's "Malek Manual" for political appointees, the administration details a number of techniques for getting around civil service laws and replacing unwanted careerists in the executive branch.[6]

Taking its cue from the Nixon administration, the Reagan administration believed that environmental and social welfare agencies were populated with Democratic partisans hired and promoted because they were dedicated to programs they were managing. Accounts of Reagan's politicizing show that he used the enhanced appointment power in the Civil Service Reform Act of 1978, natural vacancies occurring through attrition, reorganization, and program cuts, and increases in political appointees in key agencies to get control.[7] Reagan was successful at enhancing political-appointee control through the strategic use of both internal agency reorganizations and employment cuts, known as reductions-in-force (RIFs). Reagan's drive to cut employment in domestic agencies had much the same effect as more overt politicization or reorganization in some circumstances since it altered the career-appointee balance in many agencies.

The natural conclusion, given this review and well-publicized politicization episodes in both George W. Bush administrations, is that politicization is a Republican strategy, but there are two problems with this view.

First, it is difficult to make inferences without reference to cases where politicization did *not* occur. For example, if Republican presidents were behind all the cases of *depoliticization* in addition to politicization, it would be hard to draw conclusions about the relationship between Republican presidents and politicization. At the very least, this would lead to a markedly different view than that politicization is a Republican phenomenon. There are numerous cases in which Republican presidents did not politicize. Neither President Ford nor President George H. W. Bush was accused of politicizing the executive branch. Instead, President George H. W. Bush spoke in his first week in office directly to managers at the level where politicization occurs to assuage their fears, to seek pay raises for them, to encourage cooperation, and to praise their work.[8]

Second, there are alternative, more plausible explanations for the commonly recited cases of politicization. The problem with the partisan explanation is that it attributes to partisanship what is more appropriately explained by the institutional context that each president inherits. It is important to remember that much of the modern administrative state was created by Democratic presidents and Democratic majorities in Congress. As a consequence, ideological and policy commitments were locked into these agencies through personnel and statute.[9] The policies advocated and implemented by these agencies were quite different from those espoused by Republican presidents. Republican attempts to politicize social welfare agencies have less to do with politicization as a uniquely Republican strategy than with politicization as a generic presidential response in cases where agencies have policy commitments that differ from those of the president. Democrats with similar concerns act in a similar fashion. President Franklin Delano Roosevelt's suspicion of the continuing bureaucracy in his first term led him to create new agencies to implement the New Deal rather than to delegate that authority to existing agencies.[10] Roosevelt created new agencies and staffed them outside the merit system with loyal New Dealers and added those positions to the civil service later in his tenure.

Other scholars have taken the evidence of politicization by Nixon and Reagan to argue that all modern presidents, both Republicans and Democrats, have an incentive to politicize. Terry Moe argues presidents are held accountable for the performance of the whole government and respond by centralizing decision-making authority in the White House and politicizing the bureaucracy.[11] He is dubious of the responsiveness of career employees to presidential direction. Moe claims that the president is primarily a politician and is less concerned with effectiveness than with a staff structure that is responsive to his political needs. He cites the White House Office (all employees serve at the pleasure of the president) as an example of a structure that better meets the needs of the president than the Bureau of the Budget (later OMB). Moe also claims that while presidents largely inherit the basic institutional framework of the presidency, they try to make it more responsive by "manipulating civil service rules, proposing minor reorganizations, and pressing for modifying legislation . . . to increase the number and location of administrative positions that can be occupied by appointees."[12]

Hugh Heclo worries about the advent of a government of strangers and famously argues that presidents should look for neutral competence in their staff agencies, particularly the OMB.[13] By neutrality, Heclo means "giving one's cooperation and best independent judgment of the issues to partisan bosses—and of being sufficiently uncommitted to be able to do so for a succession of partisan leaders."[14] The primary means of ensuring neutrality in executive office agencies is to have them staffed by career employees with an ethos of "speak up, shut up, carry up, carry out."[15] For Heclo, the increase in appointees is ill advised and partly due to the fact that presidents do not properly understand their strategic situation. If they did, they would rely more heavily on career personnel.

Both Moe and Heclo see the increase in politicization as a potential trend. Moe seeks to describe and make sense of it while Heclo argues against it. The difficulty with the view that politicization is a trend, as Paul Light points out, is that the number of appointees is not always increasing and there is quite a bit of variation across agencies.[16] Light points out that there was actually a decline in the *percentage* of political appointees relative to civil service employment in the years between 1984 and 1992. He also notes that while some agencies like the International Trade Administration or the Office of Justice Programs have a lot of presidential appointees, others like the Patent and Trademark Office and the Bureau of Prisons have zero. What is likely, and both Heclo and Moe would probably agree, is that presidents seek more appointees in some cases and none or fewer in others.

The task, then, is to theorize about *when* and *where* presidents will seek to politicize. Of course, while multiple factors are influential in different cases, the task of theorizing is to highlight the most important factors. The Education Department and FEMA cases suggest two forces driving politicization: concerns for policy and demands for patronage.

POLICY AND PATRONAGE IN POLITICIZATION DECISIONS

Modern presidents share certain similarities based upon their constitutional and political position. This is particularly true in the modern period, when the president's behavior and outlook are defined and disciplined by the continuing professional institutional presidency and stable-party system.[17] Both Republicans and Democrats are expected to influence policy administratively through the use of personnel and presidents of both parties feel pressure to help their party accomplish its electoral goals through the shrewd distribution of patronage.

Presidents from both parties serve in the same office, with the same formal powers as their predecessors. They can veto legislation, negotiate treaties, nominate principal officers, and they are vested with a vaguely defined executive power. They serve as commander-in-chief of the armed forces, can recommend legislation, and remove insubordinate appointees. They face a similarly structured legislative branch, made up of disparate members of Congress from different districts and states. Some members of Congress share the president's preferences for policy and some do not. All chief executives ostensibly face the same judicial and constitutional constraints, although modern presidents have been aggressive in inventing new ways of circumventing these constraints, at least in the short run (for example, impoundment, executive regulatory review, signing statements). These formal powers, though subject to differing meanings over time and negotiated by interactions among the three branches, are the institutional inheritance of all presidents.[18]

The president (along with the vice president) is also the only nationally elected political official, and this influences the president's incentives in office. The president's constituency is the whole nation, and presidents are held accountable, fairly or unfairly, for the performance of the entire nation—for national security, foreign affairs, the economy, and domestic politics.[19] For example, President George W. Bush was generally blamed for the intelligence failures prior to the September 11, 2001, terrorist attacks and Iraq war, even though presidents theoretically share responsibility for national security and foreign policy with Congress and even though Bush inherited the laws, bureaucratic structures, and personnel from previous administrations. Voters consistently use economic conditions in their evaluations of presidential performance, even though presidents have very little direct control over the economy.[20] When irregularities in corporate business practices surfaced—most notably in the Enron and Worldcom corporate scandal cases—the administration felt compelled to ask the Bush-appointed chairman of the Securities and Exchange Commission, Harvey Pitt, to step down.[21] Since voters and history judge presidents for the performance of the entire federal government during their tenure, this creates incentives for presidents to ensure that policy outcomes, both legislative and administrative, are under their control.

Administrative outcomes are particularly important for presidents to control since bureaucratic officials are increasingly responsible for important policy decisions such as postwar occupation plans (Defense Department), monetary policy (Board of Governors of the Federal Reserve), the direction of antitrust policy (Justice Department), and Medicare cost estimates (Department of Health and Human Services). Some responsibility for legislative failings can be attributed by presidents to Congress, but this is rarely the case for administrative shortcomings. In 1948 President Truman successfully labeled the Republican-led Congress a "do-nothing" Congress. In 1995 and 1996 President Clinton successfully shut down the government, and the Republican majority in Congress received most of the blame. It is harder for presidents to share or shift the blame for *administrative* policy since the president is the nominal chief executive and is widely viewed as something like the CEO of the administrative state. One way presidents enhance bureaucratic control is to politicize.

Modern presidents also share similar pressures based upon their political position. Presidents serve in a key role at the head of their political party. The party's fortunes nationwide are influenced to a great extent by the president's success or failure. The president's control over personnel is a source of political capital, and how a president uses this resource can directly affect not only the electoral fortunes of his party, but also his own political fortunes and leverage for bargaining with the legislative branch.

As chapter 2 explained, politicization for policy follows a different pattern than that for patronage, involving different people and processes within the White House. Examining these two forces in politicization decisions provides a means of shedding new light on when presidents will politicize and which agencies they will target.

The Dynamics of Politicization for Policy

When new presidents assume office, they encounter a continuing, professional administrative state comprising over two million civilian employees divided into fifteen different cabinet departments and fifty-five to sixty independent agencies and their various bureaus, divisions, and offices. To manage this vast apparatus, new presidents are allocated approximately 3,000 appointees, or 0.15 percent of the federal workforce. The percentage of personnel subject to presidential appointment varies by agency. In some agencies, such as the Small Business Administration or the Department of Education, the percentage is much higher, 1.5 to 3 percent. In other agencies, the percentage is much smaller. The Department of Veterans Affairs, an agency of 236,000 persons, employs only 40 appointees (.02 percent). The Social Security Administration, an agency with 65,000 employees, has only 21 appointees (.03 percent).

This variation in politicization allows presidents different amounts of influence in the continuing bureaucracy. In some cases presidential influence can penetrate deeply into an agency. In other cases, presidents have no foothold or means of easy entrée and, as a consequence, agencies have very little interaction with or direction from the White House. Presidents, predictably, often feel as if they do not control a large enough portion of the personnel positions in the bureaucracy. President Gerald Ford said this in illuminating fashion in an interview not long after he left office:

> I think a president ought to have a little more flexibility further down in the bureaucracy, as to both the people appointed and those that can be dismissed. The American voters select a president because of what he says or promises . . . but, if he cannot reach into the bowels of a department, his decisions way up at the top will seldom be adequately implemented out in the grass roots.[22]

The feeling Ford describes is particularly acute in cases where agencies make or implement policy in an area of particular presidential interest owing to public concern, electoral consequence, or ideological predisposition.

Altering the number and penetration of appointees through replacement, layering, increasing ministerial staff, reorganizing, building parallel processes, or engaging in reductions-in-force can help presidents ensure that agencies are making policy decisions in a manner that complements and/or furthers the president's policy priorities. Placing appointees in the direct policymaking positions and increasing appointed staff to monitor program implementation, screen personnel, and help with public affairs facilitates agency consistency with the White House in message and action.

PRESIDENTS AND POLICY POLITICIZATION

Given that there are important similarities in how presidents desire to control the bureaucracy of the executive branch, theorizing generically about presidents is an appropriate and powerful tool for understanding trends in politicization over time. I make four key assumptions that will be the building blocks for the theoretical apparatus that follows. Each assumption is reasonable but not unimpeachable and I discuss the implications of relaxing two of the assumptions below. A formal derivation of the central components of theoretical apparatus that follows is included in appendix 3a.

First, I assume that presidents care about policy outcomes.[23] They care about policy either because they inherently prefer a specific public policy or because their policy choices influence how voters and historians perceive them. If an agency has a different view about policy, presidents prefer that it would be closer to their own.

Second, I assume that presidents want agencies to be competent.[24] All else being equal, presidents prefer that an agency, once given directions, is successful at carrying them out. The president prefers that agencies not make mistakes, since errors can lead to policy outcomes that are worse for the president. To illustrate, consider the president's views about budget-forecasting agencies. All presidents want competent forecasters even if they want forecasts to be biased in different directions, either optimistically or conservatively. All presidents are made worse off if forecasters cannot hit their targets, whether the target is an accurate or biased forecast.

Third, I assume that agencies themselves have views about policy but that these views can be changed by adding presidential appointees.[25] Agency views about policy are sometimes embedded in the statutes or decrees that created the agency. For example, the statute creating the Occupational Safety and Health Administration (OSHA) states that the agency is to "assure as far as possible every man and woman in the Nation safe and healthy working conditions."[26] Critically, an agency's policy views also stem from the personnel who populate it. The personnel may be Republicans or Democrats, or they may care about the mission of the agency they work for in a way that puts them at odds with the president.

Finally, I assume that agencies with a high percentage of appointees have less competence than agencies with a low percentage. Efforts to increase the number of appointees not only change policy but also hurt competence. In chapters 6 and 7 I explain more fully the reasons why appointee-filled agencies are less competent than other agencies and demonstrate this empirically. Briefly, some management expertise and skills are site-specific, gained only through experience working in a policy area or agency for some time and careerists are more likely to have this knowledge. This site-specific expertise can be an understanding of the folkways of the agency, knowledge of the informal power networks, or a familiarity with agency records, personnel, or policy processes. In addition, agencies with a significant number of appointed positions experience more executive turnover and have difficulty recruiting and retaining high-quality career professionals; these structural disadvantages hurt performance.

Starting from these four assumptions, it is possible to derive some interesting theoretical claims about presidents and their ideal numbers of appointees for different agencies. First, and again all else being equal, the larger the distance between the views of presidents and the views of agencies, the more appointees presidents prefer. The president's views about policy can be quite different from those of agencies both because presidents from different parties serve in the White House, but also because agencies themselves have strong views about policy. Adding political appointees or replacing career employees with appointees is one way of bringing the agency's preferences in line with those of the president. These appointees can be program managers or ministerial staff, and the changes are usually targeted toward the top positions of the managerial hierarchy. If the president and the agency share common views or if the disagreement between the agency and the president decreases, the preferred amount of politicization will also decrease. Fewer appointees are necessary to change agency policy when the agency's views mimic those of the sitting president.

Proposition 1. *Presidents are more likely to politicize when their policy views diverge from those of the agency.*

A second factor influencing the optimal number of appointees is how easily different agencies can accommodate appointees without influencing competence. The problem with making agencies more responsive through politicization is that such actions endanger administrative competence, moreso in some agencies than in others—some agencies can perform well with large numbers of appointees and others poorly without any appointees at all. The key performance factor that influences the president's choice is the *marginal* influence changes in appointees will have on performance. This implies that presidents will politicize or depoliticize agencies that are performing well or poorly in different cases. In some cases, adding more appointees to a poorly performing agency will cause little additional harm and, conversely, reducing the number of appointees will do very little good. In other cases, adding or cutting appointees will dramatically influence performance. In this way, concerns for performance constrain political choices about the number of appointees in given agencies at different times.

Proposition 2. *Politicization decreases as the sensitivity of agency competence to politicization increases.*

Taken together, propositions 1 and 2 suggest specific predictions about when presidents want to politicize and which agencies they will target. What is required is a way of evaluating which agencies have different policy views than the president and which agencies can most easily accommodate the addition of appointees without consequences for performance. I discuss this more fully below.

CONGRESS AND POLICY POLITICIZATION

Of course, presidential efforts to alter the number and location of appointees hinge upon the implicit or explicit approval of Congress. Congress, along with various presidents, created the statutory framework that governs the creation of appointed positions. All new Senate-confirmed positions must be created in statute. The power to use the SES and create Schedule C positions is defined broadly in law and is subject to congressional influence through legislation, appropriations, and oversight. Congressional authorization and appropriations committees can review personnel actions within agencies and give instructions through informal communication, hearings, reports, or statutory language. While presidents have significant discretion under the law, they always act with an eye toward what Congress's response is likely to be. On occasion members of Congress have publicized and resisted presidential politicization attempts through reports, hearings, threats, and language limiting the use of appropriations to pay the salaries of no more than a fixed number appointees.[27]

Congress and the president share similar concerns about policy outcomes, but these concerns can lead to different views about politicization because of institutional and partisan differences between the two branches. Members of Congress care about policy outcomes because they personally care about policy and because delivering outcomes that mirror the preferences of their districts or states enhances their reelection chances. Agencies also implement the policies crafted and funded by Congress, and members of Congress have an interest in seeing the policies they have enacted implemented effectively. They do so through administrative procedures, agency design, oversight hearings, specific statutes, and other devices to ensure that agencies implement legislation consistent with congressional preferences.[28]

While members of Congress share the president's concern for policy, and thus for the number of appointments and competence, they are less enthusiastic about appointments since appointments do not necessarily make members of Congress better off. Increasing the number of appointments or replacing careerists with appointees can aid the president in pulling an agency's policy *away* from what a member of Congress prefers. This is particularly the case if the president is conservative and the member of Congress is liberal or vice-versa.

The preferred number of appointees for members of Congress will vary based upon the ideology of the member relative to the president and the agency. When policy views differ between an agency and a member, the member is more willing to politicize. In fact, as with presidents, this is a necessary condition to support politicization in order to achieve policy change. If the agency already shares the member's views about policy, the member only stands to lose from politicization because of its effects on agency competence. In cases where the agency's views about policy diverge from the president and Congress and one or both parties want to politicize, three scenarios exist depending on the policy views of the president and Congress relative to the agency in question.

In the first class of cases, the president and Congress have policy views on opposite sides of the agency. For example, the president might consider the agency too liberal but the median member of Congress will find it too conservative. In such cases, politicization is much less likely than in cases where the two parties agree that at least *some* change is necessary. Presidents will either try to politicize but be constrained by Congress or anticipate Congress's reaction and not politicize in the first place.

In the second class of cases, the president and Congress are both more liberal or more conservative than the agency but the president is more extreme than Congress relative to the agency. In such a case, two outcomes are possible. First, the president could prefer to politicize, but Congress could oppose it because of politicization's likely effect on agency performance. Second, both branches of government could prefer to alter the number and depth of appointments to allow more presidential influence but to different degrees. The president will want more politicization than Congress. Since the preferred policy outcomes of the two branches are different, the ways the president and Congress view the tradeoff between policy and agency effectiveness differ.

In the final class of cases, both the Congress and the president are more liberal or conservative than an agency but Congress is the more extreme party. In these cases, the optimal level of politicization will be higher for Congress because it will benefit proportionally more from moving the agency's policy toward the ideal policies of the president (and, consequently, of Congress).[29]

This discussion of Congress's view of politicization suggests that less politicization will occur when the two branches disagree about agency policy. The more polarized the two branches become, the more likely agencies will be too conservative for one and too liberal for the other. In such circumstances, Congress will look with a jaundiced eye toward presidential politicization efforts since these efforts will pull the agency away from Congress. As a result, the more the president and Congress disagree about policy, the less likely politicization becomes.

Proposition 3. *The more policy views between the president and Congress diverge, the less Congress wants to politicize.*

REVISITING TWO ASSUMPTIONS

The assumptions that presidents care about policy and that agencies themselves have views about policy that can be influenced by appointees are generally accepted and were illustrated in a case study of the CSC in the last chapter. The assumptions that presidents want agencies to be competent and that adding appointees hurts competence require more discussion, however.

One possible objection is that some presidents really do not want government agencies to be competent. If presidents knew that an agency failure would lead to policy outcomes beneficial to the president, they might prefer failure over competence and politicize more. The number of cases where failure produces policy outcomes the president prefers is uncertain, however. One obvious case is health and safety or environmental regulation. We might think, for example, that conservative presidents want OSHA or the EPA to fail, thinking that a low-competence OSHA or EPA is going to regulate less. Perhaps this is true, but would presidents prefer a low-competence EPA to an EPA that shares the president's conservative ideology and is extremely competent? It is not clear. It is also worth considering whether a low-competence regulatory agency actually regulates less or whether it just regulates erratically. Equally plausible is the case that a low-competence agency produces poorly written regulations that hurt business by increasing uncertainty or by imposing unforeseen political or economic costs.[30]

Another potential objection is the claim that adding appointees might *improve* agency competence. Indeed, if appointees make agencies more competent, the president (and Congress) will find politicization a more attractive strategy. As I demonstrate in chapters 6 and 7, however, federal programs and agencies run by appointees or appointee-laden management teams perform significantly worse than those administered by career managers. This is not to say that appointees are unnecessary. Appointees can improve agency performance by counteracting inertia, bringing energy and vision, and introducing new and useful information into a stale and insular decision-making environment.[31] In many agencies the existing number of appointed positions provides exactly this type of performance-enhancing influence. Cases where adding *more* appointees in the federal government would objectively improve performance are rare, however, since all principal officers of the government are already appointed. Most agencies have passed the point where adding appointees will have a leavening influence. The history of civil service expansion, the antistatist political culture of the United States, and presidential incentives for political control have created a deeper penetration of appointees into the administrative state than is found in any other developed country, and by a large margin.[32]

The Dynamics of Politicization for Patronage

Thus far the discussion has focused on politicization decisions based on concerns about policy rather than on those appeasing patronage demands. Some of the causal factors that explain policy politicization, however, are different than those that explain patronage politicization. Presidents face constant pressure to reward supporters, repay political debts, and fulfill obligations to their party by filling agency posts with patronage appointees. Members of Congress are actively involved in this process, both by recommending persons for positions and vetting those proposed by the president.[33] These patronage pressures have predictable effects on patterns of politicization.

PRESIDENTS AND PATRONAGE POLITICIZATION

In one sense, presidents of both parties confront similar pools of potential patronage appointees. A sizeable proportion of this group is young, politically ambitious, has limited experience, and what experience they do have is for the party or one of the party's core constituencies. They have worked on the campaign, for a state party, a member of Congress, or interest group. They want a job that will give them a rewarding work experience and advance their career prospects, particularly within the party or its constellation of related groups. It was the promise of such a job that perhaps motivated them to work for the campaign in the first place.

The pool of patronage appointees does differ by competencies, however. Since the core constituencies of the two parties are different, Democratic and Republican patronage appointees have different types of background experience and find different jobs in the administration attractive. Presidential personnel officials try to match experience and qualifications of potential appointees to appropriate jobs. The less background experience, the harder it is to find them jobs. One personnel official explained, "The problem with presidential personnel in any administration is that you say (to a job-seeker), 'What do you want to do?' and they say 'I'll go anywhere.' This is completely not helpful. . . . Patronage becomes problematic when people have no idea what they want to do (but have to be placed)."[34] If potential appointees have experience working for organized labor or the U.S. Chamber of Commerce or the

Federal Farm Bureau, this signals competence for work in specific agencies. PPO officials use this information to recommend such persons for jobs in these agencies.

The pool of potential appointees also differs in the types of jobs they prefer. Young, ambitious, politically active job-seekers want jobs that will enhance their resume and future prospects. While some jobs in the administration will enhance the career of personnel from either party, other positions will be less useful helping the candidate develop the background and connections necessary to satisfy their ambitions within the party and/or its related groups. The parties differ in which agencies are attractive, given that some agencies have missions closer to the policy commitments of one party than the other. As one Republican presidential personnel official told me frankly, "Most people [Republicans] do not see Labor in their long term future. . . . You are not going to be able to make a living from that pattern of relationships."[35] Patronage appointees are better qualified for, and have more desire to work in, agencies whose policy views are similar to those of the president. While almost all personnel officials note that there are more applicants than jobs, difference in competencies and views between the parties suggest that PPO officials will have an easier time placing patronage appointees into agencies with views or policy commitments closer to those of the president or the president's party.

Proposition 4. *Patronage appointees are likely to increase in agencies whose policy views are similar to those of the president.*

CONGRESS AND PATRONAGE POLITICIZATION

What the president and his personnel officials view as patronage can benefit members of Congress in two ways. First, these positions provide members of Congress with a means by which to influence policy directly—provided, that is, that members have influence over who is selected. Up to this point I have assumed that presidential appointments pull an agency's policy closer to the ideal policy of the president, but the extent to which an increase in appointments helps the president control the bureaucracy varies. In some cases adding positions or changing the appointment authority of positions helps the president substantially. In other cases adding appointees introduces personnel who do not share the president's preferences. The more Congress plays a role in selecting an appointee, the less likely it is that the appointee exactly shares the president's policy preferences. In 1992, Richard Neustadt advised Robert B. Reich, the soon-to-be labor secretary, to "beware congressional aides since each has an agenda item all his own, or his boss's."[36]

Neustadt correctly understood that the more appointees were beholden to members of Congress, the less they were beholden to presidents.

When Congress can ensure some influence in the appointment process, their reticence about increasing appointments is mitigated. For example, consider the following statutory language from 1916:

> Provided further, That of the vacancies created in the Judge Advocate's Department by this act, one such vacancy, not below the rank of Major, shall be filled by the appointment of a person from civil life, not less than forty-five nor more than fifty years of age, who shall have been for ten years a Judge of the Supreme Court of the Philippine Islands, shall have served for two years as a Captain in the regular or volunteer army, and shall be proficient in the Spanish language and laws.[37]

According to the *New York Times*, there was only one person in the world who had these qualifications: Judge Adam C. Carson, then of the Supreme Court of the Philippine Islands.[38] He was back in the United States on leave at the time of the passage of the act and was a resident of Representative James Hay's district. Hay was Chairman of the House Committee on Military Affairs and part of the Army Organization bill conference committee. Carson was subsequently appointed to the job. This constitutes, to say the least, an unusual amount of statutory specificity in outlining an appointment.

Federal patronage has also historically been a means by which Congress secured control over federal administration locally. Members of Congress repeatedly refused to give up control over regional appointments, such as U.S. Marshals, U.S. Attorneys, and regional USDA officials, because those persons would set policy regionally in a way that was sensitive to the needs of a members' reelection coalition.[39] This was particularly true in important areas like civil rights, agriculture, and the environment. One underappreciated reason Congress was antagonistic toward merit reforms was that it decreased the body's control over agency policy. Members of Congress are more supportive of increases in the number of appointed positions when the increases allow them more direct influence over policy.

Appointed positions also help members to the extent that they help their party or individual election prospects. Members of Congress, particularly those from the president's party, are actively involved in recommending persons for appointed positions. To the extent they are successful, this can provide electoral benefits for the member. Appreciative constituents or groups express their gratitude through electoral support. Members also benefit when presidential patronage benefits their party more generally. The expansion of patronage by the other party's presi-

Table 3.1
Politicization Propositions for Government

Proposition 1	Presidents are more likely to politicize when their policy views diverge from those of the agency.
Proposition 2	Politicization decreases as the sensitivity of agency competence to politicization increases.
Proposition 3	The more policy views between the president and Congress diverge, the less Congress wants to politicize.
Proposition 4 (Patronage)	Patronage appointees are likely to increase in agencies whose policy views are similar to those of the president.

dent is opposed, however, since it provides no benefit to the member and hurts performance.

Empirical Implications

Thus far, this chapter has identified four general patterns that influence the likelihood of politicization over time (table 3.1). Specifically, presidents prefer more policy-related appointees when their policy views differ from those of the agency and when agencies can accommodate them without consequences for agency competence. The number of appointees is also likely to be higher when the president and Congress have similar views about policy. The number of patronage-type appointees will be higher in agencies that have views similar to those of the president. Each proposition can be translated into specific predictions in the real world of presidential and congressional politics by translating the general concepts of these propositions into concrete attributes of the president, Congress, or the agency. Doing so will help us both understand past politicization episodes in their broader context as well as predict when and where politicization will occur in the future.

Proposition 1: Policy Disagreement between President and Agency

Increases in policy disagreement between the president and an agency will often lead the president to increase the number of appointees in an agency. As a general matter, measuring policy disagreement between the president and an agency is difficult since there is no direct way to observe agency policy views. There are intuitive ways of checking to see whether policy disagreement leads to politicization; these involve looking at cases where the policy disagreement between the president and the bureaucracy should be largest and comparing those cases to cases where the policy disagreement should be minimal. One way to do this is to compare the amount of politicization after a party change in the White House against the amount of politicization when there has been no party change.[40] For example, did the transition from President Eisenhower to President Kennedy lead to more politicization than the switch from President Reagan to President Bush? There are good reasons to think so.

When a new presidential administration assumes office, it encounters a preexisting bureaucracy made up of hundreds of agencies with millions of employees. The new president may encounter resistance, given that the previous president had some influence over the policy views of the bureaucracy through changes in agency rules, the recruitment and promotion of sympathetic career employees, and the burrowing of political appointees into career jobs. As Richard Nixon explained to his cabinet, "I urged the new cabinet members to move quickly to replace holdover bureaucrats with people who believed in what we were trying to do. . . . [I warned that if] we don't get rid of those people, they will either sabotage us from within, or they'll just sit back on their well-paid asses and wait for the next election to bring back their old bosses."[41] If the policy views of bureaus change to conform to those of the sitting president— and surveys of federal bureaucrats show that they do—then turnover in the White House should be a clear case where the amount of policy disagreement between the president and a bureaucracy is high.

We can also evaluate whether conservative presidents politicize liberal agencies and liberal agencies politicize conservative agencies. While in office presidents will naturally govern some agencies that have views close to the president's and others unsympathetic to the president's agenda. The degree of conflict between the president and agencies can vary as a function of a number of factors, not least among them the agencies' purpose as embedded in law and personnel. Different presidents view each agency's a priori policy predispositions differently according to their ideologies. Presidents Reagan and George H. W. Bush were more concerned about the policy direction of the EPA, the Department of Education, and the Civil Rights Division of the Justice Department than was President Clinton.[42] The former presidents felt a concrete need to alter the direction of these agencies, whereas the latter's preferences were more in line with the natural preferences of these agencies. As one former Reagan administration official explained, "We did give more emphasis to those agencies [social welfare agencies] because we expected more bureaucratic resistance from them as a natural result of our agenda rather than that they were inherently worse. . . . We did not target [agencies concerned with] defense since we knew their bureaucrac[ies] would like what we were doing."[43]

While many career professionals try to operate with Heclo's ethos of "speak up, shut up, carry up, carry out," this is easier for career professionals who are sympathetic to the president's agenda. Regardless of the actual responsiveness of career professionals, presidents and their teams are usually suspicious of continuing professional personnel when they take office. By virtue of their position, professional backgrounds, experience, and personal beliefs, career employees should and do have opinions about policy, but these opinions influence how presidents and political appointees perceive employee reliability and loyalty.

Proposition 2: Sensitivity of Agency Competence to Politicization

One reason for variation in the number and penetration of appointees across agencies is that some agencies can more easily accommodate appointees than can others. Adding a handful of appointees could dramatically alter the competence of one agency while having virtually no effect in another. Politicians will permit a greater number, and deeper penetration, of appointees in some agencies than in others depending on the sensitivity of the agency's objective performance to the presence of appointees. Sensitivity to appointments can be a function of a number of factors.[44] Prominent among them are the character of agency tasks and the likely effects of politicization on the career decisions of key career personnel.

One important factor defining an agency's sensitivity to politicization is task complexity. As noted previously, President Andrew Jackson famously said that federal jobs were "so plain and simple" that all persons of intelligence could perform them with little extra training.[45] This was part of Jackson's justification for turning over a significant portion of federal jobs and giving them to his supporters. Few agencies only perform tasks today of the type described by Jackson, but the point is that some agencies perform more complicated tasks than do others. Some agencies carry out directives that require specialized activity or knowledge that is more easily disrupted by politicization since these activities cannot be done or managed equally well by people from the outside the agency. For example, some government agencies, like the National Aeronautics and Space Administration (NASA) or the Department of Energy weapons labs, are literally doing rocket science. Others, like the Bureau of Labor Statistics (BLS), the Census Bureau, and the EPA, are responsible for collecting data on the labor market, demographics, or environmental pollutants, respectively, for use in estimating complex statistical models. Older agencies like the old Federal Radio Commission, the Civil Aeronautics Board, and the Atomic Energy Commission (AEC) were engaged in regulating and promoting a new technology—radio communication, air transportation, and nuclear energy, respectively. Today the Federal Communications Commission (FCC) is regulating market access for ever-improving cable and telephone technology. The FDA is trying to decide when and if to allow experimental AIDS and cancer drugs onto the market. In these cases, slippage between what politicians decree and policy outcomes can vary a lot not only because politicians are unclear themselves about what to do, but also because the tasks are incredibly complex. Taking out a few skilled people and putting in a few less-skilled people can dramatically affect bureau performance.

A second important factor that influences an agency's sensitivity to politicization is the influence such actions have on the career decisions of agency professionals. If career professionals have attractive options outside the agency because they are eligible for retirement or because they can take comparable jobs in the private sector, small decreases in the satisfaction of work, either due to loss of policy influence, lack of access to top policy and pay jobs, or the increased influence of appointees can have a large impact on turnover within an agency's career ranks. If outside options are bad, however, career managers are more likely to stay even if work becomes less rewarding.[46] This means presidents can at times politicize with less impact on agency performance, depending upon the outside options of career professionals.

Proposition 3: Similarity of Presidential and Congressional Views on Policy

The third proposition states broadly that less politicization occurs for both policy and patronage when the policy views of the president and Congress differ. At minimum, politicization for both policy and patronage should occur more frequently in periods when the same party controls both the White House and both chambers of Congress. Members of Congress are more likely to benefit when a president from their own party is making personnel decisions, as the policies presidential appointees pursue are more similar to those of the president's partisans. As a consequence, they are more likely to actively support politicization decisions and less likely to exercise vigorous oversight of personnel decisions that reflect poorly on the president, giving presidents a freer hand in politicization.

The earlier discussion of how Congress viewed politicization also included a more nuanced view of different scenarios involving the policy views of the president and a given agency. These three scenarios have analogues in modern presidential history. In one class of cases, the president and Congress have policy views on opposite sides of the given agency. For example, during the Reagan administration, Congress was largely liberal, the president was conservative, and most agencies were somewhere in between these two extremes. Each branch viewed the administrative state with a jaundiced eye. Congress thought the departments and agencies were tools of the Republican administration, while the White House believed agencies were too closely tied to a hostile Democratic Congress.[47] During the second Clinton administration, the president was well to the left of the predominantly conservative Congress, and most agencies were, again, somewhere in between. In such cases, there is a good chance the president will want to politicize, but doing so will pull policy closer to the president's position and away from Congress. Congress would prefer no politicization or even *de*politicization, if possible. In such cases, politicization is much less likely than in cases where the two parties agree that at least some change is necessary.

In the second class of cases, the president and Congress are both more liberal or more conservative than a given agency. A good example of such a case was Eisenhower's creation of Schedule C. President Eisenhower announced in 1953 that all executive-branch positions of a confidential or policy-determining character in the civil service would be put in a new schedule where office holders would serve at the pleasure of the president. At the time this move was criticized as a patronage raid by Democrats since the order could potentially affect thousands of positions.[48] The choice was hailed by Republican members of Congress, who hoped the increased number of positions would both help Republicans get control of the bureaucracy and provide a new source of jobs for the party faithful.[49] In the end, the fears of the Democrats and the hopes of the Republicans were both unfounded. While by the end of 1956 Eisenhower had switched hundreds of positions to Schedule C, he retained the incumbents in over half of them. He also filled an additional number with employees drawn from the career ranks.[50] Eisenhower's reticence can be explained in part by his being significantly more moderate than Republican partisans in Congress, who were advocating more dramatic measures to get control of the New Deal bureaucracy.

Proposition 4: Politicization for Patronage

One of the interesting features of presidential personnel politics is that concerns for policy and patronage create different patterns of placement. Disagreement between presidents and agencies often leads presidents to increase the number and penetration of appointees in agencies with policy views that differ from his own. At the same time, the president's supporters who are seeking campaign jobs are best qualified for and desire jobs in agencies that are likely to have policy views similar to those of the president and his party.

Fortunately, tracking the differences in types of appointments can help us untangle these two types of politicization. Senate-confirmed appointees (PAS) are the most visible to Congress and the hardest for presidents to change; they also have the largest influence on policy. Senate-confirmed positions must be created in statute, and such appointees must be confirmed by the Senate; this means that Congress regularly considers these positions and who will occupy them. Schedule C positions, on the other hand, are the least visible to Congress since they are less likely to have direct authority over agencies or policy. They are the easiest positions to create and the most likely to be used to satisfy patronage obligations. Appointed members of the Senior Executive Service (SES) fall in between the other two types of appointees. They are more visible than Schedule C appointees because they regularly run federal programs, but they are less consequential to Congress than Senate-confirmed positions because presidents have the authority to staff positions they fill with appointed or career members of the SES largely at their discretion, subject to the limitations described in chapter 2. Appointed SES slots can also be used to satisfy patronage demands and SES appointees are often placed in regional director, policy-planning, and high-level public affairs or liaison positions. Appointments more relevant to policy, such as Senate-confirmed positions, should be the most likely to follow the logic of policy politicization. Schedule C appointments, on the other hand, should be the most likely of the three types of appointments to reflect patronage concerns. While Schedule C positions can be used for policy control when politicians politicize by increasing ministerial staff, these positions usually offer lower pay and less prestige. They are easier to fill with campaign staff, political supporters, and persons appointed as a way of paying off political debts.

This implies that the most policy-relevant positions, PAS positions, should follow one pattern while the most patronage friendly, Schedule C positions, should follow another. PAS positions should increase most in agencies with policy views that differ from the president, while Schedule C positions should increase most in agencies with policy views similar to those of the president and in those with policy views very different from those of the president.

Discussion

These predictions highlight the importance of several less obvious features of politicization that deserve further discussion. First, where a person sits in the political process generally influences where they stand on the wisdom of politicization. If increasing the number of appointees will help change agency policy toward a person's view of the appropriate policy, they are more likely to support it as necessary and be willing to sacrifice some competence to do it. Deciding the optimal number of appointees is impossible since the optimal number of appointees depends fundamentally upon one's ideology. Those who share the president's preferences naturally believe that more appointees are necessary to change agency policy. Those who do not share the president's views will be more suspicious of attempts to add appointees and more sensitive to the ways doing so will hurt performance.

Second, presidents do not have unlimited ability to politicize. They have limited resources, time, and attention and potential congressional action constrains them. The techniques described in chapter 2 like layering and reorganization require some ingenuity in addition to both administrative paperwork and approval by budget officers and personnel officials. Getting approvals and dealing with different agency officials takes time, negotiation, and cooperation. Politicization decisions can also be controversial, particularly if they appear to be part of a larger pattern.

Presidents also confront concrete limits on politicization since positions added to agencies cost money and can be limited in number by Congress. Presidents can slip new positions into the budget or convince Congress to either approve higher appropriations or increase caps for these purposes, but these actions take time, attention, and political capital. This is obviously easier when the majority in Congress are in the president's party. Members of opposing party in Congress can be attentive to headcounts and can see when numbers are increasing. One former personnel official explained, "If you want a flag, get a C," meaning that increasing the number of appointed positions, particularly Schedule C appointees, raises red flags for Congress.[51] Presidents must choose their battles.

Finally, it is important to remember that presidents use other administrative strategies for influencing agency policies. Prominent among these is centralization. For example, Margaret Spellings had an important role in the formation of education policy from within the White House at the start of the George W. Bush administration. Presidents who are willing to put forth the effort can use organizational processes, personal initiative, and burgeoning White House staffs to make and implement policy. Despite the presidents' best efforts to organize staff effectively for oversight, however, they often resort to politicization. President Nixon famously experimented with building a counterbureaucracy in the White House to combat the departments and agencies but he ultimately decided that politicization was a more effective means of securing control over administrative policy.[52] President George W. Bush eventually moved Spellings out into the department to implement his signature education policy, No Child Left Behind.

Presidents have also sought to use reorganization, budgets, or unilateral action to influence the direction of the bureaucracy, but these strategies often require politicization to be implemented successfully. When agency reorganizations and budgets are used as political tools to secure control, they are promulgated and implemented at the agency level by political appointees. Similarly, presidential attempts to change policy unilaterally through agency rulemaking processes are driven and implemented by agency appointees. Indeed, in 2007 the Bush administration mandated that all large agencies have a regulatory policy office headed by an appointee specifically tasked with monitoring agency rulemaking processes.[53] While presidents engage in these other strategies for administrative influence, their efforts to do should not hide the patterns of politicization described above.[54]

Conclusion

The number of appointees in the U.S. Department of Education continues to increase and its management performance continues to be lackluster.[55] In 2004 the Department of Education included 155 appointees (compared to 4,584 employees), 7 more than at the end of the Clinton administration. In the Bush administration's management grades for the 2004 federal budget, the Education Department programs came in at the bottom, second only to programs in HUD.[56] In fact, five of the ten lowest-scoring programs across the entire federal government were housed in the Education Department.

The case of the Department of Education illustrates how presidents from both parties politicize for policy and patronage. It also shows how such actions hurt agency competence. The chapter has sought to put cases like that of the Department of Education in a broader context and explain more generally why, where, and when politicization occurs. It did so through four simple propositions derived from a limited set of reasonable assumptions. The chapter also translated the general concepts in the propositions into testable predictions. The propositions and predictions are included in table 3.2.

In the next two chapters I evaluate whether this theorizing has been a productive enterprise, testing the propositions with previously untapped data. In chapter 4 I use data from what is commonly referred to as the Plum Book to examine patterns of politicization from 1960 to 2004. The chapter takes a preliminary look at the explanation provided here for when and where politicization occurs and then uses the data to examine other common views about when politicization occurs. In chapter 5 I examine year-to-year variation in the percentage and depth of ap-

Table 3.2
Politicization Predictions for Government Agencies

Proposition 1	Presidents are more likely to politicize when their policy views diverge from those of the agency.
	A) Politicization increases after party change in the White House.
	B) Liberal presidents are more likely to target conservative agencies for politicization and conservative presidents are more likely to target liberal agencies for politicization.
Proposition 2	Politicization decreases as the sensitivity of agency competence to politicization increases.
	A) Agencies with complex tasks are less politicized than other agencies.
	B) Increases in the attractiveness of outside economic options for agency employees will decrease politicization.
Proposition 3	The more policy views between the president and Congress diverge, the less Congress wants to politicize.
	A) Politicization increases during periods of unified government.
Proposition 4 (Patronage)	Patronage appointees are likely to increase in agencies whose policy views are similar to those of the president.
	A) Liberal presidents are more likely to increase patronage appointees in liberal agencies and conservative presidents are more likely to increase patronage appointees in conservative agencies.

pointees into the management teams of federal agencies using new data from OPM. These data provide a different and more nuanced measure of politicization that allows a more detailed examination of what happens in individual agencies over the course of a president's tenure. In the end, the empirical chapters together produce a rich picture of politicization as it has been commonly practiced.

APPENDIX 3A
Formalization of Propositions 1–3

In what follows, I present the basic tradeoff between ideological fealty and bureaucratic competence undergirding the verbal theory presented in chapter 3.[57] This tradeoff forms the basis of the key hypotheses from the chapter. Assume that presidents care about policy outcomes and want agencies to act in ways that will produce outcomes that presidents prefer and assume that the president and the agency have single-peaked and quadratic preferences over policy outcomes in a unidimensional policy space, so that (letting i denote player i's ideal point),

$$u_i = (x - i)^2. \tag{1}$$

Policy outcomes are determined partly by the outputs produced by the agency. Agency outputs are a function of the agency's policy preferences and its competence. The latter notion captures the idea that some agencies may have good intentions but may not be good at what they do (lack expertise or experience). Specifically, the agency will try and set policy (for example, prepare a budget, write a policy memo, or negotiate a trade agreement) exactly at its own induced ideal point, $a^\wedge$, but they cannot do so perfectly. The agency will try to implement $a^\wedge$ but the actual outcome will be $a^\wedge - \omega$ where ω is a random variable, so that

$$x = a^\wedge - \omega \ (q) \tag{2}$$

and ω has a mean 0, and a variance defined partly by q, where q is the percentage of political appointees. There are a number of possible ways to model how q influences the variance but for simplicity assume $\mathrm{var}(\omega) = mq$, where ω is uniformly distributed from $-\sqrt{3mq}, \sqrt{3mq}$. Substantively, this means that errors increase as q increases.

The agency's induced ideal policy, $a^\wedge$, is a function of its inherent ideal policy, a, the president's ideal policy (p) and the percentage of political appointees (q):

$$a^\wedge \ (q, p) = \gamma(q) p + (1 - \gamma(q)) a, \tag{3}$$

where $\gamma(q)$ is increasing in q since increasing appointees makes the president's views more influential in each agency. The amount of presidential influence in the agency's ideal policy is a function of the percentage of political appointees in the agency. Since the agency's utility is quadratic, (3) implies that the agency's optimal policy coincides with its induced ideal point.

Substituting the induced ideal point into the president's utility function gives

$$u_p = -[(1 - \gamma(q))(a - p)]^2 \tag{4}$$

and this means that the president's expected utility is

$$E(u_p) = - [(1 - \gamma(q))(a - p)]^2 - mq \tag{5}$$

where, as specified above, mq is the variance. The separability of the mean and the variance in the utility function is a property of the quadratic utility function. The value mq reflects the errors that agencies can make in trying to carry out their responsibilities. The variance is a function of q since I argue that bureaucratic competence is partly determined by the appointee percentage. Presidents have utility for mq because they prefer that agencies have more competence rather than less.

Presidents choose the optimal percentage of political appointees, q^*, so that the marginal benefits of decreasing preference divergence between the agency and the president equal the marginal costs of decreasing competence. The partial derivative with respect to q is

$$\frac{\partial u}{\partial q} = -2[(1 - \gamma(q))(a - p)]\gamma'(q)(a - p) - m, \tag{6}$$

which when solved is

$$[(1 - \gamma(q))(a - p)^2]\gamma'(q) = \frac{m}{2}. \tag{7}$$

This nicely sets the impact of preference divergence between the president and the agency against presidential concerns for agency competence if m is understood as an agency's sensitivity to the percentage of appointees. If preference divergence increases, the optimal q increases. To see this, consider that

$$[(1 - \gamma(q))(a - p)^2]\gamma'(q) - \frac{m}{2} = 0 . \tag{8}$$

By the implicit function theorem,

$$\frac{\partial q^*}{\partial(a - p)^2} = \frac{-\gamma'(q)(1 - \gamma(q))}{[(1 - \gamma(q))(a - p)^2]\gamma''(q) - \gamma'(q)(a - p)^2} .$$

This suggests that q^* increases as $(a-p)$ increases. Since $\gamma(q)$ is increasing in q, $\gamma'(q) > 0$. $(1-\gamma(q)) > 0$ by definition. Together this implies that the numerator is < 0. In the denominator the quantity is negative if $\gamma''(q) < 0$ since $(a-p)^2$, $(1-\gamma(q))$, and $\gamma'(q) > 0$. Since there are diminishing marginal returns to policization, I assume that $\gamma''(q) < 0$. Both the numerator and denominator are negative, giving a positive partial derivative. As the distance between the agency and the president increases, so does the equilibrium level of political appointees.

Proposition 1. *Politicization increases as preference divergence between the president and the agency increases.*

If the agency's sensitivity to the number of appointees increases, the optimal q decreases. To see this, consider that

$$\frac{\partial q^*}{\partial m} = -\frac{-\dfrac{1}{2}}{[(1-\gamma(q))(a-p)^2]\gamma''(q) - \gamma'(q)(a-p)^2}. \tag{9}$$

by the implicit function theorem. When solved, this is

$$\frac{\partial q^*}{\partial m} = \frac{1}{2[(a-p)^2(\gamma''(q)(1-\gamma)) - \gamma'(q)]}. \tag{10}$$

The denominator is negative if $\gamma''(q) < 0$ since $(a-p)^2$, $(1-\gamma(q))$, and $\gamma'(q) > 0$. The last of these expressions is positive because $\gamma(q)$ is increasing in q. If an agency's sensitivity to q decreases, the president's optimal level of appointees will increase.

Proposition 2. *Increases in agency sensitivity to the percentage of political appointees will decrease politicization.*

Congress and Politicization

I assume there are three primary actors, the president (P), the Agency (A), and the congressional median (C), along with Nature (N). The three primary actors have single-peaked preferences over policy outcomes in a unidimensional policy space. The agency's policy preferences are a function of the president's policy preferences, an inherent agency preference, and the level of appointees. As I suggested above (3):

$$a^\wedge(q, p) = \gamma(q)\, p + (1 - \gamma(q))\, a \tag{1}$$

The actors interact in a four-stage sequence. First, Nature chooses both a level of appointees, q_n, and a proposer, either P or C. The proposer offers a level of appointments, q_{pr}. The actor who is not the proposer then chooses whether to accept or reject the proposed q_{pr}. If the new q_{pr} is accepted, it becomes the q^* for the agency. If it is rejected, the status quo q_n remains. In the final stage, the agency sets policy with some error, the error partly being a function of q^*.

Working backward, the agency will set policy at its ideal policy since it cannot be made better off by deviating. The policy outcome will be

$$x = a^\wedge - \omega(q) \tag{2}$$

where ω is the random error associated with the agency's actions. Given this outcome, we can turn to seeing which proposals will be accepted and which will be rejected. To know this, it is necessary to describe how the actors determine their optimal level of appointees, q^*. From above (5), the president's expected utility for any configuration of q and agency preferences is

$$E(u_p) = -[(1 - \gamma(q))(a - p)]^2 - mq \qquad (3)$$

and the president chooses a q^* such that the marginal benefits of politicization equal the marginal costs in loss of agency competence.

Determining the optimal level of appointees is more difficult for Congress since presidential appointments do not always help draw an agency closer to Congress's ideal policy outcome. Like presidents, Congress cares about policy so that

$$u_c = (x - c)^2 . \qquad (4)$$

Substituting in (1) for x gives

$$u_c = -[((\gamma(q)p + (1 - \gamma(q))a) - c]^2 , \qquad (5)$$

which when solved gives the following expected utility for Congress:

$$E(u_c) = -[\gamma(q)(p - a) + (a - c)]^2 - mq . \qquad (6)$$

Congress wants an optimal percentage of political appointees, q^*, so that the marginal benefits of decreasing preference divergence between the agency and the president equal the marginal costs of decreasing competence. The partial derivative with respect to q for Congress is

$$\frac{\partial Eu_c}{\partial q} = -2[\gamma(q)(p - a) + (a - c)] \gamma'(q)(p - a) - m, \qquad (7)$$

which when solved is

$$\frac{m}{2} = -[\gamma(q)(p - a)^2 + (p - a)(a - c)] \gamma'(q) . \qquad (8)$$

This leads to a calculation of optimal appointment levels that is more contingent and complicated than that of the president. There are cases where low agency competence relative to the policy preferences of the actors leads both the president and Congress to want to keep the status quo or depoliticize. Holding these cases constant and focusing on cases where there is disagreement, Congress's preferences can be summarized in three regimes based upon the relative location of actor preferences.

DIVERGENT PREFERENCES (CAP)

Given the frequency of divided government in the United States, there are a number of cases where Congress is predominantly liberal, the president is conservative, and the administrative agency is somewhere in between. In such a case, Congress will either want no change or will want to depoliticize to limit the president's influence while the president will want to politicize in order to exert more influence over the agency. Politicizing the bureaucracy hurts Congress on both fronts since it moves policy outcomes away from their ideal policy and decreases bureaucratic competence. Congress and the president will not be able to agree and it is unlikely that politicization will occur. As preferences between the president and Congress diverge, the greater the chance that an agency will fall in between the two parties.

EXTREME PRESIDENT AND MODERATE CONGRESS (PCA)

In some cases the agency policy is either too conservative or too liberal for both Congress and the president. In such cases both branches of government may prefer more appointees, but one often wants more than the others. Consider, first, the case where Congress is more moderate than the president. In such a case, both Congress and the president may want to add more appointees but Congress prefers fewer appointees than the president.

EXTREME CONGRESS AND MODERATE PRESIDENT (CPA)

If Congress is more extreme than the president, it is possible that Congress will want more appointees than the president. In most cases, congressional preference for more appointments has been attributed to the electoral or party benefits of appointed positions for members of Congress, but there are cases where Congress prefers more appointees primarily for policy reasons. If Congress is more extreme than the president, the body may be willing to trade off more of the agency's capacity than presidents. Whereas the president is willing to abide some divergence in preference, Congress is not because the marginal benefit of policy change is higher for them than the president.

In two of the three regimes, presidents will prefer more appointees than Congress and the reason is obvious. Presidential appointees always move agency policy closer to the president's ideal policy and only coincidentally closer to Congress's ideal policy. These two regimes historically have been more common than the third since a moderate Congress has been the norm relative to the president.

Proposition 3. *The more preferences between the president and Congress diverge, the less likely it is that Congress wants to politicize.*

4

The Pattern of Politicization:
A Quantitative Overview

IN EVERY ELECTION YEAR since 1960, when John F. Kennedy squared off against Richard M. Nixon, the U.S. Congress has published *Policy and Supporting Positions*. This publication is commonly referred to as the "Plum Book," both because of its plum-like color and because it includes details about all the "plum" appointed positions in the U.S. government. The document lists every policymaking and confidential position of the federal government subject to appointment. Its publication is eagerly anticipated by campaign workers and other job-seekers hoping to secure employment in the next presidential administration for themselves or their friends. It is also good reading for political observers who like to engage in the parlor game of speculating about who might be chosen to fill available appointed slots.

For the purposes of this study, the quadrennial publication is a useful source for comparing the number of appointments over the 1960–2004 time period. It opens up exciting new possibilities to answer simple questions such as, *Which agencies are the most politicized? Which are the least politicized?*, and *Which agencies have been targeted by different administrations at different times?* that have, to this point, been hard to answer definitively.

This chapter provides a broad overview of politicization activity. It first introduces the Plum Book data and its general contours. It then uses these data to make an initial attempt to evaluate the propositions from the last chapter, particularly whether policy disagreement between the president and agencies and the president and Congress influence politicization. It supplements this quantitative analysis with a brief examination of two of the most publicized cases of politicization during George W. Bush's first term, those of the CIA and the Office of Special Counsel (OSC). The chapter concludes by using the forty-four years of data to evaluate two common views about politicization: namely, that it is increasing over time and that it is driven by Republican presidents.

The analysis utilizing the Plum Book data is the first of two that will test the propositions emerging from the last chapter. While Plum Book data have the advantage of covering a long time period, they have limitations for testing some of the propositions because of their generality, long duration, and quadrennial publication.[1] In the next chapter I introduce a second source of data on political appointments to fill out the analysis. Together, the two chapters shed important new light on how politicization is practiced by modern presidents.

A Quantitative Overview of Politicization, 1960–2004

As described in chapter 2, there are three main types of political appointments: Senate-confirmed positions (PAS), appointed positions in the Senior Executive Service (SES) and their antecedents, and Schedule C positions.[2] Table 4.1 lists the number of each type of appointee in 2004 by cabinet department and major independent agency. There is substantial variation from agency to agency. For example, although the Department of Energy, the Department of Labor, the Environmental Protection Agency (EPA), and the National Aeronautics and Space Administration (NASA) all have about the same number of employees, the number of appointees varies dramatically across the agencies. NASA has only 16 appointees, but the Department of Labor has 147—more than nine times as many. Similarly, the Department of Education has 155 appointees among only 4,584 employees—more appointees than the Department of Health and Human Services (HHS; 60,628 employees), the Department of the Interior (77,207), the Treasury Department (110,996), or even the Department of Veterans Affairs (236,427). The Departments of Education, State, Labor, and Housing and Urban Development (HUD) have the highest percentages of appointees among the cabinet departments, while those of Treasury, Defense, and Veterans Affairs have the lowest. The most politicized agencies outside the cabinet are the Office of Management and Budget (OMB) and the Small Business Administration (SBA); the least politicized are the Social Security Administration (SSA) and NASA.

The number and percentages of appointments often differ quite a bit. For example, the Department of Defense has 247 appointees, which is the third most, but it has a very low percentage of appointees because of the agency's size. This raises the interesting question of how to measure politicization. That is, if the Department of Defense had 500 appointees, it would still have a relatively low percentage of appointees, but 500 appointees is a lot in most peoples' estimation and by comparative standards. It is worth keeping this in mind when evaluating the politicization of any agency.

The two departments with the largest number of appointees are the Department of Justice and the Department of State. The surprisingly high numbers of appointees have an easy explanation, one rooted in

Table 4.1
Number of Political Appointees in 2004 by Selected Cabinet Department and Major Independent Agency

Department or Agency	PAS	Noncareer SES	Schedule C	Total Appointees	Agency Employment	Percent Appointed
Office of Management and Budget	6	13	18	37	513	7.21
Department of Education	13	20	118	155	4,461	3.47
Small Business Administration	4	14	36	56	4,156	1.35
Federal Trade Commission	5	3	5	13	1,053	1.23
Department of State	193	40	131	365	33,477	1.09
Department of Labor	19	27	101	147	15,771	0.93
Department of Housing and Urban Development	15	18	57	90	10,332	0.87
Office of Personnel Management	3	5	22	30	3,476	0.86
Broadcasting Board of Governors	7	4	6	17	2,269	0.75
Department of Energy	20	34	58	112	15,142	0.74
Federal Communications Commission	5	6	1	12	1,965	0.61
Securities and Exchange Commission	5	0	18	23	3,807	0.60
Department of Commerce	25	40	103	171	37,495	0.46
Environmental Protection Agency	14	20	30	64	17,933	0.36
Department of Justice	222	59	76	357	104,383	0.34
General Services Administration	2	17	20	39	12,773	0.31
Equal Employment Opportunity Commission	5	0	2	7	2,468	0.28
Department of Agriculture	16	41	172	229	110,981	0.21
Department of Health and Human Services	19	54	54	128	60,628	0.21
Department of Transportation	23	31	37	91	57,153	0.16
Department of Homeland Security	18	53	123	200	152,845	0.13
Federal Deposit Insurance Corporation	4	0	3	7	5,341	0.13
Department of the Interior	18	31	34	83	77,207	0.11
Department of the Treasury	32	23	35	90	110,996	0.08
National Aeronautics and Space Administration	4	4	8	16	19,242	0.08
Department of Defense	52	88	107	247	668,287	0.04
Social Security Administration	3	10	6	21	65,368	0.03
Department of Veterans Affairs	14	13	13	40	236,427	0.02

Sources: Data on appointments comes from U.S. House 2004. Employment data comes from Office of Personnel Management Fedscope Website (*www.opm.gov*), September 2004.
Note. Department of Defense includes only civilian personnel.

the history of patronage in the United States. The Justice Department includes U.S. attorneys and U.S. marshals, which are distributed throughout the fifty states and U.S. territories and which are still presidential appointees. When the Truman administration tried to move U.S. marshals into the merit system in 1952, Congress explicitly refused.[3] Historically, members of the Senate have jealously guarded the role and influence they have over the filling of these positions in their respective states. This power to influence who is appointed to these positions would be lost if they were included in the merit system. The many Senate-confirmed positions in the Department of State comprise ambassadorial positions in addition to other appointed positions. As the number of countries increases, so does the number of Senate-confirmed positions in the State Department. If U.S. attorneys, U.S. marshals, and ambassadors are excluded from the two departments, the numbers of PAS appointees return to less-surprising levels: about 36 for Justice and 38 for State.

Some of the differences in politicization are easily explained. For example, it is no surprise that the SSA has few appointees, because it was designed by Congress to be insulated from political intervention. Congress removed the agency from HHS for this reason in 1995. NASA is the nation's premier science agency, and few would be surprised that it has very few appointees, which suggests the larger question of why a science agency would have fewer appointees than other agencies. It is likely that NASA is sensitive to the addition of appointees in a way that other agencies are not. Imagining NASA with 150 political appointees instead of 16 helps one understand why science agencies are not heavily politicized. Politicization would fundamentally hurt the scientific mission of the agency and might further influence aspects of agency decision making—such as shuttle-launch decisions—that could have disastrous consequences for human life.

We can identify a couple of reasons why agencies such as the Departments of Education, HUD, and Labor might be the most politicized. First, all three departments have policy commitments closer to those of the Democratic than Republican Party and the core constituencies of these departments (that is, education associations, urban residents, and labor unions) identify more closely with the Democratic Party. The attitude of Republican presidents to programs in these departments is predictable and they respond by politicizing.

Second, each agency has a clientele, so the high numbers of appointees may be due to patronage. That is, presidents find it convenient to reward supporters with appointments in these departments as a way of satisfying patronage concerns. Democratic presidents in particular may reward supporters from their core constituency with appointments in one of these departments. Once these positions are created, they do not disappear with a change in administration. Each new administration takes the previous administration's map of appointed positions as a starting point for their own personnel process, such that even though Schedule C positions technically disappear when vacated, they are adopted by the next administration. Patronage concerns also help explain why agencies like the SBA and the Department of Commerce have a high percentage of appointees.

Not all of the data on politicization are easy to explain. For example, the EPA and HHS do not have exceptionally high numbers of appointees given their size, yet each implements controversial programs about which there is substantial disagreement between the two major parties. There are three things to consider here. First, multiple factors are at work in the politicization decision. Some of these factors—such as policy disagreements between the president and the agency, the agency's sensitivity to politicization, and the amount of agreement between the president and Congress—are discussed above. Indeed, the EPA and HHS may be less politicized because they perform complex regulatory and scientific tasks where mistakes could be very costly.

Second, within larger departments and agencies, some programs and the bureaus that implement them will be controversial and others will not. For example, while some programs in HHS are classic social welfare programs, other parts of the department, like the National Institutes of Health (NIH) and the Centers for Disease Control and Prevention (CDC), enjoy strong bipartisan support. Examining politicization of agencies at the department level can mask substantial politicization among the bureaus *within* a department.

Third, in individual cases other factors can intervene. Presidents may ignore an agency because it is not high on their priority list; or presidents may conclude that politicization would be too costly politically, given their other priorities. In the next chapter I focus on politicization one level down—at the bureau level—and estimate more complex statistical models that account for multiple confounding factors. The Plum Book data have the virtue of helping one see broad trends in politicization over time, but they do not immediately provide answers in specific cases.

One other interesting bit of information from table 4.1 is that presidential management agencies are more politicized than other agencies; the percentage of appointees in key budgeting and personnel agencies is higher than that found other agencies. The Office of Management and Budget (OMB) and the Office of Personnel Management (OPM) have two of the highest percentages of appointees (at 7.21 percent and .86 percent, respectively). In fact, the budget and personnel agencies experienced the largest percentage increases in appointees between 1960 and 2004 (table 4.2).[4] This is not surprising, given what we know

Table 4.2
Changes in Politicization 1960–2004 by Selected Agency

	Employment		PAS		Noncareer SES or NEA		Schedule C		Total Appointments		+/-	Δ %
	1960	2004	1960	2004	1960	2004	1960	2004	1960	2004		
Agencies Gaining Appointees												
Office of Management and Budget	437	513	0	6	0	13	9	18	11	37	26	4.70
Office of Personnel Management/CSC	3,568	3,476	3	3	0	5	0	22	3	30	27	0.78
Department of State	37,972	33,477	130	193	0	40	126	131	274	365	91	0.37
Dept. of Housing and Urban Dev./HHFA	11,293	10,332	3	15	0	18	56	57	59	90	31	0.35
Department of Labor	7,268	15,771	9	19	0	27	35	101	46	147	101	0.30
General Services Administration	28,861	12,773	1	2	0	17	19	20	20	39	19	0.24
Railroad Retirement Board	2,231	1,092	3	4	0	0	3	0	6	4	1	0.23
Small Business Administration	2,265	4,156	1	4	0	14	27	38	28	56	28	0.11
Department of Commerce	33,070	37,495	36	25	0	42	80	103	116	171	55	0.11
Nat'l. Aeronautics and Space Administration	15,547	19,242	2	4	0	4	2	8	4	16	12	0.06
Department of Defense	1,036,754	668,287	39	52	0	88	119	107	159	247	88	0.02
Tennessee Valley Authority	15,453	12,742	3	4	0	0	0	0	3	4	1	0.01
Department of Veterans Affairs	173,163	236,427	1	14	0	13	16	13	17	40	23	0.01
Agencies Losing Appointees												
United States Postal Service	568,896	767,616	8	9	0	0	35	0	43	9	-34	-0.01
Department of the Treasury	77,318	110,996	76	32	0	23	20	35	96	90	-6	-0.04
Department of the Interior	53,257	77,207	13	18	0	31	94	34	111	83	-28	-0.10
National Labor Relations Board	1,740	1,908	6	6	0	4	18	0	24	10	-14	-0.86
Farm Credit Administration	241	305	0	3	0	0	10	4	10	7	-3	-1.85
Fed. Mediation and Conciliation Services	336	278	1	1	0	0	9	0	10	1	-9	-2.62
Export-Import Bank	235	410	5	5	0	0	11	10	16	15	-1	-3.15

Sources: Employment data comes from Office of Personnel Management, Office of Federal Civilian Workforce Statistics. Data on appointments comes from U.S. House 1960, 2004.

Note: Table lists all agencies that gained appointees in both number and percentage between 1960 and 2004. It also includes all agencies that lost appointees in both number and percentage during the same time period. Omitted agencies either experienced no change or had a change in number but not percentage appointed or vice versa. Agencies with only PA appointees also omitted. Department of Defense includes only civilian personnel.

historically about presidents' attempts to get control of the levers of government. For example, assistant secretaries of administration, which were once career employees, are now routinely political appointees.[5]

Changes between 1960 and 2004

Comparing the number of appointees in 1960 to 2004 provides a means of evaluating how significant the growth has been and where the change has occurred. Apart from OMB and OPM, agencies experiencing large increases include the Departments of State, HUD, Labor, and Commerce. In some agencies the growth occurs primarily in Senate-confirmed (PAS) positions. The appointee increase in the Department of State from 1960 to 2004, for example, is composed largely of new PAS positions, a significant portion of which are ambassadorships. The number of PAS positions increases from 3 to 15 with the elevation of the Housing and Home Finance Agency to cabinet status as HUD. The number of PAS appointees in the Veterans Administration (VA) increases from 1 to 14, partly due to its elevation to cabinet status. The number of PAS positions increases from 9 to 19 in the Department of Labor. The proliferation of PAS positions in HUD, Labor, and the VA reflects politicization by layering and replacement. These agencies have added more deputy, under-, and assistant secretaries during this time period.

In other agencies an increase in Schedule C positions explains the proliferation in appointees. The number of such positions grows from 35 to 101 in the Department of Labor and from 27 to 38 in the SBA. The Department of Commerce adds 23 new Schedule C positions. These increases occurred even though many positions were removed from the schedule in 1966 and placed into what would eventually become the Senior Executive Service (SES). This increase in Schedule C positions has historically helped to satisfy patronage demands in addition to expanding presidential influence.

The creation of the SES during the Carter administration also helps explain the increase in appointees in many agencies. While the SES includes many positions that were classified as Schedule C positions in 1960, the creation of the SES also added a significant number of new appointed positions. It provided a means for presidents to place appointees at lower levels in the bureaucracy and thereby exert more control. It also provided presidents a new political resource through increased patronage opportunities. The largest number of appointed SES members allocated to agencies in existence in 1960 was in the Departments of State, Defense, and Commerce.

Changes between 2000 and 2004

More recently, the George W. Bush administration increased the number of appointees by 350 positions over the level at the end of the second Clinton administration. The increase was to be expected since Clinton was in his second term and Bush was from a different party. Clinton had eight years to change agency policies and to identify career employees sympathetic to his views on policy. Appointees also had ample opportunity to burrow into career positions across the executive branch. Bush was accordingly suspicious of the continuing bureaucracy. Bush also had the advantage of serving with a Republican-majority Congress for part of his term, whereas Clinton faced an opposition Congress during his second term. This made it easier for Bush to politicize.

Table 4.3 includes a list of agencies that both gained and lost the largest percentage of appointees between 2000 and 2004. Interesting variation is found within the aforementioned 350-appointee increase. For instance, the number of PAS appointees does not change significantly between 2000 and 2004. This is not surprising since PAS positions must be created in statute. The increases or decreases in PAS slots often reflect the creation of new agencies or bureaus within specific agencies. For example, in 2000 the Department of State included an Office for the Ambassador-at-Large for the Newly Independent States. This office was eliminated prior to the publication of the 2004 Plum Book. Changes in PAS positions can also reflect more traditional politicization, however. A case in point is the creation of a deputy administrator within the National Nuclear Security Administration that allowed political control one level lower down in the Department of Energy bureaucracy.

The biggest changes in the number of appointments occur among the SES and the Schedule C positions, and this can be seen most clearly in the Departments of Labor, Education, and Commerce. The biggest departmental decreases were in the Departments of Agriculture and Energy. In some agencies the increase occurs almost entirely in Schedule C positions. This is the case for both the Department of Commerce and the Department of Labor, where the administration added only 1 appointee to the SES but added 54 and 51 Schedule C positions, respectively. In others, the increase in appointees is due to increases in SES managers. In the Department of Education, for example, 5 new appointees were added to the SES.

Increasing the number of SES and Schedule C appointees is a viable means of politicizing in order to change an agency's policy views. A disproportionate increase in Schedule C positions, however, usually indicates patronage-driven politicization. Given the predominance of Sched-

Table 4.3
Changes in Politicization 2000–2004 by Selected Agency

	Employment 2000	2004	PAS 2000	2004	Noncareer SES 2000	2004	Schedule C 2000	2004	Total Appointments 2000	2004	+/-	Δ %
Agencies Gaining Appointees												
Office of Science and Technology Pol.	33	31	5	3	3	4	3	6	11	13	2	8.60
Federal Housing Finance Board	107	120	5	5	0	0	0	8	5	13	8	6.16
U.S. Commission on Civil Rights	77	62	0	0	2	1	8	9	13	14	1	5.70
Office of National Drug Control Policy	123	112	5	5	3	2	11	14	19	21	2	3.30
Office of Management and Budget	511	513	6	6	7	13	9	18	22	37	15	2.91
Office of Special Counsel	105	106	1	1	1	1	3	5	5	7	2	1.84
Overseas Private Investment Corp.	195	210	10	10	0	0	2	6	12	16	4	1.47
Commodity Futures Trading Com	574	502	5	5	3	0	6	12	14	17	3	0.95
Nat'l. Foundation on Arts & Humanities	373	384	3	3	6	5	7	11	16	19	3	0.66
Department of Labor	16,040	15,771	17	19	26	27	47	101	91	147	56	0.36
Department of Education	4,734	4,461	15	13	15	20	117	118	148	155	7	0.35
Small Business Administration	4,150	4,156	4	4	11	14	27	38	42	56	14	0.34
Office of Personnel Management	3,780	3,476	3	3	6	5	13	22	22	30	8	0.28
National Credit Union Administration	1,021	904	3	3	0	0	5	6	8	9	1	0.21
Department of Commerce	47,652	37,495	25	25	41	42	52	103	118	171	53	0.21
National Transportation Safety Board	419	430	5	5	1	1	5	6	11	12	1	0.13
Environmental Protection Agency	18,036	17,933	14	14	19	20	8	30	41	64	23	0.13
Agencies Losing Appointees												
International Trade Commission	384	361	6	6	0	0	15	10	21	16	-5	-1.04
Federal Maritime Commission	123	129	5	5	0	0	5	3	10	8	-2	-1.93
Farm Credit Administration	285	305	3	3	0	0	10	4	13	7	-6	-2.27
Council of Economic Advisers	30	29	3	3	0	0	4	3	7	6	-1	-2.64
Trade and Development Agency	37	41	1	1	0	0	2	1	3	2	-1	-3.23
Fed. Mine Safety and Health Rev. Com.	46	40	5	5	0	0	5	3	11	8	-3	-3.91
Council on Environmental Quality	21	24	3	1	0	0	3	3	6	4	-2	-11.90

Sources: Employment data comes from Office of Personnel Management, Office of Federal Civilian Workforce Statistics. Data on appointments comes from U.S. Senate 2000; U.S. House 2004.

Note. Table lists agencies that gained appointees in both number and percentage between 2000 and 2004 from biggest percentage increase down.

ule C increases in the Departments of Labor and Commerce, the General Services Administration (GSA), and the SBA, patronage pressures were undoubtedly influential.

Testing Theoretical Propositions about Politicization

With the major contours of politicization in the modern presidency clear, I turn to evaluating the factors that lead to changes in politicization. The last chapter provided two distinct predictions about *when* politicization would occur. Specifically, politicization will increase when the policy views of presidents and agencies diverge and when Congress and the president have similar policy views. The Plum Book data provide easy, intuitive means of evaluating these two propositions.

Policy Disagreement between President and Agency

One means of testing the prediction that policy disagreement between the president and an agency leads to increases in appointees involves looking at cases where the policy disagreement between the president and the bureaucracy should be largest and comparing those instances to cases where the policy disagreement should be minimal. One can do this by comparing the amount of politicization after a party change in the White House against the amount of politicization when there has been no party change.[6] For example, did the transition from President Eisenhower to President Kennedy lead to more politicization than the switch from President Reagan to President Bush?

According to the Plum Book data, transitions from a Democratic president to a Republican president or vice versa lead to increases in the number and percentage of appointees. Substantively, party change in the White House leads to an average increase of about 300 appointees (figure 4.1). This suggests that policy disagreement between the president and the bureaucracy increases politicization by a noticeable amount. Indeed, the increase of about 350 positions in the transition from the Clinton administration to that of George W. Bush was to be expected given the presidents' different policy views.

When the transfer of power is within one party, such as when George H. W. Bush succeeded Ronald Reagan, there is a smaller increase in the number of appointees. Interparty transitions lead to an average increase in appointees of about 150 positions. This increase reflects the pressure all new presidents feel to get control of the government, even when the previous president was from the same party. The pressure to politicize is obviously not as strong as when a party has changed, but

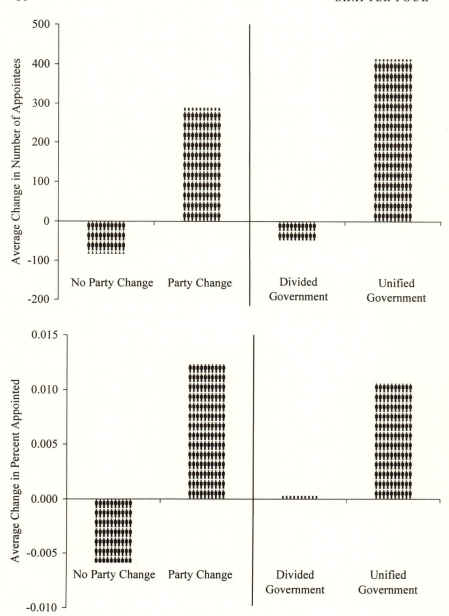

Figure 4.1 Average Change in Number (above) and Percentage (below) of Appointees by Party Change in White House and Unified Government, 1960–2004

differences in policy views within the party can still make politicization attractive. In the United States, people with very different views about policy and competing factional and personal loyalties can coexist within the same party. Each party is a large amalgamation of disparate groups defined by issues, demographic characteristics, geography, self-interest, and other factors that are lumped together because of a need to win elections. This can make presidents uncomfortable with the continuing bureaucracy, even one managed for years by their co-partisans. Recall that New Deal southerners like Lyndon Johnson coexisted with northeastern-ers like John F. Kennedy in the Democratic Party. Similarly, in the Republi-can Party moderate northerners like George H. W. Bush served in the same party as conservative (transplanted) westerner Ronald Reagan.

Second-term presidencies witness a decline in the number of ap-pointees. The number of appointees decreases by about 150 positions on average. This decline may be attributed in part to the difficulty a second-term president has recruiting and retaining appointees, but also to the sitting president's success in changing policy as well as the adminis-tration's improved ability to recruit talented and like-minded careerists into top management positions.[7] Duration in office gives presidents the ability to change agency policy priorities through statute, administrative rulemaking, and budgets. It also provides the president and his subordi-nates time to learn more about the agency and the personnel at the agency who can work with the administration because of either similar policy views or a flexible bureaucratic ethos. If presidents are successful at changing agency policy and finding and promoting sympathetic ca-reer managers, they do not need as many appointed positions.

While all transitions invariably lead to some policy disagreements be-tween the White House and specific agencies, transitions (including a change in party) have the potential to generate the largest and most numerous policy disagreements. We should not be surprised, then, to find that appointees are most likely to be added after a party change in the White House. The larger the change, the larger the increase in politicization.

Policy Agreement between President and Congress

Of course, the success of presidential politicization efforts depends upon the willingness of Congress to go along. Indeed, one type of appointed position, that requiring Senate confirmation, can only be created or eliminated by explicit congressional action.[8] Other types of appointed positions, while normally created by administrative action, are subject to oversight by Congress. Presidential discretion is limited by the antici-pated response of Congress to presidential politicization decisions.

When Congress and the president share the same party or the same views about policy, Congress is more willing to create appointed positions and less likely to object when presidents create more appointed positions by executive action.

Figure 4.1, above, also graphs the change in the number and percentage of appointed positions during 1960–2004 by whether or not the two branches of government are controlled by the same party (that is, unified or divided government). When the president and Congress share the same party, the change in politicization is substantially larger than during periods of divided government. Indeed, on average the number, though not percentage, of appointees declines during periods of divided government. During four-year periods of unified government there is an average increase of close to 400 appointees. This increase partly reflects an agreement about policy between the two branches. Increasing the number of appointees makes it more likely that the bureaucracy will produce policies in line with the policy views of the president *and* Congress. Increasing the number of appointees also helps the party reward supporters with jobs, particularly those supporters with connections to members of Congress.

A Closer Look at Two Cases

Looking at the numbers of appointees in specific agencies or at different points in time can obscure the specific cases where this number increased. Hidden among the numbers in the previous discussion of changes from 2000 to 2004 are two of the most publicized cases of politicization during the George W. Bush administration, that of the CIA under Porter Goss and of the Office of Special Counsel (OSC) under Scott J. Bloch. Looking more closely at these two cases provides an opportunity both to test the propositions from the last chapter but also to illustrate how and why politicization occurs in concrete cases.

Porter Goss and the CIA

In the summer of 2004 President George W. Bush nominated Porter Goss to succeed George Tenet as the Director of the CIA. Goss was easily confirmed by the Republican-controlled Senate (77–17). After his confirmation, Goss brought with him a number of political appointees from Capitol Hill to help him run the agency.[9] Conflicts quickly arose between Goss's new team and career staff at the CIA.[10] In order to put his stamp on the agency, Goss froze top careerists out of high-level decision making, asked some senior personnel to leave, and issued explicit instructions to CIA personnel to "support the administration and its policies in our work."[11]

Goss's actions and the tense relationship between his appointees and top career professionals reduced agency morale and created significant attrition among top career managers at the CIA. The Director of Central Intelligence, the Executive Director (third in command), and the head of the analysis branch all departed. In total, about 20 top career managers within the agency left after Goss's arrival.[12] The new director encouraged, or at least expected, some of these officials to leave, but he was also put on the defensive by the extent of the exodus. His actions disrupted the agency's operations, damaged its institutional memory, and caused a decline in human capital. For Goss, however, the loss of key top-level managers was a price he was willing to pay to get control of the agency.

The "Gossification" of the CIA, while praised by some, was widely decried on parts of Capitol Hill and by the press.[13] Members of Congress were divided about whether politicization of the CIA was a necessary tactic for reining in an unresponsive government agency or whether it was a dangerous example of bad management with potentially disastrous consequences for national security. Senator John McCain (R-AZ) called the CIA a "dysfunctional" and "rogue" agency and argued that Goss should do "whatever is necessary" to reform the agency.[14] Generally, those members of Congress who shared the administration's views about policy took McCain's view. Those who opposed the administration took the latter view. Representative Jane Harman (D-CA) warned of an implosion at the CIA, and Senator Evan Bayh (D-IN) said, "Anytime you've got top people dropping like flies when we're facing serious risks, you have to be concerned."[15]

Goss resigned by mutual agreement with the White House in May 2006 and was replaced by intelligence veteran Michael Hayden. While President Bush publicly praised Goss's tenure, saying Goss had led "ably" and noted his efforts to increase the number of analysts and operatives, Democrats hailed his departure as good news for the agency. Rep. David Obey (D-WI) stated, "His management style has been wrecking the country's most important intelligence agency. I hope that whoever is selected to take his place will rebuild agency morale and competence."[16]

Scott J. Bloch and the OSC

Scott J. Bloch began his five-year term as head of the Office of Special Counsel (OSC), an agency created to protect federal employees from prohibited personnel practices, in January 2004. He assumed control at an interesting time for the agency. The OSC had recently handled a number of high-profile whistleblower cases.[17] The publicity surrounding these cases and the events related to the 9/11 terrorist attacks led to an increase in cases sent to the agency by federal employees. Bloch succeeded a Clinton-appointed Democrat, Elaine Kaplan, who had been credited by one federal-employees group with revolutionizing the office and making it a "safe harbor" for whistleblowers.[18] Kaplan had been an advocate for federal employees, but her tenure had created a substantial backlog in OSC cases. Kaplan said, "A more thorough investigation requires more time. There is no simple fix for this—it is a balancing problem."[19]

Bloch, a former official in the Justice Department and the newly created Office of Faith-Based and Community Initiatives, came in with his team of political appointees and was immediately enmeshed in two controversies.[20] First, he ordered a review of the OSC's legal authority to protect gays from discrimination and removed statements about their legal protections from the agency's website. When this action was leaked to the press, the office became the subject of national news reports, congressional criticism, and a public response from the White House.[21] Bloch believed that long-time career employees in the Washington office leaked the information about his actions to the press. This firestorm was followed by a Government Accountability Office (GAO) audit in March of 2004 on the extent of the backlog at OSC. The GAO report concluded that a large percentage of cases had not been processed quickly enough to satisfy statutorily imposed time limits and that the OSC should "provide Congress with a detailed strategy" describing how the office would deal with this problem.[22] While Bloch had not been in office when the backlog was created, the GAO report brought increased negative attention to the agency.

As part of his effort to reduce the backlog of cases, Bloch conducted a review of agency operations along with his senior management team. His review prompted a reorganization of agency structure and processes. His focus on case-disposition was a significant policy change since it necessarily meant a less-aggressive pursuit of all cases, particularly cases that were not clear-cut. Most objectionable to critics, however, were the personnel actions associated with the reorganization.[23] Bloch's reorganization created a new regional OSC office in Detroit and required the transfer of a dozen Washington office employees to field offices in Detroit, Oakland, and Dallas.

According to a complaint filed by some of the affected employees and watchdog groups, the personnel actions were targeted at long-term career employees critical of Bloch's management, particularly those suspected of leaking his plans to the press. Three government watchdog groups wrote to Congress that "the way that the 'reorganization' is being implemented leads to the inescapable conclusion that existing career staff are being purged."[24] No employees hired during Bloch's tenure, including those that had been hired from outside the career service, were asked to transfer. The agency did not ask for volunteers, and employees who did not mind moving were not allowed to trade places with those who were asked to transfer. Employees were given ten days to make a decision about whether or not to transfer to one of the other offices and sixty days to complete the move. If they refused their new assignment, they would be fired. Critics charged that there were seven vacancies already in the Washington, D.C., office and that it would be cheaper and more efficient to fill these vacancies directly in the district offices rather than paying to move existing employees. Bloch, for his part, denied any attempt to target specific employees.

Bloch's actions were the subject of some controversy. He was forced to defend his actions to interest groups, Congress, and the press.[25] In March 2005 some of the affected employees filed a complaint against Bloch with the support of employee-watchdog groups and the Human Rights Campaign. The latter group joined the claim on the basis of the assertion that Bloch targeted employees who complained to the media or a labor union about how sexual-orientation cases were being handled.[26] Claims and counterclaims were made about the success of his efforts to reduce agency backlogs and whether those actions amounted to anything more than closing cases without appropriate sensitivity or review. In the aftermath of Bloch's reorganization, turnover and attrition increased. Of the twelve employees asked to move, ten left the agency and two retired. This delayed the opening of the Detroit field office.[27] A review by Republican House members Tom Davis (R-VA) and Jon Porter (R-NV), however, ended with their stating, "We continue to be impressed with the sincerity and pragmatism with which you and all your staff approach your jobs."[28]

These two cases illustrate three important points about politicization. First, policy disagreement between Bush appointees and career personnel was the motivation for politicization. The CIA was politicized because the Bush administration and Goss were suspicious of the CIA's loyalties and did not believe that the CIA's views on policy and practice coincided with their own. Indeed, many in the administration and Congress believed the CIA to be out of control and the source of embarrassing leaks during the 2004 campaign.[29] In the OSC case, there was real policy disagreement between Bloch and the career staff. At least part of the holdover career staff preferred more deliberate case-processing focused on worker protections, particularly cases involving sexual orientation or whistleblower complaints. Bloch and his team preferred quicker processing and less attention to these types of cases. These disagreements were inextricably linked with Bloch's reorganization proposal.

Second, politicization was made easier by the fact that the president's party controlled Congress. In both cases, members of Congress responded predictably to the administration's actions. In the CIA case Republicans lined up behind the administration while Democrats lambasted Goss. In the OSC case Democrats and moderates in Congress were those most concerned about Bloch's actions, while conservatives seemed less attentive to the issues raised and more satisfied with Bloch's explanation. This is not surprising given the core constituencies and ideological views of the parties involved. Federal employees' unions are part of the core of the Democratic Party constituency, and Democrats have been more protective of government workers in the last fifty years. On the other hand, Republicans, who have advocated making federal jobs more competitive and tying pay to performance, have been more enthusiastic about the Bush administration's attempts to reshape the civil service system. Goss would have had to step more gingerly and Bloch might not have pursued his reorganization had Democrats been in control of one or both chambers of Congress. In both cases, the similarity in Congress's and the president's policy views created a political environment where politicization was more possible than it would have been otherwise.

Finally, the cases illustrate that where one stands on politicization depends upon where one sits in the political process. In the CIA and OSC cases Republicans were more supportive of both Goss's and Bloch's actions while Democrats were more critical. Tellingly, Democrats were also those most concerned about how the actions of Goss and Bloch would influence agency competence. Those who were least likely to approve of the policy change brought by the politicization were also the most likely to be concerned about competence. Fundamentally, it is difficult to talk about the "right" number of appointees precisely because one's opinion on the proper number of appointees depends partly upon ideology. Those with policy views closer to the president will be more sympathetic to the president's plight and believe that adding appointees can be a useful strategy for getting control of a wayward or misguided agency. Those with policy views that diverge from those of the president will see the politicization strategy itself as misguided.

Testing Competing Views

The evidence that politicization occurs when there is policy disagreement between the president and the bureaucracy and when the president and Congress are from the same party confirms two of the predictions from the earlier chapter. To have more confidence in these findings, however, it is necessary to compare them against competing views. The two most common views about when politicization occurs are that it has increased steadily over time and that the increase is driven primarily by Republican presidents.

Has Politicization Increased Over Time?

The limited amount of empirical work on politicization supports the view that politicization is increasing. For example, Paul Light documents an increase in management layers in the federal government—what he calls "thickening"—and assesses both the causes and consequences of this phenomenon. He argues that some of this "thickening" is due to the increasing number of political appointees added to the government by the president and Congress. Light does, however, note that the increase has not been steady or even across agencies. The Volcker Commission similarly reported a noticeable expansion in the number of political appointments. In 1989 the commission counted 3,000 political appointees compared to barely over 200 in 1933. They conclude that all of the expansion cannot be explained by growth in the size and responsibilities of the federal government. From 1933 to 1965 they claim the number of Senate-confirmed appointees grew from 73 to 152. From 1965 to 1989, however, the number increased to 573, a rate much faster than the rate of growth in the size of government. When it reconvened in 2003, the commission concluded that the increase in political appointees they had documented in 1989 had continued into the Clinton administration.[30]

The problem with existing counts, however, is that they tend to focus too much on Senate-confirmed (PAS) positions. Simple counts of the number of PAS positions can be misleading. These counts include appointments to advisory boards, positions filled by part-time employees, and persons who serve without compensation. If the additional appointments are entirely in advisory posts or jobs outside the cabinet in part-time positions, this would imply a significantly different conclusion than that offered by the Volcker Commission.[31] Focusing on PAS positions also ignores the broader universe of appointed positions, which is where politicization usually occurs. For example, when President Nixon was accused of politicizing the bureaucracy, he was not being accused of increasing the number of PAS positions. Rather, the concern was that he was changing career positions to appointed positions by *administrative* action.

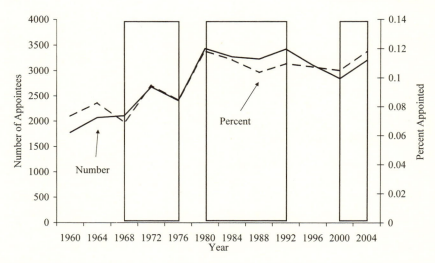

Figure 4.2 Total Number of Federal Government Appointees and Percentage Appointed, 1960–2004

Note: Boxed areas represent Republican presidents. Includes salaried PAS, Schedule C, Noncareer SES, and NEA appointments.
Source: U.S. Congress. *Policy and Supporting Positions, 1960–2004.*

Figure 4.2 graphs the total number and percentage of appointees from 1960 to 2004, including PAS, noncareer SES appointments and their predecessors, as well as Schedule C appointees. It excludes unsalaried and part-time positions. The graph demonstrates a clear increase in appointees between 1960 and 1980 with a slight dip between 1972 and 1976. This implies that the conventional view about the increase in appointees is partly right. There are more appointees in 2004 than there were in 1960, and there was a relatively steady rise from 1960 to 1980. The number of appointees does not increase after 1980, however, and this is surprising given that most of the scholarly debate about politicization arose in the 1980s.[32] Indeed, the decline in the number of appointees after 1980 would be even more pronounced if not for the increase in the number of appointees in the George W. Bush administration. The number of appointees declined from a high of 3,435 in 1980 to 2,845 by the end of the Clinton administration.

The sharpest increase in the number of appointees occurs in the transitions from Johnson to Nixon and from Ford to Carter. The increase in appointees under Nixon is manifested most clearly in the social welfare agencies and stems from Nixon's broader attempts to get control of a bureaucracy he mistrusted. The administrative apparatus of government grew substantially under Johnson, who, along with Kennedy, populated both the new agencies created during the Great Society as well as the existing bureaucracy. By the time Nixon assumed office the agencies of government had been under Democratic control for eight years.

The increase from Ford to Carter is a bit more enigmatic. The low number of appointees in the Ford administration partly reflects post-Watergate attrition. The Republican administrations of Nixon and Ford had a harder time recruiting and retaining political appointees after the Watergate scandal and the resignation of President Nixon. The increase during the Carter administration is due partly to filling existing vacant positions and also to the creation of new cabinet departments (Education, HHS, and Energy) and the SES.[33]

The dramatic expansion in the number of appointees during the Carter administration raises the question of whether the increase indicates that government is growing and new bureaucracies are being created or whether it reveals politicization, as is being discussed here. To aid the examination of this possibility, figure 4.2 also includes the percentage of appointees relative to the total number of federal civilian employees. The expansion of government cannot be the explanation for the increase in the number of appointees during the Carter administration since the percentage of appointees relative to employment shows the same pattern as the total number. In fact, one of the main differences between the two figures is that the decline in politicization after 1980 is even more pronounced when looking at percentages. This suggests that the pattern in the number of appointees is not a result of fluctuations in federal employment. In fact, if we consider the growing contracting workforce as part of the federal workforce, the decline in politicization after 1980 would be even more pronounced.[34]

Looking at the total number of appointments obscures where the changes are occurring. If we break down the number of appointees by type over this same time period, it is clear that some types of appointments are increasing and others are decreasing (figure 4.3). There has been an increase of about 90 PAS positions between 1980 and 2004. About a third of these positions were added with the creation of the VA and the DHS. While PAS positions increased, the number of appointed SES managers and Schedule C appointees decreased. Down from a high of 828 appointees in 1980, the SES includes only 700 appointees in 2004. There are also 200 fewer Schedule C appointees in 2004.

In sum, it is not a fair characterization of the data to say that the number of appointees is increasing steadily over time. While the number of appointees is higher today than in 1960, a then-versus-now comparison ignores substantial variation over time and across types of appointees. The number of appointees has actually declined since 1980, and the

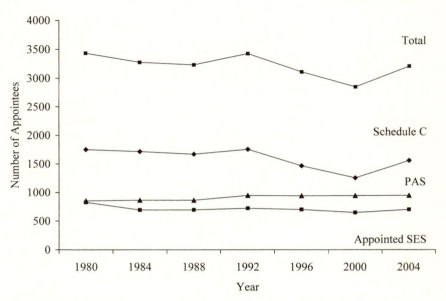

Figure 4.3 Total Number of Presidential Appointments, 1980–2004

Note: Excludes unsalaried or part-time PAS positions.
Source: U.S. Congress. *Policy and Supporting Positions, 1980–2004.*

drop is among noncareer SES and Schedule C appointees, precisely the category of appointees used most often for politicization.

Is Politicization a Republican Strategy?

If we look at the raw numbers or percentages of appointees during the 1960–2004 time period, we find more appointees serving during Republican administrations than Democratic administrations. Republican administrations average about 140 more appointees than Democrat administrations. This, however, reflects the fact that Republicans serve after the period when the increase in appointees took place. Republicans served in sixteen out of the twenty-four years after 1980, the peak of politicization.

Looking at the simple trends in politicization over time also reveals that both Democrats and Republicans politicize the bureaucracy. The increase from 1960 to 1980 occurred during the administrations of Democrats Kennedy, Johnson, and Carter and also during that of the Republican Nixon. The number of appointments did decrease under Clinton, but they also decreased under presidents Ford and Reagan. Appointments actually increase slightly more on average under Democrats. This is not to suggest that Republicans such as Nixon and Reagan, or Eisenhower before them, did not politicize or benefit from the increase in appointments by presidents who preceded them. President Reagan, for example, made use of the politically appointed positions created by Carter, particularly those in the SES, to change the bureaucracy's course. Reagan OPM director Donald J. Devine lauded the benefits associated with the creation of the SES for the Reagan Administration.[35] In addition, the Republican presidents accused of politicizing did politicize some, but not all, agencies; and their politicization was not consistent across the government or across their terms. The same, however, is true for Democrats. This leads to an important conclusion: politicization is not a partisan phenomenon in the sense that it is a tool of one party but not the other. On the contrary, it is a strategy for bureaucratic control employed by presidents from both parties.

Conclusion

The very real conflicts illustrated by cases like those of the CIA and the OSC play out across the government in different types of agencies—large and small agencies, politically controversial agencies, and agencies that are havens for patronage. Although incidents of politicization are not perfectly predictable, this chapter has demonstrated that politicization can be described by broad and consistent patterns over the more than forty years between the end of the Eisenhower administration in 1960 to the Bush administration in 2004.

Some of the increase in the number of appointments can be attributed to pressures stemming from party change in the White House. The greater the level of perceived policy disagreement between the president and the continuing bureaucracy, the greater the incentive the president has to increase the number of appointees in both managerial and staff positions. Indeed, there can be quite a bit of perceived disagreement between a new administration and the holdover bureaucracy, particularly when the new party has been out of power for several elections.

The president's plan to alter the number of appointed positions through techniques such as layering, adding ministerial staff, reductions-in-force, or reorganizing requires at least the tacit cooperation of Congress. This is easier when the majority in Congress supports the president's views on policy. Not surprisingly, during the second half of the last century, more appointees were added when the two branches were controlled by the same party. When the government was divided between the parties, the number of appointed positions actually declined slightly on average.

Despite popular perceptions to the contrary, politicization has neither increased steadily over time nor increased primarily during Republican administrations. The raw number and percentage of appointments did increase more or less steadily through the Carter administration, but no subsequent president has exceeded Carter's levels. Although the number of appointments increased noticeably with the transition from President Clinton to President George W. Bush, the number of appointments actually increased during both Democratic and Republican administrations in the period from 1960 to 2004.

These data and their analysis have provided an important first step in evaluating the theoretical claims of chapter 3 and the existing literature. That said, we are limited in what we can accomplish with the Plum Book data since it does not lend itself to easy econometric analysis. One limitation is that the long time period makes categories of political appointments incomparable.[36] Unfortunately, these different types of appointments are central to understanding distinct patterns of politicization attributable to concerns for policy versus demands for patronage. The long time period also makes measuring key concepts difficult because good personnel data are not available prior to the end of the Reagan administration.[37] In addition, the quadrennial nature of the publication makes evaluating the rhythms of politicization within administrations impossible and makes tracking agencies over time difficult, particularly at the subagency level.[38]

These factors do not eliminate the usefulness of the Plum Book data for testing theory and evaluating common views, but they do limit the ways in which it can be used. Fortunately, OPM has collected data year by year and agency by agency in a manner that allows for better measures of all of the key concepts. While the time period covered by this data is shorter (1988–2005), there are actually more years of data to facilitate the estimation of appropriate econometric models.

The next chapter uses OPM data to examine year-to-year variation in the percentage of appointees in the management teams of federal agencies. It examines agencies one step below the large cabinet departments. For example, rather than evaluating the Department of Justice as a whole, the chapter examine the management teams of individual bureaus, such as the Federal Bureau of Investigation (FBI), the Bureau of Alcohol, Tobacco, Firearms, and Explosives (ATF), and the Drug Enforcement Administration (DEA) over time. It also uses statistical techniques to try to determine what factors influence the degree of politicization with the appropriate controls. These new data provide an important supplement to the analyses in the current chapter.

5

The Pattern of Politicization:
A Closer Quantitative Analysis

IN JANUARY 2007 President George W. Bush issued an executive order mandating that all departments and large agencies have an office of regulatory policy review headed by a presidential appointee.[1] The purpose of the office is to review and control informal guidance documents issued by agencies. These documents explain how agency rules will be enforced and provide more detail about what regulated parties need to do to comply with regulations. The Bush administration worried that informal guidance was being used by agencies to subvert the intentions of the administration in regulatory enforcement.

Even though the president's power was arguably at its lowest ebb, given his low approval ratings and a new Democratic majority in the House, he politicized. Apart from a few newspaper articles, the president's action received little attention.[2] The order was quickly overshadowed by the scandal surrounding the administration's removal of nine U.S. Attorneys.[3] This episode is representative of how less visible instances of politicization can escape widespread attention. While they might escape public notice, they are still visible in the quantitative data, which is one of its advantages. This chapter continues the quantitative analysis of politicization patterns but does so in a more precise fashion.

While the last chapter examined data from the Plum Book, this chapter examines new data from OPM's Central Personnel Data File (CPDF). The data include information on political appointments for 256 agencies over the eighteen-year period from 1988 to 2005. While these data have the disadvantage of only being available back to 1988—thus facilitating a close look at only three presidencies (those of George H. W. Bush, Bill Clinton, and George W. Bush)—they complement the data in the last chapter in a number of ways.

First, the short time period makes it possible to track and compare different types of appointments over time. This is essential for disentangling policy-motivated politicization from patronage-driven politicization. The short time period also allows one to get assessments of agency policy views that are comparable across agencies and time. This provides a means of evaluating whether Democratic and Republican presidents treat liberal and conservative agencies differently.

A second advantage of the CPDF data is that they allow for a finer-grained analysis of politicization. Data on the number of appointments are available at the bureau level, one step below the department level. In the federal government most large departments include a score of self-contained, subordinate agencies or bureaus. The Department of the Interior includes bureaus such as the U.S. Fish and Wildlife Service, the Bureau of Land Management (BLM), and the U.S. Geological Service. The Treasury Department includes the U.S. Mint, the Internal Revenue Service (IRS), and the Alcohol and Tobacco Tax and Trade Bureau. One difficulty in analyzing politicization in the last chapter was that there was substantial variation in politicization within departments across the different bureaus. The CPDF data provide an opportunity to exploit these differences and more precisely test when and where politicization occurs. For example, it can be useful to know that within the Department of Agriculture, the Rural Housing Service has more than 50 appointees, whereas the Agricultural Research Service has none at all, or that within HHS, the Administration on Children and Families has 21 appointees while the CDC has but 1.

The CPDF also includes annual information about the management status and type of work (professional, technical, blue-collar, and so forth) of all federal civilian employees across the government. These data provide better measures of the key concepts discussed in chapter 3, including politicization itself and sensitivity of agency performance to politicization.

The chapter proceeds deliberately. It first provides an overview of the OPM data similar to that provided for the Plum Book data. It then reviews the four propositions about politicization and explains how the concepts in these claims are measured. The next section describes the details of econometric models used to test the propositions. The chapter then presents the results of the models and discusses their implications for both the propositions and alternative views of politicization. It concludes by summarizing the findings and putting them in a larger perspective.

Politicization below the Waterline: An Overview

Table 5.1 lists the most politicized agencies as of September 2005 using the number of appointees relative to the number of managers as the measure of politicization.[4] The table also lists the raw numbers of employees, managers, and appointees of various types. As the table suggests, some agencies, particularly smaller ones, have as many or more appointees than managers—even under this generous definition of "manager." For example, the Appalachian Regional Commission has 2 managers but 4 appointees: 2 Senate-confirmed federal co-chairs and 2

Table 5.1
Most Politicized Management Structure in 2005 by Size of Agency

Department	Bureau	Employment	Managers	PAS	Noncareer SES	Sched. C	% Mgrs Appointed
Small Agencies (<500 employees)							
IND	Appalachian Regional Commission	10	2	2	0	2	200.0
EOP	Office of Science and Technology Policy	30	8	2	4	6	150.0
HUD	Faith-Based and Community Initiatives	8	2	0	0	2	100.0
EOP	Council of Economic Advisers	24	4	1	0	3	100.0
EOP	Office of National Drug Control Policy	123	23	3	2	16	91.3
Medium-sized Agencies (500–5,000 employees)							
EOP	Office of Management and Budget	477	75	6	10	18	45.33
DOJ	Office of Justice Programs	628	116	5	3	11	16.38
USDA	Risk Management Agency	505	59	0	2	6	13.56
IND	Commodity Futures Trading Commission	511	96	5	0	7	12.50
COM	International Trade Administration	1,772	434	1	11	40	11.98
HHS	Administration on Children and Families	1,324	180	3	9	9	11.67
Large Agencies (5,000–20,000 employees)							
USDA	Rural Housing Service	6,174	858	0	2	50	6.06
USDA	Farm Service Agency	5,740	1,184	0	6	61	5.66
State	Department of State	24,482	3,950	31	36	120	4.73
Energy	Department of Energy	14,973	3,683	18	31	78	3.44
IND	Environmental Protection Agency	18,398	2,369	8	23	38	2.91
Very Large Agencies (>20,000 employees)							
IND	National Aeronautics and Space Administration	18,786	2,647	2	7	14	0.87
HHS/IND	Social Security Administration	66,145	6,716	3	9	5	0.25
DHS	Bureau of Customs and Border Protection	41,849	5,971	1	2	7	0.17
DHS	Bureau of Immigration and Customs Enforcement	14,628	2,044	0	1	2	0.15
Interior	National Park Service	23,904	4,268	1	1	4	0.14

Source: Office of Personnel Management, Central Personnel Data File (*CPDF*), September 2005.
Note: The Departments of State and Energy were not disaggregated by OPM into their subcomponents.

additional appointed policy advisors (Schedule C). The Office of Faith-
Based and Community Initiatives, located within HUD, had 2 managers
and 2 Schedule C appointees.

Not surprisingly, several of the most politicized agencies in the federal
government are agencies in the Executive Office of the President (EOP).
These agencies include the Office of Science and Technology Policy,
the Council of Economic Advisers, and the Office of Management and
Budget (OMB). The EOP also includes the Office of National Drug Control Policy, created in 1988 under President Reagan, set up by President
George H. W. Bush, and later politicized by President Clinton.[5] One explanation for the politicization of the EOP agencies is the importance
of loyalty to the president. The president wants his staff to be both
loyal and competent, and in these sensitive positions loyalty is particularly important.

The table shows that small agencies have higher percentages of appointees than larger agencies. This suggests that a larger percentage of
appointees may be necessary in smaller agencies than in larger agencies.
For example, to control a small agency with 2 managers, a president
may need 50 percent of the managers to be appointed, whereas in an
agency like the U.S. Air Force, which has 20,000 managers, 13 appointees, or .04 percent of the management team, might have the equivalent influence.

Several of the smaller agencies with the most appointees relative to
the number of managers are commissions. For example, the Appalachian Regional Commission and the Commodity Futures Trading Commission both have high numbers of appointees. Commissions are typically managed by 3 to 7 persons, rather than by a single person. Often
commissioners are selected by presidential appointment for fixed and
staggered terms, and no more than half the members can be from one
political party.[6] This gives commissions the appearance of being politicized in the sense that there are a relatively large number of appointees
relative to the number of managers, but this is misleading. Staggered
terms limit the appointment power of any sitting president. Fixed terms
limit the president's removal power, and party-balancing or other membership requirements are intended to limit the pool of available appointees and give the commission some semblance of partisan balance.
The Federal Reserve is an example of an agency that has an appointed
board but by all accounts is well insulated from presidential politics relative to other agencies.

Many agencies have no appointees at all. In September 2005, 51 of
210 agencies had no appointees. Some agencies had no appointees because of vacancies in PAS positions or other management positions the
administration intended to fill with an appointee.[7] Others had no ap-

Table 5.2

Selected Agencies with No Appointees in September 2005, by Size

Department	Bureau	Employment	Managers
Small Agencies (<500 employees)			
COM	Bureau of Economic Analysis	497	76
USDA	Coop. St. Research, Education, & Extension Service	437	48
HHS	Agency for Healthcare Research and Quality	306	28
TREAS	Financial Crimes Enforcement Network	291	40
IND	Federal Mediation and Conciliation Service	274	23
Medium-sized Agencies (500–5,000 employees)			
DOD	Defense Contract Audit Agency	4,112	710
GSA	Federal Supply Service	3,008	633
TREAS	Bureau of Engraving and Printing	2,297	390
TREAS	Financial Management Service	2,137	283
TREAS	Bureau of the Public Debt	1,919	297
Large Agencies (5,000–20,000 employees)			
DOD	Defense Finance and Accounting Service	13,388	2,191
HHS	Indian Health Service	13,354	1,488
Interior	Indian Affairs	10,622	1,313
DOD	Defense Contract Management Agency	10,535	1,037
USDA	Agricultural Research Service	9,392	710
Very Large Agencies (>20,000 employees)			
DHS	Transportation Security Administration	57,081	7,222
USDA	Forest Service	41,483	6,075
DOD	Defense Logistics Agency	21,501	2,890

Source: Office of Personnel Management, Central Personnel Data File (*CPDF*).

Note: A number of agencies have no appointees. Agencies listed on table had highest employment in their category.

pointees because they are administered by career managers and staff. Table 5.2 provides examples of different-sized agencies that had no appointees as of September 2005. This set of agencies is interesting for a number of reasons. First, several of the agencies—such as the Bureau of Economic Analysis, the Agency for Healthcare Research and Quality, and the Agricultural Research Service—are research-oriented agencies. In research and scientific agencies, political appointees would have a hard time doing the work required and the pool of potential appointees qualified to oversee the work of these agencies is likely small. This suggests that agencies with complex tasks like research and development or science appear more sensitive to politicization and are thus in general less politicized.

Second, in a number of agencies on the list scandals have occurred, are prone to occur, or are particularly costly if they do occur. For example, the Bureau of Indian Affairs has been the subject of a very visible lawsuit brought by several Native American tribes because of the bureau's mishandling of trust funds.[8] The Defense Contract Audit Agency, the Federal Supply Service, the Defense Finance and Accounting Service, and the Defense Contract Management Agency are all agencies dealing with procurement, where the potential for scandals or improper political tampering is quite high. Treasury Department agencies such as the Financial Management Service, the Bureau of the Public Debt, and the Bureau of Engraving and Printing manage the federal government's money, collect its delinquent debts, borrow money for government operations through the selling of bonds and notes, and design and print Federal Reserve notes, identification cards, and naturalization certificates. The potential for scandal or fraud in all of these activities is also high. Even before the adoption of the Pendleton Act in 1883, these jobs were normally performed by continuing professional personnel who stayed in the Treasury Department from administration to administration.[9]

Changes in Politicization, 1988–2005

Patterns of politicization change significantly over the 1988–2005 time period. Figure 5.1 graphs the average change in politicization by agency size. One pattern that emerges clearly is the natural rhythm of politicization during a president's tenure in office. In the first year of a president's term, there appears to be little politicization or even a decrease in appointee percentage, particularly after a party change in the White House. Politicization subsequently increases in the second and third years of a president's term, when presidents fill out their administration teams. In contrast, politicization often declines in the fourth year of a president's term as well as in a president's second term.

The first-year decline is seen starkly in 1993, President Clinton's first year in office, with its notoriously labored transition.[10] A decrease in politicization is also seen in 2001, the first year of George W. Bush's presidency. In 1989, the first year of the George H. W. Bush administration, however, there was no decline in appointee percentage. This reflects both the success of President Bush's transition staff and the fact that a transition from one Republican presidency to another is likely to be smoother than one involving presidents from different parties. Not only could the newly elected president rely on some holdovers from the Reagan administration—about one-third of his appointees had served under Reagan—but he also inherited a bureaucracy that had been staffed and influenced by a Republican president for eight years, one that was significantly more conservative and Republican than that inherited by his predecessor.[11] In 1997 and 2005, the first year of Clinton's and George W. Bush's second terms, respectively, there was also no across-the-board decline in politicization. The demands of office are different in second terms: presidents already have a team in place when they start their second term, and they have had four years to influence the necessary departments and agencies.

The party transition, whether the George H. W. Bush-to-Clinton transition or the Clinton-to-George W. Bush transition, led to an *immediate* decline in politicization. Ultimately, however, *party changes appear to create increases in politicization over all*. Initial decreases in politicization are followed by two to four years of increasing appointee percentages. At first glance, this appears consistent with our expectation that presidents will politicize more when they perceive significant disagreement between themselves and the bureaucracy, which is greatest after a party change and early in a president's tenure. The decreases in politicization across a president's term also suggest that presidents need to politicize less as they get control of agencies and have success identifying, promoting, and relying on sympathetic career managers. As the perceived disagreement between presidents and agencies decreases, so does politicization.

Looking at simple averages over time masks substantial variation across agencies in which politicization is occurring. Table 5.3 lists the agencies where politicization increased the most by presidency. It compares the number and percentage of appointees in 1988 and 1992 for President George H. W. Bush, in 1992 and 1996 for President Clinton, and in 2000 and 2004 for President George W. Bush. Notable increases in appointees during the George H. W. Bush administration occurred in stereotypically "liberal" agencies—those engaged in activities such as economic regulation (Federal Maritime Commission), labor relations (National Mediation Board), consumer affairs (Consumer Product Safety Commission), occupational safety (Occupational Safety and Health Review Commission), and government-directed volunteerism (Action).

President Clinton added a large number of appointees in the Department of Agriculture: three different bureaus within the department had significantly more appointees in 1996 than they had in 1992, at the end of the George H. W. Bush administration. Part of the increase was due to patronage, since the president and vice president were both from rural states with significant agricultural constituencies and Secretary of Agriculture Mike Espy, who previously had been a member of Congress, had his own network of supporters he wanted to bring into the department.

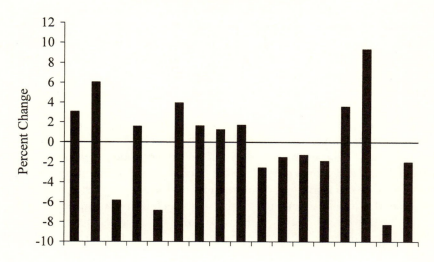

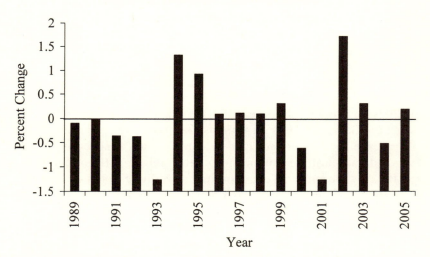

Figure 5.1. Change in Politicization over Time by Size of Agency, 1988–2005

Large Agencies (5,000 to 20,000 Employees)

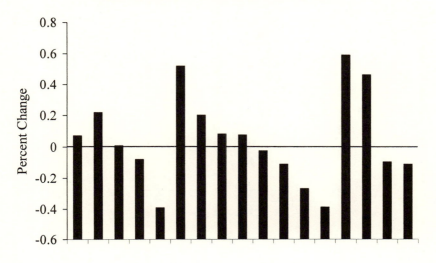

Very Large Agencies (> 20,000 Employees)

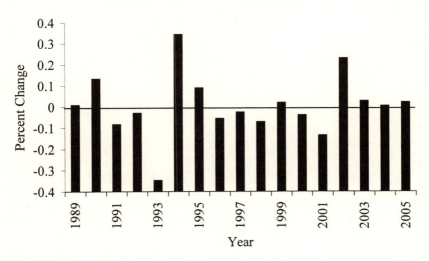

Figure 5.1. (*cont'd*)

Table 5.3

Agencies Politicized Under Presidents George H.W. Bush, Bill Clinton, and George W. Bush

Department	Bureau	Employment	Managers	PAS	Noncareer SES	Sched. C	% Mgr. Appointed
President George H. W. Bush							
IND	Federal Maritime Commission	211	48	4 (+4)	1 (+1)	9 (+9)	29 (+29)
IND	National Mediation Board	57	14	3 (+2)	0 (0)	2 (+2)	36 (+29)
IND	Occupational Safety and Health Review Commission	77	28	3 (+3)	2 (+1)	4 (+4)	32 (+29)
COM	U.S. Travel and Tourism Administration	66	18	0 (0)	2 (0)	5 (+3)	39 (+25)
USDA	Human Nutrition Information Service	120	23	0 (0)	1 (+1)	2 (+2)	13 (+13)
EOP	Office of Science and Technology Policy	47	12	2 (+2)	4 (+3)	7 (+5)	108 (+8)
IND	Action	425	118	3 (+3)	1 (0)	9 (+5)	11 (+7)
HUD	Public and Indian Housing	205	36	1 (+1)	0 (−1)	6 (+4)	19 (+7)
IND	Consumer Product Safety Commission	547	99	3 (0)	3 (+1)	11 (+2)	17 (+4)
IND	Merit Systems Protection Board	328	87	4 (+1)	3 (+1)	5 (+1)	14 (+4)
President Bill Clinton							
HUD	Community Planning and Development	235	21	1 (+1)	0 (−1)	10 (+4)	52 (+42)
USDA	Rural-Business Cooperative Service	151	53	0 (0)	2 (+2)	12 (+7)	26 (+22)
USDA	Rural Utilities Service	380	64	1 (0)	1 (−1)	7 (+7)	14 (+11)
DOD	Defense Advanced Research Projects Agency	157	105	0 (0)	6 (+6)	0 (0)	6 (+6)
IND	Office of Personnel Management	3,867	411	3 (+2)	9 (+2)	15 (+3)	7 (+5)
COM	International Trade Administration	1,650	498	4 (+1)	21 (+5)	28 (+2)	11 (+3)
USDA	Grain Inspection, Packers & Stockyards Admin.	914	160	0 (0)	2 (+2)	1 (+1)	2 (+2)
IND	National Science Foundation	1,245	278	1 (−1)	7 (+4)	0 (0)	3 (+1)
IND	Federal Trade Commission	950	525	5 (0)	7 (+4)	4 (−1)	3 (+1)
COM	Patent and Trademark Office	5,418	554	3 (+1)	1 (+1)	3 (+1)	1 (+1)
President George W. Bush							
EDUC	Office of English Language Acquisition	43	7	0 (0)	1 (+1)	3 (+2)	57 (+43)
EOP	Office of National Drug Control Policy	124	26	5 (+4)	2 (−1)	14 (+3)	81 (+21)
COM	Economic Development Administration	226	31	1 (+1)	2 (0)	5 (+2)	26 (+16)
IND	National Foundation on the Arts and Humanities	423	79	50 (+10)	5 (−1)	11 (+4)	84 (+14)
IND	Federal Housing Finance Board	115	28	0 (0)	0 (0)	5 (+4)	18 (+13)
COM	Nat. Telecommunications and Information Admin.	283	39	0 (−1)	2 (+2)	3 (+3)	13 (+11)
EOP	Office of the U.S. Trade Representative	213	38	5 (+2)	3 (−2)	6 (+3)	37 (+9)
DOJ	Office of Justice Programs	608	112	6 (+5)	4 (−1)	6 (+4)	14 (+8)
EOP	Office of Management and Budget	506	83	3 (−2)	13 (+3)	15 (+7)	37 (+8)
HUD	Federal Housing Commissioner	820	78	2 (+2)	2 (+2)	5 (+2)	12 (+7)

Source: Office of Personnel Management, Central Personnel Data File (*CPDF*).

Note: Table compares agency in 1992 and 1988, 1996 and 1992, and 2004 and 2000. It excludes cases where increase occurs entirely in Senate-confirmed positions.

Under President George W. Bush, some of the largest increases were in bureaus within the Department of Education, HUD, and the National Endowments for the Arts and Humanities. Like his predecessors, George W. Bush also increased the number of appointments in part of the Department of Commerce, known colloquially as "Bush Gardens" during his father's administration.

The agencies targeted by the three presidents reflect each administration's concerns both for policy and for patronage. For example, the conservative presidents did seem to target some reputedly "liberal" agencies, but they also added appointees to agencies that are regularly larded with patronage appointments, like Commerce and the SBA.[12]

These three presidents also strategically targeted federal management agencies such as OPM and OMB. This is nothing new. As the last chapter indicated, modern presidents recognize the importance of controlling human resources and budgets. A presidentially directed OPM facilitates presidential control of the bureaucracy since OPM determines whether new positions can be filled by Schedule C appointees, allocates SES positions across the executive branch, decides whether or not to allow appointees to burrow into the career service, and monitors agency compliance with civil service rules and procedures. A politicized OMB allows for presidential influence in areas such as budgets, regulation, and rulemaking; the assessment of program performance; and economic forecasting.

Evaluating Four Propositions of Politicization: Measures and Methods

These data provide an opportunity to evaluate the predictions emerging from chapter 3. Specifically, they provide a means of examining whether politicization increases when the president and agencies disagree about policy and whether it decreases when they agree. It also provides a means of testing whether an agency's sensitivity to politicization influences the degree of politicization and whether executive-legislative polarization influences politicization practices. Tracking the patterns of different types of appointees across agencies and administrations will also provide a means of determining whether patronage-driven politicization follows different patterns than that driven by concerns for policy. The focus of the analysis will be the values listed in the far right column in tables 5.1, 5.2, and 5.3, above, for the number of appointees relative to the number of managers. My expectation is that these factors will explain variation in the politicization of management teams, both across agencies, and across time.

Policy Disagreement between President and Agency

One key reason presidents politicize is that they believe an agency either does not share their views about policy or is unresponsive to the White House. It is difficult to compare agency views about policy with those of the president in a systematic way. The last chapter examined the politicization practices of presidents after a party change in the White House against presidents serving after same-party transitions or in second terms. It showed that presidents presiding after a party change, when the level of disagreement between the president and the bureaucracy is presumably greatest, politicized more than other presidents.

Another means of determining whether presidents politicize agencies with policy views dissimilar to their own is to see whether more liberal presidents target traditionally conservative agencies and more conservative presidents target traditionally liberal agencies. Advances in techniques for rating the liberalism-conservatism of presidents using positions on votes provide a more precise means of measuring political views than a simple party label. They allow one to distinguish Ronald Reagan's conservatism from the more moderate presidency of George H. W. Bush in a way that a party label cannot.[13] They also provide a common metric upon which to evaluate the liberalism-conservatism of presidents relative to Congress.

While we have ready estimates of the liberalism and conservatism of presidents and members of Congress based upon their records, it is difficult to determine which agencies are liberal and which are conservative. In some cases, one can reasonably deduce from an agency's mission or history whether it is more liberal or conservative. For example, social welfare agencies such as those housed in the Department of Labor, HUD, and HHS have core policy commitments closer to the platform of the Democratic Party than to that of the Republican Party. Similarly, one might reasonably expect that the armed services and agencies dealing with business are more conservative, and thus more closely allied with the platform of the Republican Party.

Rather than attempt to identify agencies that tend to be liberal consistently, conservative consistently, or neither, I relied on the expertise of academics and Washington observers. With the help of a colleague I identified a set of thirty-seven experts in American bureaucratic politics among academics, journalists, and Washington think-tanks.[14] We sent them a list of eighty-two departments and agencies with the following directions:

> Please see below a list of United States government agencies that were in existence between 1988 and 2005. I am interested to know which of these agencies have policy views due to law, practice, culture, or tradition that can be charac-

terized as liberal or conservative. Please place a check mark (✓) in one of the boxes next to each agency—"slant Liberal, Neither Consistently, slant Conservative, Don't Know."

We received twenty-three responses to the request (a response rate of 62 percent), and used these expert survey responses—adjusting for the degree of expertness (discrimination) and different thresholds for what constitutes a liberal or conservative agency—to get estimates of which agencies are consistently liberal or conservative.[15] Table 5.4 lists the agencies determined to be liberal or conservative based on whether they could be statistically distinguished from moderate agencies using the survey responses. The interaction of presidential ideology measures with agency ideology measures provides a direct way of testing whether policy disagreement between the president and the agency leads presidents to prefer more appointees.

Sensitivity of Agency Performance to Politicization

Presidents' choices about where to politicize are determined not only by agency policy views, but also by how politicization will influence agency competence. Competence concerns can influence the number of appointees both directly and indirectly. Presidents recognize the need for continuing professional personnel with a long-term perspective, expertise in government work built through experience, and site-specific knowledge. This constrained their behavior during the spoils period, when presidents chose not to turn over key positions in government and pushed for reform long before Congress was willing to assent.[16] In their own staffs, presidents do not rely entirely on political appointees. Although the White House is filled with employees who serve at the pleasure of the president, the executive clerk is a continuing professional, and professional staffs carry over in most of the other components of the EOP, including OMB and the Office of the U.S. Trade Representative.[17] Presidents also recognize that politicizing agencies like the U.S. Mint or the Secret Service could lead to disastrous outcomes in the form of currency scandals or injuries to public officials.

Concerns for competence can also influence presidents indirectly. Members of Congress are often more sensitive to the effects of politicization on agency performance because their views on policy differ from those of the president. Presidents are less likely to politicize if they anticipate an adverse reaction from that body due to competence concerns.

We have surmised that some agencies can bear more appointees than others without consequences for competence, but which agencies are they? The performance of agencies with complex tasks or demands for

Table 5.4
Liberal, Moderate, and Conservative Agencies Based Upon Expert Surveys, 1988–2005

Liberal	Moderate	Conservative
African Development Foundation	Broadcasting Board of Governors/USIA	Commodity Futures Trading Commission
Appalachian Regional Commission	Department of Agriculture	Council of Economic Advisers
Commission on Civil Rights	Department of Energy	Defense Nuclear Facilities Safety Board
Consumer Product Safety Commission	Department of Justice	Department of Commerce
Corporation for National and Community Service	Department of State	Department of Defense
Council on Environmental Quality	Department of Transportation	Department of Homeland Security
Department of Education	Department of Veterans Affairs	Department of Interior
Department of Health and Human Services	Executive Residence at the White House	Department of the Air Force
Department of Housing and Urban Development	Farm Credit Administration	Department of the Army
Department of Labor	Federal Communications Commission	Department of the Navy
Environmental Protection Agency	Federal Election Commission	Department of the Treasury
Equal Employment Opportunity Commission	Federal Housing Finance Board	Export-Import Bank of the United States
Federal Labor Relations Authority	Federal Maritime Commission	Federal Deposit Insurance Corporation
Federal Mediation and Conciliation Service	Federal Mine Safety and Health Review Commission	National Security Council
Merit Systems Protection Board	Federal Retirement Thrift Investment Board	Nuclear Regulatory Commission
National Foundation on the Arts and the Humanities	Federal Trade Commission	Office of Management and Budget
National Mediation Board	General Services Administration	Office of National Drug Control Policy
National Science Foundation	Inter-American Foundation	Office of the U.S. Trade Representative
Occupational Safety and Health Review Commission	National Aeronautics and Space Administration	Overseas Private Investment Corporation
Peace Corps	National Archives and Records Administration	Securities and Exchange Commission
Social Security Administration	National Capital Planning Commission	Small Business Administration
U.S. Agency for International Development	National Credit Union Administration	Trade and Development Agency
	National Labor Relations Board	U.S. International Trade Commission
	Office of Administration	
	Office of Government Ethics	
	Office of Personnel Management	
	Office of Science and Technology Policy	
	Office of Special Counsel	
	National Transportation Safety Board	
	Pension Benefit Guarantee Corporation	
	Railroad Retirement Board	

high expertise tends to be sensitive to the addition of appointees. Because the work of many federal agencies is complex, we need to be aware of the subtle differences among them in order to identify sensitive agencies. One way to see variation in work complexity is to examine the composition of agency workforces. OPM tracks the number of federal employees across agencies by broad categorizations of agency type: *professional, administrative, clerical, technical, blue-collar,* and *unknown.* Two of these work categories are relevant to evaluating agency task complexity: the percentage of workers classified as "professional" and the percentage classified as "technical."

OPM states that "professional" positions are white-collar occupations that require specialized knowledge in a particular field. Qualifications are often demonstrated through education at the bachelor's level or higher in a nongeneral field. The work requires the application of a body of knowledge to specific circumstances in order to make "new discoveries and interpretations" and to improve "data, materials, and methods."[18] Professional employees include economists, lawyers, and engineers.[19] The percentage of professional employees varies across agencies; 25 percent of an average federal agency's workforce is composed of professionals. The Rural Housing Service, however, has over 6,000 employees, but only 3 to 4 percent of these employees are professionals. Most of its employees are in administrative jobs, involved in providing grants and loans for housing and community facilities. Similarly, the SSA employs over 60,000 people, of which only 5 percent are professionals. More than 40,000 of the agency's employees are administrative personnel who make eligibility and claims determinations, largely in local Social Security offices. In the Nuclear Regulatory Commission, on the other hand, over 60 percent of the employees are classified by OPM as being "professional." NASA (65 percent), the SEC (66 percent), and the FDA (70 percent) are agencies with even higher percentages of professionals. Increases in the percentage of agency employees in professional occupations should be correlated with lower levels of politicization.

According to OPM, occupations classified as "technical" are white-collar jobs generally in support positions that are nonroutine and require extensive practical knowledge gained through experience on the job or specific training at a level generally below that denoted by a college degree.[20] Technical occupations include computer operations, forestry technicians, photographers, research assistants, food inspectors, and certain types of nurses. As in the case of forestry technicians or food inspectors, they often have site-specific knowledge that is hard to replace from outside the agency.[21] In other cases, such as computer operators or research assistants, large numbers are reflective of complex technical work. Some established agencies with high percentages of technical employees

include the Food Safety and Inspection Service (73 percent), the Forest
Service (52 percent), the Council of Economic Advisers (42 percent),
and the Defense Finance and Accounting Service (41 percent). Agencies
with lower percentages of technical employees include the Defense Legal
Services Agency (1 percent), the Surface Transportation Board (1 percent), and the Defense Advanced Research Projects Agency (1 percent).

The availability of good outside economic options for career professionals also influences the extent to which agency competence is sensitive to politicization. If senior agency personnel have attractive outside
options, changes in politicization can generate harmful departures in
the career workforce. Comparing the wages of SES employees to comparable private-sector earnings provides one means of measuring outside
options.[22] If SES wages decline relative to private-sector earnings, politicization should go down. If SES wages increase, however, politicization
should increase.

Policy Agreement between President and Congress

The president's optimal number of appointees frequently differs from
that of the median member of Congress because they have different
views about policy. The last chapter evaluated whether disagreement between the two branches limited politicization by comparing periods of
unified and divided government. While the number and percentage of
appointments decreased slightly during periods of divided party control,
unified government led to increases of about 450 appointees across the
government on average. Of course, this figure is influenced heavily by
the creation of the SES during the Carter administration. During Carter's term the number of appointments increased by more than 1,000
positions, and approximately 400 of these positions were newly created
SES positions. If we remove the Carter administration from the calculations, the estimated increase in the number of appointments during unified government is closer to 165 positions. From 1988 to 2005, there
were five years where the same party simultaneously controlled the White
House and both chambers of Congress (1993–1994 and 2003–2005).
These two periods of unified government occur during years when other
confounding factors are at work. The first period of unified government
(1993–1994) was concurrent with President Clinton's slow transition.
The second period (2003–2005) includes the only year in the sample
that saw both unified partisan control and a second-term president—
one of the disadvantages of examining a shorter timer period.

While unified/divided government provides an intuitive measure of
agreement and disagreement between the executive and legislative
branches, ideal-point estimates provide a more precise means of measur-

ing polarization between the branches.[23] The extent of executive-legislative polarization can vary substantially during both periods of unified and divided government. Such a measure can capture the influence of a conservative coalition existing between Republicans and conservative Democrats or Democrats and liberal Republicans. These cross-party coalitions can diminish the difficulties of divided government or increase the difficulties of governing during periods of unified government.

Patronage Politicization

A final factor driving politicization is the need to place campaign supporters and party workers. This pressure should be reflected in appointment patterns, particularly differences between PAS and Schedule C positions. Senate-confirmed appointees (PAS) are the most visible to Congress and the hardest for presidents to change; they also have the largest influence on policy. PAS positions must be created in statute, and such appointees must be confirmed by the Senate; this means that Congress regularly considers these positions and who will occupy them.

Schedule C positions are the least visible to Congress since they are less likely to have direct authority over agencies or policy. They are the easiest positions to create and the most likely to be used to satisfy patronage obligations. While Schedule C positions are used to enhance policy control, they usually offer lower pay and less prestige than PAS or SES positions. Schedule C positions are easiest to fill with campaign staff, political supporters, and persons appointed as a way of paying off political debts.

As chapter 3 emphasized, liberal presidents increase patronage positions more in liberal agencies and conservative presidents increase patronage positions more in conservative agencies. This is due to fact that liberal (conservative) campaign supporters are more likely to have background qualifications and job aspirations that make them easier to place in liberal (conservative)-leaning agencies.

Econometric Models of Politicization

In what follows I use the data to estimate econometric models of politicization.[24] The models provide a means of testing the four propositions while accounting for other possible sources of variation in politicization. The models control for presidential ideology and a possible trend to once again evaluate the most common views about politicization.[25] They control for normal within-term dynamics by including the log of the year of the president's term.[26] The models also control for important differences among agencies discussed above. Specifically, they include the log of agency employment to capture differences in agency size.[27] They include controls for whether the agency is a commission,[28] is in the EOP,[29] is independent,[30] or part of a larger department but not in a bureau (for example, office of the secretary) to capture important differences in structure that influence the number of appointees.[31] Agencies with these features should have higher-than-normal levels of politicization.[32] The models also control for whether each agency has its own personnel system or has a personnel system without SES positions to account for differences in appointee level attributable to differences in personnel systems.[33]

The models have two other useful features described in more detail in the section below. First, as in tables 5.1–5.3, above, they measure politicization as in the number of appointees relative to the number of managers. They do so, however, in a fashion that allows that larger agencies have larger numbers, but smaller proportions, of appointees.

Second, the models are flexible enough to allow for changes in key variables to have short-run or permanent effects on politicization levels. For example, it is possible that a change from a Democrat to Republican in the White House will produce a short-run increase in the number of appointees in the EPA or HUD, but that ultimately the number of appointees will go back to its original level once the new president has established control. Alternatively, it is possible that this party change in the White House increases the number of appointees in these agencies for the duration of the president's term. Since we have no concrete expectation about whether the effects are short- or long-term, models flexible enough to allow the data to speak for itself are appropriate.

This analysis also has one major limitation: namely, the shorter time period. This can be limiting in several ways. First, the data are comprised primarily of three presidents, one Democrat and two Republicans.[34] This makes generalizing across presidencies difficult. It is hazardous to generalize from Bill Clinton to all Democrats and from the two Bushes to all Republicans. For example, we know that politicization decreased during the Clinton administration even though it increased under every other Democratic president since 1960. Second, the short time period means that it can be hard to disentangle causal factors that are correlated with this time period. It is it difficult to discern, for example, whether politicization increases because the government is unified or because the party in the White House has changed. During this time period, all periods of unified government save one occur during a presidential term where there has been a party change in the White House.

With these caveats in mind, the data provide a new look into the politicization practices of modern presidents. In the next section I provide the details of the econometric models of politicization, and would encourage those readers to whom such issues of methodology are of minimal interest to move ahead to the following section.

METHODS: DETAILS OF ECONOMETRIC MODELS

The data from table 5.1 suggest that a greater *number* of appointees but a smaller *proportion* are present in larger agencies. To model this I measure politicization as:

$$\frac{y_{i,t}}{m^{\lambda}_{i,t}} \qquad (1)$$

where $y_{i,t}$ is the number of appointees in agency i at time t and $m_{i,t}$ is the number of managers in agency i at time t.[35] The greek letter λ represents a parameter whose estimated value should be $0 < \lambda < 1$ if the proportion of appointees necessary to manage larger agencies is, indeed, smaller.

Taking logs and including covariates gives:

$$\log y_{i,t} = \lambda \log m_{i,t} + X_{i,t}\beta. \qquad (2)$$

Since $y_{i,t}$ is often 0 and $m_{i,t}$ is occasionally 0, I add 1 to both $y_{i,t}$ and $m_{i,t}$ to facilitate the taking of logs.[36]

To account for both short- and long-run effects, I estimate a series of error correction (EC) models. The standard EC model is:

$$\Delta y_{i,t} = \Delta X_{i,t}\beta - \varphi(y_{i,t-1} - X_{i,t-1}\gamma) + \varepsilon_{i,t}, \qquad (3)$$

where $\varphi(y_{i,t-1} - X_{i,t-1}\gamma)$ is the EC term. In equilibrium $y_{i,t-1} = -X_{i,t-1}\gamma$. Changes in $X_{i,t-1}\gamma$ result in long-run changes in the number of appointees, $y_{i,t-1}$. When there has been a shock that throws $(y_{i,t-1} - X_{i,t-1}\gamma)$ out of equilibrium, φ reflects the rate at which a process returns to equilibrium.[37]

Substituting in equation 2 gives:

$$\Delta \log y_{i,t} = \Delta X_{i,t}\beta_k + \Delta \log m_{i,t}\beta_l$$
$$- \varphi \left(\log y_{i,t-1} - \lambda \log m_{i,t-1}\gamma_p - X_{i,t-1}\gamma_j \right) + \varepsilon_{i,t}. \qquad (4)$$

I multiply out (4) and estimate the following equation via OLS to obtain estimates of the short-run effects, the EC mechanism, and λ:

$$\Delta y_{i,t} = \Delta X_{i,t}\beta_k + \Delta \log m_{i,t}\beta_l - \beta_0 \log y_{i,t-1} + \beta_p \log m_{i,t-1} + X_{i,t}\beta_j + \varepsilon_{i,t}, \qquad (5)$$

where β_0 is φ, β_p is $\varphi\lambda$, and β_j is $\varphi\gamma$ in equation 4.[38] Since the panels have different variances based upon size and errors could be correlated across agencies (errors in agency i at time t are correlated with errors in agency j at time t), I report panel corrected standard errors.[39]

To interpret the coefficients from model 4 in table 5.5, I transform them back into ECM format so that:

$$\Delta y_{i,t} = -0.09 \Delta PARTYCHANGE_t - 0.04 \Delta UNIFIEDGOVERNMENT_t + \quad (6)$$
$$0.11 \Delta \ln(AGENCYMANAGERS_{i,t}) + 0.26 \Delta \ln(AGENCYEMPLOYMENT_{i,t}) +$$
$$0.07 \Delta REPUBLICANPRESIDENT_t - 0.07 * [\ln APPOINTEES_{i,t-1} -$$
$$1.43 PARTYCHANGE_{t-1} - 0.57 UNIFIEDGOVERNMENT_{t-1} -$$
$$0.001 \ln(AGENCYMANAGERS_{i,t-1}) - 0.14 \ln(AGENCYEMPLOYMENT_{i,t-1})$$
$$- 0.00 REPUBLICANPRESIDENT_{t-1} - 0.29 COMMISSION_i, - 0.29 EOP_i$$
$$+ 0.14 NOTITLE5_i + 0.86 NOSES_i - 0.86 INDEPENDENT_i -$$
$$2.14 \text{"}OTHER\text{"}BUREAU_i + 3.14 \ln(YEAROFTERM_{i-1}) - 0.00 TREND + C]$$

Evaluating Four Propositions of Politicization: Results

The model estimates provide the opportunity to look closely at the politicization patterns of three presidents, George H. W. Bush, Bill Clinton, and George W. Bush. They provide a means of testing the different propositions relating to politicization along with competing views and are a valuable complement to the analysis in the preceding chapter. They also illustrate two general features of politicization in the federal government that will help make sense of the discussion to follow.

First, while larger agencies have greater numbers of appointees, the *ratio* of appointees to managers is significantly smaller.[40] For example, in an agency with 10 managers and 50 employees—like the Economics and Statistics Administration (ESA) within the Department of Commerce— presidents may feel like they need 2–3 appointees (20–30 percent of the managers) to run the agency. As a proportion of the management team in a larger agency like OPM, however, 20–30 percent is more than necessary for an equivalent amount of control. Indeed, in OPM, which has about 385 managers and 5,000 employees, an equivalent number of appointees, in terms of influence, is closer to 10 appointees than the 95 that would be 25 percent of the management team. In thicker hierarchies not all of the additional managers are making policy-relevant decisions, so the proportion of appointees necessary to run an agency is smaller. In the ESA and OPM, appointees assume the positions with the most policy influence. Proliferating the number of appointees in positions of lower pay and responsibility produces fewer policy benefits for the administration although it can help satisfy demands for patronage.

Second, the influence of different factors varies by agency depending upon its degree of politicization to start with. For example, if party change in the White House is estimated to increase the number of appointees by a single appointee in each agency, this does not mean every

Table 5.5
ECM Models of Politicization, 1988–2005

	Schedule C	Noncareer SES	PAS	Total	Total
	(1)	(2)	(3)	(4)	(5)
Short Term Effects					
Δ Party Change in White House	−0.09**	−0.06*	−0.02*	−0.09**	—
Δ Difference in Wages	—	—	—	—	0.12**
Δ Unified government	0.00	−0.09**	0.01	−0.04	−0.10
Δ ln(Agency managers+1)	0.05	0.19**	0.05*	0.11**	0.10**
Δ ln(Agency employees)	0.20**	0.08	0.12**	0.26**	0.25**
Δ Republican president	0.07	0.01	0.08**	0.07	0.04
Permanent Effects (EC Mechanism)					
ln(Political appointees) $_{t-1}$	−0.08**	−0.13**	−0.10**	−0.07**	−0.07**
Policy Disagreement: President-Agency					
Party Change in White House $_{t-1}$(0,1)	0.07*	0.11**	0.01	0.10**	—
Sensitivity of Agency Performance					
Difference in Wages $_{t-1}$	—	—	—	—	0.10
Policy Disagreement: Congress-President					
Unified government $_{t-1}$(0,1)	0.02	0.00	0.04**	0.04	0.01
Controls					
ln(Agency managers+1) $_{t-1}$	−0.01	0.02	0.02*	0.01	0.00
ln(Agency employees) $_{t-1}$	0.02	0.00	−0.00	0.01	0.01
Republican president $_{t-1}$(0,1)	0.05	0.03	0.02	0.05*	0.00
Commission (0,1)	−0.01	−0.05**	0.05*	0.02	0.02
Executive Office of the President (0,1)	0.03	0.06**	0.01	0.02	0.02
Agency-Specific Personnel System (0,1)	−0.03	−0.06	0.01	−0.00	−0.01
Personnel System without SES (0,1)	−0.03	—	−0.03	−0.04	−0.06**
Independent (0,1)	0.06*	0.08**	0.07**	0.07*	0.06*
"Other" Bureau (0,1)	0.17**	0.20**	0.12**	0.15**	0.15**
ln(Year of Term)	−0.13**	−0.18**	−0.11**	−0.20**	−0.22**
Year (0–17)	−0.01*	−0.01**	−0.003**	−0.01*	0.00
Constant	0.08	0.11**	0.06	0.16**	0.20**
N	3381	3106	3385	3381	3172
Agencies	253	231	253	253	252
R^2	0.11	0.19	0.11	0.18	0.17

Note: Dependent variable Δ ln (political appointees$_{i,t}$+1).
 * significant at the .10 level; ** significant at the .05 level in two-tailed tests. T-statistics calculated using panel-corrected standard errors.

agency will get a single-appointee increase. Rather, agencies that already have a high number of appointees, such as large agencies or offices of the secretary in large departments, will likely get several new appointees. Other agencies that have no appointees or only a few may be unaffected.

Policy Disagreement between the President and Agencies

One key reason presidents politicize is that they believe an agency either does not share their views about policy or is unresponsive to the White House. The first means of evaluating this statement was to look at politicization practices of presidents after a party change. The model estimates in table 5.5, above, replicate the analysis from the last chapter with this new data and indicate that a party change in the White House leads to an immediate decline in politicization, and then a long-run increase that lasts throughout the new president's term. The initial decline after a party change confirms the difficulties associated with these transitions. For instance, incoming presidents can count on fewer holdovers, and the process of filling out management teams across the government is slowed by the distractions of the transition, by bargaining among factions over patronage, and by the learning process associated with taking control. If the incoming party has been out of power for a period of time, the pool of available appointees tends to be smaller. One personnel official explained it this way: "It was difficult to set up the process [at the start of the Clinton administration]. It was difficult at times to get people in. Democrats hadn't been in power for twelve years. People from the Carter administration were doctors and lawyers and most didn't want to come back or couldn't afford to because they would have [had] to take a pay cut."[41] In second-term or same-party transitions, a larger set of Washingtonians are available to serve the administration, including junior appointees who gained experience through service in the last administration or term.

The pattern associated with a presidential term after a party change is more broadly reflected in figure 5.2, which uses a sample agency to illustrate the effect of a party change on politicization. The sample agency is a reasonably sized agency of about 1,500 employees. It could be the Food and Nutrition Service ([FNS]; Agriculture), the Federal Technology Service (GSA), Health Resources and Services Administration (HHS), or the Administration on Children and Families (HHS).

Let us focus on the first of these, the FNS. This Agriculture Department agency runs, among other things, the Food Stamp Program. A party change in the White House can be expected to add 1–2 more appointees to the agency. Adding new appointees can affect the agency substantially because they assume the top policy and pay positions in the

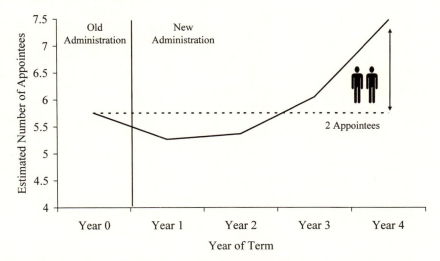

Figure 5.2. Impact of Party Change in the White House on Number of Appointees in Medium-Sized Agency (1,500 Employees)

managerial hierarchy. For example, in 2006 the FNS had 2 appointees in its management team in addition to the administrator.[42] The deputy administrator for Special Nutrition Programs was an appointed member of the SES, and the deputy administrator for Communications and Governmental Affairs was a Schedule C appointee. Career managers administered the other parts of the FNS.

After a party change, the incoming president might bring in an appointed member of the SES or a Schedule C appointee to run the politically salient Food Stamp Program directly, replacing the current career manager of the program. The president could also reasonably be expected to add a Schedule C appointee to be the Consumer and Community Affairs Director for the Communications and Governmental Affairs operation or create a new position that would be filled by an appointee with a portfolio pieced together from existing activities or new programs. The addition of these 2 appointees could significantly influence both the public profile and the activities of the agency. An appointed head of the Food Stamp Program could push the president's agenda for either easing or making more restrictive eligibility requirements for food stamps, and the new appointee in the public affairs position could sharpen the consistency of the agency's message and popularize the president's activities and approach. Both appointees can significantly influence the experience and perception of the Food Stamp Program and the agency for clients, stakeholders, and the public at large.

To the management team in a 10,000-person agency, such as the BLM (Interior), Natural Resources Conservation Service ([NRCS]; Agriculture), FDA (HHS), or the National Oceanic and Atmospheric Administration ([NOAA]; Commerce), a party change in the White House could be expected to bring a bigger change, depending on the agency's initial degree of politicization. In an agency like NOAA, for example, where a larger number of positions are filled by appointees (20), the effect will be larger (figure 5.3). NOAA's appointed positions include the Senate-confirmed undersecretary and assistant secretary posts as well as a dozen deputy assistant secretaries, directors, assistant administrators, general counsels, and various staff positions. In such an agency—one with more executives, managers, separate directorates, and layers—adding a larger number of appointees is much easier; one would estimate an increase of closer to 6 positions.

Of course, the extent to which the president or his subordinates seek to politicize agencies like the FNS, BLM, or NOAA depends on the extent to which they care about the policies they implement and their assessment of what will happen if these agencies continue on autopilot with the current number of appointed positions.

It is also true that if presidents politicize those agencies with which they have policy disagreements, they are depoliticizing agencies whose

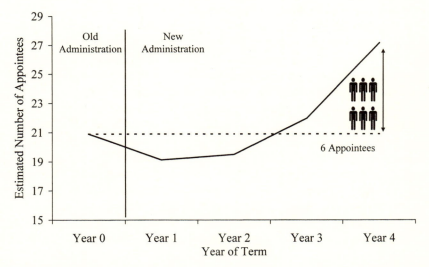

Figure 5.3. Impact of Party Change in White House on Moderately Politicized Agency (10,000 Employees)

Note: Agency started in 75th percentile in number of appointees. Simulated effects calculated, holding all other factors constant.

leadership they trust. This can happen in a number of ways. First, presidents can depoliticize directly by refusing to add discretionary appointments such as Schedule C appointments, by reorganizing with the intent to put careerists in control, by replacing appointed SES members with career SES members, by selecting career officials for appointed positions, or strategically leaving appointed positions vacant.[43] Second, depoliticization can occur by default when no appointees are added to a growing agency. Third, presidents can ask department heads to set aside more SES positions as career-reserved positions. Career-reserved positions cannot be filled by appointees, and a status change away from career-reserved requires explicit approval from OPM. Finally, presidents and Congress can strategically leave vacant important positions. Vacant appointed positions, in the absence of an appointee, will normally be filled by a career deputy.[44]

TARGETING LIBERAL OR CONSERVATIVE AGENCIES

Another means of determining whether presidents politicize agencies with policy views dissimilar to their own is to see whether liberal presidents target conservative agencies and conservative presidents target liberal agencies. The model estimates in table 5.6 indicate that PAS appointees increased more in liberal than conservative agencies under George H. W. Bush and George W. Bush.

For President George H. W. Bush and President George W. Bush, the increase in PAS appointees amounts to about one-third of an appointee added to the average liberal or moderate agency. In other words, an additional Senate-confirmed appointee was added to every third liberal or moderate agency. For conservative agencies, however, the appointee increase is smaller and of shorter duration. The advent of a Republican administration is estimated to increase the number of PAS appointees by one-tenth of an appointee for conservative agencies. Across the executive branch, the advent of a Republican administration is estimated to increase the number of PAS appointees by 50 positions in liberal or moderate agencies compared to only 10 in conservative agencies. The number of PAS appointees is estimated to go back to its previous level in the conservative agencies but not in liberal or moderate agencies.

If we look just at the largest, most politicized agencies, the patterns become clearer. Under one of the Bush presidencies, the number of PAS appointees is estimated to increase by between 1 and 2 positions in liberal agencies such as EPA, the U.S. Agency for International Development (USAID), or HUD.[45] In more conservative agencies such as the Overseas Private Investment Corporation or the Department of the Treasury, how-

Table 5.6
ECM Models of Politicization, 1988–2005

		Noncareer		
	Schedule C	SES	PAS	PAS
Short-Term Effects				
Policy Disagreement: President-Agency				
Δ President's Conservatism*Agency Conservatism	—	—	0.01	—
Δ President's Conservatism*Liberal Dept.	0.22**	0.01	—	−0.02
Δ President's Conservatism *Conservative Dept.	0.19**	0.11**	—	0.01
Sensitivity of Agency Performance to Politicization				
Δ % Technical in Agency Employment	−0.34	−0.03	0.00	0.02
Δ % Professional in Agency Employment	−0.61**	0.07	−0.24*	−0.25*
Policy Disagreement: President-Congress				
Δ Preference Distance House-President	0.23	0.40**	0.05	0.04
Controls				
Δ ln(Agency managers + 1)	0.05	0.18**	0.06*	0.06*
Δ ln(Agency employees)	0.21**	0.08	0.11**	0.11**
Δ President's Conservatism	−0.08	−0.02	0.06	0.08**
Permanent Effects (EC Mechanism)				
ln(Political appointees) $_{t-1}$	−0.08**	−0.14**	−0.11**	−0.11**
Policy Disagreement: President-Agency				
President's Conservatism*Agency Conservatism$_{t-1}$	—	—	−0.02**	—
President's Conservatism*Liberal Dept.$_{t-1}$	0.04	−0.01	—	0.01
President's Conservatism *Conservative Dept.$_{t-1}$	0.05	0.03	—	−0.04
Sensitivity of Agency Performance to Politicization				
% Technical in Agency Employment$_{t-1}$	−0.15	−0.20**	−0.16**	−0.14**
% Professional in Agency Employment$_{t-1}$	−0.03	0.03	0.00	0.00
Policy Disagreement: President-Congress				
Preference Distance House-President$_{t-1}$	−0.32	−0.32*	−0.14**	−0.14**
Controls				
Agency conservatism	—	—	−0.00	—
Liberal agency (0,1)	0.00	0.01	—	0.03
Conservative agency (0,1)	−0.00	−0.00	—	0.03**
ln(Agency managers+1)$_{t-1}$	−0.01	0.01	0.02*	0.01
ln(Agency employees)$_{t-1}$	0.02	0.01	0.00	0.00
President's Conservatism$_{t-1}$	0.01	−0.02	0.05*	0.03
Commission (0,1)	0.00	−0.05**	0.06**	0.05*
Executive Office of the President (0,1)	0.03	0.08**	0.03	0.01
Agency-Specific Personnel System (0,1)	−0.03	−0.07	−0.00	−0.00
Personnel system without SES (0,1)	−0.04*	—	−0.03	−0.03
Independent (0,1)	0.05	0.07*	0.06**	0.07**
"Other" Bureau (0,1)	0.17**	0.21**	0.12**	0.12**
ln (Year of Term)	−0.09**	−0.13**	−0.09**	−0.09**
Year (0–17)	−0.01	−0.01	−0.003*	−0.004**
Constant	0.29	0.30**	0.16	0.13**
N	3381	3106	3385	3385
Agencies	253	231	253	253
R²	0.11	0.18	0.11	0.11

Note: Dependent variable Δ ln(political appointees$_{i,t}$+1).
  * significant at the .10 level;
 ** significant at the .05 level in two-tailed tests. T-statistics calculated using panel-corrected standard errors.

ever, the expected increase is slightly less than one-half of an appointee per agency.

A similar pattern appears for Bill Clinton, except that appointees generally decline during his administration. In the midst of the decline, however, the number of PAS appointees is markedly higher in conservative agencies than liberal or moderate agencies. PAS appointees are estimated to decline by a quarter of an appointee for the average liberal or moderate agency but decline by only .07 appointees for a conservative agency. In the larger, traditionally liberal agencies mentioned above, the decline is estimated to be about 1–1.5 appointees in liberal or moderate agencies compared to less than 0.4 of an appointee in the traditionally conservative agencies.

The different politicization pattern for more liberal-leaning and more conservative-leaning presidents demonstrates how policy disagreement between the president and agencies influences politicization choices. Presidents add more appointees and keep more appointees in agencies that have policy views that differ from their own.

Sensitivity of Agency Performance to Politicization

While policy disagreement plays a key role in politicization decisions, such decisions do not occur in a vacuum. Presidents and Congress forecast how politicization will influence the ability of the agency to do what it has been asked to do. Sometimes personnel officials are sensitized to concerns for competence through painful experience. For example, mismanagement of the Indian Trust Fund and procurement scandals have led to decreases in politicization in the Bureau of Indian Affairs and government-contracting agencies. In other cases, personnel officials are constrained more intuitively. They have never thought consciously about dumping appointees into the CDC or the Bureau of Economic Analysis. When asked about their decisions, personnel officials explain that it is hard to find appointees who are qualified to work in these agencies. Presumably, presidents and their personnel officials could politicize these agencies and fill them with unqualified appointees but the costs in terms of performance would be too great. While personnel officials explain their choices in terms of the availability of qualified appointees, the problem is really with the agencies themselves. If agency tasks were not complex or did not require substantial professional experience, technical expertise, or site-specific knowledge, personnel officials could find an ample supply of appointees and politicize without consequences for performance. Instead, the likely impact of adding appointed positions for agency competence constrains how politicization choices are made and does so more in some agencies than in others.

In the models, sensitivity of agency competence to politicization is measured in two ways: complexity of agency tasks and the availability of good outside economic options. The models use the percentage of professional and technical employees as proxies for task-complexity and demonstrate that increases in professional and technical employees are correlated with decreases in politicization. Agencies with more complex tasks, that require specialized skills, site-specific knowledge, experience, and the exercise of discretion, are less politicized than other agencies. A one-standard-deviation increase in either the percentage of professionals or technical employees is estimated to decrease politicization by between one-quarter and one-half of an appointee in the average agency. The effects of a one-time change are expected to diminish slowly over time for a change in professional employees. For technical employees, however, the resulting change in politicization levels is permanent.

To put results for professional employees in context, consider that from 1988 to 2005, the percentage of federal employees that were professionals varied substantially within each agency, about 10 percent on average. Some agencies experienced a decline: professional occupations declined 10 percent in the Foreign Agricultural Service and 23 percent in the Substance Abuse and Mental Health Services Administration. Others, such as the SEC and the Patent and Trademark Office, experienced large increases (20 and 25 percent, respectively) in the percentage of employees in professional occupations. In the sample, about one-third of the agencies had their highest percentages of professionals ever in 2005, compared to only 6 percent in 1988. Given the increasing volume and complexity of government work, the percentage of professionals is likely to increase. Part of the explanation for the decline in politicization since 1980 is likely the increasing complexity and volume of government work reflected in the persistent increase in professional occupations in the federal workforce.

For technical-employee percentages, the models show that agencies with a high percentage of technical employees have lower politicization levels. Figure 5.4 graphs the expected number of appointees for the average agency by the percentage of the agency's employees in technical occupations. As the percentage of technical employees increases, the number of appointees decreases. While the average agency has 3 to 4 appointees, agencies with higher percentages of technical occupations, for example 30–40 percent, are estimated to have only 1–2 appointees.

Together the results for professional and technical occupations suggest that agencies with tasks that require a significant number of professional or technical personnel have lower politicization levels. This implies that in agencies whose tasks require professional training, where

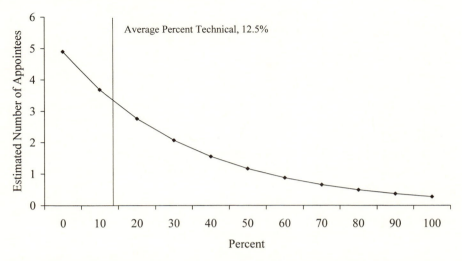

Figure 5.4. Estimated Number of Appointees for Average Agency by Percentage of Technical Employees, 1988–2005

skills are learned on the job, or where skills are hard to acquire in the private sector, the levels of politicization are lower.

If we measure sensitivity of competence to politicization by looking at the availability of good private-sector options for career employees, the results are similar.[46] In cases where politicization will lead to significant harm to agency competence, politicization decreases. Increases in private-sector earnings relative to SES wages decrease politicization. Model estimates suggest that a permanent one-standard-deviation increase in private-sector earnings relative to SES salaries is estimated to decrease politicization by 1–2 appointees in the average agency. This amounts to between 250 and 500 positions across the government. This suggests that presidents and Congress politicize less when there is a real possibility that doing so will lead a large number of career employees to leave government service. When career professionals have attractive outside options, as they did during the economic boom at the end of the Clinton administration, politicization can lead to significant departures among long-time career employees.

On the other hand, a permanent one-standard-deviation decrease in private-sector earnings relative to SES wages is estimated to increase politicization by 1–2 appointees per agency. When career employees have fewer options, as they did during the recession at the end of the George H. W. Bush administration, politicization is a more attractive strategy since it is less likely to lead to significant departures.

Policy Agreement between President and Congress

The model estimates also indicate that politicization decreases when the president and Congress have different views about policy. A change in interbranch polarization equivalent to that experienced by Clinton after the 1994 midterm elections (which brought Republicans to power in Congress) is estimated to decrease the number of appointees by 1–2 appointees in the average agency. Conservatively, this means a decrease of 250 positions across the government. As before, the agencies most likely to be influenced are those that start with large numbers of appointees.

The results in tables 5.5 and 5.6, above, also suggest that the relationship between interbranch polarization and politicization is the most robust for PAS appointees. This makes sense given that Congress must both create these positions and confirm personnel to serve in them. PAS positions include secretaries (including deputy, under-, and assistant secretaries) and some commissioners, administrators, and bureau chiefs—the most significant positions at the top of the management hierarchy. Appointees serving during a period of interbranch comity also are less likely to experience political conflict resulting from disagreements between political superiors in the White House and Congress. They will serve longer tenures. The aggregate effect is that periods of unified government lead to increases in the number and percentage of appointees across the government.

The reason for the decline in politicization when Congress and the president disagree is straightforward. Members of Congress benefit less from presidential politicization when the president does not share their views about policy. Presidents use appointees to pull policy away from what the majority in Congress wants. They also use patronage to benefit the minority. Opposition Congresses are therefore more likely to monitor and constrain politicization efforts. A recent column by Paul Krugman expresses this sentiment colorfully. He writes: "As I said, none of this is surprising. The Bush administration has been purging, politicizing and de-professionalizing federal agencies since the day it came to power. But in the past it was able to do its business with impunity; this time Democrats have subpoena power, and the old slime-and-defend strategy isn't working."[47] What Krugman writes has been true for over forty years. Presidents have had a freer hand in politicizing when the majority in Congress had views close to those of the president. When the majority has opposing views, however, Congress has limited the number of appointees through oversight and publicity as well as specific statutory language and slow confirmations.[48]

Patronage Politicization

The final proposition is that presidents will increase patronage appointees in agencies that have policy views close to their own. While all three types of appointees can be used to influence policy, Schedule C posts are the most likely to be used to reward campaign supporters and satisfy demands for patronage. If politicization patterns for Schedule C appointees differ from other types, particularly PAS appointees, this is good evidence that both policy and patronage are at work.

Model estimates confirm that politicization patterns differ for PAS and Schedule C appointees. Figure 5.5 graphs the estimated influence of a new Republican administration on the number of PAS and Schedule C appointees for relatively politicized agencies. The patterns are significantly different for PAS and Schedule C appointees. The advent of the new administration leads to an increase in both PAS (top of the figure) and Schedule C appointees (bottom of the figure) in liberal agencies. This confirms our expectations about how policy disagreement between the president and agency would influence politicization. It shows how appointees are a means for the new administration to get control of agency policy.

Schedule C appointees also increase in *conservative* agencies, however, suggesting that patronage is also at work. The advent of either the George H. W. Bush or George W. Bush administration is estimated to increase the number of Schedule C appointees by one-half an appointee in the average liberal or conservative agency compared to a slight decline in a moderate agency. This amounts to an increase of about 150 Schedule C appointees scattered throughout liberal and conservative agencies.

The difference in politicization patterns for Schedule C and PAS positions is instructive. Republican presidents add to the numbers of PAS appointees in liberal agencies because of Republican concerns about liberal agencies' policy views. Schedule C positions, however, get added to both the most liberal and the most conservative agencies for reasons of both policy and patronage.

To compare the types of politicization that occur in liberal and conservative agencies under Republican presidents, consider the cases of the NEA and the SBA. The NEA was considered by the expert raters as "liberal" and has been a frequent Republican target for budget cuts or elimination.[49] The endowment funds arts activities in the fifty states through grants to organizations and individuals and is run by a chairperson nominated by the president and confirmed by the Senate to a fixed four-year term. In 2000 the NEA had 7 appointees, including a Senate-confirmed chair, 2 deputy chairs who were appointed members of the SES, and 4 other appointees who were in public affairs (appointed SES) and staff

PAS Appointees

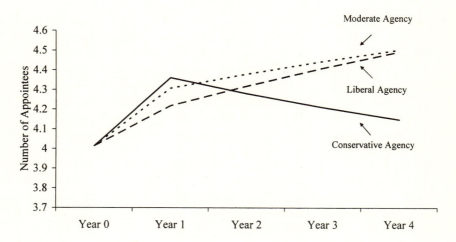

Schedule C Appointees

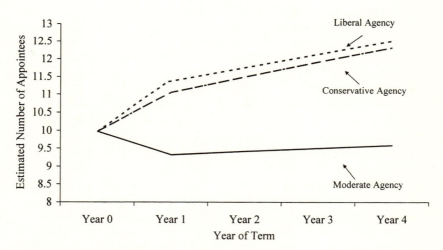

Year of Term

Figure 5.5. Different Patterns for Policy and Patronage: Change in Agency Politicization by Type of Appointee in Conservative Administration

Note: Estimates based upon agency in 75th percentile of politicization and all other factors held constant.

positions (Schedule C), such as executive secretary and staff assistant.[50] By 2004, however, the agency had 10 political appointees.[51] In addition to the chair (PAS) and deputy chairs (appointed SES), Schedule C appointees filled the positions of general counsel, director of development, and director of research and analysis as well as 2 positions in public affairs. The new positions were not staff positions, but they appeared oriented toward ensuring that the NEA continued in the conservative direction it had taken in the aftermath of scandals involving the funding of controversial works by Robert Mapplethorpe and Andres Serrano.[52]

In the SBA, on the other hand, the pattern appears to be different. The SBA's stated mission is to serve the interests of small business. It is run by an administrator nominated by the president and confirmed by the Senate. The SBA was labeled conservative by our raters, and in 2000, at the end of the Clinton administration, the SBA had 42 political appointees: it had 4 PAS appointees, 11 SES appointees, and 27 Schedule C appointees. This is a large number of appointees by any count, but it is particularly large for an agency of its size (4,300 employees). A high percentage of the appointed members of the SES and the Schedule C appointees filled ministerial staff, public affairs, and regional director positions. SBA has independent offices for Congressional and Legislative Affairs, Communications and Public Liaison, and Field Operations, each of which is headed and staffed with appointees. The SBA understandably has a reputation for being larded with patronage appointments.[53]

By the fall of 2004, the number of SBA appointees increased to 56 positions (4 PAS, 14 noncareer SES, and 38 Schedule C).[54] Some of the biggest changes following the end of the Clinton administration were made in the Office of the Administrator. The office was reorganized substantially to suit the new administration. The offices of Chief Financial Officer (career) and National Ombudsman (appointed) were moved out of the administrator's office, and one temporary position lapsed. The position of Chief Operating Officer was switched from a career to an appointed position, and a new White House Liaison position was created and staffed by an appointed member of the SES. Five new Schedule C positions were added, including positions such as Policy Advisor, Director of Scheduling, Special Assistant, Assistant Administrator for the Office of Policy and Planning, and Senior Advisor to the Chief Operating Officer; 4 out of 5 of these positions were increases in ministerial staff. Other significant increases occurred in the Office of Congressional and Legislative Affairs (4 positions) and the newly created Office of Strategic Alliances (4 positions).

The bulk of the president's politicization of the SBA involved appointees moving into positions with less direct policy responsibility than was the case in the NEA. Noting the various positions filled with ap-

pointees across the agencies helps us understand the differences between politicization for policy reasons and politicization for patronage.
President George W. Bush added appointees to the liberal NEA to ensure
consistency with his views for what the NEA should be funding. His appointments in the more conservative SBA appear on their face to be
driven by patronage.

For President Clinton the politicization patterns look similar except
that appointees are generally declining during his administration. President Clinton maintained higher numbers of PAS appointees in conservative agencies than either moderate or liberal agencies. Liberal and moderate agencies, however, had higher levels of both SES and Schedule
C appointees. The different patterns for the most policy-relevant and
patronage-relevant appointees suggests that the two processes are also at
work in the Clinton administration.

Interestingly, however, both liberal and conservative agencies are estimated to have fewer Schedule C appointees than moderate agencies during the Clinton administration. The decline in Schedule C appointees
in liberal and conservative agencies is somewhat surprising and inconsistent with both expectations and what the other presidents did.

MODEST EFFECTS IN THE SENIOR EXECUTIVE SERVICE (SES)

For the SES appointees, the effects of political factors is modest. The
patterns that do exist reflect modest patronage politicization. The advent
of the Clinton administration is estimated to have increased the number
of SES appointees by one-quarter of an appointee in liberal agencies
and decrease the number of appointees by one-fifth of an appointee
in conservative agencies. This is a difference of close to one-half of an
appointee in the average agency based upon agency ideology. Across the
government, this amounts to a modest 12-appointee increase in liberal
agencies and a 15-appointee decrease in conservative agencies. In contrast to the Democrat Clinton, the Republican presidents increased the
number of SES appointees in conservative agencies but decreased them
in liberal agencies. The fact that these three presidents put marginally
more appointed SES members into agencies with ideologies close to
their own suggests that whatever politicization did occur in the SES was
often for patronage. This is consistent with the addition of SES appointees in the SBA case described above.

There are two reasons why changes in SES appointees are modest compared to changes in other types of appointees. First, career members of
the SES have tenure rights for at least three months after a new executive
takes over an agency. This means that incoming presidential administrations have to wait to make key changes. Presidents not willing to wait may
choose to politicize through other means. Second, presidents can use

the flexibility in the SES to choose sympathetic careerists from the SES to do the same job as an appointee would. Careerists have the advantage of both bureau-specific expertise and longer tenure.

In sum, however, the evidence suggests that concerns for both policy and patronage were driving politicization during the 1988–2005 time period. All three presidents placed more policy-relevant appointees in agencies that did not share their policy views, confirming our expectation that disagreements between the president and agencies would increase appointees. Two of the three presidents increased Schedule C appointees in both liberal and conservative agencies, suggesting that appointee increases were not only for reasons of policy, but also for purposes of patronage.

Exploring Alternative Views and Additional Findings

The models shed additional light on other common views of politicization. Notably, no upward trend in appointments is discernible between 1988 and 2005. Model estimates consistently show an overall decline in presidential appointments. This reinforces the finding from chapter 4 that political appointments increased between 1960 and 1980 but have remained relatively steady or have declined slightly since then. The models do suggest, however, that President George H. W. Bush and George W. Bush politicized more than President Clinton. Agencies averaged 1–2 additional appointees during the presidencies of George H. W. Bush and George W. Bush than in the Clinton administration. Government-wide, this amounts to about 250–500 more appointees in each of these Republican presidencies. This is also consistent with what we saw in the last chapter. From the the George H. W. Bush presidency to that of Clinton, appointments declined; then, from the second Clinton term to George W. Bush's presidency, there was an increase of about 350 positions. So, while over the last forty or so years both Democrats and Republicans have increased the number of appointments, Clinton did not. In fact, several Clinton administration officials interviewed volunteered that they were under clear instructions not to exceed President George H. W. Bush's numbers and were "always under pressure to reduce" the number of appointees. Clinton's politicization was targeted to specific agencies.

Additional Findings

Several other model estimates are worth noting, among them how differences among agencies in administrative structure and situation in the executive branch influence the baseline number of appointees in each agency. Agencies in the EOP, commissions, independent agencies, and the parts of larger departments that are not in distinct larger bureaus (for example, the office of the secretary) have higher percentages of appointees than are found in other agencies. An agency in the EOP will have 1–2 more appointees than a comparably sized agency outside the EOP. This reflects the extra weight that presidents place on loyalty in their staff agencies as well as the free hand with which Congress allows presidents to shape and reshape their own staffing. The EOP includes such agencies as OMB, the Council of Economic Advisers, the National Security Council (NSC), and the Office of the U.S. Trade Representative.

Commissions by definition have more top executives, so it is no surprise that they tend to have more appointees than other comparably sized agencies. Commissions tend to have 1–2 more appointees than comparably sized agencies that are organized as administrations. In addition to the commissioners themselves, appointees often fill positions as executive directors, general counsels, congressional liaisons, and staff to each of the commissioners.

The higher proportion of appointees in offices of the secretary and unaffiliated parts of large departments indicates politicization by layering. These parts of large agencies and departments are estimated to normally host 40–45 more appointees than other agencies; in 2005 they varied from 18 appointees (VA) to 170 appointees (Department of Defense). To manage large departments presidents tend to proliferate deputy-, under-, and assistant secretaries and the ministerial staff that attends to them, such as chiefs of staff, special assistants, and general counsels. The unaffiliated parts of larger departments also include smaller offices—such as legislative affairs, intergovernmental affairs, general counsels, inspectors general, public affairs, and policy and strategic planning—that are often filled by appointees but have relatively few managers and employees.

Independent agencies are estimated to have 9 more appointees than comparably sized agencies that are part of larger departments. So, comparably sized agencies such as the FDA and the EPA are estimated to have different numbers of appointees based upon their location in the bureaucratic hierarchy. An agency like the FDA will have fewer appointees since it is under a hierarchy of deputy-, under-, and assistant secretaries as part of a larger department. The raw numbers of appointees in such agencies is not indicative of the extent of political influence in these agencies.

Agencies that have been granted authority to create personnel systems outside the traditional Title 5–based civil service are no less politicized than other agencies, except to the extent that they have no SES equivalents. Agencies with personnel systems that do not include SES positions normally have 1–2 fewer appointed positions.[55] Two factors are at work in this larger pattern: first, that agencies outside Title 5 might have fewer appointees indicates that agencies with their own personnel systems already allow executives more control over the hiring, promoting, and firing of agency personnel, thus reducing the need for appointees for policy control; and second, some agencies have been granted exemptions from Title 5 because of their special employment needs. The VA, for example, requested such authority to help it recruit and retain top medical personnel, which are hard to hire within the civil service regulations.

Discussion and Conclusion

In general, the quantitative analysis has helped confirm what was suggested by earlier argumentation, anecdote, and the Plum Book data used in chapter 4. Politicization followed the patterns set forth by the four propositions. It increased predictably when presidents perceived policy disagreement between themselves and the continuing bureaucracy. Compared to within-party transitions and second terms, party-change transitions led to increases in appointments after a first-year decline. This was one of the most robust findings across the models and it demonstrates how a president's perceptions of policy disagreements or disloyalty in the bureaucracy can drive politicization. The examination of liberal and conservative agencies confirmed that presidents are more likely to target agencies that do not share their policy views. They do so most prominently with PAS and Schedule C appointees.

Both Republicans and Democrats were sensitive to how politicization would influence agency performance. As the percentage of professional and technical employees in an agency increased, the number of political appointees decreased. Agencies that perform more complex tasks have lower levels of politicization than other agencies since it is harder for appointees to replicate the performance of career employees in the agency. Similarly, as outside economic options improve for careerists relative to their current salaries, politicization also decreases.

Politicization increases when the president and the majority in Congress share the same views about policy, such as when the same party controls both the presidency and Congress. The increase in appointments during periods of unified government over the 1960–2004 period was replicated in this data, particularly for PAS positions. Members of Congress are more willing to increase the number of appointees when they are confident that the president will select appointees with policy views similar to those of the majority in Congress.

Finally, patronage-type appointments increase more in agencies that have policy views similar to those of the president. For all three presidents in this dataset, appointees in the SES were most likely to be added to agencies that shared the president's policy views. For two of the three presidents, Schedule C appointees not only increased in agencies with different policy views, but also increased in agencies that shared the president's policy views. These findings help confirm what the interviews suggested: namely, that two processes related to both policy and patronage are at work in the appointment of presidential personnel.

As the case with the regulatory policy offices at the start of the chapter suggested, quantitative analysis can illuminate less visible instances of politicization. This is important since it is frequently difficult to observe politicization. Presidents and their appointees cloak politicization efforts in new dramatic programs with fancy titles, in reorganizations nominally intended to improve efficiency, or in plans to cut agency employment through reductions-in-force. It can be difficult for the press, Congress, or other interested observers to identify politicization because these same types of activities happen regularly with no intent to politicize.

One agency whose politicization did not get widespread public attention until it was too late was the Federal Emergency Management Agency (FEMA). The last few chapters have sought to answer the first question that motivated this study: namely, *Why do some agencies have more appointees than others?* In the next two chapters, I address a second: namely, *How do political appointments influence federal management performance?*

6

Politicization and Performance: The Case of the Federal Emergency Management Agency

No CASE more visibly illustrates the influence of politicization on performance and the importance of this topic than that of the Federal Emergency Management Agency (FEMA). The agency's poor response to Hurricane Katrina had dramatic consequences for the lives of disaster victims living on the Gulf Coast. Congressional, academic, and journalistic reviews of the agency's performance after the event targeted, among other things, the large number of appointees in the agency. They suggested that better leadership and a quicker, coordinated response could have saved hundreds of lives and prevented substantial human suffering.[1] This is not the first time the agency's performance invited criticism of its appointee-laden management structure; the scathing assessments of FEMA after Katrina were eerily similar to those made after hurricanes Hugo and Andrew in 1989 and 1992. According to these sources, FEMA has had a long-standing problem with politicization that has hurt performance and made it difficult for the agency to sustain reform. This chapter and the next explore the relationship between appointees and performance, beginning with a discussion of the performance of appointees vis-à-vis careerists, and then moving to the ways these factors have played out in FEMA, notably in its response to Hurricane Katrina.

Appointees, Careerists, and Management Performance

There are legitimate and competing views about whether presidential appointees or career executives are better for competent agency performance. On the one hand, a long tradition holds that political appointees drawn from outside the civil service bring needed energy and responsiveness to federal management.[2] According to this view, the public sector's low wages and its lack of pay-for-performance salary structures push the best and the brightest workers into the private sector.[3] Employees who know they are competent prefer a pay scheme that rewards high performers, while those who are less competent seek a salary structure that is less directly tied to performance. To the extent this is true in the aggregate, the best workers will choose the private sector over government work because the private sector is more likely to reward them for their performance. Civil service rules and regulations that stymie efforts to recruit, train, and retain good managers only lessen the attractiveness of federal work for potential employees, such that appointees drawn from the private sector arguably are, in aggregate, more talented than their careerist counterparts.[4]

The distinct means of appointment and prior background experience create systematic differences between the two populations of federal executives. Appointees and careerists view the policy world through a generalist or specialist lens, respectively. Appointees have a closer connection to political stakeholders' preferences. Career executives, on the other hand, are more likely to start low in a bureau's hierarchy, spend a significant portion of their career in that agency, and develop substantive expertise in the policy area they manage. Consequently, appointees are less likely to see the world through the bureau's eyes, but rather through those of elected officials. Furthermore, the fact that appointees can be removed by the president at any time for any reason makes them more responsive than their careerist counterparts, who are protected from removal by procedural rights and appeals.

On the other hand, a substantial literature has lauded the management advantages of promoting career executives. Indeed, the very motivation for the creation of the merit system was to establish a more competent, professional administration of government.[5] Career executives are more likely to have subject-area expertise, public management skills, and the immunity from politics necessary for both long-term planning and the cultivation of professionalism.[6] Each of these characteristics arguably improves management. Subject-area expertise and bureau-specific experience facilitate monitoring and program implementation. An employee who has worked in an agency before he or she becomes its manager is more familiar with the agency's policy decisions, personnel, processes, and culture; this makes monitoring, planning, and leading significantly easier.

In this view, careerists are more likely to succeed by virtue of having *public* management experience. Many generic management skills are difficult to transfer from the private sector to government because of the important differences between the two work environments.[7] Effective federal management requires knowledge of the uniquely public environment of agency work as well as the skills to navigate that environment. Public-sector work occurs in a political environment where the success or failure of an endeavor can depend fundamentally on the building and maintenance of coalitions.[8] Federal managers must therefore understand their political environment and be able to use their negotiation and diplomacy skills to convince people over whom they have no formal authority to cooperate with them. They need to understand arcane topics like public budgeting, rulemaking, and personnel-system guidelines. They operate under the unique constraints imposed by the political calendar and the difficulties of measuring outcomes in public-sector work. The public nature of agency work also necessitates that agency managers have the political communication skills to reach stakeholders, the public, and employees in a manner that is rarely required in the private sector.

Clearly, the two views about the relative merits of appointees and careerists are not mutually exclusive. A number of studies have examined how appointees and careerists can work together creatively and productively and, indeed, the right balance of appointees and careerists in an agency might allow the one to correct the biases, lack of knowledge, or experiential shortcomings that characterize the other.[9] Of course, the desire for political control and patronage expectations influence the balance of appointees and careerists across the government, so the mix of appointees and careerists is not only determined by a desire for professional competence, and therein lies the larger story.

The Hidden Effects of Politicization on Performance

Whatever valid arguments these two views might offer, they fail to address an underlying problem created by political appointees: namely, that maintaining a high number of appointees can hurt agency performance even if all of the appointees selected are of consistently high quality. Politicization creates predictable problems for organizational management that go deeper than the persons filling management positions at any given time. It makes it difficult for agencies to recruit and retain high-quality civil servants; it reduces incentives for careerists to develop expertise; and it leads to increased management turnover—three factors that can hurt performance even under the best of conditions.

Federal employees enter public service for any number of reasons. Some are attracted to the relatively stable or reasonably salaried jobs or to the generous and reliable pension plan.[10] Much of what we know about the civil service, however, implies that many people enter public service because they care about policy and want to make a positive contribution to the nation and its government.[11] But regardless of an employee's motivation to become a public servant, politicization makes the job less attractive. If a large or increasing number of top jobs in an agency are available only to an appointee class, it is hard to recruit new, bright employees to agency work. It is also hard to retain competent, hard-working employees who are attractive to other employers because of their expertise, experience, and demonstrated quality. Both new recruits and current employees can forecast their career trajectory; they know what their career prospects are, and they can see that in heavily politicized agencies, the most fulfilling jobs (in terms of pay and policy influence) are not available to them. One high-level careerist described the effects of appointees' taking career jobs this way: "There is a demoralizing situation when there are qualified career personnel who are forced out by political appointees who have not paid their dues within an agency by coming up through the ranks."[12] Good careerists, or potential careerists, leave the public sector or do not come to it in the first place.

The net result of politicization, then, is to make it hard for an agency to build capacity or even to keep its current capacity from eroding. The issue is not just that on average appointees might not be as good at public management as career managers; what is equally important is that politicization creates a situation in which the quality of *careerist* managers and employees in the politicized agency also suffers due to problems with recruitment and morale. This is articulated nicely by one frustrated Foreign Service officer who wrote,

> We have had a recent exodus at the top of our service as some of our best senior personnel—people who have been trained and paid at taxpayer expense—find they have no future in the Foreign Service because people whose only qualification is the size of their political contributions have preempted positions that career officers had spent a lifetime preparing to occupy. They leave, and the United States loses valuable assets. It is having a corrosive effect on some of our brightest younger and mid-level officers who no longer have the spur of a good chance at ultimately holding positions at the highest leadership levels.[13]

The quality of career employees in politicized agencies is determined by departures and recruitment difficulties as well as by the incentives generated by the work environment. To do most federal jobs well, particularly at the management level, site-specific knowledge is essential. This knowledge includes expertise in specific policy areas, familiarity with key stakeholders, an understanding of the folkways and informal power relationships of the agency and its policy arena, and aspects of federal work as mundane as how the accounting, records, and personnel systems work. Obtaining this type of knowledge requires both time and effort on the part of the employee.[14] Politicization creates an environment where there are few motivations for both careerists and appointees to develop this site-specific expertise or to engage in professional development. This is true for the careerist, because the probability of being denied jobs with higher pay and more policy influence lessens the motivation to acquire such expertise; it is true for the appointee because the job may well be short-lived, making specific expertise relatively useless whether for the present job or a future one outside the agency. Career managers who are denied jobs with higher pay and more policy influence have fewer reasons to acquire the expertise that would normally increase their chances of getting just these types of jobs. The net result is lower performance by careerists in the politicized agency.

Politicization also hurts agency performance by increasing management turnover both immediately and in the long run. While the average CEO in the private sector stays on the job for five to seven years, PAS appointees' tenures average about twenty-four months and lower-level appointees tend to serve for an even shorter duration.[15] Increased turnover creates leadership vacuums, sends mixed signals about agency goals, and diminishes an agency's commitment to reform, resulting in generally poorer performance.[16] Appointees are often in office just long enough to establish new priorities and start new initiatives—but not long enough to see them through to completion. Long-serving careerists, many of whom have their own ideas for growth and improvement, must stand by and watch the revolving door of appointees coming and going, knowing that their own efforts toward new initiatives may well be wasted in the constant flux of transition and adjustment. They are naturally cautious. One Department of Defense civilian with government experience described it this way: "We start, we stop, we reverse, but we seldom move ahead for any period of time. One loses interest after a few years."[17] Turnover also disrupts working relationships among functionally related agencies and programs. Newly formed teams fall apart because of executive turnover. New participants have to be selected, integrated into the team, and brought up to speed, slowing down the pace of work.

When Appointees Improve Performance

Of course the claim that increasing appointments hurts performance must be reconciled with the fact that presidents occasionally add appointees to *improve* performance. What, then, explains this contradiction? First, as noted in earlier chapters, political actors' views about competence and policy are inextricably linked, so a very competent person who is engaging in what political actors perceive to be the wrong policy is often viewed as being incompetent. Similarly, an unqualified person who is doggedly pursuing what political actors perceive as the right policy can be viewed as the only competent person working in an agency. Former Reagan aide Lyn Nofziger has said, "As far as I'm concerned, anyone who supported Reagan is competent."[18] Therefore, when political actors talk about making appointments to improve managerial effectiveness, we should be cognizant that this idea of improvement likely includes having the "right" policy views.

Second, it can be the case that a very competent appointee can come in and improve performance for as long as he or she serves in that position. The deleterious consequences of politicization on performance may not show up until later, when a second or third appointee has assumed office and the ripple effects of the politicization have played themselves out. While some programs are fortunate enough to be administered by very competent appointees, it is much less common that programs are administered by a string of effective appointees. Even agencies and programs that are able to attract top-quality appointees on a regular basis still suffer in the process. Politicization means more managerial turnover. New appointed positions often engender additional appointed positions, and the deeper penetration of appointees means that fewer high-level, policy-relevant, and well-paying jobs are available to career employees. Eventually, this leads top-quality people to leave for jobs where they can have more of an influence or earn higher pay, as discussed above. In short, politicization can be a short-term strategy for improving performance, but its long-term consequences are pernicious.

Third, in some cases, adding an appointee can legitimately improve performance by balancing out the shortcomings of the careerist managers in an agency. Appointees can improve agency performance by counteracting inertia, bringing energy and vision, and introducing new and useful information into a stale and insular decision-making environment.[19] For example, budget forecasting at the state level is more accurate in agencies where appointees and careerists are both present. All-appointee agencies tend to be inaccurate because they are too optimistic, while all-careerist agencies tend to be inaccurate because they are too conservative. Those agencies that maintain a balance of appointees and careerists produce the most accurate forecasts because they do not fall into the errors typical of either type of personnel.[20] In many agencies the existing number of appointed positions provides exactly this type of performance-enhancing influence. Cases where adding more appointees in the federal government objectively improve performance are rare, however, since all principal officers of the government are already appointed and most agencies have passed the point where adding appointees will have a leavening influence. The history of civil service expansion, the antistatist political culture of the United States, and presidential incentives for political control have created a deeper penetration of appointees into the administrative state than is found in any other developed country.[21]

In short, although ostensibly politicians occasionally add appointments to improve performance, they often conflate competence and policy views or overvalue the short-term benefits of a specific appointee relative to the long-term effect of adding another appointed position. In the United States federal government, increasing the number of appointees hurts performance more often than it helps.

Politicization and Performance: The Case of the Federal Emergency Management Agency (FEMA)

To look at the relationship between appointees and performance more concretely, I turn now to an in-depth examination of FEMA's history, from its creation through its involvement in Hurricane Katrina. Using a variety of sources, including agency histories, press accounts, and government documents, I retell FEMA's history, trying to provide a faithful narrative of the multiple factors that influenced FEMA's recent performance. Amidst the complex picture that emerges, the influence of politicization on performance is a prominent and undeniable theme.

Hampered by Design

The Federal Emergency Management Agency (FEMA) was created on April 1, 1979, after Reorganization Plan No. 3 (1978) went into effect. The reorganization plan, and subsequent executive orders that helped implement it brought together over one hundred disparate federal disaster-relief programs with the civil defense responsibilities of the Defense Civil Preparedness Agency.[22] Carter's creation of FEMA was partly a response to a request from the National Governors Association that the federal government centralize federal emergency functions.[23] A series of high-profile disasters in the 1970s had stretched state capacity and highlighted the shortcomings in the local-state-national interface in disaster response.[24] President Carter expressed hope that the new agency would consolidate "emergency preparedness, mitigation, and response activities" and "strengthen our ability to deal effectively with emergencies" by unifying these activities in one agency responsible directly to the president and Congress.[25]

From the start the new agency had to overcome several difficulties. First, FEMA had a large number of appointees. Carter's reorganization plan stipulated that the new agency would have 8 PAS appointees.[26] By the end of the Carter administration, FEMA had 31 appointees managing 3,400 employees. In addition to the 8 PAS appointees stipulated by the reorganization plan, there were 13 SES appointees and 11 Schedule C appointees.[27] This was close to three times the average number of appointees for an agency this size.

Not only did FEMA have an exceptionally large number of appointees for its size, but it lacked Washington prominence, a factor that influenced the quality of its appointees.[28] For presidents (and most other politicians), emergency response is usually only politically relevant during or after a crisis. If an agency is not part of the president's agenda but has a lot of appointed positions, the Presidential Personnel Office (PPO) will fill the agency according to *its* agenda. PPO sees positions in such agencies as lower-echelon slots to be filled with lower-echelon political appointees after other, more important executive positions have been filled. This means regional political directors, home-state political officials, and other committed campaign personnel with limited background experience to qualify them for other jobs have historically received positions in FEMA.

A second inherent difficulty for any president has been how to balance and integrate the agency's civil defense and natural disaster-response functions. The United States has had an aggressive civil defense program since the end of World War II—the primary mission of the Defense Civil Preparedness Agency being a response to nuclear attack—and for many stakeholders, civil defense was, and is still, the most important mission of FEMA. For others, however, coordinating the government's response to disasters of all types, including earthquakes, hurricanes, and tornadoes, has been seen as FEMA's primary mission. In his statement creating FEMA, President Carter supported the latter view. He endorsed an "all-hazards" approach for disaster response, meaning that there is a fundamental similarity in preparing for and responding to emergencies of various types from terrorist attacks to floods.[29]

Despite the president's vision for emergency management, internecine struggles related to the dual civil defense and natural disaster-response roles have plagued the agency from the beginning. The divide was reflected in an organizational separation within FEMA between the National Preparedness Programs Directorate and the rest of the agency. Money funneled into civil defense, continuity-of-government, and defense activities for information technology (IT) was not shared with other directorates out of concerns for secrecy.[30] For example, while the IT system developed was adaptable and could have integrated noncivil defense—related FEMA activities, agency executives refused to make it accessible to support general emergency management functions because of security concerns. This ultimately had consequences for agency response to Hurricane Hugo and the Loma Prieta, California, earthquake in 1989, when the agency was swamped with tens of thousands of paper applications for assistance.[31]

Managing the conflicts between civil defense and natural disaster response has been complicated by entrenched cultural differences in the agency.[32] The reorganization brought together defense department per-

sonnel committed to the civil defense, emergency management professionals, and personnel involved in firefighting science and grants programs. Each of these constituencies had its own vision for FEMA, and
the differences among these were exacerbated because they coincided
with organizational splits between the National Preparedness Programs
Directorate, the State and Local Programs and Support Directorate, and
the United States Fire Administration, along with personnel-system splits
between those with and without security clearances. In 1993, for example, 1,900 of the agency's 3,000 employees had security clearances.[33] As
one participant observed, "It was like trying to make a cake by mixing
the milk still in the bottle, with the flour still in the sack, with the eggs
still in their carton."[34] These divisions meant that the disparate parts of
FEMA would not naturally cooperate, which in turn contributed to a
perception of zero-sum competition for budgets among the agency's directorates.[35] As late as 1993 an external review of FEMA complained that
FEMA had an unclear mission, never really merging the disparate cultures and missions of the agency into one.[36]

Finally, FEMA has had to respond from the start to a difficult legisla-
tive-oversight environment. While the national government's civil defense and natural disaster-response programs were consolidated under
the FEMA umbrella, the agency's creation did not unify congressional
oversight. From the start at least five different Senate committees confirmed its appointees and twenty different committees had jurisdiction
over its programs.[37] One study estimated that two-thirds of legislators
served on a committee that exercised jurisdiction over at least one of
FEMA's programs.[38] This means that throughout its history each committee and subcommittee involved in the confirmation, budgeting, and
oversight process would articulate specific requests, policy views, and parochial concerns. They would ask for and receive assurances that FEMA
programs would be implemented according to their wishes. Informal
understandings would be consummated about what the agency would
do and what goals would receive priority. The difficulty, of course, is that
the different bodies asked the agency to do different things and directed
them without concern for other legislative requests or the agency's overall mission. No one committee could take a comprehensive look at the
number and qualifications of the agency's appointees or their views on
FEMA's priorities, contributing to the persistence of large numbers of
appointees in the agency.[39]

Politicization and Its Consequences

Under inspired leadership FEMA might have overcome these challenges,
but the appointee-heavy management structure made it less likely that
such leadership would emerge, and indeed contributed to its problems.

Throughout the 1980s the number of appointees to the agency when it was fully staffed hovered between 30 and 40. Appointees filled the senior-management posts, the public affairs operation, and the General Counsel's office. They also filled all of the regional director positions and a number of staff positions.

The large number of appointed positions led to frequent vacancies in top management positions since political appointees on average stay for only two years. There was rarely a time when at least one of the important appointed posts was not vacant. The number of FEMA appointees fluctuated noticeably around elections since the PPO strategically leaves positions vacant prior to midterm elections to provide positions for departing members of Congress and their staffs.[40] President George H. W. Bush did not appoint a permanent head of FEMA until August of 1990, nineteen months after his inauguration.[41] Other senior positions were vacant over a year into the new term.

The low status of the agency meant that less-experienced political types filled agency jobs. Few appointees in FEMA, and in fact none of the agency's directors between 1979 and 1992, had had previous emergency management experience. In 1983 the agency's third in command resigned over allegations that FEMA had spent $170,000 renovating a FEMA building he would be using as a residence.[42] In 1985 director Louis Giuffrida resigned in response to investigation by two House subcommittees looking into allegations of waste, fraud, and abuse.[43] The investigations specifically targeted possible favoritism in contracting and improper spending.[44] In 1992 the agency's executive director was removed in response to administrative missteps and revelations that he had tried to force a homosexual agency employee to produce a list of all homosexuals working in the agency.[45]

The cumulative effects of these management problems soured appointee-careerist relations. Appointees targeted career executives with personnel transfers, referred to as "administrative Elbas."[46] One senior careerist was transferred five times in eighteen months after falling out of favor. As a consequence of politicization and poor performance in the management structure, agency morale was extremely low by the end of the George H. W. Bush administration. More than half of the employees surveyed said they would take another job if offered and only one in five said the agency was well managed.[47] It was during this period that employees at FEMA headquarters unionized.[48]

The agency's inability to cope with its own management, let alone manage a genuine emergency, was reflected in its response to three major natural disasters in the 1989–1992 period, Hurricane Hugo, the Loma Prieta earthquake, and Hurricane Andrew. When these disasters hit, the combination of inherent management difficulties and the cumulative effects of poor appointee leadership left the agency ill equipped to respond.[49]

Hurricane Hugo hit the U.S. Virgin Islands, Puerto Rico, and the Carolinas in September 1989, when 7 of 8 top FEMA posts were still vacant or filled in an acting capacity. A significant amount of the responsibility for response resided with the associate director for state and local programs, Grant C. Peterson, at least four levels down in the FEMA hierarchy. Peterson, described by FEMA employees as a capable manager, had had no previous emergency management experience prior to his appointment to FEMA. He had been campaign manager for Reagan/Bush in Spokane, Washington, in 1980.[50]

The hurricane left scores dead and tens of thousands of persons homeless. It did an estimated $13.6 billion in damage. FEMA's response was slow and bureaucratic. For example, as the hurricane sped toward Puerto Rico, the governor of the island sent the proper request forms to FEMA only to have them returned by regular mail when a FEMA Washington employee noticed that the governor had failed to check one section of the form. The returned form did not reach the governor until after Hugo hit. The governor was forced to refile the forms and return them once again through the mail, holding up federal aid for days.[51] Persons seeking assistance were subjected to delays and requests for detailed cost assessments.[52] Food and clothing supplies did not reach some affected areas until fully six days after the hurricane had hit.[53] Disaster victims and public officials in the Carolinas roundly criticized FEMA's tardy, bureaucratic response. Senator Ernest F. Hollings (D-SC) did not waste words, calling FEMA's staff "the sorriest bunch of bureaucratic jackasses I've ever known."[54]

One month later the 6.9 magnitude Loma Prieta earthquake struck northern California, causing numerous deaths, thousands of injuries, and $6 billion in property damage as buildings and roadways collapsed.[55] FEMA's response by most accounts was better than its response to Hugo but was still seen as too little too late, and distinctly lacking in compassion. The agency was predictably overwhelmed by paper applications for disaster assistance.[56] Then-Congressman and future Secretary of Transportation Norman Mineta (D-CA), frustrated by FEMA's response, concluded that FEMA "could screw up a two-car parade."[57]

Despite the ferocious criticism of the agency in response to the two disasters in 1989, the agency could not sustain reform. The most severe blow for the agency came after its fumbled response to Hurricane Andrew in 1992. The category 5 hurricane hit Florida on August 24 and destroyed 85,000 homes, left 250,000 persons homeless, and 1.3 million without electricity. The disaster caused $43.7 billion in damage. The agency arrived late, and when it did manage to get its services in place they proved insufficient. As with Hurricane Hugo, some of the delay in response resulted from FEMA's belief that it had to wait for a gubernatorial request for aid. Governors are often reluctant to request aid because of the costs. States are obligated to pay a portion of the disaster-response bill and when the federal government intervenes, governors have less control over how much is obligated. They also worry about the political consequences of giving up command authority.

After Hurricane Andrew landed, many believed that a major crisis had been averted since it hit south of Miami.[58] In reality, many of the state's emergency workers were among those affected by the crisis, making it impossible for them to respond or pass along information about the extent of the crisis to state and federal officials. With state capacities stretched, FEMA dithered. It did not assess the damage itself or pressure the state to accept federal aid. Criticism mounted, and three days after Andrew landed Dade County Director of Emergency Preparedness Kate Hale said in a live press conference, "Where the hell is the cavalry on this one? We need food. We need water. We need people. For God's sake, where are they?"[59]

President George H. W. Bush got the message, circumvented FEMA director Wallace Stickney, and asked then-Transportation Secretary Andrew Card to organize a response that included close to 20,000 troops. When FEMA help began to arrive four days after the hurricane made landfall, it was late, disorganized, and again insufficient.[60] Aid stations were overwhelmed as lines stretched literally for miles and mobile medical aid stations were delayed. By almost all accounts, FEMA's response to Hurricane Andrew was a failure. This was a brutal blow for the agency, particularly since it came on the heels of poor performances in Hurricane Hugo and the Loma Prieta earthquake.

The response from the public and Congress was predictable. Hurricane victims posted signs saying, "What do George [H. W.] Bush and Hurricane Andrew have in common? They're both natural disasters."[61] Pete Stark (D-CA) derided the agency for its "Keystone Kops performances during the Loma Prieta earthquake, Hurricane Hugo, and other natural disasters" and attributed the agency's poor performance to its "becoming a turkey farm for flunkies and political supporters."[62] One *Washington Post* article referred to FEMA as "the agency everyone loves to hate" and a congressional report called it a "federal turkey farm."[63] Some experts and members of Congress, including Stark, proposed eliminating FEMA altogether.[64] Congress asked for, and received, extensive evaluations of FEMA by the National Academy of Public Administration (NAPA) and the GAO;[65] ten different committees asked the GAO for reports.[66] Hearings in the aftermath of the response focused on legislatively mandated reform. Senator Barbara Mikulski (D-MD) proposed legislation that recommended cutting the number of appointees, creating a more formal device for White House involvement, returning to an all-hazards approach, improved rapid-response capability inside the agency and through interagency teams, and a revision of the federal response plan.[67]

The Witt Revolution

Senator Mikulski's efforts were overtaken by the 1992 presidential election of Bill Clinton. President Clinton, recognizing the political harm to President George H. W. Bush created by FEMA's faulty response to the three major disasters during his administration, selected James Lee Witt to run the agency and elevated FEMA to cabinet status in 1996. According to Witt, "The president knew something had to be done and he said, are you going to be able to do it?, and I said, yes, I'll fix it."[68] Witt, who had served as head of the Arkansas Office of Emergency Services, was the first FEMA director to have emergency management experience prior to appointment. Witt was not only an experienced emergency manager, he was also politically savvy. Witt took seriously the recommendations included in the NAPA report, GAO testimony, and, importantly, the Mikulski legislation. He pledged to make a number of important reforms during his confirmation and worked tirelessly to cultivate members of Congress and state public officials as well as publicize agency activities.

He made a number of important changes in FEMA. Among the most important of these was Witt's reduction by one-third of the number of appointees. According to Witt, "The White House didn't like that, but the president didn't mind."[69] Another change was Witt's direct involvement in the selection of subordinate appointees, in direct contrast to previous agency head Wallace Stickney, who was appointed after 31 other appointed positions in the agency had been filled.[70] This meant Witt could screen appointees for competence and experience. On Witt's recommendation Clinton appointed Deputy Administrator Robert M. "Mike" Walker and Executive Associate Director for Response and Recovery Lacy E. Suiter. Walker was formerly undersecretary of the Army where he had responsibilities over the Department of Defense's response to domestic disasters. Suiter had thirty years of emergency management experience, twelve as director of Tennessee's Emergency Management Agency.[71]

This clout, derived from cabinet status and Witt's personal relationship with the president, allowed him more influence over appointments and thus more opportunity to avoid the appointment and retention patterns associated with lower-echelon appointments.[72] Witt proved himself able to keep appointees on the job longer than had previously been the case, allowing them to learn their jobs and apply that knowledge more effectively. Witt himself served for the full two terms of Clinton's presidency. Other top FEMA appointees such as Suiter, Associate Director Kay Goss (who was responsible for preparedness, training, and exercises), Director of Policy and Regional Operations Michelle M. Burkett, U.S. Fire Administrator Carrye B. Brown, and four of the agency's regional directors served over six years.

But perhaps the most strategic change during Witt's tenure was the shift of focus away from civil defense and toward a proactive, all-hazards approach to emergency response.[73] The words "all-hazards, comprehensive emergency management" became the stated mission of the agency. Witt advocated a broader definition of the Stafford Act, the act that authorizes FEMA's disaster response. Specifically, Witt and senior agency personnel determined that the act allowed for the mobilization and prepositioning of personnel and resources prior to an event when sufficient evidence indicated that an event was likely. This would potentially shorten the response times that had plagued FEMA in response to hurricanes Hugo and Andrew.

Witt reorganized the agency around this newly articulated vision. He significantly deemphasized civil defense. He eliminated the National Preparedness Programs Directorate and distributed its programs throughout the agency. He shifted personnel and resources away from civil defense and reduced the number of personnel with security clearances. He increased resources allocated to mitigation, response, and recovery and used grants to state and local governments as a means of both building relationships between FEMA and state and local emergency service providers and encouraging state and local disaster preparation. He broke down preexisting employee divisions by rotating senior managers to new jobs, changing the IT structure, creating diverse rapid-response units, and assigning agency personnel specific roles in emergencies. As part of these changes FEMA overhauled and automated its disaster assistance program to make it faster and more flexible.[74] According to one review of the period, " 'all hazards' became a mantra that, when combined with organizational changes, turned FEMA into a streamlined, professional natural disasters preparation and response clearinghouse."[75]

Witt's notable reinvention of FEMA was augmented by increased public relations activities. Witt expanded public relations staff and resources to improve performance in three areas. First, the agency started trying to gauge public opinion of its performance through response report cards and surveys of disaster victims. Second, the agency sought to increase its public information activities in order to sensitize the public to emergencies, encourage the public to make choices like buying flood insurance, and better inform the public about FEMA's role so that the gap between what FEMA delivered and what they were expected to deliver would be smaller.[76] Finally, Witt conducted extensive political outreach. During his first few months on the job, Witt contacted the chairs of all the committees that had a stake in FEMA's reorganization and met with legislators like Stark that had proposed eliminating or reorganizing the agency through statute. He created correspondence units whose mandate was to respond to letters from members of Congress or governors in ten days or less. During crises he was proactive about contacting the affected members of Congress to keep lines of communication open.[77] Noting that disasters were "political events" Witt also oversaw FEMA during a time when federal disaster declarations increased dramatically. Both the number and type of disasters expanded, including "snow emergencies" to which previous presidents had refused aid. Increased efficiency delivering disaster assistance helped drive FEMA's popularity.[78]

The success of Witt's transformation of FEMA was seen in public response to two major disasters in the 1990s, the 1993 Midwestern flood and the 1994 Northridge, California, earthquake. From April 1–July 31, 1993, persistently heavy rain fell on the middle part of the country, in excess of ten times the normal amount for that time of year. The Mississippi and Missouri rivers and their tributaries could not contain the run-off, resulting in severe flooding in nine states. Thousands of acres of farmland were under water and the flooding damaged hundreds of roads, levees, bridges, and dams. Forty people were killed and property damage was estimated at $10–15 billion.[79]

FEMA's response to this disaster was much better than before and it received wide acclaim for its response. Emergency teams and coordinating officials were on hand early, in some cases less than twelve hours after reports of flooding. The agency moved resources into place without waiting for state requests. They communicated regularly throughout the period with state and local officials. FEMA also simplified the disaster-assistance application process by providing toll-free numbers. More than three-quarters of the applications were processed through this new means. FEMA's efforts were bolstered by significant community outreach, including the aforementioned report cards. Witt also asked members of Congress from the affected states to call him if they had concerns.[80]

The response from the affected areas, the press, and members of Congress was consistently positive. One state emergency management director said, "This is the first time we have had this kind of coordination in my experience. . . . They think like we do, not like bureaucrats."[81] An article in the *New York Times* reported that in a series of short interviews with disaster victims at a few aid locations in Missouri, not one had criticized FEMA. The article went on to say, "By almost every measure, Mr. Witt's early performance managing the flood response is being received well by flood survivors, local officials and members of the agency staff."[82] These reports were representative of the positive press the agency received and members of Congress from both parties were similarly enthusiastic about FEMA's response, both in the immediate aftermath and in hearings that followed.[83]

On January 17, 1994—only about six months after the Midwestern flood—the agency faced another natural disaster. A major earthquake centered in the Los Angeles area—California's second major quake in only five years—caused severe damage to major arterial roadways, bridges, buildings, and homes, and to water, gas, and power systems. Sixty-one people were killed and hundreds more were injured. The quake caused an estimated $30 billion in damage.

FEMA emergency personnel arrived quickly and spent the first two days after the earthquake helping with search and rescue. Within fifteen minutes of the quake FEMA officials were in contact with state and local emergency services personnel and coordinating assistance from various federal agencies. Emergency response teams from FEMA began arriving ninety minutes after the quake. A telephone registration center to receive disaster assistance applications was set up by the next day.[84] They began coordinating response activities, setting up disaster-relief efforts, and publicizing where people could get help through community outreach, including a television program and disaster newspaper.[85] While there were some lines for receiving aid and problems finding Spanish-speaking volunteers to help with disaster assistance, the agency was generally praised for its response. The agency had arrived quickly, set up relief centers, and publicized their efforts. The California Emergency Management director said, "FEMA has clearly exorcised the ghost of Hurricane Andrew. This is not the same operation."[86] The *Los Angeles Times* published a poll showing that 70 percent of emergency-shelter residents approved of the federal government's response.[87] In 1994 FEMA surveyed 5,000 disaster victims and 80 percent approved of the agency's performance.[88]

FEMA was also praised for its response to other disasters during the 1990s, including the 1993 California wildfires, the 1995 bombing of the Alfred P. Murrah Federal Office Building in Oklahoma City, and severe weather affecting twelve states in 1997.[89] In short, by almost all accounts, FEMA under Witt experienced a dramatic turnaround. While there were nagging concerns with financial management and the disaster-declaration process, Witt and FEMA were widely praised in response to the major crises in the 1990s and journalists and academics turned their attention to explaining the "FEMA Phoenix," FEMA's "Renewal and Revitalization," and FEMA as an example of reinventing government.[90] One history of FEMA summarized,

The once scandal-ridden and sclerotic Federal Emergency Management Agency (FEMA) experienced a dramatic turnaround [after 1992]. The agency morphed from a caricature of the ills of bureaucracy into a model of effective federal administration. Politicians who previously blamed the agency for its slow and inefficient response to disasters came to depend on the agency to lend credibility to their own efforts.[91]

There was perhaps no greater measure of the agency's improved stature than the fact that politicians actually sought out opportunities to be seen with FEMA officials during disasters to enhance their own public standing.[92]

What, then, brought about this remarkable change? The answer lies in part in Witt's reforms: good management, shrewd politicking, and energetic leadership. But it also lies in the structural change that brought Witt and the experienced, long-serving team he created to the fore: namely, a depoliticized management structure. President Clinton selected a leader with the appropriate background experience and allowed that appointee to cut the number of appointees, select subordinate officials who, if they were not careerists, ended up looking like careerists in background experience and job tenure. These actions in turn created an environment where the quality and performance of career employees improved. Career employees took more responsibility, took more risks, and had a much better understanding of how their job fit into FEMA's overall mission.[93]

George W. Bush Takes Over

Though candidate George W. Bush publicly lauded Witt for his performance during the first presidential debate in 2000, once Bush became president he chose to replace him with Joseph Allbaugh. Allbaugh was Bush's chief of staff in Texas and 2000 election campaign manager. Bush stated in his announcement of Allbaugh that the nominee had proven to be a competent manager and had worked with him at the state level to respond to a number of emergencies.[94] Witt had been a very popular FEMA director and Allbaugh's appointment was understandably met with some trepidation by career employees. The head of the agency's union complained, "There are plenty of Republican emergency managers, fire chiefs, or police chiefs around. And they pull this guy who's a campaign manager?"[95]

Allbaugh's appointment also signaled a change in policy at FEMA. Despite Bush and Allbaugh's praise for Witt, significant policy differences had been emerging between Republicans and Democrats during the Clinton administration. First, many Republicans felt that civil defense had been dangerously downgraded in the "reinvented FEMA." As one long-time FEMA employee explained, "Some will say he [Witt] introduced 'all-hazards.' I say he reduced the importance of some hazards at the expense of others."[96] As concerns about terrorism increased during the Clinton administration, FEMA steadfastly resisted a role in domestic terrorism response and training.[97] There is disagreement among Witt and others about why this occurred, but agreement that FEMA was poorly equipped to assume new responsibilities in this area. Consequently, one of Allbaugh's first actions in office was to create an Office of National Preparedness to train first responders in domestic terrorism response and coordinate the federal government's response to such incidents.[98]

Second, many fiscal conservatives argued that FEMA had become a federal giveaway program. They believed that disaster declarations had become a form of pork-barrel spending, one particularly sensitive to presidential election politics. During congressional hearings Allbaugh himself said, "Many are concerned that federal disaster assistance may have evolved into both an oversized entitlement program and a disincentive to effective state and local risk management. Expectations of when the federal government should be involved and the degree of involvement may have ballooned beyond an appropriate level."[99] Allbaugh gave further evidence of a change in FEMA policy early in 2001 when, during a visit to flooded Davenport, Iowa, on the Mississippi River, he publicly questioned whether the federal government should continue bailing out river towns like Davenport that refused to take steps independently to prepare for flooding.[100]

The desire for policy change coincided with a change in management environment and public and presidential attention to emergency response. By the end of the Clinton administration, the number of appointees in FEMA had begun to creep upward once again. Figure 6.1 graphs the number of appointees in the agency from 1980 to 2004. It also includes the number of vacancies in executive policymaking positions since simple counts of the number of appointees do not reflect the full extent of politicization. For example, the graph shows only 24 appointees in FEMA in 1988 but that is because there were 8 vacancies in positions such as Chief of Staff and General Counsel. The graph illustrates a number of relevant aspects of the FEMA management environment that President George W. Bush inherited. First, it shows the number of appointees in FEMA compared to the average number for agencies with 2,500–5,000 employees; as previously noted, FEMA had two to three times as many appointees as most agencies its size. Second, there was a decline in appointees under Witt, as noted above, from 35

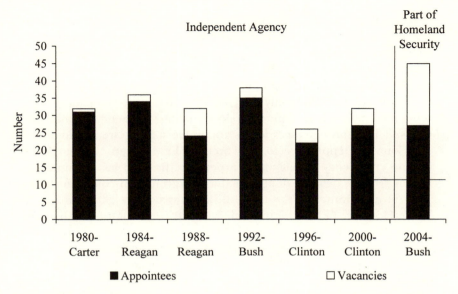

Figure 6.1. FEMA Appointees and Vacancies in Policy and Supporting Positions, 1980–2004.
Sourde. U.S. Congress, *Policy and Supporting Positions,* various years.

at the end of the George H. W. Bush administration to 22 at the end of Clinton's first term. Finally, it illustrates a slight increase from 1996 to 2000 of about 5 positions, suggesting a trend back to a higher number of appointees.[101]

The George W. Bush administration inherited a FEMA that had 27 appointees as of the fall of 2000. By the fall of 2002 the agency had 38, more than at any other time in its history. The biggest increase was in Schedule C appointees, which increased from 5 in the fall of 2000 to 15 in 2002. New positions were added in the General Counsel's office, the External Affairs Directorate, and the Information Technology Services Directorate. The new appointees filled roles as staff assistants, speechwriters, and White House Liaison.[102] There were also 4 more appointees added to the corps of senior executives in the agency. Given the type of appointees added, the increase appears driven primarily by patronage. In 2004, according to the figure, the numbers appear to decline. As I explain below, however, many of the appointee positions were vacant in the fall of 2004 and the graph underestimates the true politicization of FEMA once it had been absorbed into the newly formed Department of Homeland Security (DHS) since the move layered new department-wide appointees *on top* of FEMA.

When Bush assumed office, FEMA not only had a high number of appointees but the agency had also lost visibility. Since there had not been any catastrophic national emergencies of the magnitude of Hurricane Andrew for several years, FEMA management was not high on the president's agenda. According to the *Washington Post*, Joe Allbaugh had been "exiled" to FEMA only after losing out in a power struggle with other members of Bush's inner circle, signaling the agency's diminished status.[103] The consequences for its appointee staffing are striking: General Counsel, Deputy Director, and eventual FEMA head, Michael Brown had no emergency management experience prior to his appointment; Patrick Rhode, Brown's deputy, had a background in communications prior to his advance work for the Bush campaign in 2000 and for the White House;[104] FEMA Deputy Chief of Staff Brooks Altshuler had also done advance work for the 2000 Bush campaign and similarly lacked any emergency management experience; and Daniel Craig, who became director of recovery for FEMA, was previously head of the Eastern Regional Office of the U.S. Chamber of Commerce.[105] In fact, during Brown's tenure at FEMA, only one person in the front office had any emergency management experience prior to assuming their post and this person was serving in an acting capacity.[106] FEMA regional directors similarly had very little emergency management experience.[107] According to one congressional investigation, Brown's leadership team also lacked even "basic management experience and the leadership ability" necessary to direct federal response to a catastrophic event.[108]

This change in policy and management environment was accompanied by budget cuts. In its first budget, the Bush administration proposed cutting $200 million from FEMA's budget, primarily in mitigation activities (mitigation activities are those targeted toward preventing loss of life and property in advance of a disaster, that is, moving people out of vulnerable locations such as flood plains or taking action to protect structures in those locations).[109] FEMA programs that were cut included Project Impact, a popular Witt creation that educated and gave grants to make communities more disaster-resistant.[110] The Bush administration sought to eliminate inefficient and redundant federal programs across the government and FEMA officials had a difficult time providing systematic evidence that its mitigation programs were effective.

Allbaugh's FEMA faced its first big test in the wake of the September 11, 2001, terrorist attacks on the World Trade Center, Pentagon, and related plane crash in Pennsylvania. FEMA's initial response was lauded but ongoing recovery efforts were criticized by legislators from the affected areas in New York. By almost all accounts FEMA's response to the attacks was excellent, with personnel and resources in place quickly.

Lawmakers heaped praise on FEMA, while others described their response to the Pentagon attacks as "superb."[111]

FEMA personnel were involved not only in search and rescue but also recovery, determining eligibility for and distributing disaster aid and assistance. It was in the recovery process that FEMA received the most criticism. FEMA was criticized for mistakes in eligibility determinations, errors in allocation of recovery funds, and for taking too long to get aid to disaster victims.[112] It was also criticized for poor coordination with private charities, creating additional confusion in the recovery process. In fairness, some of the criticism was inevitable, given the emotionally charged environment in which difficult decisions must be made quickly, and in view of the balance FEMA had to achieve between compassion and fairness in applying program guidelines. Among the criticisms of the agency leveled by New York—area disaster victims was the shortchanging of aid requests from self-employed artists and its refusal to pay the cost of make-up school days and other costs affecting the New York City school system.[113] A report from the agency's Inspector General subsequently concluded that the agency could have been both fairer and more flexible in helping people who suffered economic loss as a result of the attacks. The report further says that the agency's inability to comprehend the indirect economic effects of the attack hampered its ability to deliver aid quickly and effectively.

Yet while some subsequent reports suggested the agency's response had not engendered public confidence and referred to the multiple 2004 hurricanes in Florida as a chance for FEMA to prove itself after its poor response to 9/11, the general assessment of the agency's performance remained positive.[114] Histories of the 9/11 period describe FEMA as having "stepped up and responded well" and FEMA's response as "relatively well-regarded."[115] The reforms instituted by Witt and praised by both candidates during the 2000 elections had left the agency in good shape to respond when the attacks happened. It bears mentioning that at the time of the attacks, the agency had only 9 appointees and that Allbaugh himself was not in Washington, D.C.[116]

FEMA Moves to the Department of Homeland Security

However one judges the agency's response, the events of 9/11 set in motion a political process that would move FEMA into the newly created DHS. In November 2002, Congress enacted legislation merging twenty-two separate agencies and 170,000 employees into the new department. FEMA's move into DHS further politicized an already appointee-laden agency by layering still more appointees on top of FEMA's existing management structure. This politicization facilitated a dramatic mission-shift in the agency away from an all-hazards approach back to civil defense, particularly domestic terrorism. The move of FEMA into a larger department also decreased the prestige of FEMA jobs and forced FEMA to compete for power and resources with other parts of DHS. The effect of the move into DHS and the politicization that came with it was to make it more difficult to recruit and retain both appointees and career professionals. Morale plummeted, relationships between FEMA and state emergency services agencies weakened, and the changeover created confusion about whether FEMA itself or DHS had control during catastrophic events. These changes ultimately damaged the agency's ability to respond to Hurricane Katrina.

The most obvious change created by the act was to put FEMA under a new infrastructure of appointed leaders, including the Secretary and Deputy Secretary and their staffs. In the fall of 2004, the office of the DHS Chief of Staff alone included 16 appointees, not counting 61 others working in the Office of the Secretary: those working for the Executive Secretary (9), the Assistant Secretary for Public Affairs (24), the Director for State and Local Affairs (7), the Assistant Secretary for Legislative Affairs (14), and various employees working directly for the Secretary and Deputy Secretary (7). Whereas Allbaugh reported directly to the president, the new head of FEMA would report to a cabinet secretary. One state emergency management official claimed that "Witt's greatest impact was the fact that he linked FEMA to the executive branch, the Executive Office of the President, and the President. Witt had access."[117] At the time of the reorganization, many doubted whether FEMA under DHS would have the same type of access. This type of access is an essential resource since response to catastrophic emergencies requires the cooperation and participation of other departments and agencies such as the Departments of Defense, HHS, and Agriculture that are much larger than FEMA. Political muscle from the president is often necessary to get this kind of cooperation and coordination.

Even though more appointees were layered on top of FEMA, FEMA itself lost 5 PAS appointee slots when it moved into DHS. These were replaced by SES appointees and Schedule Cs. Figure 6.1 shows that in the fall of 2004 FEMA had 27 appointees. If this were an accurate reflection of the agency's politicization, it would indicate that the agency had returned to its appointee-level in 2000. But in fact, the agency had significantly more than 27 appointed positions since a number of positions held by appointees were vacant at the time the numbers were collected. Among the positions vacant were the Administrator for Mitigation, the Assistant Secretary for Policy and Planning, and 6 regional directorships. By a conservative count 8 of the vacant positions were appointee positions, giving the agency *at least* 35 appointee slots, significantly more than in 2000. This was in addition to the new layer of appointees above FEMA in DHS.

Politicization hurt agency management and morale. FEMA Director of Response Eric Tolbert said, "The impact of having political [people] in the high ranks of FEMA . . . that's what killed us, was that in the senior ranks of FEMA there was nobody that even knew FEMA's history, much less understood the profession and the dynamics and the roles and responsibilities of the states and local governments."[118] In a January 2005 report by a nonprofit consulting firm hired to diagnose problems in FEMA response, senior career managers confidentially expressed concerns about the number of appointees, their lack of experience, and the regular vacancies and turnover that accompanied appointee management. These were consistent reasons raised to explain poor FEMA performance.[119]

Since DHS appointees were primarily focused on domestic terrorism, FEMA was under tremendous pressure to change its mission. While the new FEMA inside the department was originally supposed to be "like FEMA on steroids", the agency lost a series of bureaucratic turf fights in 2004 and 2005 that gutted it and made it into a weakened response and recovery agency rather than an all-hazards preparedness and response agency.[120] FEMA lost its preparedness functions, personnel, and budget. Grant-making power had been an essential part of FEMA's success since the offer of federal money was the primary means by which FEMA could get state and local emergency services agencies to do what FEMA desired. It provided state and local officials incentives to work cooperatively with FEMA. Removing these functions from FEMA and placing them in another part of DHS meant both that more money would go explicitly for terrorism response and that FEMA would quickly lose leverage with states and localities.

No longer in charge of disaster preparedness, FEMA lost its unifying vision. As one reviewer explained, "The genius of the all-hazards, all-phases concept was its ability to unite the different parts of the disaster timeline—preparation, response, recovery, mitigation—into a single notion of preparedness."[121] The mission that galvanized the agency under Witt had dissolved. The stovepipes that had existed prior to Witt's appointment reemerged within DHS, making it harder for the different parts of disaster preparedness and response to work together.

These changes in mission, budget, and power, coupled with structural changes, made FEMA's top jobs less prestigious. After the move into DHS the FEMA administrator had less power, lower pay, and greater layers of bureaucracy overhead. When FEMA was independent, FEMA's Director could go directly to the White House with policy concerns. Now the head of FEMA was one of twenty-two parts of a larger department and its integrity as an agency was subject to the decisions of other appointees. When FEMA Director Allbaugh learned of the decision to move FEMA into DHS, he decided to quit. As one long-time FEMA career manager explained, "Joe signed on to be agency head, not to play second fiddle. . . . He didn't want to be reporting to anybody but the president."[122] The pay of the FEMA Director also declined from an executive level II salary to an executive level III salary, a decline of $12,500 per year. Pay grade is also a sign of status and this change was another sign of the decreasing status of the agency.

Accompanying the decline in pay and status of the FEMA director's job was the added difficulty of having to compete for resources with other parts of the department. FEMA not only lost out in struggles over preparedness responsibilities but competition for budgets influenced the ability of the agency to replace lost employees, maintain the capacity of its reservist workforce, ensure the readiness of its national response teams, and train National Defense Medical System and Urban Search and Rescue teams. These teams were significantly below capacity and poorly trained due to budget constraints prior to Hurricane Katrina.[123]

The cumulative effect of the politicization of FEMA and its move into DHS was devastating. Evidence of growing problems was apparent as early as the fall of 2002, a year and a half into the Bush administration, when the DHS legislation was being debated and enacted. The agency that had once been lauded as a model was now ranked the worst place to work in the federal government according to data from the Federal Human Capital Survey.[124] In early 2004 the head of FEMA's union wrote to twenty legislators arguing that since the start of the Bush administration, experienced professional managers were leaving and being replaced by contractors or inexperienced newcomers. He further wrote that "funds are being misspent, morale has fallen, and our nation's emergency management capability is being eroded." He cited a union survey that indicated that 60 percent of FEMA headquarters employees would probably leave for another job if offered one.[125] His claims were confirmed by the 2004 version of the Federal Human Capital Survey, which suggested that DHS was the second-worst place to work in the federal government.

Turnover and vacancies in key positions increased.[126] Allbaugh's departure was followed by the exits of other agency appointees. The move into DHS also created an unparalleled turnover among career managers inside the agency. Among those leaving were some of FEMA's most senior managers, including the career officials in charge of response, recovery, and preparedness at the time of the 9/11 attacks.[127] These personnel frequently were not replaced or, in other cases, succeeded by those with less experience or persons in an interim capacity. In the fall of 2004,

17 of the 46 policy-relevant and supporting positions in the agency were vacant, including the Chief of Operations in the Response Division, Chief of Individual Assistance in the Recovery Division, Chief of Public Assistance in the Recovery Division, and Deputy Director of Preparedness. Vacancy rates among all agency employees hovered between 15 and 20 percent.[128]

In short, increasing politicization that occurred prior to, and was then exacerbated by, the move into DHS caused numerous problems that directly influenced how FEMA eventually responded to Hurricane Katrina. The increase in appointed positions contributed to inexperience and unfamiliarity with disaster response at the highest reaches of FEMA and DHS. It generated persistent vacancies and management turnover. These factors made it difficult for the agency to fight for budgets within DHS, engage in long-term planning, and maintain readiness and response capabilities. It also made it hard for DHS and FEMA to develop and implement a workable plan for emergency response for a catastrophic event like Katrina. DHS had not worked out the details or sufficiently rehearsed its emergency response plan prior to Katrina's landfall in late August 2005.[129] While the agency's response to the 2004 Florida hurricanes during the campaign season had been competent, the agency's Katrina response revealed just how troubled the agency had become.[130]

Hurricane Katrina

A catastrophe of Katrina's magnitude would have been difficult for any response agency to handle. Consider the requirements: the instantaneous mobilization of an agency's disparate resources; the political clout to muster help from departments as varied (and turf-conscious) as Defense, HHS, Transportation, and HUD; the coordination of whatever efforts these added resources would supply; and the effective coordination of all these with state and local emergency services agencies in the affected states, as well as with whatever private charities might become involved. Nor does the failure of FEMA under such circumstances mean that the blame lies solely with that agency; there is plenty of blame to spread around elsewhere. Levees were poorly constructed and maintained. The evacuation order for New Orleans came too late. State and local officials planned and responded poorly. Part of the failure, however, resides squarely with FEMA. The agency's response was slow, error-prone, poorly coordinated, and resulted in incalculable misery and suffering.[131] Ultimately, Michael Brown had to be removed and authority for the recovery efforts was placed in the hands of Coast Guard Vice Admiral Thad W. Allen.

Subsequent evaluations of FEMA's performance look strikingly like those that followed Hurricane Andrew in 1992. Critiques focused on unclear responsibilities and lines of authority during catastrophic events; confusion about when the federal government can and should supersede state authority; insufficient planning, training programs, and predisaster exercises; inadequate response and recovery capabilities; and a failure in executive leadership.[132] One reason for confusion about relative responsibilities and lines of authority was the difficulty implementing (some might even say reading) the 426-page National Response Plan (NRP). The Homeland Security Act mandated that DHS create a new plan to clarify roles in catastrophic events. The NRP was incomplete and insufficiently rehearsed prior to Katrina's landfall, the result being that the various elements of the local, state, and national response were unclear as to their roles. Only one large-scale national exercise rehearsing the NRP had taken place prior to Katrina and this exercise demonstrated clearly "a fundamental lack of understanding for the principles and protocols set forth in the NRP."[133]

According to the NRP, the Secretary of Homeland Security is responsible for declaring which events qualify as "events of national significance" and is the primary official responsible for coordinating a response. At the time the hurricane made landfall, it was unclear what constituted "national significance" and emergency responders at all levels were uncertain as to their roles.[134] For example, the NRP gave the Secretary authority to assume a more aggressive federal role in events of Katrina's magnitude but DHS head Michael Chertoff seems to have been unaware of the severity of the crisis and also his authority under the NRP. He did not declare Katrina an "event of national significance" until August 30, the day after Katrina had made landfall.[135] The Department of Defense prepared a response according to its understanding of the NRP and waited for FEMA to make requests for assistance. Two days after Katrina's landfall, emergency management officials in Louisiana and the National Guard were still receiving basic NRP training to get them up to speed.[136] The full rules of engagement for catastrophic events were not supposed to be released until October.[137]

In retrospect, one can see that FEMA's move into DHS caused problems on at least two levels. First, it was at least partly responsible for the unfortunate timing of the NRP's release. If the agency had been run by professionals and funded appropriately, progress on the NRP could have been swifter. This would have allowed for more widespread understanding of the rules governing agency response, and for practice exercises on a national level in anticipation of events like Katrina. A second and related consequence of moving FEMA into DHS was confusion about power and authority in response to catastrophic events. Chertoff was working from home on August 27, the day he was first informed of the potential crisis. He wrote a memo delegating response authority to FEMA head Michael Brown the day after Katrina hit and deferred to the White House and Brown rather than actively taking charge.[138] In the aftermath of the hurricane, Brown argued that he did not have the authority he needed to coordinate an effective response. Chertoff, however, argued that the authority he had given Brown under the NRP was sufficient to give Brown whatever authority was necessary. In the midst of this confusion, the Homeland Security Operations Center (HSOC) was supposed to gather, coordinate, and distribute reliable information to decision makers but failed to do so. One reason for this was that Brown refused to communicate with Chertoff, choosing instead to speak with White House staff. This contributed to DHS having insufficient information about what was happening on the ground.[139]

Another reason for the delayed federal response was misunderstanding about the severity of the storm. Previous simulations, warnings from the National Hurricane Center, and public statements by FEMA itself all indicated clearly that a crisis was at hand. The head of the National Hurricane Center took the unusual step of calling governors directly. Yet, local, state and federal officials, however, seemed unresponsive to simulations and forecasts about the likely extent of the crisis, a reaction that lingered even after the Hurricane made landfall and the levees were breached. To some extent, this may have been due to a lack of information since, as during Hurricane Andrew, many first responders in the affected states were themselves victims of the hurricane. These included police and fire departments as well as National Guard units and medical personnel. As the subsequent Senate report explains,

> With local and state resources immediately overwhelmed, rapid federal mobilization of resources was critical. Yet reliable information on such vital developments as the levee failures, the extent of flooding, and the presence of thousands of people needing life-sustaining assistance . . . did not reach the White House, Secretary Chertoff, or other key officials for hours, and in some cases more than a day.[140]

The federal government hesitated, waiting for specific requests from the states yet the states themselves did not know the extent of their need. This was despite all of the evidence FEMA, state and local officials, and the media had prior to the hurricane's landfall and the fact that the federal government explicitly had in the NRP the legal power to respond without a request from state authorities.[141]

The response was also slow partly due to a lack of capacity within FEMA. When responders finally did reach the area, there were too few of them. The emergency response team sent to New Orleans was new, untrained, and ill equipped. Medical personnel deployed to New Orleans lacked sufficient medical equipment and had limited training. Only one team was actually in place in the Gulf region to provide immediate medical care after the hurricane.[142] Others were called up late, languished for days waiting to be assigned, and then, upon arrival were overwhelmed.[143] Urban search and rescue teams existed on a barebones budget and had no water-rescue capabilities. This inhibited their ability to reach the large number of New Orleans residents stranded by the flooding.[144]

Because state and local officials were overwhelmed and because the federal government did not aggressively step in, gaps in communication and predictable confusion emerged. FEMA Director Brown, for example, did not know that thousands of persons had sought refuge at the New Orleans Convention Center and had been there for days without supplies. Different parts of the response set up competing chains of command.

Ultimately, there was a failure in executive leadership. Top executives in FEMA, the DHS, and White House did not understand what was commonly understood by hurricane experts, FEMA professionals, and had been demonstrated by FEMA exercises prior to Katrina. It was widespread knowledge that even a category 3 hurricane could threaten thousands of lives and leave hundreds of thousands stranded in New Orleans.[145] Brown himself waited five hours after Katrina's landfall to call in disaster-response teams.[146] He did not pre-position sufficient personnel and resources. Only one FEMA official was in New Orleans when Katrina hit.[147] Critical disaster supplies such as water, food, and ice were not tracked and did not reach some locations until ten days after the Hurricane.[148] Even when confronted with dire predictions by FEMA staff Brown was unresponsive.[149] If Brown and his team had more disaster experience Brown might have grasped the severity of the crisis and prepared a more appropriate response much sooner. He would have advised Chertoff of his responsibilities under the NRP and pleaded more aggressively for White House intervention. The recovery might have proceeded much more smoothly. Instead, FEMA was unprepared, disorganized, and poorly equipped, just as it had been in 1992.

Summary

Most of the blame in the aftermath of Hurricane Katrina was targeted at FEMA Director Michael Brown. By all accounts, Brown's performance was poor. He had no previous emergency management experience before coming to FEMA; indeed, Brown had been an attorney active in the Republican Party and head of the International Arabian Horse Association when he was brought to the agency by Allbaugh, his college roommate.[150] Understandably, DHS Secretary Michael Chertoff and President Bush also received criticism for selecting Brown. They, in turn, were blamed for being slow to recognize the severity of the crisis, and for being reactive rather than proactive.

Subsequent analyses of what went wrong point to FEMA's changing mission, low budgets, personnel problems, inadequate training, and other factors. These factors undoubtedly influenced FEMA's response capability but they are better understood as symptoms of a larger malady—politicization. If FEMA had had fewer appointed positions and more presidential attention, there would have been better-qualified appointees, less executive turnover, and a greater focus on emergency response and recovery. Reducing the number of appointees would have generated more stable leadership since career professionals would have then assumed important management positions. Presidential personnel would have been more likely to place better-qualified persons in the agency. Stable leadership would have made it easier for the agency to cultivate internal leaders, argue for budgets, build enduring relationships with state and local officials, and design and implement long-term plans and training exercises. Enhanced career prospects, stable leadership, and better-qualified appointees also would have improved morale among career employees. While reform efforts can target the symptoms of FEMA's underperformance—inadequate budgets, the contents of the NRP, or the qualifications for the FEMA Directorship—and will likely improve performance, a better approach would be to target what is generating these symptoms and start by reducing the number and penetration of political appointees into the agency.

One conclusion that should *not* be drawn from FEMA's experience, however, is that all appointees should be removed; the performance of James Lee Witt should silence those arguments. As his example indicates, appointees can bring energy, responsiveness, and the political leverage that is often necessary to secure budgets, change law, or build coalitions crucial for policy implementation. It is unlikely that the FEMA of the 1980s and early 1990s could have been transformed into that of the mid-1990s without strong political leadership. Up until Witt's arrival, FEMA's functions had been stovepiped into civil defense and emergency response directorates, and it took the kind of political connections that Witt brought to the table to break down those barriers to effective management. One of Witt's noted accomplishments was his success at generating risk-taking behavior and accountability among career professionals. Witt was also extremely successful building and cultivating relationships among FEMA, state and local officials, members of Congress, and the administration. Beyond a doubt, Witt's connection to President Clinton was instrumental in FEMA's rise.

Conclusion

As the FEMA example illustrates, politicization affects performance in two critical ways. It systematically influences the types of people who are selected to run government agencies and it generates hidden effects on the morale, tenure, and incentives of career managers. While appointees can bring new perspectives, a broader vision, and private management experience to a given agency, they are less likely to have agency experience, policy-area expertise, and public management skills than their careerist counterparts. Even if appointees and careerists were identical in background and ability, the transitory nature of political appointments hurts an agency's overall performance, disrupting policy implementation, executive monitoring, breaking up interagency teams, and leaving important programs without representation in the political and budget processes. Appointees are routinely given the highest-paying jobs and those with the most policy influence. When the most rewarding jobs are no longer accessible to careerists, they are less likely to stay, to invest in site-specific training and expertise, or to even choose to work for an agency in the first place.

Both effects are aptly represented in the FEMA case. Witt aside, the appointees selected to run FEMA consistently lacked emergency management experience, and many lacked even basic management skills. The politicized management structure generated consistent vacancies, low morale, and difficulties in conceptualizing and implementing reforms. As such, the history of FEMA provides an in-depth look at the pathologies of politicization. As we have seen, sometimes the full effects of politicization do not come to light until there is an extraordinary failure; and by almost any measure, FEMA's performance in the case of Hurricane Katrina qualifies as such.

To what extent can we generalize about the influence of politicization from this case? FEMA's competence is more sensitive to politicization than some agencies and less sensitive than others, which makes its experience more applicable to some agencies than others. For FEMA to function effectively requires the coordination and mobilization of huge amounts of resources and personnel in the event of a disaster. Advanced planning and standard operating procedures are necessary to accomplish this successfully. These procedures have to be flexible enough to accommodate different types of small and large incidents in diverse locations. Effective response also requires strong, long-term relationships with state and local emergency management officials and comprehensive planning. To manage FEMA well requires an understanding of the agency's tasks and procedures, and of how these procedures relate to complex contingencies. Appointees with little disaster experience are at a natural disadvantage understanding this system well enough to implement it effectively.

While managing FEMA does not require the specialized knowledge required to run the CDC or the FDA, to take two examples, it is nonetheless substantial. One feature of FEMA's work that makes it less sensitive to politicization is the availability of trained emergency management professionals in local and state agencies. If presidents select trained emergency management professionals as appointees, politicization's harmful effects are mitigated. This is borne out by the experience of FEMA under Witt, who both cut the number of appointees and selected qualified people for those appointments he retained, and by all measures raised the profile and competence-level of what historically has been a much-maligned agency.

7

Politicization and Performance: The Larger Pattern

THE CASE of FEMA detailed in the previous chapter raises the important question of how political appointments influence management across the U.S. federal government more generally. This chapter examines the influence of appointees on federal management performance in hundreds of cases by analyzing two new datasets that provide different measures of performance. The first dataset is comprised of the Program Assessment Rating Tool (PART) scores—a numerical measure of program performance—innovated during the George W. Bush administration. The second dataset includes responses from the Federal Human Capital Survey (FHCS), a survey of federal employees that includes questions about employee perceptions of agency leadership, management, and work climate. The chapter includes some of the first systematic analysis to date on the relationship between politicization and performance.

The chapter proceeds deliberately. It first explains why large-scale studies of the relationship between appointees and performance have been difficult to execute. It then describes how the dataset comprised of PART scores provides a useful means of overcoming these difficulties. The chapter examines the backgrounds of appointed and career managers who have had programs evaluated in the PART process to see whether the two types of managers have significantly different qualifications. It then compares the PART scores of programs administered by appointees to those headed by careerists to see whether appointee-run programs get systematically lower PART scores. The chapter then examines which of the differences between appointees and careerists matter for performance, particularly the ability to translate the wishes of political actors into clear policy and program goals. Next, it uses the data from the FHCS to verify the robustness of the PART findings concerning the relationship between appointees and performance. The chapter concludes with the implications of these findings for the larger argument of the book, modern presidential staffing practices, and policy debates surrounding how to improve federal management performance.

Testing the Influence of Appointees on Management Performance

Empirically evaluating competing views about the relationship between appointments and performance has been difficult, and as a consequence we have little systematic knowledge of this important issue.[1] Stories about shortsighted, inexperienced, unqualified appointees abound.[2] Similarly, numerous accounts describe unresponsive and incompetent career managers who operate in individual agencies or cycle through multiple positions in government.[3] Not much research exists that tries systematically to arbitrate among these competing anecdotes.[4] The evidence we have that looks across large numbers of agencies focuses on the performance of various agencies engaged in macroeconomic forecasting. This evidence is mixed but suggests that some balance of appointees and careerists is best for performance. It is not clear, however, whether evidence from forecasting agencies is applicable to other types of agencies.[5]

One reason research that examines a broader set of agencies is scarce is that it is difficult to define good management or performance. For administration officials a definition of good management must include responsiveness to the president's policy agenda. Members of Congress, clients of the agency, and other interested parties are likely to have different definitions of good management. A second difficulty is comparing executives and agencies against one another, given that agencies have different mandates, operating environments, and constraints. Doing a comparative study of executive performance is an awesome task. It requires an acceptable definition of good performance, an identification of the universe of federal bureau chiefs, an acceptable grading scheme, willingness on the part of federal executives to participate, and an approach that is sensitive to differences among federal programs. Given these constraints, it is no surprise that large-N evaluations of comparative management performance have been difficult to execute.

The Program Assessment Rating Tool (PART) system implemented during the George W. Bush administration and the Federal Human Capital Survey (FHCS) provide two new means of overcoming the substantial difficulties in testing competing views about whether appointees or careerists are better for management and of evaluating the relationship between appointments and performance more generally. The PART system defines good performance in a defensible, transparent, and largely policy-neutral way. It attempts to take into account variations in management environment, and federal managers are required to participate. This means we have performance data on a sample of programs and managers that is large enough and representative enough to make statistically reliable claims about this important relationship. The FHCS similarly is given to over 200,000 federal employees throughout the bureaucracy. It has a reasonable response rate so that average evaluations of performance are available for each agency.[6] Publicly available data on agency functions, size, and employment provide a means of accounting for differences in management environment for evaluations of performance; thus, the unique influence of politicization on performance can be identified.

PART Program Evaluations and Management Performance

The PART system is a grading scheme used by the Office of Management and Budget (OMB) to evaluate the performance of federal programs numerically.[7] It was developed through the Federal Advisory Commission Act process in cooperation with the President's Management Council, the National Academy of Public Administration, and other interested parties from the administration, Congress, and the nonprofit sector. Four categories of performance receive grades from 0 to 100 based on a series of 25–30 yes-or-no questions filled out jointly by agencies and the OMB examiners.[8] The questions cover such aspects of good management performance as whether programs have a limited number of specific goals, whether people are held accountable for results, and whether performance is measured. Ultimately, programs are also asked to demonstrate whether they are performing well. Their ability to do this is the most important part of their PART evaluation.

The responses to these questions are totaled into raw scores in four categories of performance. These raw scores are weighted and combined for a total numerical score (0–100) and overall categorical grade—*ineffective, results not demonstrated, adequate, moderately effective,* and *effective*.[9] The four categories are as follows:

- *Program Purpose and Design* (weight = 20 percent): to assess whether the program design and purpose are clear and defensible.
- *Strategic Planning* (weight = 10 percent): to assess whether the agency sets valid annual and long-term goals for the program.
- *Program Management* (weight = 20 percent): to rate agency management of the program, including financial oversight and program improvement efforts.
- *Program Results* (weight = 50 percent): to rate program performance on goals reviewed in the strategic planning section and through other evaluations.[10]

The administration graded 234 programs (20 percent) for the FY 2004 budget, 176 more for the FY 2005 budget, and 206 programs for the

FY 2006 budget. The remaining federal programs were scheduled to be graded in the FY 2007 and 2008 budgets.[11] The total scores vary quite a bit. For the cohort graded in the FY 2006 budget, the average score is 62.78 and the minimum and maximum are 13.82 and 96.7, respectively. The highest- and lowest-scoring programs FY 2004–2006 are included in table 7.1. It is interesting to note that the National Science Foundation, which has never had a Schedule C appointee or an appointee in its corps of Senior Executive Service (SES) managers, has five programs in the top ten. On the other hand, four of the ten lowest-scoring programs come from the Department of Education, the most politicized cabinet department.

Does PART Measure Performance Reliably?

Evidence from interviews with OMB and agency officials and comparisons of PART scores to other measures of performance demonstrates that the scores, while not perfect, measure real differences in objective performance across federal programs.[12] While PART has some demonstrated problems—including evidence of unequal standards for low or high grades across programs, variation in OMB examiner expertise, poor or inconsistent program definition across programs, and different amounts of managerial control in different types of programs—this does not diminish the system's usefulness for evaluating comparative management quality, provided one proceeds carefully.[13]

Briefly, if the errors or mistakes in the PART grades are random—say one program is awarded too many points and another too few points—this inaccuracy will wash out when one looks at all the programs together. If the situation is worse—say the mistakes in giving grades are nonrandom—this is also not a problem so long as we can devise appropriate ways of accounting for these biases or establish that the problems in the grades are unrelated to the key subject of interest, namely, whether a bureau chief is an appointee or careerist. For example, suppose all social welfare programs like those in HUD or HHS were graded down unfairly. While this would not be an admirable grading scheme, this bias in grading would not influence our conclusions so long as all social welfare programs, both those administered by careerists and appointees, get downgraded equally.

The worst-case scenario for inference would be if the errors in grading were related to whether a program is administered by a careerist or an appointee. Even in this case, however, the bias is likely to lead to higher grades for *appointees*. If the administration wanted to favor one group of managers over another in the PART process, it would favor appointees since the administration's reputation is more closely tied to the perfor-

Table 7.1
Highest- and Lowest-Scoring Federal Programs on the PART, 2002–2004

Dept.	Bureau	Program	Year	Program Purpose & Design	Strategic Planning	Program Mgt	Program Results	Total
State	Educational and Cultural Affairs	Global Educational & Cultural Exchanges	2004	100	100	100	93	96.7
OPM	Office of Inspector General	FEHBP Integrity	2003	100	100	100	93	96.7
Treas	Engraving and Printing	New Currency Manufacturing	2003	100	100	100	92	95.9
NSF		Polar Tools, Facilities, and Logistics	2004	100	100	100	91	95.3
DHS	Secret Service	Protective Intelligence	2004	100	100	100	90	95.2
NSF		Facilities	2003	100	100	100	90	95.1
NSF		Information Technology Research	2003	100	100	100	90	95.0
NSF		Nanoscale Science and Engineering	2003	100	100	100	90	95.0
NSF		Biocomplexity in the Environment	2004	100	100	100	89	94.5
DOD	Air Force	Depot Maintenance	2004	100	100	86	93	93.8
HUD	Housing	Housing for Persons with Disabilities	2002	40	43	18	13	22.4
HUD	Housing	Housing for the Elderly	2002	40	43	18	13	22.4
DoEd	Elementary and Secondary Education	Impact Aid Payments for Federal Property	2004	60	0	50	0	22.0
DoEd	Vocational and Adult Education	Vocational Education State Grants	2002	20	43	67	0	21.7
DoEd	Special Ed. Rehabilitative Services	IDEA Preschool Grants	2002	40	0	56	0	19.2
DoEd		Federal Perkins Loans	2003	20	50	33	0	15.7
VA	Veterans Benefits Administration	Compensation	2002	20	0	57	0	15.4
DOJ	Office of Justice Programs	State Criminal Alien Assistance	2003	40	0	33	0	14.7
Interior	(Multiple)	LWCF Land Acquisition	2004	20	13	43	0	13.8
Interior	Bureau of Indian Affairs	Tribal Courts	2003	40	25	0	0	10.5

Note. Total score is weighted average of raw scores for Program Purpose and Design (20%), Strategic Planning (10%), Program Management (20%), and Program Results (50%).

mance of its appointment selections than to that of career bureaucrats.[14] Taken as a whole, the management grades provide a unique opportunity to analyze the causes of variation in management quality, but we should use these grades carefully, noting the possibility that the grades are biased in favor of appointees.

Comparing Appointees and Careerists Using PART Scores

For each of the 614 programs graded, OMB produced a worksheet that lists both a department and a bureau administering the program. I found the names and appointment authorities of agency heads for each bureau using the *Federal Yellow Book* and the Plum Book.[15] In total, 245 different bureau chiefs administer the 614 graded federal programs. Appointment-status information was available for 242 of the 245 managers. Of these, 62 percent were Senate-confirmed (PAS) political appointees, 11 percent were politically appointed members of the Senior Executive Service (SES), and 25 percent were career SES managers.[16] A summary of the differences in background characteristics between careerists and appointees of various types is included in table 7.2.

The backgrounds of appointed and career bureau chiefs are significantly different. Appointees have more private or nonprofit management experience and are much more likely to have worked in Congress or the White House before accepting their current post. They also have slightly higher levels of education on average and are more likely to be generalists, having worked in other departments prior to their current job. In contrast, careerists are the most likely to have worked in the bureau they manage, to have the most public management experience, and to have the longest tenures in their current position. This latter characteristic implies that appointee-run federal programs experience more managerial turnover than do programs administered by careerists.

The work environments of these managers also differ significantly. Appointees manage the largest bureaus in terms of budgets and number of programs, although not necessarily employment. Appointees in the SES manage bureaus with the smallest average employment. Not surprisingly, appointees work in the most-politicized bureaus. While only 3 percent of the managers in careerist-run bureaus are appointed, 10 percent of managers are appointed in appointee-run bureaus.

Program performance does appear to be affected by whether a bureau chief is an appointee or a careerist, as shown in figure 7.1, which graphs the total PART scores of federal programs by the type of manager.[17] Programs administered by appointees have significantly lower average PART scores than programs run by career managers. When de-composed, these

Table 7.2
Background Characteristic by Manager Type

Variable	Career Manager	Appointed SES Manager	Senate-confirmed (PAS)
Manager Background			
Education (0–3)	1.89	1.88	1.99
Previous bureau experience (0,1)	0.71	0.37	0.25
Experience in another federal department (0,1)	0.18	0.19	0.36
Public management experience (0,1)	0.91	0.59	0.77
Private sector management experience (0,1)	0.04	0.52	0.46
Tenure as bureau chief (Months)	38.3	16.7	20.0
Worked in Congress (0,1)	0.05	0.15	0.19
Worked in the White House (0,1)	0.00	0.11	0.08
Management Environment			
Programs graded (1–13)	1.52	3.44	2.73
Average budget of program graded (millions)	$411	$1,267	$2,206
Bureau employment (10–222,715)	8,247	2,993	17,069
% managers appointed in bureau (0–75)	3%	10%	10%
PART Score			
Program Purpose and Design	88.25	84.24	86.15
Strategic Planning	71.37	66.28	70.15
Program Management	84.01	81.75	77.94
Program Results	56.07	39.14	47.42
Average Total PART grade (0–100)	69.58	58.66	63.50

Note: N=242. Education levels (0–3) are high school, bachelors, masters, and doctorate degree. Employment data is available on only one-half of all bureaus. The number of cases for bureau employment are N=25, 18, and 102, respectively. The number of cases for % managers appointed is N=22, 17, and 101, respectively.

scores show that the greatest disparities between appointees and careerists exist in the program-management and program-results sections of the PART evaluation. This is some of the first evidence we have that programs run by appointees are at a disadvantage, and it fleshes out the anecdotal connection mentioned above between appointees and performance in the National Science Foundation and Department of Education cases.

Figure 7.2 graphs total PART scores by the percent of managers in an agency that are appointed.[18] The downward-sloping line shows the correlation between increasing politicization and lower PART scores. More-politicized agencies get lower performance evaluations. Lower PART scores are found not only among programs in bureaus whose top executives are appointees, but also among those in bureaus where appointees penetrate deeply.

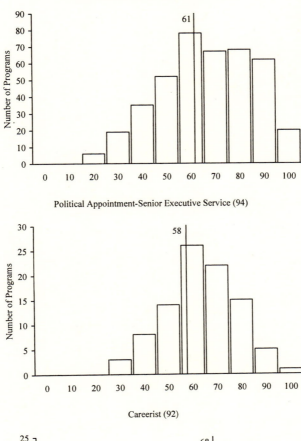

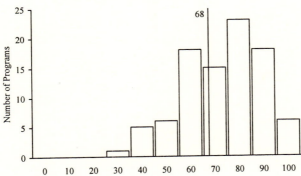

Figure 7.1. Total PART Score by Manager Type, FY 2004–2006

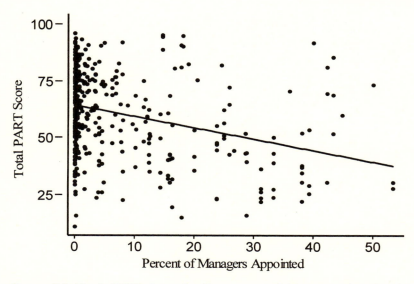

Figure 7.2. Total PART Score by Percentage of Managers Appointed, FY 2004–2006

Statistical Models of PART Scores

Of course, the difference in PART scores could be due to a number of factors unrelated to the management performance of appointees or careerists. One possible alternative explanation for the observed differences in scores is that the programs and agencies administered by appointees are unlike those headed by career managers. For example, appointee-run bureaus tend to be larger and the programs they administer more expensive and these aspects could explain the apparent performance gap.

Other characteristics of federal programs to consider are their sizes and purposes. Some programs, like Supplemental Security Income (Social Security Administration [SSA]), are direct federal programs providing services or benefits to the population directly. Other programs, like the Acid Rain program in the Office of Air and Radiation (Environmental Protection Agency [EPA]), are regulatory programs. Some of the variation in PART scores could be related to the differences in what the programs do, for programs vary substantially in type: 30.5 percent of the programs graded were direct federal programs; 18.1 percent were competitive grant programs; 16.3 percent were block-grant and formula-grant programs; 14.1 percent were research-and-development programs; 9.6 percent were capital-assets and service-acquisition programs; 6.8 percent were regulatory programs; 3.8 percent were credit programs; and 1 percent were combination programs.[19] Programs also vary substantially in size. Some programs have budgets as small as $1 million (for example, the B. J. Stupak Olympic Scholarship Program) and others as large as $270 billion (for example, Medicare).[20] Appointees tend to administer larger programs, and they are most likely to manage block- or formula-grant programs, research-and-development programs, and direct federal programs.

In addition to spanning a range of purposes and sizes, federal programs also vary in their political history or content. The difficulty of managing a program might be at least partly influenced by the political climate at the time the agency was created. Political scientist Terry Moe argues, for instance, that federal program design is the result of a struggle among political actors and that this struggle can result in structures and processes that are not effective.[21] It is possible that federal programs created during a period of divided-party government (59 percent of cases) might be systematically less effective than those created during a period of unified government.

Not only do these programs vary significantly, but the agencies that administer these programs differ in important ways, too. We saw in table 7.2 above, that appointee-run bureaus tend to be larger than those run by careerists, and they also tend to be responsible for a larger number of programs. Agencies also range in thickness at the top: some agencies have larger numbers and greater percentages of managers relative to employees.[22] Some bureau chiefs in this data are insulated from political pressure by fixed terms (7 percent of cases). Others administer programs as commission chairs (3 percent of cases).[23] As we saw in the last chapter, some agencies are more traditionally liberal or conservative than others.[24] If scores from the PART assessment, which was designed and implemented during a Republican administration, are influenced by politics, liberal agencies could get systematically lower scores than conservative agencies. Finally, agencies' unique histories and cultures influence the ease or difficulty of management. For instance, managing in the Department of the Interior is significantly different from managing in the Department of Defense because of each department's distinctive histories, personnel systems, management imperatives, and cultures.

The best way to determine whether discrepancies in performance between appointees and careerists can be traced to characteristics of the two populations is to estimate statistical models with appropriate controls so that we can rule out other competing explanations. This facilitates parsing out the peculiar influences of management type on PART scores while accounting for the influence of other factors—like program size and management environment—on the scores, as well.

One potential complication in this analysis is that presidents may choose to put an appointee or careerist into a job precisely because of the difficulty or ease of the job. If this is the case, it is hard to attribute to either appointees' or careerists' responsibility for high or low performance because the performance level was determined before they got into the job. It is worth noting, of course, that this only matters for the findings here if political appointees were put into all the toughest jobs, in which case poor performance by appointees is related not to differences between appointees and careerists, but rather to differences in the types of programs they manage. To account for this possibility, I estimate models that control for distinguishing characteristics of the programs themselves. I also estimated models where appointee or careerist management (or percent of managers appointed) is modeled directly along with the program's performance. In these models, I could not reject the hypothesis that the estimates were the same as in the more straightforward models, so I proceed to describe the simpler models.[25] I discuss the models used in examining PART scores in greater detail in appendix 7A, below.

Appointees versus Careerists Redux

The results of the statistical models confirm what was demonstrated in figures 7.1 and 7.2, above: namely, programs administered by appointees get systematically lower PART grades than careerist-administered programs even when we control for differences among programs, substantial variation in management environment, and the policy content of programs themselves. Model estimates are included in table 7.3 and they indicate that programs administered by appointed managers get grades five to six points lower than those administered by careerists. To put these findings in perspective, imagine two comparable programs, one managed by an appointee and the other by a careerist: the performance bonus seen in the (hypothetical) latter, careerist-run program would move the program's PART scores ranking from the 50th percentile to the 65th, or from the 75th percentile to the 90th.

This finding—that programs administered by appointees get systematically lower grades than programs run by career managers—is important because it is among the first systematic evidence we have that appointee-run federal programs do not perform as well as careerist-run programs. As is, the data confirm the underlying logic for the creation of the merit system, and yet these results may actually *underestimate* the true benefits of career management if the administration has biased the PART grades in favor of appointees. It should be noted that appointees are not trying to make programs fail. If I analyze only conservative agencies, those supported by a Republican administration, the deleterious consequences of appointees for PART scores are even more pronounced.[26]

Table 7.3
Models of Federal Program PART Score, FY 2004–2006

	(1)	(2)
Politicization		
Appointee (0,1)	−5.52** (2.88)	—
% of Managers Appointed	—	-0.54** (0.13)
Program Characteristics		
Ln(Program Budget)	0.65 (0.71)	0.53 (0.72)
Block-Formula-Grant (0,1)	−11.19** (4.45)	−18.72** (4.48)
Capital Assets and Service Acquisition (0,1)	−18.51** (5.46)	−19.58** (5.11)
Competitive-Grant (0,1)	−18.98** (3.85)	−19.58** (3.88)
Credit (0,1)	−12.28* (6.77)	−13.20 (6.83)
Direct Federal (0,1)	−17.87** (4.14)	−18.00** (4.20)
Mixed (0,1)	−19.82** (5.84)	−21.05** (5.93)
Regulatory (0,1)	−12.98** (4.73)	−13.22** (4.71)
Bureau Characteristics		
Fixed-Term (0,1)	11.49** (5.09)	10.60** (5.07)
Commission (0,1)	0.83 (8.52)	0.51 (8.50)
# Programs Evaluated	−0.45 (0.37)	−0.50 (0.37)
Agency-Specific Personnel System (0,1)	2.93 (3.93)	2.36 (3.94)
Ln(Employment)	−0.47 (1.95)	−0.26 (2.17)
Ln(Managers)	−1.01 (2.03)	−1.21 (2.29)
Political Characteristics		
Created under Divided Government (0,1)	−1.81 (2.23)	−1.90 (2.21)
Agency Liberalism-Conservatism	2.28 (1.52)	2.47 (1.50)
Constant	93.50** (8.90)	89.72** (8.56)
N (Observations, Managers)	328, 125	330, 126
F (14, 209; 15, 209)	6.14**	6.04**

Note. Excludes extreme values of % managers appointed (> 99th Percentile). ** significant at the $p < 0.05$ level; * significant at the $p < 0.10$ level in two-tailed test. Robust standard errors adjusted for clustering on managers reported.

If we examine the effects of politicization more generally (table 7.3, column 2), we continue to get similar results. Agencies with higher percentages of appointees in their management teams are found to get systematically lower PART scores. Increasing politicization by 10 percentage points decreases the estimated PART score by 4–5 points. Therefore, if the average program receives a score of 61.7 from the OMB, increasing the percentage of managers appointed in that program by 10 percentage points would be expected to decrease the PART score to 57.7. Similarly, if identical programs are placed in different bureaus staffed with with 0 percent, 10 percent, 20 percent, and 30 percent appointees, the programs' scores are estimated to be 61.7, 57.7, 53.7, and 49.7, respectively—just on the basis of the extent of politicization. It is important to note that these outcomes have nothing to do with either political opinions about what the programs do or the responsiveness of the agency. Politicization here influences only performance.[27]

Looking at PART scores in this more sophisticated and nuanced way also reveals a number of interesting facts about the scores and factors that influence performance. First, research-and-development programs get the highest grades; grant programs get the lowest. Second, programs administered by bureau chiefs who serve for fixed terms get systematically higher PART scores, 11–12 points higher than other programs. This implies that some insulation from presidential control may enhance traditional management. Finally, while the calculations for programs created during periods of divided government and for traditionally liberal agencies suggest that these programs get lower PART scores, these results are not statistically significant. Similarly, differences in management environment, such as agency size, the number of managers, whether an agency is a commission or administration, and program budget are all uncorrelated with program performance.

Explaining the Appointee-Careerist Gap

While the statistical analysis tells us that programs administered by appointees get lower grades, it does not tell us *why* this is the case. The descriptive statistics in table 7.2 indicate a number of important differences between appointees and careerists. As noted previously, appointed managers have higher levels of education, more private or nonprofit management experience, and significantly more public affairs experience. Appointed managers are also more likely to be generalists, having worked in the federal government outside the bureau they currently manage. Careerists, meanwhile, are more likely to be specialists and to have work experience in the bureau they manage; they are also more likely to have public (as opposed to private) management experience. Careerists serve longer tenures on average, which means that programs administered by appointees experience more executive turnover.

To determine which of these factors matter for performance, I re-examine the data, focusing on the characteristics of the managers themselves in place of whether the bureau chief is an appointee or a careerist. I examine education level and whether the bureau chief has worked outside the bureau in another federal department, has private management experience, or has worked in either Congress or the White House. I also consider whether managers have worked in the bureau before, how long managers have served in their current position, and whether they have had public management experience.

I include these estimates in table 7.4. Importantly, these new analyses help explain why careerist-run programs get higher PART scores and also illuminate where previous public affairs experience might help. The background characteristics that favor appointees—such as higher education levels or business experience—do not appear to matter for program performance. Two of the background characteristics that favor

Table 7.4
Federal Program PART Score, FY 2004–2006 by Background

	Total PART Score	Raw Program Purpose and Design Score
Bureau Chief Characteristics		
Bachelors (0,1)	9.59** (3.86)	2.72 (13.12)
Masters (0,1)	3.21 (3.72)	4.11 (12.70)
PhD (0,1)	1.41 (4.60)	7.23 (13.17)
Worked in Another Department (0,1)	1.57 (2.38)	−5.08 (4.02)
Private Management Experience (0,1)	−1.10 (2.11)	−5.44 (3.77)
Worked in White House (0,1)	3.20 (4.24)	14.87** (7.47)
Worked in Congress (0,1)	0.32 (2.08)	12.94** (5.16)
Bureau Experience (0,1)	5.46** (2.30)	3.72 (4.10)
Months Serving as Bureau Chief (0–182)	0.21* (0.12)	0.17 (0.21)
Months Serving as Bureau Chief^2	−0.002 (0.001)	0.001 (0.002)
Previous Public Management Experience (0,1)	−0.54 (2.61)	8.27* (4.36)
Bureau Characteristics		
Fixed Term (0,1)	12.82** (4.56)	11.69 (8.10)
Commission (0,1)	−0.38 (6.20)	14.22 (14.40)
# Programs Evaluated	−0.45 (0.33)	0.23 (0.60)
Agency-Specific Personnel System (0,1)	−2.18 (2.85)	−18.60** (8.40)
Political and Program Characteristics		
Created under Divided Government (0,1)	−3.10* (1.84)	−1.02 (3.59)
Agency Liberalism-Conservatism	1.38 (1.25)	1.17 (2.14)
Ln (Program Budget)	0.67 (0.53)	−0.65 (1.03)
Constant	64.69** (5.41)	113.18** (15.35)
N (Observations, Managers)	459, 199	459
F (22, 218; 24, 201; 26, 123)	5.61**	62.81**
Number of Right-censored Observations	—	237

Note. ** Significant at the .05 level, * Significant at the .10 level in two-tailed test. Robust standard errors adjusted for clustering on managers reported. Program type indicator estimates omitted. Column 1 includes estimates from an OLS regression where total PART score was regressed on the independent variables listed. Column 2 includes estimates from a Tobit model of raw Program Purpose and Design (PPD) scores from the PART. I estimate a Tobit since the PPD scores are bounded at 100 and a number of programs scored at 100, suggesting censoring.

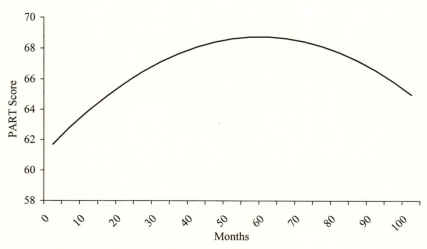

Figure 7.3. Estimated Total PART Score by Manager Tenure

careerists do appear to matter, however: previous bureau experience and length of tenure.

Bureau chiefs who worked in the bureau before they assumed their management position are estimated to add 4–5 points to their program's total PART score. Presumably, their knowledge of programs, processes, structures, and personnel facilitates monitoring, reduces the start-up costs associated with a new management position, and helps them know better how to measure and manage performance. Previous bureau experience may also bring specialized policy knowledge that helps facilitate management oversight. One implication of this finding is that it is prudent to either recruit managers from the career service or select appointees who have served in previous administrations in similar positions.[28]

Of course, after a period of time all managers can learn how a bureau and its programs operate, although their knowledge will not, perhaps, be as intimate as that of a person who came up through a bureau's ranks. The longer a bureau chief has been at the head of a bureau, the better her program's performance.[29] In figure 7.3 I graph the estimated influence of job tenure on a PART score. Increasing management tenure by ten months increases the PART score of a program by 2–2.5 points, which suggests that the early months produce the largest return in terms of performance. The relationship between tenure and performance flattens out over time, so additional months of tenure are not nearly as helpful after four or five years on the job as they were in the first twelve months. Based on the point estimates from the models in table 7.4, above, after fifty-five months in a job (between four and five years), additional months have no added benefit. For most bureau chiefs, then, longer tenure improves performance.[30]

Interestingly, previous public management experience was not significantly related to management performance. Similarly, previous work experience in a department outside the department where the bureau chief currently works also does not significantly improve PART performance. Work experience in multiple federal positions does not by itself improve performance, either. There are three possible explanations for these disconnects. First, and most obviously, generalists who move in and out of different positions are no better than specialists at managing. General experience does not make up for a lack of specific bureau knowledge. Second, it is possible that generalists do perform better but that this measure of work history also captures the influence of those managers who have been shifted around to various positions because of past failures. Third, it may be the case that generalist managers are appointed to run the toughest programs. It is impossible to disentangle these three explanations from this data, but these results provide no evidence that generalists are better managers on average.

As noted earlier, two primary advantages held by political appointees are higher levels of education and previous experience working in the White House or Congress, yet neither of these characteristics correlates with improved performance in the PART ratings. I could not reject the view that education had no influence on management performance, except for the evidence that managers with a bachelor's degree perform better than those with only a high school education. Of course, it may be that only the most talented people among the set of less-educated employees make it into these management positions. This would dampen the influence of education on performance. Managers with higher levels of education may be able to get management positions without undergoing the same type of screening that applies to those without degrees. Private management was also uncorrelated with PART performance, bolstering public management scholars' claim that private management experience does not necessarily transfer to the public sector given the significant discrepancies between the two environments.

In the main analysis, previous work experience in Congress or the White House, or any public administrative position, was also uncorrelated with management performance. A reasonable expectation a priori is that bureau chiefs with public affairs experience would be more sensitive to the wishes of political stakeholders and that this should improve management. I did some additional analysis of just the raw program purpose and design scores from the PART evaluation, estimating the same type of statistical models I describe above (table 7.4, column 2). This

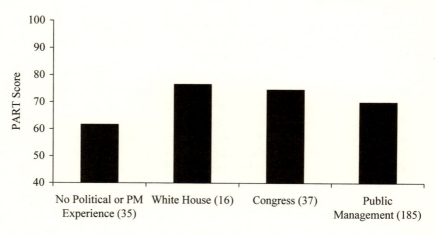

Figure 7.4. Estimated PART Program Purpose and Design Score by Political Experience of Managers (236 Total)

subsection of the PART evaluation asks questions such as, *Is the program purpose clear?* and, *Is the program optimally designed to address the national interest, problem, or need?* Interestingly, in these analyses previous public management experience, work in Congress, and work in the White House *does* significantly improve the manager's ability to craft a program purpose and design that is clear and acceptable to the OMB. As suggested by figure 7.4, previous experience of this type is estimated to increase a program's raw program and purpose score by 8.5–14 points, which is an increase of almost one standard deviation in some cases. Managers with White House, congressional, or previous public management experience are better able to take the statutes, rules, and orders that authorize their programs and translate them into clear program definitions. Political connections and experience do appear to have some benefits in managing in a political environment. Unfortunately, however, this experience does not carry over to strategic planning, program management, or generating program results—the nuts and bolts of bureau management.

In sum, then, the PART results are both important and interesting. They demonstrate that appointees get systematically lower PART management grades than careerists and agencies with higher percentages of appointees in the management team get lower PART scores. They confirm the claims of previous scholars that increasing the number of appointees could have negative effects on management. And they illustrate the tradeoff presidents make when politicizing: that is, increasing the number of appointees can increase agency responsiveness, but adding appointees tends to hurt management performance. The systematic differences between career managers and appointees that explain why careerists get higher grades are their previous bureau experience and their longer tenure in management positions. The advantages that appointees have over careerist bureau chiefs—such as higher levels of education, private management experience, and work in other departments outside the bureau—are not significantly related to PART scores. Public affairs experience does seem to help with one aspect of public management: translating political wishes into a clear program purpose and design.

Appointees and Management Performance: Federal Human Capital Survey

The PART scores analyzed above provide one way of measuring federal program performance, but there are others that do not depend upon the specific instrument created and implemented by a given administration. Data from the Federal Human Capital Survey (FHCS) provide another way of measuring performance that uses evaluations by federal employees across the government. It is a useful means of verifying the robustness of the key PART score findings. The combination of the FEMA case study (see chapter 6 in the present volume), the PART scores analysis, and the FHCS data, if consistent, will provide convincing evidence of politicization's influence on performance.

In the summer of 2002 and the late fall of 2004, the Office of Personnel Management (OPM) surveyed over 200,000 and 275,000 federal employees, respectively, across the government about different aspects of their work environment. Included within the survey were questions about the level of respect federal employees had for the senior leaders of their organization and about the presence or absence of organizational features associated with good management. I selected the questions from the survey that were most directly related to leadership, management, and work climate.[31] There is substantial variation across agencies that provides insight into which agencies are being led and managed well and which agencies are having difficulty. In total, employees in 178 and 191 agencies were surveyed in 2002 and 2004, respectively; 162 agencies were surveyed in both years.

Included in table 7.5 is a list of the best- and worst-evaluated agencies in leadership, management, and work climate across the government according to federal employees. The table lists the percentage of each agency's employees that agree or strongly agree with statements such as, *I hold my organization's leaders in high regard*, and, *In my organization, leaders generate high levels of motivation and commitment in the workforce.*[32] Noticeable

Table 7.5
Highest and Lowest Evaluations of Leadership, Management, and Work Climate in the 2004 Federal Human Capital Survey (FHCS)

Dept.	Bureau	(1)	(2)	(3)	(4)	(5)	(6)	(7)	Avg.
Treas	Office of the Inspector General	72.7	66.4	76.2	85	76.6	75.2	67.8	74.3
NASA	Lyndon B. Johnson Space Center	69.8	58.3	68.5	86.5	76.3	79.7	79.6	74.1
NASA	John F. Kennedy Space Center	68.2	58.1	66.4	8.37	71.9	81.0	76.0	72.2
Treas	Office of the Comptroller of the Currency	59	47	68.5	88.3	68.8	80.5	77	69.8
VA	Office of the Inspector General	71	58.8	67.7	76.5	66.3	69.8	66.5	68.1
NASA	George C. Marshall Space Flight Center	60.1	52.6	62.5	81.8	68.4	76.7	74	68.0
GSA	Public Buildings Service	58.6	50.6	72.6	78.1	69.4	73.0	70	67.5
GSA	Federal Supply Service	60.2	54.9	77.3	77.2	63.7	72.3	66.5	67.4
EPA	Region 9—San Francisco	50.8	41.9	66.9	81.1	57.9	85.2	83.9	66.8
DOT	Federal Highway Administration	62	44.8	70.4	78	65.2	75.6	71.5	66.8
DoEd	Spec. Education and Rehabilitative Serv.	35.5	23.7	53.9	66.4	47.7	40.4	35	43.2
OPM	HCLMSA	31	27.6	54.2	59.3	48.4	42.5	32.5	42.2
IND	Holocaust Memorial Museum	33.5	26	42.9	61.9	43.2	45.6	40.9	42.0
Treas	Financial Crimes Enforcement Network	35.9	24	34	58.7	31.8	54.7	51.9	41.6
DoEd	Office of Postsecondary Education	30.8	24.1	52.4	55.8	36.2	46.8	40.5	40.9
HUD	Federal Housing Commissioner	39.8	27	45.8	50.7	40.8	46.4	34.7	40.7
Interior	Bureau of Indian Affairs	43.5	25.5	34.8	55.4	36.4	48.6	35.8	40.0
DOD	Defense Security Service	21.4	18	46.6	68.8	43.5	44.1	36.2	39.8
Interior	Office of the Solicitor	27.8	17.3	25.7	76	30	54.8	46	39.7
IND	Broadcasting Board of Governors	31.9	22.6	33.8	59.6	35.3	42.3	35	37.2

(1) "I hold my organization's leaders in high regard" or "I have a high level of respect for my organization's senior leaders (Strongly Agree, Agree)," for 2002, 2004, respectively.

(2) "In my organization, leaders generate high levels of motivation and commitment in the workforce (Strongly Agree, Agree)."

(3) "Managers review and evaluate the organization's progress toward meeting its goals and objectives (Strongly Agree, Agree)."

(4) "The workforce has the job-relevant knowledge and skills necessary to accomplish organizational goals (Strongly Agree, Agree)."

(5) "Managers promote communication among different work units (for example, about projects, goals, needed resources)," or "Managers promote communication among different work units (Stongly Agree, Agree)," for 2002 or 2004, respectively.

(6) "I recommend my organization as a good place to work (Strongly Agree, Agree)."

(7) "How would you rate your organization as an organization to work for compared to other organizations? (One of the Best, Above Average)."

among the highest-evaluated agencies are some of the historically least politicized agencies in government, including those in the National Aeronautics and Space Administration (NASA) and in the Department of Veterans Affairs (VA). Two of the top agencies are Inspector General offices within larger departments; these are insulated from politics by design. As with the PART scores, among the lower-scoring agencies were two bureaus in the Department of Education and one bureau in the Department of Housing and Urban Development (HUD), the second-most-politicized department in the government. Not surprisingly, the list also includes the Bureau of Indian Affairs (BIA) and the Office of the Solicitor within the Department of the Interior. BIA is the target of well-publicized and ongoing litigation for its egregious mishandling of the Indian Trust Fund.

Each of the agencies in the dataset is coded according to whether they are led by an appointee. Of these agencies, 65 percent were headed by an appointee, 17 percent by career managers, and 18 percent by military officers. The average agency's management team was comprised of about 3 percent appointees.[33] Whether agencies are run by appointees or careerists appears to matter for employee evaluations of leadership, management, and work climate. Figure 7.5 graphs federal employee evaluations of leadership, management, and work climate by whether the agency was run by an appointee or careerist. On each question federal employees evaluate the leadership, management, and work climate or their agency more highly if their agencies are run by career managers. This same relationship holds if I look at overall politicization. Employees in agencies with high percentages of appointees are less likely to agree when prompted that they have a high level of respect for their organization's senior leaders or that their senior leaders engender high levels of commitment or motivation in the workforce. They are also less likely to believe that these leaders hold the organization accountable, provide staff with the necessary skills to fulfill its mandate, or promote communication among work units. These beliefs lead to less general satisfaction in the workplace and federal workers in more politicized agencies are less likely to believe their agency compares favorably with other organizations and to recommend their job as a good place to work.[34]

Statistical Models of Employee-Survey Responses

As with the PART scores, the differences in performance observed in the simple graph could be due to omitted factors that are correlated with whether or not an agency is run by appointees or careerists. To disentangle the unique influence of appointee management on performance, more complicated statistical models are necessary. I estimate

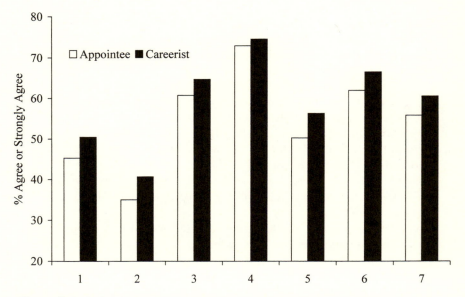

Figure 7.5. Federal Employee Evaluations of Leadership, Management, and Work Climate by Appointment Authority, 2002–2004

(1) "I hold my organization's leaders in high regard," or "I have a high level of respect for my organization's senior leaders," for 2002, 2004, respectively.
(2) "In my organization, leaders generate high levels of motivation and commitment in the workforce."
(3) "Managers review and evaluate the organization's progress toward meeting its goals and objectives."
(4) "The workforce has the job-relevant knowledge and skills necessary to accomplish organizational goals."
(5) "Managers promote communication among different work units (for example, about projects, goals, needed resources)," or "Managers promote communication among different work units," for 2002 or 2004, respectively.
(6) "I recommend my organization as a good place to work."
(7) "How would you rate your organization as an organization to work for compared to other organizations?" (One of the Best, Above Average)

such models, including controls for differences in management structure, agency size, and type of agency work. As in my analysis of the PART scores, I have to be concerned about the possibility of alternative explanations or that appointees are placed into the agencies that are hardest to run. I deal with these issues and the details of model estimation more fully in appendix 7B, below.

Table 7.6 includes estimates from seven models. The model numbers correspond to the questions listed at the bottom of the table. Models one and two deal with leadership, three through five with management,

Table 7.6
Federal Agencies and Employee Evaluations of Leadership, Management, and Overall Work Climate, 2002–2004

	Leadership			Management		Work Climate	
	(1)	(2)	(3)	(4)	(5)	(6)	(7)
Politicization							
Appointee (0,1)	-6.06**	-5.71**	-3.67*	-0.87	-5.79**	-6.02**	-4.82**
% Managers Appointed	-0.35	-0.42*	-0.18	-0.56**	-0.46***	-0.48*	-0.71**
% Managers Appointed[2]	0.01**	0.01**	0.00	0.02**	0.01**	0.02**	0.02**
Controls and Constant							
Military officer (0,1)	-6.42**	-6.82**	-6.51**	-3.70*	-5.22**	-5.18**	-4.58**
Ln(Employment)	-0.29	-0.43	-0.16	-0.52	-0.51	-0.16	0.40
Ratio of Managers to Employees	0.17	-3.05	-5.13	0.32	2.24	-1.80	-1.46
Commission (0,1)	0.28	2.13	-8.27*	2.71	-3.12	1.46	2.49
Fixed-Term (0,1)	0.18	-1.20	4.86**	-0.75	0.05	-0.58	-1.46
Agency-Specific Personnel System	2.57	4.31**	-4.01**	1.42	2.43**	3.54*	3.83*
Defense (0,1)	2.82	2.14	6.44**	4.29**	0.13	-3.26	-4.51**
Regulatory (0,1)	0.39	0.86	3.70*	3.30**	1.36	3.59*	2.79
Science/Technology (0,1)	2.46	2.40	-0.59	3.22**	3.19*	6.74**	4.05**
Manager in Acting Capacity (0,1)	0.19	-0.12	2.10	-0.85	-0.19	-3.54	-2.15
2002 Survey (0,1)	-1.96**	-6.16**	9.57**	-2.10**	-2.48**	-5.37**	-4.79**
Constant	43.34**	56.66**	61.44**	78.30**	60.48**	62.62**	65.16**
N	262	262	262	262	262	262	262
F (14 df)	6.25**	12.48**	18.37**	3.88**	5.15**	7.37**	8.32**
R^2	0.19	0.28	0.34	0.16	0.22	0.29	0.28

Note. Standard errors clustered on agency.
* significant at the .10 level,
** significant at the .05 level in two-tailed tests.
(1) "I hold my organization's leaders in high regard" or "I have a high level of respect for my organization's senior leaders (Strongly Agree, Agree)," for 2002, 2004, respectively.
(2) "In my organization, leaders generate high levels of motivation and commitment in the workforce (Strongly Agree, Agree)."
(3) "Managers review and evaluate the organization's progress toward meeting its goals and objectives (Strongly Agree, Agree)."
(4) "The workforce has the job-relevant knowledge and skills necessary to accomplish organizational goals (Strongly Agree, Agree)."
(5) "Managers promote communication among different work units (for example, about projects, goals, needed resources)," or "Managers promote communication among different work units (Stongly Agree, Agree)," for 2002 or 2004, respectively.
(6) "I recommend my organization as a good place to work (Strongly Agree, Agree)."
(7) "How would you rate your organization as an organization to work for compared to other organizations? (One of the Best, Above Average)."

and six and seven with overall work climate. Importantly, the results demonstrate that agencies headed by appointees get systematically lower evaluations in the FHCS just as they did in the analysis of the PART scores. The average percentage of employees agreeing or strongly agreeing with statements such as, *Leaders generate high levels of motivation and commitment, Managers promote communication among different work units,* and *I recommend my organization as a good place to work* is 5–6 points lower than in careerist-run agencies even when controlling for a host of factors. The influence of appointee management is largest in evaluations of leadership and overall work climate.

If politicization is measured as the percentage of an agency's management team that is composed of appointees, the results are similar. As the percentage of appointees in the management team increases, the average employee evaluation decreases.[35] In figure 7.6 I graph the estimated influence of appointee percentage on evaluations of performance. Increasing the percentage of appointees in the management team from the average to one standard deviation above the average decreases the number agreeing to any of the questions by 1–4 percent. Of course, there are exceptions to the general pattern. For example, OMB and the Office of the Secretary of Defense both received high evaluations even though they each had one of the highest percentages of appointees. What is instructive about these cases, however, is that while these agencies are politicized, career employees have a lot of responsibility, work in an exciting environment, and have influence over policy. For example, budget examiners influence PART scores, budgets, and management reforms in their portfolio areas. In most politicized agencies morale is low partly because of a lack of influence or opportunities for advancement.

In sum, politicization is associated with poorer performance in almost all cases. Agencies headed by Senate-confirmed (PAS), noncareer Senior Executive Service (SES), or Schedule C appointees get lower evaluations than other agencies. Similarly, agencies with management teams composed of high percentages of appointees get systematically lower evaluations. This evidence provides important confirmation of the evidence provided by both the study of FEMA in chapter 6 and of the PART scores in the first part of the present chapter. These three sources of data provide a means of triangulating on an important empirical regularity—politicization hurts performance.

Conclusion

Apart from anecdotal evidence like that surrounding the FEMA case analyzed in chapter 6, it has been difficult to evaluate claims about the rela-

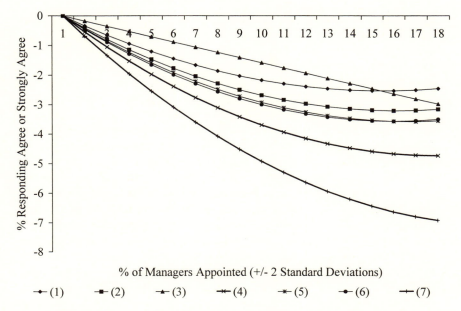

Figure 7.6. Influence of Politicization on Employee Evaluations of Agency Performance

(1) "I hold my organization's leaders in high regard," or "I have a high level of respect for my organization's senior leaders," for 2002, 2004, respectively.

(2) "In my organization, leaders generate high levels of motivation and commitment in the workforce."

(3) "Managers review and evaluate the organization's progress toward meeting its goals and objectives."

(4) "The workforce has the job-relevant knowledge and skills necessary to accomplish organizational goals."

(5) "Managers promote communication among different work units (for example, about projects, goals, needed resources)," or "Managers promote communication among different work units" for 2002 or 2004, respectively.

(6) "I recommend my organization as a good place to work."

(7) "How would you rate your organization as an organization to work for compared to other organizations?" (One of the Best, Above Average)

tionship between appointments and performance. This chapter has used the Bush administration's Program Assessment Rating Tool (PART) scores and the Federal Human Capital Survey (FHCS) to systematically evaluate this relationship. The innovation has been both in the use of the new data and in connecting the data to information about politicization and characteristics of managers themselves. This analysis demon-

strates that appointees get systematically lower PART scores than careerists and federal employees in politicized agencies are less likely to say
their agencies are led and managed well or are good places to work.
Previous bureau experience and longer tenure in management positions
explain why careerist-run programs get higher grades. The advantages
that appointees tend to have over careerist bureau chiefs, such as higher
levels of education, private management experience, and work in other
departments outside the bureau, are not significantly correlated to performance. Public affairs experience, however, does seem to help in one
aspect of public management: translating political wishes into a clear
program purpose and design.

The chapter's findings are consistent with two trends in modern presidential staffing. First, an in-and-out system has developed in the last
twenty-five years. Increasingly, presidents are relying on persons who
move frequently in and out of government positions to staff important
policymaking posts in their administrations. This implies that political
actors understand the value of choosing appointees with previous bureau
or department experience when filling appointments.[36] For example, a
number of high-level appointees who served in the George W. Bush administration had served in previous administrations, including Anthony
Principi (Veterans), Condoleezza Rice (National Security Council
[NSC]), Donald Rumsfeld (Defense), and Anne Veneman (Agriculture).
Second, recent administrations have self-consciously promoted from
within during their second terms partly as a way of building a farm team
of both future elected office holders and future agency officials.[37]

The systematic results demonstrating the appointee-careerist management gap have implications for our understanding of the federal government's response to Hurricane Katrina and current debates about reducing the number of appointees. They suggest that the influence of
appointees on FEMA performance, examined elsewhere in this volume,
is generalizable to other programs and agencies. In FEMA, politicization
led to successive waves of inexperienced managers, high turnover, and
insufficient long-term planning. The agency had a hard time recruiting
and retaining qualified personnel to run important programs and the
absence of consistent leadership, proper training, and useful exercises
left the agency bureaucratic, unresponsive, and generally ill prepared.
The results examined in this chapter suggest that politicization is having
a similar influence on other agencies.

One implication of this research is that reducing the number of political appointees is one means of improving performance. While few argue
that we should eliminate all appointees, the need for bureaucratic control and historical demands for patronage appear to have pushed the
number of appointees beyond the numbers optimal for governmental
performance from the perspective of most voters. Short of reducing the

number of appointees, this research suggests other means of improving performance. Presidents could focus more on ensuring the competence of the people they select or focus on selecting people who are willing to serve longer than most appointees do. The president could improve performance, for example, by recruiting managers from the career service and recruiting appointees who are "in-and-outers," executives who have served in previous administrations in similar positions.

Why, then, do presidents politicize when doing so is bad for performance? It is possible that presidents and their staffs misunderstand the influence of politicization on performance. While this may be true in some cases, it is likely that presidents also politicize because to do so has other benefits, including the control it allows presidents over agency activities and the opportunities it provides presidents to reward political supporters. Presidents are personally held accountable for the functioning of the entire executive branch. This being the case, they will want to make certain that the people they select are making the important decisions. Presidents are also under immense pressure to maintain support for themselves and their party through the distribution of jobs. This dynamic generates persistent politicization that leads to poor management performance not only in FEMA, as noted above, but across the government as a whole.

APPENDIX 7A
Model Estimation: PART Scores

This appendix describes the model estimation used for the PART score analysis in this chapter, identifying the difficulties in model estimation and the methods employed to overcome these problems. This model estimation presents six primary difficulties: nonindependent observations, missing data, potential endogeneity, measurement problems with the dependent variable, omitted variable bias, and right-censoring of the dependent variable in one case.

First, there are multiple observations on each bureau chief, which means that the observations are not independent—a violation of the traditional Gauss-Markov assumptions. To account for this I report robust standard errors clustered on each bureau chief. I have also estimated models using each bureau chief as one observation and the average score of the bureau chief as the dependent variable. These results generally confirm the conclusions of the chapter and are available upon request.[38]

Second, some data for a few of the control variables, such as divided government at the time of creation, are missing because it is difficult to identify start dates for many programs. I estimate multiple models including or excluding the controls to show that the results are generally robust. Tables including simpler specifications are likewise available upon request.

Third, whether or not a program is administered by a careerist or an appointee may be endogenous. In other words, the same variables that predict the PART score could also predict whether a bureau is headed by a careerist or an appointee. For example, it is possible that all difficult-to-manage programs are run by appointees and all easy-to-manage programs are run by careerists. If this is the case, any relationship between appointment status (appointee or careerist) and PART score could be spurious because the ultimate cause of the low PART score would be the inherent difficulty of the program itself, not whether the manager is an appointee or a careerist. While it is not clear that appointees are more likely to be chosen to administer the most-difficult programs, this concern must be taken seriously. All models attempt to control for the management environment, including the characteristics that would make a program or bureau comparatively difficult or easy to manage. I also estimated a set of instrumental variables regressions where the appointment authority of the bureau chief is estimated along with the effect of appointment authority on PART score. In these regressions I could not reject the null hypothesis that the original OLS coefficients were consistent. As such, I report the OLS estimates.[39] These estimates are also available upon request.

A related problem is that estimates of the influence of tenure on program performance could be endogenous. If a program is very difficult to manage, this could influence not only how long a manager serves, but also the program's PART score; thus, it can be difficult to parse out the distinct influence of tenure on the PART score. I estimated a model where tenure was instrumented and could not reject the null hypothesis that the original OLS estimates were consistent. The difficulty in this case was finding regressors that predict tenure but not PART score. Fortunately, the natural sequencing of PART evaluations provides two such regressors. Some programs were evaluated in 2002 (for the FY 2004 budget), some in 2003 (for the FY 2005 budget), and some in 2004 (for the FY 2006 budget). If the selection of programs was indeed random, then when the programs were evaluated *should not* matter for the PART score but *should* matter for tenure, since tenure for bureau chiefs is shorter the earlier they are evaluated. I used both a Hausman test and the auxiliary regression approach described in the previous footnote to determine whether the instrumental variables specification/model was appropriate for the main text.[40]

It is also possible that appointees want programs to fail. This would drive PART scores down, but not because of a lack of competence. To account for this possibility I control for program content using indicators for program type (regulatory, block-grant, and so forth), department, and partisanship of the Congress and president at the time the program was created. I also estimate models on split samples based upon program content to see whether the influence of appointees on performance is greater for programs Republicans are less likely to support. I first estimated models excluding programs created under unified Democratic control to see whether the coefficient on appointee management gets smaller. Since the PART scores were produced by a Republican administration, political appointees should be more likely to want to run down or eliminate programs created by Democrats. This implies that the coefficient on appointee management will be larger and negative when programs created under unified Democratic control are included. I find just the opposite. When I *exclude* these programs, the coefficient on appointee management is much larger and negative. Second, I have estimated models only on conservative agencies to see whether the coefficient on appointee management or appointee percentage gets smaller.[41] The coefficient estimates are again negative, larger, and statistically significant. Together, these analyses suggest that appointees are not purposefully grading down programs they want to fail.

There is variation across departments that may not be picked up by the other control variables. I therefore estimate models with fixed effects for department. There are fifteen indicators added to the specification, one for each department and independent agencies are the base category. When models are estimated with fixed effects, the results are similar except that the coefficient on appointee manager is larger and the coefficient on appointee percentage is smaller and marginally significant ($p<0.11$; $p<0.07$) in two-tailed tests. In models of background characteristics, however, the key coefficient estimates have the same sign but are smaller and lose significance. It is hard to tell how much of the weakening of the results comes from multicollinearity associated with the fifteen additional indicators.

Finally, I report estimates from a Tobit model in table 7.4, above, since the dependent variable—raw program purpose and design scores—is bounded at 100 and a number of programs received grades of 100 on the PART evaluation.

APPENDIX 7B
Model Estimation—FHCS Data

This appendix describes the specification and methods for the FHCS data analysis. I include controls for differences in management structure, agency size, and type of agency work. Since the key independent variable is whether the agency is run by an appointee or a careerist and we want direct comparisons, I include a control for whether or not the agency is run by a military official who is neither a career civil service employee nor a political appointee (0,1; 17 percent). This means that career civil service managers are the base category. I also include controls for the log of agency employment (mean 8.03, s.d. 1.41); the ratio of managers to employees (mean 0.14, s.d. 0.10); whether or not agencies are commissions (0,1; 3.5 percent); whether agencies are headed by appointees who serve for fixed terms (0,1; 8.5 percent); and whether or not the agency has its own personnel system (0,1; 26.7 percent).[42] I include controls for agency function—defense (0,1; 28.3 percent); regulation (0,1; 23.4 percent); and science/technology (0,1; 12.8 percent)—since these different functions may be easier or harder to manage and appointees are less likely to manage all three types of agency.[43] Finally, I include controls for whether the manager was serving in an acting capacity at the time of the survey (0,1; 8.3 percent), and an indicator for whether the survey was the 2002 survey (0,1; 44.7 percent).

Since the dependent variable is continuous and is more or less normally distributed, I estimate a series of OLS regressions. I adjust the standard errors for clustering on the agencies themselves since there are two observations for 162 of the agencies. I have also estimated models with each panel separately and with fixed effects for department and the results are similar.[44]

There are two difficulties in estimation. First, as with the PART data, there is some missing data. The missing data in the models stems from the lack of personnel data for some agencies. The OPM does not provide personnel data for some agencies, including the major subcomponents of either the Department of State or the Department of Energy. It does so for all other cabinet departments. While I have survey results from these agencies, I do not have data on the number of employees, managers, or appointees.[45] I estimate multiple models including or excluding the controls to show that the results are generally robust. Tables including simpler specifications are available upon request.

A second difficulty is that appointees may be chosen to run the most difficult agencies to manage. If this is the case, the estimated relationship between appointees and performance would be spurious since what is causing poor performance is not appointee management but the difficulty of managing the agency in the first place. There are several responses to this concern. First, one reason why we estimate models with controls is to try to account for the effects of differences in management environments on performance. Second, it is difficult to know whether careerists or appointees would be preferred in cases where programs are hard to manage. Third, I have examined the change in the appointee percentages from 2002 to 2004 to see if it is correlated with the change in employee evaluations during that same time period. If appointees were put in charge of the most difficult programs to run to improve their performance, increasing percentages of appointees should correlate positively with changes in employee evaluations. In all models, changes in appointee percentages were negatively correlated with changes in employee evaluations, suggesting that appointees are probably not added to improve poorly performing agencies. These models are not estimated precisely. While the coefficient on change in appointee percentage is significant at the .05 or .10 level (two-tailed) in four of the seven models, I could not reject the null of no improvement over a constant-only model in six of the seven models. These estimates are likewise available upon request.

Finally, a standard means of handling endogeneity is to estimate two-stage models where the endogenous variable is estimated directly. In this case it is difficult to find regressors that are correlated with appointee percentages and not performance, a requirement for identification. With that caveat, I use measures of the politics at the time the agency was created as instruments, including war (0,1), year of the president's term (1–4), presidential second term (0,1), and party change in the White House (0,1) as instruments and estimate the model with two-stage least squares. I could not reject the null that the two-stage least squares estimates were equal to the coefficients in the regressions in simpler models.[46] I therefore rely on the estimates in the text.

8

Learning the Lessons of Politicization

THE EVIDENCE from the Federal Emergency Management Agency (FEMA) (see chapter 6, above), Program Assessment Rating Tool (PART) scores (see the first part of chapter 7, above), and Federal Human Capital Surveys (FHCS) (see the second part of chapter 7, above) demonstrates that politicization hurts performance across the government, sometimes dramatically and to catastrophic effect. Why, then, do presidents add political appointments to departments and agencies when the consequences of doing so appear harmful? The solution to this puzzle is that presidents have to ensure bureaucratic responsiveness and generate support for their candidacy and programs through the distribution of patronage. They are willing to trade some competence in order to get agencies to do what they want them to do and to build political support.

This is a key irony of bureaucracy in a democratic government. Some insulation from political control is necessary to make the bureaucracy effective—to help it cultivate expertise, develop long-term perspective and planning effectiveness, and to provide the institutional memory that keeps the government running from election to election. What makes it effective makes it less subject to political control and less useful as a source of political power.

The study's explanation for the causes and consequences of politicization has implications for our overall understanding of American politics, activities referred to as "politicization" in other contexts, and policy debates surrounding the federal personnel system. This final chapter discusses these implications in light of what has been learned.

Politicization: What Have We Learned?

This study set out to address two important questions about the American political system. First, why do some agencies have many appointees and others few? And second, how do political appointments influence management? Common answers to these questions are worth reviewing in the light of the evidence brought forth thus far. The view that politicization is increasing over time is partly correct: the number of appointees is greater in 2006 than it was in 1960. The increase in appointed positions halted in 1980, however, and since that time the number of appointees has decreased slightly. There has been a noticeable increase in the number of Senate-confirmed (PAS) positions since 1980 but the increase has occurred primarily in unsalaried, part-time, and advisory positions or positions outside the cabinet.

The claim that Republican presidents politicize and Democratic presidents do not is incorrect. Democrats have increased the number and percentage of appointees as much as Republicans. While both Richard Nixon and George W. Bush increased the number of appointees, so did Kennedy, Johnson, and Carter. While there was a decline in appointees under Clinton, there was also a decline under Ford and Reagan. Republicans and Democrats do politicize differently, however, and tend to target different agencies. Republican presidents are most likely to increase the number of policy-relevant appointees in traditionally liberal agencies while Democrats are more likely to do the same in traditionally conservative agencies. Patronage, however, follows the opposite pattern with Republicans, for whom more patronage appointments are made in the traditionally conservative agencies, whereas for the Democrats, a larger number of patronage appointments are made in the traditionally liberal agencies.

The empirical evidence reveals no support for the view that presidents subscribing to the New Public Management politicize more than presidents that do not. While the management philosophies of Reagan, George H. W. Bush, Clinton, and George W. Bush were probably influenced by the New Public Management, the number of appointees declined both in numbers and as a percentage of federal employment during their combined tenures. Presidents of different ideologies do prefer different techniques for obtaining bureaucratic control, however. Liberals are more likely to build parallel processes or increase ministerial staff as a means of politicizing since these techniques avoid direct confrontation with government employees and their unions. Those adopting conservative ideologies are less concerned with antagonizing federal employees and unions and are more inclined to politicize through replacement and reductions-in-force (RIFs).

Rather than increasing steadily or in response to party or management ideology, politicization varies predictably across agencies and over time. Politicization is the result of both presidents' drive for political control of the bureaucracy and the regular demands of patronage. Increasing the number of appointees allows presidents to influence agency planning, personnel, and processes, including rulemaking and budgeting. Control of these management factors allows presidents to change public policy administratively. As chapter 2 demonstrated, the politicization of the Civil Service Commission (CSC) and Office of Personnel Management (OPM) by presidents Carter and Reagan allowed the presidents to change the emphasis of federal personnel policy away from merit system protection to executive management. Presidents must also find jobs in the administration for supporters. The proliferation in advisory positions, boards, and commissions outside the cabinet help satisfy some of this pent up demand for jobs. In other cases agencies such as FEMA, the Department of Commerce, and the Small Business Administration (SBA) are made heavy with appointed positions.

Members of Congress are often willing partners to politicization. In cases where their views coincide with those of the president, they tend to support more presidential influence in the bureaucracy. As one former member explained, the assessment of whether or not to support the president's creation of appointed positions revolved around whether or not to "empower him (the president) to do this policy change. . . . Am I trying to advance that kind of agenda or block that kind of agenda?"[1] If the president and the agency disagree about policy, the agency and that member of Congress are also likely to disagree. The ability of members of Congress to influence the selection of appointees through confirmation proceedings or other leverage with the president provides members a means of placing their favorites into administration jobs, thereby influencing policy themselves. Members of Congress regularly make influential appointment recommendations. Powerful members even occasionally hold up confirmations until presidents acquiesce to appointing congressional favorites to other posts. As for the president, policy and patronage considerations make appointees attractive to members of Congress. Indeed, when Congress had more influence over patronage, they were the major force resisting the expansion of the merit system.

Members of Congress who do not share the president's views about policy or partisanship are less sanguine about presidential appointees since presidents use them to change policy away from what these members want. Presidents do so at the expense of agency competence—a double blow. Presidents also use the positions for electoral gain to the detriment of the member's party. The ability of any faction in Congress to constrain the president's politicization efforts is limited by the composition of Congress. During periods of unified party control the number of appointees has increased significantly more than in periods of divided party control.

As the FEMA case illustrates, politicization harms agency competence. Appointees often do not have the background or qualifications of their careerist counterparts. Careerists are more likely to have prior agency experience and they stay for longer tenures. These background advantages provide careerists a better understanding of agency programs, budgets, and processes and make management and program-oversight easier. An overabundance of appointees also creates less visible impediments to performance. Penetration of appointees into agency management teams generates higher rates of executive turnover, difficulty recruiting and retaining career professionals, and reduces the incentives for career professionals to work hard and develop useful expertise. The combination of these factors means that there is a tradeoff with politicization—presidents get more control but at the expense of performance.

The tradeoff between achieving policy change and preserving bureaucratic competence drives politicization in three ways. First, politicization increases when presidents believe that the policy views or priorities of specific agencies differ from their own. This is seen most visibly in data that show that presidents politicize most after party changes in the White House and that Republican presidents target agencies widely perceived as liberal and Democratic presidents target agencies widely regarded as being conservative. Conversely, the penetration of appointees diminishes when presidents believe agencies share their views about policy. Second, some agencies are more or less prone to politicization than others based upon their ability to incorporate appointees without consequences for performance. Finally, the number of appointees increases when presidents and the majority in Congress see the world through the same partisan or ideological lens. Congress is less concerned about politicization and more willing to let presidents increase the number of appointees when the president will select appointees with policy views similar to those of the majority party in Congress.

Politicization and American Democracy

These empirical findings have implications for democratic theory, political efforts to control the bureaucracy, and our understanding of the modern presidency. Politicization choices reflect long-standing tensions in any democracy between empowering the state to be effective and controlling that same power. In the United States, this tension is complicated by a unique constitutional system and political history that have sought to weaken rather than enable the administrative state. The administrative state is the child not of the Constitution but of the politicians selected, constrained, and empowered under the Constitution's guidelines. When the U.S. Congress and the president make choices about politicization, they are choosing between less-expert and more-expert bureaus. They are also choosing between more-responsive and more-autonomous bureaus. Their choices result in an administrative state that, in one sense, is less efficient than it could be. It could be more expert, more professional, better managed, and more effective; however, it would also be more autonomous, less subject to democratic control, and more dangerous to liberty.

We might be tempted to argue that, in a different sense, the administrative state *is* efficient. It reflects a reasonable tradeoff between the benefits of democratic control and the benefits of expertise, capacity, and professionalism. This is partly right but it is too simple. Presidents persistently prefer more appointees than most perfectly informed voters would want and a significantly higher percentage than in other well-functioning developed nations. This is the case for a number of reasons. The first, and most obvious, reason is that presidential views about the number of appointees are influenced by their concerns for patronage. Voters that are not active in politics or candidates for patronage posts themselves are naturally less enthusiastic about such positions.

Second, each president starts with the last president's number of appointees as a baseline number rather than evaluating in a holistic manner the proper number and location of appointed positions. There are always more job-seekers than jobs available and the pace of transition and staffing makes impractical efforts to evaluate the wisdom of maintaining specific appointed positions. The default for new administrations is to accept the existing appointed positions as given and make incremental changes from that baseline. This means that presidents that actually need fewer appointees to control policy often maintain higher levels than they need to satisfy patronage demands. This is not to say that presidents do not depoliticize. They do in response to scandals, management concerns, or trust in career professionals, but they do so slowly and incrementally and they are more likely than voters to value the appointed position as a means of rewarding a supporter.

Third, presidents discount the long-term impact of politicization on agency performance more than most voters. The president's time horizon is defined most immediately by what is happening at the moment, but ultimately by the length of a presidential term. Presidents politicize as a solution to an existing problem and reap the political rewards immediately but do not bear the full cost of the action after they have left office. The hidden impact of politicization often does not become manifest until the second or third appointee fills a new position. When the office has lost the president's direct interest, presidential personnel will fill the position with a lower-tier appointee, suitable for the declining status or importance of the position. Executive turnover, vacancies, and difficulties in recruitment and retention of career professionals are the delayed hidden costs created by politicization.

Finally, political support or opposition to existing levels of politicization coincides with the support or opposition to the president. A significant portion of the public and Congress latently support the existing number of appointed positions because they provide a means for the president to control the executive branch. Efforts to reduce the number of appointees must overcome the opposition of the president and a significant portion of Congress. The Office of Special Counsel (OSC) and CIA cases nicely illustrated how views about politicization efforts varied depending upon ideology. Conservatives were more likely to support President George W. Bush's politicization efforts while liberals were more critical and worried about the influence of such actions on agency performance.

These cases illustrate not only how views about optimal levels of politicization vary depending upon ideology but also the importance of politicization for democratic theory. At the heart of democracy is the responsiveness of government to the people. An insular professional bureaucracy is unlikely to be responsive to voters as articulated through elections and elected representatives. An overly politicized bureaucracy, however, cannot be responsive because it is not effective. Such a management structure will not provide an environment in which necessary professionalism, institutional memory, and expertise can develop. It hinders long-term planning and makes program implementation difficult. Determining the causes and consequences of politicization helps us understand democratic government and can guide decisions about the appropriate depth and penetration of appointees.

Political Control of the Bureaucracy

Investigating politicization has illuminated an important strategy for bureaucratic control. Executive-branch agencies make policy, and the legitimacy of their decisions depends upon control by the people through their elected officials. They take the vague and sometimes conflicting mandates of Congress and the president and translate them into policy. In cases where laws or political directions are well understood, agencies simply implement law. In cases where the law is less clear, agencies interpret the law and apply it according to their understanding. They are told to determine what "safe" levels of a particular toxin are and take steps to regulate it. They are told to enforce civil rights law but must determine what the law means and how to allocate resources to such efforts given other mandates. In cases where agencies have been delegated authority to solve a more general problem, agencies prescribe law.

Political actors use a variety of tools, including administrative procedures, monitoring, and budgets, to rein in the bureaucracy because of its influence over policy. Personnel are an important component of any political control strategy. Agency executives, both career and appointed, determine the types of policies selected, whether these policies align with the interests of Congress and the president, and whether they satisfy agency stakeholders and clients. Up to this point, however, the strategy of politicization has been murky. This study has described the mechanics of politicization, explained when it occurs, and demonstrated how it both changes policy and hurts management performance.

Politicization and the Modern Presidency

The study's evidence also provides important insights into the modern presidency. Presidents are held accountable for the functioning of the entire government, and this book has sought to provide new insights into how presidents use appointments to accomplish their goals as both chief executive and party leader. It has revealed the tradeoff that presidents make between control and competence in the bureaucracy and why presidents from different parties politicize differently. Presidents are neither aggressively increasing the number of appointees across the board nor are they differentiated by partisanship in their willingness to employ this tool. Presidents of different parties do target different agencies for politicization since presidents naturally hold individual policy views.

Looking at politicization has refocused attention on how much the modern personnel process is driven by concerns for patronage. Presidents use this important resource to help them overcome limitations in other, more formal sources of power. The distribution of patronage provides rewards for those who have demonstrated support for the president and in this way holds the president's fragile coalition together. One personnel official described his job in the following way: "I saw that job [PPO director] as a surrogate for the president, absorbing pressures from all constituencies. . . . My job was basically political. . . . Balance the conflicting interests on the position, the interest groups, the professional groups, competence, adherence to administration policy."[2] The thousands of jobs available for distribution provide a means for presidents to hold supporters in line, signal policy commitments, and accomplish their policy goals. A Nixon aide explained, "Symbolic appointments of people will do almost more to move groups to you than any issue will. If you name their leader to a key post, suddenly you have access to a whole group that you didn't have before—or you can loosen a group's ties to the opposition."[3] The present study of politicization has helped refocus

attention on the fact that presidential sources of power are limited and
that presidents are political actors that use political means such as patronage to accomplish policy goals.

Politicization in a Broader Context

I initially defined "politicization" as the increase in the number and penetration of political appointees. In other contexts, however, scholars have
used the term to describe related practices associated with political intervention in administration, including that of recruiting appointees only
on the basis of party loyalty, involving civil servants in political fights, and
making appointment and promotion decisions in the civil service on the
basis of political attitudes. Indeed, these are just the type of actions that
are at the center of the 2006–2007 scandals in the Department of Justice
(DOJ). Partisan rather than performance considerations led to the removal of nine U.S. Attorneys. The White House targeted U.S. Attorneys
who were not loyal to the president personally or ideologically and replaced them with persons with stronger political or partisan connections,
such as Tim Griffin, a former aide to presidential adviser, Karl Rove, who
was made U.S. Attorney in Arkansas.[4] DOJ officials also selected *career*
attorneys on the basis of their political views in violation of merit system
principles.[5] One potential criticism of a focus solely on the number of
appointees is that it obscures more subtle forms of political manipulation.

While the focus on appointees is important in its own right, the findings have broader relevance to other forms of political intervention. For
example, data from the FHCS reveal a strong correlation between the
number of appointees in the management team and other indicators
of "politicizing-type" activity.[6] There is a correlation between appointee
leadership and whether federal employees report that:

- Arbitrary action, personal favoritism, and coercion for partisan political
  purposes are tolerated.
- Prohibited personnel practices are tolerated.
- They fear reprisal for disclosing a suspected violation of a law, rule, or
  regulation.

This correlation between the number of appointees and employee perceptions of politicizing-type activities suggests that the number of appointees is symptomatic of larger patterns of behavior. The factors that
lead to increases in the number of appointees probably lead to increases
in other forms of political intervention into administration. For example,
policy disagreement between the president and the agency should increase the likelihood that appointees will be selected on the basis of

ideology, that civil servants will be promoted on the basis of policy views, that political intervention will intrude into neutral policy analysis or adjudication, and that temporary Senior Executive Service (SES) positions, strategic vacancies, or interns will be utilized as backdoor appointees. This was certainly the case in DOJ. Between 2000 and 2004 the number of appointees increased by 59 positions. The increased penetration of appointees into DOJ was symptomatic of larger attempts to make DOJ's policy views more conservative and satisfy demands for Republican patronage. Indeed, the increase in appointees was probably a precursor to these other forms of politicizing-type activity.

What about implications for the political-career balance in other contexts? Political scientists have described an increase in the number of political appointees in top bureaucratic posts in a number of different countries, including Australia, Britain, Finland, France, Germany, Japan, and Spain, since the 1970s.[7] For example, in Australia there has been an increase in political ministerial staff, more involvement by the Prime Minister in the selection of higher-level civil servants, and shortened tenure for department heads. One of the first acts of the government of John Howard in 1996 was to replace 6 of the 20 department heads, some with persons brought in from outside the civil service (although most had experience in the departments in the past).[8] In Britain Margaret Thatcher's ascension heralded an increasing role for the Prime Minister in the selection of higher-level civil servants. The British politicization debate was reinvigorated by New Labour's appointment of 53 political advisors, compared to 38 under the previous government, and Prime Minister Tony Blair's attempt to appoint his Chief of Staff, Jonathan Powell, as his principal private secretary (normally a civil service position).[9] In Germany there has been an increase in external recruitment for top administrative posts, politically induced temporary retirements, and lateral reshuffling of higher-level civil servants, particularly after party turnover.[10]

Each of these countries has a different political history and government structure than does the United States, making generalizations perilous. Where modern governments are similar, however, these findings are at least suggestive. For example, legislatures in many countries—not just the United States—have delegated increasing amounts of policymaking authority to bureaucracies as the work of government has grown in volume, scope, and complexity. Governments must exercise control over these newly empowered bureaucracies and one means of securing additional control is through politicization.

A cause of politicization that likely translates cross-nationally is policy disagreement between the governing party and the permanent bureaucracy. When this disagreement swells, pressures to rein in the bureaucracy through politicization increase. This is one reason why politicization often accompanies party turnover. New governments seeking policy change find the permanent bureaucracy a protector of the status quo and try to get control of the bureaucracy by politicizing it. Those ministries most directly influenced are those most important to the incoming government and those whose competence is least sensitive to politicization.

It is unclear whether politicization is bad for performance in these different contexts but the evidence thus far suggests that it is. On the one hand, adding appointee influence could conceivably have a leavening influence on performance in contexts where civil servants are risk-averse, parochial, and unresponsive. As one personnel official told me, "No one [in the career civil service] ever got punished for not taking risks."[11] In addition, the bad effects of politicization should be minimized since starker lines are drawn between civil service and political appointees and appointees often have more previous experience as shadow ministers.

On the other hand, the effects of politicization on the career trajectories, incentives, and the influence of career civil servants are generic. When appointees are brought in from outside the civil service and they replace careerists or are layered on top of them, natural problems arise from executive turnover, difficulties recruiting and retaining career professionals, and reduced morale and incentive to develop expertise. The existing evidence suggests that politicization damages the ability of governments to deliver important goods and services and delegitimizes the state in the eyes of citizens.[12] It shows that developing countries with meritocratic recruitment have higher rates of economic growth and more competent bureaucracies.[13] Of course, it is important to remember that politicization can still be desirable even if it harms the bureaucracy. Sometimes bureaucracies need to change course, and politicization, with all of its attendant effects, is the only way to do it.

Policy Implications

Since the penetration of appointees into the bureaucracy is a natural response to the incentives and pressures of political actors, reform is no guarantee that these pressures will be eliminated. As one former personnel official told me, "Look, people want people they trust. If you don't let them have them, they will pervert the merit system and this is worse than just letting them have the appointees."[14] Still, the study's findings have undeniable implications for federal personnel policy, including proposals to cut the number of appointees, add qualifications to important appointed positions, and delegate more authority to agencies to create their own personnel systems.

Reduce Appointees

The most obvious solution to politicization's adverse effects on agency performance is to cut the number of appointees. Efforts to reduce the number of appointees should be done thoughtfully and with a clear recognition of the adverse consequences of doing so. Several considerations should be taken into account. First, political appointees are an absolutely essential part of democratic government. Political appointees ensure the democratic character of public policy decisions made by bureaucracies. They also provide electoral accountability for bureaucratic decisions. They help translate the wishes of elected officials into clear program guidance and can correct the biases of careerist professionals by making them less conservative and pushing them to see the bigger picture.

Second, the growth in political appointments has occurred unevenly across the executive branch. Some appointed positions are always important and deserve the time and care presidents and Congress put into selecting and vetting nominees. These positions tend to attract the first tier of presidential appointees. The Presidential Personnel Office (PPO) spends a lot of time searching for appropriate candidates for these positions, often engaging the efforts of professional recruiters in the process. These are not the types of positions that have been proliferating. Rather, a significant portion of the increase in PAS positions has occurred outside the cabinet, often in advisory, part-time, or minor-agency positions. The growth inside the cabinet in the number of deputy, under-, and assistant secretaries has been modest: about 65 positions. This increase, however, partly stems from the creation of new agencies, such as the Department of Veterans Affairs (VA) and the Department of Homeland Security (DHS).

While this study has often focused on PAS positions, there are also SES and Schedule C positions to consider.[15] Since these last two types of appointees do not require Senate confirmation, they attract less attention. Proposals for cutting the number of appointees explicitly or implicitly target different types of appointees. Some persons suggest cutting the number of PAS positions and others recommend cutting lower-tier SES or Schedule C appointees. Another possibility is across-the-board cuts without reference to type. Cutting different types of appointees, however, will have different effects on the political system and performance. For example, cuts in the number of Schedule C appointees will not ease the burden of filling and confirming the 1,000 + PAS positions.

Third, the large number of appointed positions provides other democratic political benefits. The promise of a job in a new administration creates incentives for citizens to participate in campaigns. The possibility of going to Washington to work for a new administration induces college students, business people, and some retirees to take one to two years off from their normal life to become involved in the political process. Those who do are more likely to stay mobilized throughout their lives.[16] The promise of appointed positions also provides a credible means by which presidents can express their commitment to interest groups that their views will be represented in the administration, and thereby secure the groups' support, manpower, and resources. The promise of a job in the new administration provides an important means for presidential aspirants to conduct campaigns.

Appointed positions also provide presidents a political bargaining tool that helps them govern once in office. Legislating and governing is difficult in the American separation-of-powers system. In addition to the checks and balances built into the Constitution, Senate filibuster rules mean that supermajorities are required to enact most legislation. Coalitions must be formed and compromises reached among legislators divided by party, caucus, committee, and diverse constituencies. The president's formal powers for overcoming these barriers are meager. Presidents have to rely on informal powers of persuasion, moral leadership, and bargaining. Historically, appointed positions have been an important bargaining resource presidents have employed to overcome resistance, forge coalitions, and secure party discipline. Efforts to cut the number of appointed positions will reduce the ability of presidential candidates to generate resources during the campaign and bargain once in office.

Given these considerations and the evidence provided in the present study, efforts to reduce the number of appointees should be targeted toward different levels and types of appointees. First, cuts should initially target appointed positions at the bureau or program level. Bureaus, offices, divisions, and programs run by careerists get systematically higher evaluations by the administration and federal employees than their appointee-run counterparts. This does not imply that all appointed bureau-chief positions should be converted to careerist positions or that all appointees are worse managers. Rather, the appointment authority for positions at this level should be given a hard look across the government.

Reducing appointees at the bureau level, however, will do little to remedy the increase in subcabinet appointments, such as deputy, under-, and assistant secretaries, layered on top of the career service in the past forty years. These positions have been created for a variety of reasons including politicization, agency merger without a reduction in appointed positions, and growth in programmatic responsibilities. A second goal of reductions in appointees should be to re-evaluate these positions across the cabinet departments and find a means of reducing their number. One potential remedy is to adopt a cap on the number and type of PAS appointees in each department and allow presidents flexibility in determining which executive positions should be filled by candidates requiring the approval of the Senate. Other positions can be filled by members of the SES. For example, the legislation creating the DHS provides for 12 assistant secretary positions with no specified functions in addition to a number of others where the functions are specified.[17] While this is a statutory novelty, it provides a means of preserving executive flexibility, encourages presidents to identify and utilize careerists, and achieves the goal of reducing the number of appointees.

Third, cuts should be considered in the number of Schedule C appointees. Many of the functions carried out by Schedule C appointees are handled by career professionals in other agencies. The empirical evidence indicates that Schedule C appointees are more likely to go into agencies with policy views similar to those of the sitting president, confirming that many Schedule C appointees are placed primarily for patronage reasons. Schedule C appointees can be reduced with the least influence on the president's ability to control the bureaucracy.

Cuts could also be made where the largest increases have occurred: namely, in part-time, commission, and advisory posts. Many of the new positions created as part-time or advisory positions outside the cabinet are used by presidential personnel to reward wealthy donors or persons connected to the campaign not fit or unwilling to take other positions. Cutting these positions will usefully reduce the number of PAS positions but will not improve performance in agencies like FEMA, OPM, or the Department of Justice. The principal benefit of cutting such posts is that doing so will allow new administrations to more efficiently allocate their time to vetting the positions that remain. On the other hand, if a significant portion of these posts exist for the purpose of fulfilling patronage obligations, it is arguably better to satisfy patronage demands this way rather than by placing supporters in jobs with more policy influence.

Efforts to cut appointees should target those agencies where the cuts will do the most to improve performance. Since some agencies can bear more appointees than others without harm to competence, it makes sense to cut appointees first in agencies where doing so will have the largest marginal effect. Specifically, cuts should be considered in agencies where career professionals in the agency have good outside economic options, where agency tasks are complex but politicization is high, and in agencies with important public safety responsibilities.

Appointee reductions are likely to significantly improve performance in agencies where career professionals have viable outside economic options, either because their expertise is in demand in the private sector or because they are eligible for retirement. Reducing the number of appointees will increase the number of top jobs in pay and responsibility available to career professionals. Increasing access to top jobs makes it more likely that careerists will stay, invest in expertise, and work productively. It will also make it easier for these agencies to recruit bright young people to work and build careers in the agency. One way to compensate for high private-sector wages is to provide meaningful work, policy influence, and a professional work environment. Federal personnel data can illuminate which agencies have the highest percentages of the workforce eligible for retirement and exit surveys of federal employees can provide useful information about which agencies and occupations are experiencing the largest number of defections to the private sector.

Appointee reductions should also improve performance in agencies where the number of appointees is out of balance with the complex nature of agency work. Agencies that perform difficult tasks like rocket science or complex statistical models will be more sensitive to changes in levels of politicization since some jobs cannot be done or managed equally well by people from the outside the agency. Reducing appointees in such agencies is likely to significantly improve performance. Two examples of agencies that should be evaluated in this regard are NASA and the National Oceanic and Atmospheric Administration (NOAA). The work of NASA has only become more complex over time, yet the number of appointees has quadrupled, from 4 to 16, between 1960 and 2004. It was one of these appointees who resigned in 2006 after a controversy erupted over his attempts to limit the access of journalists to one of NASA's climate scientists.[18] NOAA is a federal agency primarily concerned with the oceans and earth's atmosphere. It includes the National Weather Service (NWS) and performs important scientific research but has close to 20 appointees, significantly more than other comparable agencies.

Appointee reductions should also be considered in agencies critical to public safety. Some agencies that are instrumental for public safety, including the FBI and the Secret Service, already have few appointees. Others are relatively politicized. As with FEMA, the politics of agency design can leave these agencies with significantly more appointees than their size or functions merit. Invariably, agencies that start with lots of appointees get loaded down with lower-tier appointees, particularly when the agency's policy area is off the president's agenda. Even if all of the appointees are excellent managers, agencies with appointee-laden management structures suffer from harmful executive turnover, difficulties recruiting and retaining good career professionals, and poor long-term planning.

Given the high costs of failure, relatively politicized agencies with responsibility for public safety such as FEMA, DHS, and the Department of Defense should be considered for reductions. As chapter 6 demonstrated, FEMA operated much more effectively when the number of appointees was cut. In DHS the large number of appointees (approximately 200) resulted from the fact that agencies merged into the new department kept their appointees. At least one department critic has argued that it is the politicized management structure of DHS that is slowing progress toward remedying significant vulnerabilities in port, rail, and chemical plant security.[19] In the Department of Defense, the number of appointees also seems to be out of balance with agency tasks. Even though the Department of Defense has reduced in size by hundreds of thousands of employees since the end of the Cold War, the number of appointees has stayed roughly the same.

Cuts in appointees will come at a cost. Some responsiveness to the president and Congress will be lost. The incentives to work for and support presidential candidates will decline and presidents will have less leverage in the political system. These costs, however, will be at least partly offset by improvements in performance. The quality of appointees will improve with more time and attention in selection. Careerist performance will improve since there will be less executive turnover, higher morale, and greater incentives to join and stay in the service of a federal agency. In the end, presidents may find the bureaucracy more responsive since it will be more competent.

Add Qualifications to Appointee Positions

Short of reducing the number of appointees, some political actors have proposed adding explicit qualifications to key executive-branch jobs. For example, in the aftermath of Hurricane Katrina, Congress mandated in a 2006 homeland security spending bill that the FEMA director have demonstrated general management and emergency management experience. Similarly, Reps. Nancy Pelosi (D-CA) and Henry Waxman (D-CA) introduced the "Anti-Cronyism and Public Safety Act," which mandates that appointees with public safety responsibilities have minimum qualifications for their posts. The National Academy of Sciences was considering recommending similar policies for appointees to head the Food and Drug Administration (FDA). The empirical evidence in the last chapter demonstrates that managers with longer tenures and previous experience get systematically higher evaluations. If proposals to add qualifications to appointed positions make appointees look more like careerist managers, the proposals could help.

The difficulty with adding qualifications to appointed positions, however, is that they are hard to legislate effectively. Either the qualifications are so general as to not be binding or the strictures are too binding and worsen the recruitment problem. The former problem is more common than the latter. For example, the much-maligned former FEMA director

Michael Brown *would* have been qualified for the FEMA job according to the relatively stringent requirements envisioned by either the 2006 homeland security spending bill or the Pelosi-Waxman bill.

The 2006 spending bill mandates that the FEMA director have "five years of management experience and demonstrated emergency management skills."[20] Since Brown had management experience within FEMA, as chairman of the board of the Oklahoma Municipal Power Authority, and in his role in the International Arabian Horse Association, he probably would have satisfied the management requirements of the 2006 spending bill. His experience in FEMA as general counsel and deputy director would have been sufficient evidence to demonstrate emergency management skills.

The Pelosi-Waxman bill recommended that the head of FEMA and other public safety positions have "proven credentials relevant to the position; a superior record of achievement in one or more areas relevant to the position; and training and expertise in one or more areas relevant to the position."[21] At the time Brown assumed his position as the head of FEMA, he had been the agency's general counsel and deputy director. The agency had responded well to the 9/11 terrorist attacks and the 2004 Florida hurricanes. His previous experience within FEMA provided credentials and a record of achievement.

Indeed, any FEMA manager with significant agency experience could satisfy these requirements, particularly in the eyes of an acquiescent or sympathetic committee. If an unfriendly committee was looking for a way to reject Brown's nomination, they might have been able to use the proposed language to do so, but then again, an unfriendly committee would not need this language to reject a nominee.

Attaching background requirements to top executive positions also does not deal with the overall politicization in an agency's management team. Wallace Stickney was appointed to head FEMA in the George H. W. Bush administration after 31 subordinate appointed slots had already been filled. Attaching qualifications to the top job does not guarantee that the agency head will have influence over the number and qualifications of subordinate appointees.

The case of FEMA illustrates the other danger with legislating qualifications for nominees. If not written carefully, they could become too stringent and exacerbate recruitment problems. White House personnel officials uniformly noted that jobs requiring scientific or technical backgrounds were the hardest to fill because finding persons with these backgrounds who met other criteria was very difficult. By legislating specific backgrounds, Congress is shrinking the pool of available appointees. This makes the recruitment search more difficult and can lengthen the amount of time it takes to fill these positions. For example, in the aftermath of Hurricane Katrina, it took seven months to fill the vacancy at FEMA created by Michael Brown's departure. Seven prospective appointees turned down the job, delaying efforts to reform and revitalize the agency.[22] Making the task of filling this job more onerous could create additional problems.

Fragmentation of Federal Personnel System

The influence of efforts to cut political appointees or attach qualifications to appointed jobs must be evaluated in the context of ongoing dramatic changes in the federal personnel system. Whereas close to 90 percent of federal employees were under one traditional civil service system in the middle of the twentieth century, at present less than 50 percent are included in the traditional merit system. Agencies have asked for, and received, permission to create agency-specific personnel systems better adapted to the agencies' specific needs. During the George W. Bush administration, Congress granted DHS and the Department of Defense this authority. The effect of these changes is to give managers increased flexibility in hiring, pay, and personnel actions, including promotion, demotion, transfers, and firing. Furthermore, private contractors have played a steadily increasing role in what traditionally had been government work. The effect of these changes is to blur the line between appointees and careerists and fundamentally transform the federal personnel system.

The ongoing transformation has the potential to increase executive control and improve the ability of managers to secure the job-relevant skills necessary to accomplish their agency's mission. Similarly, there are a number of federal jobs that can be performed effectively by the private sector. While true, this ongoing transformation from a one-size-fits-all personnel system to a fragmented personnel system resembling an at-will system raises a number of concerns. First, the proliferation of agency-specific personnel systems may enhance control at the agency level but it will hinder centralized control. Increasing the number of different personnel systems means that very few people, if any, understand how they all work and relate to each other. Government-wide initiatives are hard to implement across these different systems. Monitoring compliance with merit system principles is more difficult since specific knowledge of the different systems is required to monitor them effectively. Indeed, in the aftermath of the Civil Service Reform Act of 1978, the delegation of examining authority to executive-branch agencies was very difficult for OPM to monitor because of differences across agencies. Historically, increased fragmentation of personnel responsibilities has created significant monitoring problems.[23]

Second, the move toward flexibility in the federal personnel system means that civil servants will have fewer incentives to invest in training, experience, and site-specific expertise. The original motivation for the creation of the merit system was to create a workforce of competent professionals with expertise to carry out the mandates of elected officials. Public-sector work requires site-specific knowledge, long-range planning, institutional memory, and stability. If the civil service increasingly resembles an at-will workforce like the corps of political appointees, this will have predictable consequences for performance.

Conclusion

The politicization of the bureaucracy is not an issue that attracts a lot of attention. Perhaps it is because, as Jimmy Carter said, "This stuff is boring." To most of the voting public, details about how the executive branch works and is staffed are obscure. Information about the number of appointees in various agencies is hard to come by and frequently difficult to connect to performance. Personnel issues are unlikely to influence elections. Congress rarely mobilizes behind personnel reform in the absence of some focusing event. Historically, politicization has only become salient after large-scale public studies, well-publicized hearings, or crises make a clear connection between staffing patterns and bureaucratic performance. The two studies produced by the National Commission on the Public Service and the hearings in the aftermath of Hurricane Katrina once again have made charges of politicization or cronyism politically salient and provided opportunities for Congress to systematically reconsider the number of appointees in government agencies.

These issues should be researched, understood, and addressed. They are too important to be subject to fate or left as a byproduct of other political decisions—as FEMA's response to Hurricane Katrina, and its terrible toll in human suffering, should continue to remind us.

Notes

Chapter One
Politicization in Theory and Practice

1. U.S. Senate 2006, 2.

2. For a sampling, see, for example, U.S. Senate 2006; Adams, Rebecca, "FEMA Failure a Perfect Storm of Bureaucracy," *CQ Weekly*, September 12, 2005, 2378; Cooper and Block 2006.

3. Adams, "FEMA Failure a Perfect Storm of Bureaucracy"; U.S. Senate 2006, 14–1.

4. Hsu, Spencer S., "Leaders Lacking Disaster Experience," *Washington Post*, September 9, 2005, A1; James, Frank, and Andrew Martin, "Ex-officials say weakened FEMA botched response," *Chicago Tribune*, September 3, 2005 (online edition); U.S. Senate 2006; U.S. Government Accountability Office 2006; Anrig 2007; Roberts 2006.

5. See, for example, Dunn 1997, Heclo 1975, Rose 1987, Suleiman 2003. Krister Stahlberg (1987, 378) notes that "politicization may be portrayed in terms of extent, how many positions are filled politically and how deep in the administrative hierarchy does politicization extend its influence, and—in terms of the intensity of politicization—how blatant is the patronage, the disregard for normal recruitment procedures."

6. National Commission on the Public Service 1989.

7. For textbook recitation of this belief, see Fesler and Kettl 2005, 214; Stillman 2000, 184. For examples of newspaper accounts, see Causey, Mike, "Agencies Adding More Political Jobs," *Washington Post*, October 24, 1973, C23; Kilborn, Peter T, "Hail to the Senior General Deputy Assistant Chief," *New York Times*, April 26, 1984, B10. For a more skeptical view of whether appointees are increasing, see Maranto 1998a, 1998b. See also Ingraham et al. 1995, who show a leveling off in the number of appointees at the end of the Reagan administration.

8. Light 1995. Light's particular focus is "thickening" in government, which he defines as an increase in the number of management positions both vertically (layers) and horizontally in the executive branch. This is something different from politicization, since management positions are filled primarily by civil servants. Thickening can have the effect of depoliticizing or politicizing depending on the career-appointee makeup of the new positions added. Light notes an increase in thickening and names an increase in the number of appointed positions as one cause among many. It is unclear from Light's study, however, whether the growth in appointees outstrips the growth in federal employment and agency programmatic responsibilities.

9. Aberbach and Rockman 2000 contest the notion that there is a quiet crisis in federal administration. While they find a slight decline in morale in their survey of top federal officials from 1970 to 1991–92, the overall level of job satis-

faction is quite high. They also find that top federal officials in the career service are better educated than ever before and have significant previous experience in government.

10. They document that President Kennedy had 286 positions at the rank of secretary, deputy secretary, undersecretary, assistant secretary, or administrator. At the end of the Clinton administration there were 914 such positions.

11. Moe 1985. For a related argument about how all presidents have an administrative strategy for hierarchical control, see Ingraham et al. 1995.

12. Nathan 1975, 1983. See also Anrig 2007; Durant 1992; Heclo 1975, 1977; Goldenberg 1984; Newland 1983; Rosen 1983.

13. Suleiman 2003, 43–47.

14. See, for example, Cohen 1998; Dunn 1997; Heclo 1975, 1977; Kaufman 1965; National Commission on the Public Service 1989, 2003; Suleiman 2003. See, however, Maranto 1998a, 1998b, 2001, 2005; Moe 1985; and Lynch, Edward J., "No, We Don't Have Too Many Political Appointees," *Government Executive*, April 1991, 54–55. A number of works discuss how appointees bring energy and responsiveness to government and how and whether appointees and careerists can work productively together. See, for example, Bok 2003; Dunn 1997; Golden 2000; Krause, Lewis, and Douglas 2006.

15. For the examination of short appointee tenures and their impacts, see Boylan 2004; Brauer 1987; Chang et al. 2000, 2003; Heclo 1977; Mackenzie 1987; Mann 1965; National Commission on the Public Service 1989; Stanley, Mann, and Doig 1967.

16. Heclo 1977.

17. Suleiman 2003.

18. Weber notes, "The 'political master' finds himself in the position of 'dilettante' who stands opposite the 'expert,' facing the trained official who stands within the management of administration. . . . Every bureaucracy seeks to increase the superiority of the professionally informed by keeping their knowledge and intentions secret" (1946a, 232–33).

19. For examples, see Carpenter 2001; Carpenter and Whittington 2003; Kaufman 1976; Krause 1999; Moe 2004.

20. By science of administration, Wilson meant expertise in the organization and methods of government offices. See Wilson 1887; de Tocqueville, Alexis, *Democracy in America*, ed. J. P. Mayer and Max Lerner (New York: Harper and Row, 1966 [1835]), 191–92; Weber 1946b.

21. Weber 1946b, 95.

22. Wilson 1887, 210.

23. Long 1949, 1954; Mosher 1968. See Epstein and O'Halloran 1999 and Huber and Shipan 2002 on delegation generally.

24. Congress delegated authority to the president in 1801 to issue rules relating to trade with Native American tribes. Later Congress granted to the Treasury Secretary the power to regulate the importation of goods into the United States. The actual language stated that the secretary would "establish regulations suitable and necessary for carrying this law into effect; which regulations shall be binding." There is discretion inherent in almost all directions given to adminis-

trative actors, and increasing amounts of policy authority are delegated to the bureaucracy. See Kerwin 1990, 7.

25. Mosher 1968, 1.

26. See, for example, Arnold 1979; Epstein and O'Halloran 1999; Huber and Shipan 2002; McCubbins, Noll, and Weingast 1987, 1989; McCubbins and Schwartz 1984. See also Balla 1998; Carpenter 2001; Howell 2003; Howell and Lewis 2002; Lewis 2003; Moe 1989; and Moe and Wilson 1994 for more skeptical views about the extent to which Congress can control administrative outcomes.

27. Canes-Wrone 2006; Howell 2003; Mayer 2001.

28. Arnold 1998; Benze 1985; Carpenter and Lewis 2004; Lewis 2002; Mayer 2001.

29. For work on how presidential appointees can influence agency policy, see Moe 1982, 1985; Randall 1979; Stewart and Cromartie 1982; Wood 1990; Wood and Anderson 1993; Wood and Waterman 1991, 1994. For works that explain how presidents use increases or decreases in appointments to influence the bureaucracy, see Durant 1992; Heclo 1977; Moe 1985; Nathan 1975, 1983. For work that describes the politics of civil service, see Carpenter 2001; Gailmard and Patty 2007; Libecap and Johnson 1994; Skowronek 1982.

30. Moe 1982, 1985; Randall 1979; Stewart and Cromartie 1982; Wood 1990; Wood and Anderson 1993; Wood and Waterman 1991, 1994. The exception to this general statement is the number of excellent works on presidential personnel operations and transitions that describe patronage pressures. See in this regard Burke 2000, 2003; Henry 1960; Patterson and Pfiffner 2001, 2003; Pfiffner 1996; Weko 1995.

31. For the classic treatment of this argument, see Neustadt 1990 [1960].

32. Henry 1958, 21, notes that the focus in appointments had shifted from a debate about merit versus spoils in 1933 to a debate about control. The Bureau of the Budget had an active and capable management division working on government organization and advising the president how to manage effectively the dramatically expanded executive branch. Congress passed the Legislative Reorganization Act in 1946, mandating that House and Senate committees exercise "continuous watchfulness" over agencies in their purview.

33. This is reflected in the granting of reorganization authority to President Franklin D. Roosevelt first in 1939 and also in the creation of three commissions on administrative management: the Brownlow Committee in 1937, the first Hoover Commission in 1947, and the second Hoover Commission in 1955. See Arnold 1998 for a good review of these commissions and comprehensive reorganization planning in general.

34. Department of Education numbers come from U.S. Senate 2004, U.S. House 2000. The politicization of the Department of Education received the most scrutiny in the Clinton administration. See Pasternak, Judy, "White House Appoints Loyalists to Education Department Posts," *Los Angeles Times*, October 3, 1999, B10; and Jackson, Robert L., "Education Secretary Vows to Rid Agency of 'Mismanagement, Fraud,' " *Los Angeles Times*, April 21, 2001, A15. For details on the CIA, see Pincus, Walter, and Dana Priest, "Goss Brings 4 Staffers From Hill to CIA," *Washington Post*, October 1, 2004, A4; Priest, Dana, and Walter Pincus, "Deputy Chief Resigns from CIA," *Washington Post*, November 13, 2004, A1;

Priest, Dana, "Shake Up at CIA Headquarters Continues," *Washington Post*, November 15, 2004 (online edition); and Pincus, Walter, "Changing of the Guard at the CIA," *Washington Post*, January 6, 2005, A3. For details on the Office of Special Counsel, see Lee, Christopher, "Head of Worker Protection Office is Accused of Retaliatory Transfers," *Washington Post*, January 11, 2005, A13; Lee, Christopher, "Dispute and Whistleblower Office," *Washington Post*, February 24, 2005, A19; Barr, Stephen, "Agency's Reorganization Results in Accusations, Employees Leaving," *Washington Post*, March 18, 2005, B2.

Chapter Two
The Nature and History of the Modern Personnel System

1. Kluttz, Jerry, "The Federal Diary: Whims of Politics Govern Conservation, Gabrielson Charges," *Washington Post*, December 3, 1953, 25.
2. For details of the "Jobs for Republicans," or "Willis," directive, see Kluttz, Jerry, "White House Seeks Jobs for GOP Favorites," *Washington Post*, October 27, 1954, 1, and "Ike Defends GOP Plans for Job Hunt," *Washington Post*, October 28, 1954, 1.
3. Van Riper 1958, 12–16.
4. White 1954, 347.
5. While selection for office during this period is properly characterized as stemming largely from concerns for fitness, the earliest presidents also made appointments influenced by other factors, as well. These included veteran status, regional demands in the distribution of offices, jobs given to honor public persons, positions allocated to friends or the worthy elderly, and appointments made in exchange for political support. See Kaufman 1965.
6. As quoted in White, 1954, 318.
7. The practice of rotation after intraparty transfer of the presidency actually started with Millard Fillmore, who replaced Taylor Democrats with Fillmore Democrats. See Kaufman 1965.
8. White 1958, 31.
9. Kaufman 1965, 30.
10. White 1954, 362.
11. Wilson 1887.
12. Skowronek 1982.
13. There had been sporadic attempts in specific departments to employ merit requirements before the 1883 enactment of civil service legislation. These experiments were usually short-lived and hardly impinged on patronage practices. For example, in 1853 Congress required that applicants for clerical offices in Washington pass exams establishing their merit. The implementation of the law was irregular, given that the responsibility for creating and administering the exams was left up to the departments. In addition to these "pass exams," a number of departments at different times instituted examination systems of their own. There were tests for entrance to the military surgeons as early as 1814, and the Treasury Department had exams for accounting positions before 1853. See Van Riper 1958, 68–71.

14. As late as the 1870s one member of Congress observed, "During the last twenty-five years, it has been understood, by the Congress and the people, that offices are to be obtained by the aid of senators and representatives, who thus become the dispensers, sometimes the brokers of patronage. . . . [The Tenure of Office Act] has virtually resulted in the usurpation by the senate [*sic*], of a large share of the appointing power [that] has resulted in seriously crippling the just powers of the executive, and has placed in the hands of senators and representatives a power most corrupting and dangerous" (Garfield, James A., "A Century of Congress," *Atlantic Monthly* 40 [237]: 61). The act was repealed in 1887 during the Grover Cleveland administration.

15. For a good discussion of the politics surrounding the Grant Civil Service Commission, see Skowronek 1982, 56–59.

16. During its short existence, the commission designed rules governing appointments to the civil service, established examining boards, and introduced competitive examinations in a limited way in the Washington departments, the New York customhouse, and the New York post office.

17. The president's own lukewarm support for civil service reform was demonstrated by his appointment patterns after the 1872 elections. The commission's first chairman, George William Curtis, resigned when Grant appointed prominent patronage supporters to important spoils positions, including the surveyor of customs for the Port of New York.

18. The historical account of Hayes, Garfield, and Arthur is drawn more or less directly from Kaufman 1965, Van Riper 1958, and U.S. Office of Personnel Management 2003a. For a good discussion of the differing explanations for the passage of the Pendleton Act, see Theriault 2003. For fine histories of the national federal bureaucracy and development of civil service, see also Carpenter 2005, Johnson and Libecap 1994, Nelson 1982, Raadschelders and Lee 2005.

19. President Grant's Interior Secretary, Jacob Cox, had tried to implement a competitive examination-based merit system in the Patent Office, Census Bureau, and Indian Office, but he resigned under pressure before the year was out; see Kaufman 1965.

20. See Skowronek 1982; White 1958.

21. Van Riper 1958, 105.

22. Van Riper notes that "the personnel problems of the federal service were to be solved at this time primarily by controlling the entrance into the public service. If the 'front door' could be regulated, the 'back door' would take care of itself. Little thought was yet given by the central personnel agency—or anyone else—to the government employee after he once became a member of the civil establishment" (ibid., 147). There was no agency enforcing violations of "back door" removals, and while the commission did police political removals, it had little formal power to act. In 1912 Congress codified the original McKinley order of July 27, 1897, restricting removals (37 stat 555).

23. The Pendleton Act included provisions barring political assessments on office holders, and an attorney general's opinion had prohibited direct personal approaches for contributions but allowed requests for donations by mail; see Van Riper 1958, 186. Enforcement of these prohibitions on political activity was difficult and irregular.

24. 22 stat 403, section 7. Of course, Congress also retained the right to include or exclude jobs in the merit system by legislation.

25. Some of the expansion of the merit system happened automatically through the growth of government agencies. Section 6 of the Pendleton Act mandates that employees in customshouses or postal offices with more than fifty employees be included in the merit system. As agencies grew, more jobs were automatically included in the system. Johnson and Libecap 1994 argue that between 1884 and 1903, 35 percent of the growth in the merit system can be attributed to this natural growth; the remainder was due to presidential order. Their estimate of the automatic growth may be high if new agencies were created by Congress under the merit system or Congress enacted legislation to expand the system during this period.

26. White 1958.

27. Ibid., 307.

28. Prior to the passage of the Pendleton Act, there was limited unionization among blue-collar workers in craft unions that paralleled those in the private sector; see Johnson and Libecap 1994, West 2006.

29. This makes sense given that 63 percent of all federal civilian employees worked in the Postal Department in 1891; see Johnson and Libecap 1994, 78.

30. Ibid., 79; Mosher 1968, 179.

31. See Carpenter 2001, 169; West 2006, 12.

32. The act was partly a response to "gag orders" placed on federal employees by presidents Theodore Roosevelt and Taft in the early 1900s, prohibiting them from lobbying Congress directly, primarily for pay raises. The orders required that employees communicate to Congress only through department officials. See Johnson and Libecap 1994, 67–68; Mosher 1968, 179.

33. In 1896 the National Association of All Civil Service Employees formed but the most aggressive unionization of white-collar workers did not occur until after passage of the Lloyd-Lafollette Act.

34. The National Federation of Federal Employees (NFFE) was originally chartered by the American Federation of Labor (AFL). The NFFE split from the AFL in 1931 over a recommendation by the Civil Service Commission (CSC) to extend the merit system to all federal jobs. The NFFE supported the recommendation but it was opposed by leaders of craft unions within the AFL, who saw the proposal as a threat to their representation of skilled workers. Craft-union leaders preferred organization by skill, not by industry, and they believed expansion of the merit system would lead to the organization of federal workers generically or by agency, rather than by type of occupation. The AFL chartered the American Federation of Government Employees (AFGE) as a response in 1932. See Mosher 1968, 179; West 2006, 13–14.

35. Johnson and Libecap 1994, 68. The 1923 and 1949 Classification Acts established the modern white-collar pay system known as the General Schedule (GS) in order to ensure equal pay for equal work. The General Schedule is comprised of a series of grades and pay steps within each grade. The grades comprise pay rates associated with jobs requiring different levels of skill or experience. Pay increases within the grades were determined by efficiency ratings. Over time, however, time in a pay grade became used as the primary means of determining

increases within the pay grade on the theory that a person's value increases with experience. According to OPM, during 1950–1978, "Pay advancement within a grade becomes more uniform. The system of pay increases or decreases based upon efficiency ratings is replaced by a system that makes time in grade the primary determinant of within-grade advancement" (U.S. Office of Personnel Management n.d.).

36. Mosher 1968, 179–80.

37. West 2006, 14.

38. Johnson and Libecap 1994.

39. During the New Deal, Congress and the president created close to 60 new agencies (100,000 employees) outside the merit system, and only 5 were populated with employees approved under competitive examinations administered by the CSC. See Van Riper 1958, 320. David and Pollock 1957 note that Congress "repeatedly killed legislative proposals to place the employees of these New Deal agencies under civil service regulations" (51).

40. Particularly influential in expanding merit system coverage was the enactment of the Ramspeck Act (1940). The act gave the president the authority to include within the merit system all positions except those in the Tennessee Valley Authority (TVA), the Work Projects Administration (WPA), Senate-confirmed (PAS) appointees, and assistant U.S. attorneys. The act eliminated almost all of the exceptions to the merit system added since the passage of the act. It complied with the recommendation of the President's Committee on Administrative Management (that is, the "Brownlow Committee"), which recommended the expansion of the merit system "upward, outward, and downward." President Franklin Roosevelt's subsequent executive orders extended the merit system to all posts except temporary posts, jobs excepted by the CSC (Schedule A and B jobs), and those excluded in the Ramspeck Act (that is, PAS positions, positions in the TVA, WPA, and assistant U.S. attorneys). See U.S. Office of Personnel Management 2003a, 81–82.

41. There is some question as to how much influence the early act had based upon the fact that many of the jobs classified early on were the jobs that were least important to party officials, including departmental jobs in Washington, D.C., and jobs requiring technical expertise. The latter group of jobs included those in the Weather Bureau, medical officers, and jobs in the Fish Commission. The CSC also relied heavily on activities in field that it had no ability to monitor due to funding and staffing shortages. See Carpenter 2001, 46; Skowronek 1982, 72.

42. Source: U.S. House 1976a, 305–6. This percentage includes all civilian positions in the executive branch not specifically exempted from the competitive service by statute, executive decree, or CSC decision.

43. See U.S. General Accounting Office 1995a.

44. In 2004, 49.9 percent of the federal civilian workforce (2,735,359 employees) was in the traditional merit system. See Stanley and Niemi 2006. If the personnel reforms are implemented in DHS and the Department of Defense, approximately 600,000 additional employees will be removed from this system, leaving about 28 percent of the federal workforce under the traditional merit system.

45. Source: U.S. Office of Personnel Management 2003b; U.S. Department of Defense 2004.

46. Historically, different departments employed hourly employees through pay systems based on local wage surveys. This led to a proliferation of different, confusing, and often unequal pay systems for about 600,000 hourly workers. In 1965 President Lyndon Johnson asked the CSC in cooperation with federal agencies to develop one coordinated federal wage system for hourly workers—the result was the Federal Wage System. See U.S. Office of Personnel Management 2003a, 13–14.

47. U.S. Office of Personnel Management 2003b.

48. Currently, if an employee is to be suspended without pay for fourteen days or more, demoted, or fired, she must be notified thirty days in advance. She has a right to appeal to the agency head and have a response within ten days. She can then appeal to the Merit Systems Protection Board, and eventually the circuit court or the Court of Claims, if pay is at issue. Job protections of this sort did not come into existence until the Lloyd-Lafollette Act (1912). This act guaranteed that employees could not be removed or suspended without pay "only for such cause as will promote the efficiency of the service." There was no appeal procedure enforcing this act until it was given to veterans in the Veterans Preference Act (1944). This right of appeal was extended to all employees in the merit system by John F. Kennedy in 1962 through executive order, and it was codified in the Civil Service Reform Act (1978). Employees have a number of other protections including whistleblower, privacy, and free-speech protections established in law and jurisprudence. I borrow this discussion from Dresang 2002, particularly chap. 13.

49. This discussion excludes an additional category of appointees—PA appointees. This category of appointee is constituted almost exclusively by advisory-commission personnel or White House Office employees. Technically, the Senior Executive Service (SES) is part of the "competitive service," but OPM counts SES positions as excepted. As defined by Section 2103 of Title 5, the " 'excepted service' consists of those civil service positions which are not in the competitive service or the Senior Executive Service." Since the SES system is distinct from the provisions of the classical competitive system, it probably makes more sense to consider them as something distinct from this system. See U.S. General Accounting Office 1997a.

50. In *Buckley v. Valeo* (1976) the Supreme Court wrote that "any appointee exercising significant authority pursuant to the laws of the United States is an 'Officer of the United States,' and must, therefore, be appointed in the manner prescribed by 2, cl. 2, of that Article." This implies that personnel in a strictly advisory capacity, such as presidential aides, are not principal officers and therefore not constitutionally required to be nominated and confirmed. See Hogue 2005, 80–82. In *Morrison v. Olson* (1988) the court acknowledged how difficult it is to determine the line between principal and inferior officers, but gave four guidelines: "(1) Can the officer be dismissed by a higher executive-branch official? (2) Are the officer's duties certain and limited? (3) Is the officer's jurisdiction limited? (4) Is the officer's tenure limited?" If the answer to these questions is yes, this suggests the officer is more inferior than principal. The quotation and

discussion are drawn from Rosenbloom 1997, 163–64. In *Edmonds v. U.S.* (1997) the court further ruled that the term " 'inferior officer' connotes a relationship with some higher-ranking officer or officers below the president." This seems to suggest not only that each agency needs only one layer of advice-and-consent positions to satisfy constitutional requirements, but also that any other official who is part of a hierarchy not administered by a Senate-confirmed official should be himself considered a "principal" officer. See Hogue 2005, 80–82.

51. U.S. House 2004.

52. The key exceptions are the Justice Department (222) and the State Department (193). These numbers are a bit misleading, however, since they include 186 U.S. Attorneys and U.S. Marshals and 135 ambassadors.

53. There are also a small number of limited-term (LT) and limited-emergency (LE) members of the SES. Limited-term appointments are time-limited appointments that do not require SES certification and can last for up to three years. Limited-emergency appointments are limited to eighteen months. There are caps on the number of such positions an agency can have relative to its total SES allocation. These authorities are used for temporary jobs (for example, for a special project) or instances where a post needs to be filled immediately. They are to be filled by "career or career-type" federal civil service employees. There is some disagreement among personnel officials as to whether these are used as a back door means of politicizing. One federal personnel official told me, "Over the years, I have found that the LT appointment authority is often used as a back door appointment mechanism for would-be political appointees, especially when an agency does not wish to bring undue attention to itself or it it has reached the 25 percent limit for noncareer appointments."

54. Presidents and agency heads select personnel to fill these positions subject to the further limitation that some SES positions are designated as "career reserved." Agencies designate certain positions as "career reserved" if the agency believes these positions require impartiality or the public perception of impartiality. Examples include law enforcement or auditing positions. These positions can only be filled by career employees in the SES. About one-half of all SES positions are currently designated as "career reserved." Once a position has this designation it can only be changed by action of OPM. Every two years agencies submit to OPM an executive-resource inventory detailing their requests and justification for the number of SES slots the agency needs. OPM reviews these requests and allocates a number of SES slots. The agency may allocate these SES slots among its component parts as it sees fit. These slots are filled by persons from the SES.

55. Career personnel in the SES have rank in their persons as opposed to rank in their jobs. This allows them to be moved around while retaining status. So, for example, career SES employees can serve in PAS or other positions but retain reemployment rights in the SES when they leave those positions.

56. U.S. Office of Personnel Management 2003c.

57. White House Office of the Press Secretary, "President Names 34 Appointees at 13 Departments and Agencies," White House, July 22, 1993.

58. This was not a new motivation. Historically, allowances have been made to ensure that positions of a policymaking or confidential nature could be filled by persons sympathetic to the policy aims of the current administration. Prior to

the creation of the SES in 1978, there was a system of about 4,000–4,500 non-career (NEA) and career executive (CEA) positions at approximately the same level as persons in the SES would fill. By law, one-quarter of these positions could be filled by noncareer persons. The NEA-CEA system, instituted in 1966, was preceded by a less formal system overseen by the CSC, wherein top positions that were not PAS positions could be filled by what would be called "Schedule C" appointees.

59. Schedule A positions existed at least as far back as the early 1900s, when a long list of positions technically in the classified service but "excepted" from examination were called the Schedule A. In 1910 the Schedule A was divided into Schedule A and Schedule B, with basically the same distinction between the two then as today. See Van Riper 1958, 196, 214.

60. Telephone interview with Emily Sheketoff, September 29, 2006.

61. One additional conceptual difficulty is that some jobs in agencies with otherwise standard personnel systems are filled by people appointed under an "excepted" personnel system. For example, Foreign Service officers are appointed outside of the competitive system defined by Title 5, but they are detailed to jobs in agencies like the U.S. Agency for International Development (USAID), the Department of Defense, the Department of Agriculture, and the Department of Commerce. Similarly, employees from the Panama Canal Employment Service Authority are appointed to jobs in the General Services Administration (GSA) and various parts of the Department of Defense. See GAO 1997a, chap. 2.

62. See ibid., 30.

63. U.S. Office of Personnel Management 2003b, table 9.

64. Gore 1993; National Commission on the Public Service 1989, 2003.

65. Interestingly, the statute also apparently provides the president with the ability to fill some assistant secretary slots without requiring Senate confirmation. See Hogue 2004.

66. Each agency is allocated a number of SES "spaces" every two years. If presidents want to add a *new* job to be filled with an appointed member of the SES, they must first determine whether this is possible given the number of SES allocations in the agency. Has the agency used all of its allocations? If all of the agency's allocations have been used, the agency will have to ask OPM for a special additional allocation.

67. Schedule C authority used to be attached to positions rather than persons, so that there were commonly vacancies in Schedule C positions. This appears to have changed in the 1980s.

68. For a good overview, see Patterson and Pfiffner 2001.

69. As quoted in Weko 1995, 26.

70. "The General Personnel Process," received via personal communication from Clay Johnson, October 25, 2006.

71. As quoted in Pfiffner 1996.

72. Mann 1964.

73. Interview with Pendleton James, New York, October 10, 2006.

74. For a good example in a concrete case, see Devroy, Ann. 1989, "High-Level Government Jobs Reserved for Bush Supporters," *Washington Post*, January 14,

1989, A1; Solomon, Burt, "A Long Time Bush Aide Takes Charge of Peopling," *National Journal,* January 21, 1989, 140.

75. Telephone interview with Mark Hunker, September 26, 2006.

76. Telephone interview with Bob Nash, January 8, 2007.

77. Interview with Pendleton James, New York, October 10, 2006; interview with Brad Patterson, Bethesda, Maryland, October 9, 2006; email correspondence with Chase Untermeyer, October 24, 2006.

78. This anecdote was recounted by Jan Naylor Cope, telephone interview, October 30, 2006.

79. Email correspondence, October 24, 2006.

80. Patterson and Pfiffner 2001. See also Devroy, Ann, "Envoys Without Experience," *Washington Post,* July 18, 1989, A1.

81. Eventually, Dan Fenn assumed responsibility for suggesting competent people ideologically sympathetic to the president's agenda while patronage was handled in Larry O'Brien's congressional-relations shop. See Weko 1995, 26. For President Johnson the division was reflected in the role of John Macy and the president himself. Macy, who was also head of the CSC, was involved in recruiting top people to execute the Great Society programs and patronage concerns were handled through more traditional means, including utilization of Johnson himself, who had a great memory for people and details. In the Nixon administration Fred Malek set up two distinct staffs. President Ford did not have this explicit division in PPO, partly because he had no campaign debts to repay, but President Carter did. The executive-recruitment operation of President Carter was limited since he originally promised cabinet-style government and had given secretaries control over the selection of their teams. The administration later sought to reassert control over all policy-relevant appointments with the selection of Arnie Miller to head presidential personnel. While Miller's operation did very little recruiting for top executive positions in the manner of professional recruiters, he was heavily involved in balancing competing demands on these top executive posts. "We just didn't have the capacity. . . . The kind (of recruiting) I do now did not exist then." He further explained, "My job was basically political . . . balance the pressures from conflicting interests on the position, the interest groups, the professional groups, evaluating competence, capacity for loyalty and agreement with administration policy." Apart from the selection of candidates for top policy positions, Miller's operation included a unit that recommended people connected to the campaign for lower-level appointee positions. President George H. W. Bush's division between the needs of recruiting for top executive posts and patronage were reflected in the creation of the Schedule C Project to place Bush supporters in administration jobs. Telephone interviews with Arnie Miller, October 18, 2006, and October 27, 2006; telephone interview with James B. King, September 22, 2006; interview with Brad Patterson, Bethesda, Maryland, October 9, 2006. See also National Academy of Public Administration 1984; Patterson and Pfiffner 2001; Pfiffner 1996, 140; Weko 1995.

82. Interview with Clay Johnson, Washington, D.C., October 25, 2006.

83. Telephone interview with J. Veronica Biggins, December 4, 2006.

84. Democrats comprised 47 percent of supergrade (GS 16–18) career managers in the Nixon administration, compared to 17 percent Republicans and 36

percent independents. A large percentage of the Democrats at this level worked in departments with large social service expenditures, like the Office of Economic Opportunity, the Department of Housing and Urban Development (HUD), or the Department of Health, Education, and Welfare. They were the most liberal in both their views about the proper role of government in the provision of social services and their perceptions of inequities in representation. See Aberbach and Rockman 1976, 459.

85. Maranto and Hult 2004.

86. See Rourke 1997, 183, who argues, "Thus as American bureaucracy has become much more professionalized in recent years, . . . it has also become increasingly politicized. These converging trends have greatly expanded the number of situations in which professionals today may have to take actions or make decisions that are inconsistent with their own standards of professional conduct."

87. See Corwin 1939 for a general discussion of congressional delegation of authority to subordinate administrative officials and the executive power of the president to remove officials and ensure that the law is faithfully executed. For examples of cases where subordinate officials have questions about the legality of policy direction from different presidential administrations, see Salamon and Abramson 1984, particularly their discussion of the administrative presidency during the Reagan administration, and Clayton 1992, which provides a history of the Attorney General's office.

88. Somers 1965, 80.

89. Ibid., 81.

90. "Federal Political Personnel Manual," 8903–9050.

91. "Former Chief of Agency Drops to 4th," *Washington Post,* July 23, 1954, 26.

92. Kluttz, Jerry, "The Federal Diary: Whims of Politics Govern Conservation, Gabrielson Charges," *Washington Post,* December 3, 1953, 25.

93. This technique has also been used in later administrations. At the start of the Carter administration, for example, several agencies sought to change the appointment authority of certain important career jobs. Specifically, they sought to make departmental administrative officer jobs appointed positions. Several agencies also sought to extend political appointments to the field offices, where positions were filled by career employees. See Causey, Mike, "Political Aides See Shift," *Washington Post,* May 25, 1977, C2.

94. Originally there were few specific rights for persons whose job designations were switched from career to appointed, but this apparently changed by the time of the Nixon administration. The "Malek Manual" includes the claim that replacement is less effective because employees often had the ability to stay in jobs after the appointment authority had been changed.

95. "Federal Political Personnel Manual," 8903–9050.

96. In the early 1980s this technique was used successfully by Interior Secretary James Watt to get control of the Office of Surface Mining (OSM) and the Solicitor's Office. Both department bureaus were targeted by the Heritage Foundation for their conservation "zealotry" before the Reagan administration assumed office. Watt announced a reorganization of the OSM to move its technical services division from Denver, Colorado, to Caspar, Wyoming, and transferred a number of lawyers from one coast to another. The net effect of these actions was heavy

233

attrition among both lawyers and OSM personnel. See Thornton, Mary, "How Interior is Changing, From the Inside," *Washington Post*, January 8, 1982, A21.

97. Pear, Robert. 1992, "Clinton's Promise of Cleaning House Worries Some Career Civil Servants," *New York Times*, November 15, 1992, A26.

98. Nongeographic transfers require a fifteen-day advance written notice and geographic transfers require consultation and a sixty-day advance written notice; see U.S. Office of Personnel Management 2001.

99. O'Toole, Thomas. 1977, "Chief Geologist's Downfall," *Washington Post*, November 13, 1977, A6.

100. Ibid.

101. See Heclo 1975; Heclo 1977, 78–81; U.S. Senate 1964.

102. See Heclo 1975 and U.S. Senate 1973.

103. See Causey, "Political Aides See Shift."

104. Light 1995.

105. For a good example, see Blumenthal, Sidney, "Quest for Lasting Power," *Washington Post*, September 25, 1985, A1.

106. See Cook and Polsky 2005, 593.

107. See Durant 1992, 37, for a discussion of RIFs as one part of the Reagan administration's strategy for gaining control of the bureaucracy.

108. Mosher, Lawrence. 1982, "Environmental Quality Council Trims Its Sails in Stormy Budget Weather," *National Journal*, July 24, 1982.

109. See Davies 1984.

110. Harris, Shane. 2005, "Political Official to Serve as Acting Commissioner of FTS," *Government Executive*, January 24, 2005 (online edition, available at www.govexec.com).

111. For details of the "Jobs for Republicans," or "Willis," directive, see Kluttz, "White House Seeks Jobs for GOP Favorites," and "Ike Defends GOP Plans for Job Hunt."

112. Kluttz, Jerry, "The Federal Diary: Government Aides Doubt Legality of Jobs-for-GOP Plan," *Washington Post*, October 29, 1954, 27; see also Causey, Mike, "Probe Bares 400 Illegal HUD Hirings," *Washington Post*, October 16, 1974, B13, for another example.

113. 109 Stat 703 (December 15, 1995).

114. For details, see U.S. General Accounting Office. 1995b.

115. Causey, Mike, "GOP Officials on Hit List," *Washington Post*, May 13, 1977, B2.

116. Roberts, Steven V., "Many Reaganites Now Find the Capital Is a Nice Place to Work," *New York Times*, January 9, 1989, A14.

117. Greve, Frank, "Hundreds of Bush's Appointees Change Stripes to Save Jobs," *Houston Chronicle*, January 9, 1993, 6.

118. Telephone interview with James B. King, September 22, 2006.

119. See, for example, U.S. House 2006a.

120. Havemann, Judith, "Top Federal Jobs 'Politicized,' " *Washington Post*, August 6, 1987, A1.

121. U.S. General Accounting Office 1995b, 1997b, 2000.

122. U.S. Congress 2006a.

123. On occasion Congress will change the appointment authority of appointed positions from one type of appointee to another. In particular, Congress will require Senate-confirmation of positions that were previously appointees without Senate-confirmation. Two examples of this were top executive positions in OMB in the 1970s. See Heclo 1977.

124. Lewis 2003.

125. The language goes on to limit the ability of the department to detail their appointees outside the department. With one exception, I have only uncovered this language applied to the Department of Transportation. I have also seen it included in appropriations language for the Office of the U.S. Trade Representative in one instance. For an example, see 104 P.L. 50, Section 311.

126. Telephone interview with Steve Cohen, November 28, 2006; Ban and Ingraham 1984, 14. For an excellent history of OPM, see Lane 1992.

127. Telephone interview with Carol J. Okin, October 27, 2006.

128. Ban and Ingraham 1984, "Introduction," 1.

129. Ingraham 1992, 23.

130. Kramer, Larry, "Carter to Offer Plan to Reform Civil Service," *Washington Post*, February 26, 1978, A1.

131. Peirce, Neal R., "Civil Service Reform is Spreading," *Washington Post*, December 17, 1977, A19.

132. Rosen 1982–83, 8.

133. Strout, Richard L. 1978, "Civil Service Reform: First in a Century," *Christian Science Monitor*, September 12, 1978, 1; "President Carter: 'The State of Our Union is Sound,' " *Washington Post*, January 20, 1978, A14.

134. The Merit Systems Protection Board (MSPB) is an agency that hears employee appeals over personnel actions. The OSC is charged with protecting whistleblowers and investigating allegations of prohibited personnel practices. They bring cases before the MSPB. The Federal Labor Relations Authority is a quasi-judicial body that resolves disputes involving labor-management relations in the federal government, such as the negotiability of collective bargaining agreements. For a review of the legislative history, see Ingraham 1984 and Sugiyama 1985.

135. As OPM's official history explains, "Among its primary aims, the Civil Service Reform Act of 1978 sought to strengthen Presidential control over the Federal bureaucracy" (U.S. Office of Personnel Management 2003, 167). See also Rosenbloom 1979, 171; Sawyer, Kathy, "Plan Aimed at Making Government Responsive," *Washington Post*, March 3, 1978, A1.

136. Telephone interview with Steve Cohen, November 28, 2006; Ban 1984, 49.

137. Telephone interview with Doris Hausser, November 30, 2006. For a review of CSC investigations into these agencies, see Sugiyama 1985, 3.

138. Telephone interview with Doris Hausser, November 30, 2006.

139. For a clear discussion, see Reid, T. R., "Reagan Has Power to Remold Bureaucracy," *Washington Post*, November 19, 1980, A1.

140. Two ran the White House Fellows program. One served as an executive director to a presidential commission to recommend ways to get private-sector executives into government.

141. U.S. House 1976b; U.S. Senate 1980.

142. Causey, Mike, "The High Turnover: OPM's Revolving Door," *Washington Post*, July 5, 1979, C2.

143. Ibid.

144. Ibid.

145. Ibid.

146. Rosen 1982–83.

147. According to some, Devine was Reagan's most conservative appointee. See Barker, Karlyn, "Personnel Chief Draws Fire," *Washington Post*, November 23, 1981, B1; Dillin, B., "Devine Quits; Conservatives Feel Sting of Another Loss," *Christian Science Monitor*, June 7, 1985, 3.

148. Barker, "Personnel Chief Draws Fire."

149. Telephone interview with Doris Hausser, November 30, 2006; Lane 1988–89; Ban 1984, 53–54.

150. Lane 1988–89, 342; Ban and Marzotto 1984, 155.

151. Lane 1992, 110.

152. Telephone interview with Donald J. Devine, September 13, 2006.

153. Dillin, "Devine Quits."

154. Devine 1987; telephone interview with Steve Cohen, November 28, 2006; telephone interview with Carol J. Okin, October 27, 2006.

155. U.S. House 1976b; U.S. Senate 1980.

156. Telephone interview with Doris Hausser, November 30, 2006. It should be noted that almost without exception the careerists I interviewed reported good relations with Devine and generally distanced themselves from those who chafed under his directorship.

157. U.S. House 1976b, 1984; U.S. Senate 1980. To double-check the Plum Books I also used the *U.S. Government Manual* in 1980 and did background research on the associate directors in 1980. For four of the five associate directors, I could confirm that they were careerists rather than appointees.

158. Perl, Peter, "OPM Chief Hit for Politicking," *Washington Post*, April 21, 1984, A3. For a discussion of the controversy over Devine's tenure, see also Causey, Mike, "Democrats Balk at 2nd Devine Term," *Washington Post*, April 2, 1985, A7.

159. Causey, Mike, "OPM Director Names 5 Regional Assistants," *Washington Post*, November 5, 1982, B2.

160. According to one career OPM manager, the "federal workforce had a vitriolic hatred of Devine due to the policy changes being made" (telephone interview with Carol J. Okin, October 27, 2006).

161. Barker, Karlyn, "AFGE Demands Resignation of OPM Chief," *Washington Post*, November 18, 1981, A5.

162. Telephone interview with Steve Cohen, November 28, 2006.

163. Specifically, careerists referred to difficulties monitoring the merit system and the need to "reinvent the wheel" due to Devine's refusal to rely on existing career professionals. Telephone interview with Steve Cohen, November 28, 2006; telephone interview with Doris Hausser, November 30, 2006.

164. United States General Accounting Office 1989.

165. U.S. Merit Systems Protection Board 1989, i, 23.

166. See, for example, the President's Private Sector Survey of Cost Control (the Grace Commission) and Goldenberg 1985, 84–85.

167. Lane writes, "It did not further merit principles. It did not become the primary management office for the president. Public personnel management at the federal level was not transformed into modern human resource management" (Lane 1992, 111). See also Zuck 1989.

168. Agresta, Robert J. 1994, "OPM Needs a Mission—Not a Funeral," *Government Executive*, September, 1994, 70.

169. Telephone interview with Doris Hausser, November 30, 2006; telephone interview with Carol J. Okin, October 27, 2006.

170. Zeller, Shawn, "MSPB to Close Offices, Lay Off Employees," *Government Executive*, December 10, 2003; "Susanne Marshall (Interview)" *Federal Times*, November 10, 2003

Chapter Three
Why, When, and Where Do Presidents Politicize the Bureaucracy?

1. Pasternak, Judy, "White House Appoints Loyalists to Education Department Posts," *Los Angeles Times*, October 3, 1999, B10.

2. I count all Senate-confirmed (PAS), noncareer Senior Executive Service (SES), and Schedule C appointments to full-time, nonadvisory positions as political appointments. See U.S. Congress, *Policy and Supporting Positions*, various years.

3. Pasternak, "White House Appoints Loyalists to Education Department Posts."

4. See particularly Heclo 1977; Nathan 1975, 1983; Weko 1995. One motivating force behind President Nixon's approach to the presidency was that he feared disloyalty embodied in the personnel left over from the preceding Kennedy and Johnson administrations. In an informal instruction manual for new Nixon administration political appointees, White House aide Fred Malek claimed politicization techniques were justified since the Kennedy and Johnson administrations had "raped" the career service during their tenure. Malek was referring primarily to three real or alleged actions by the previous Democratic administrations. First, the Kennedy administration, with the help of outside management consultants, had identified every position (career and noncareer) that was an important "pressure point" for influencing the executive branch. Kennedy aide Larry O'Brien then researched the background of every incumbent in these positions and allegedly removed all of those not loyal to the Kennedy administration within 180 days of Kennedy's inauguration. Second, President Johnson had reinstated a dual-hatting personnel system by naming Civil Service Commission (CSC) Chairman John Macy as a special assistant to the president for personnel. As special assistant, Macy was responsible for personnel matters of all types, including recruitment and, to a lesser extent, patronage. Yet as CSC chairman, he was responsible for the integrity of the merit system, a seeming conflict of interest. Finally, the Johnson administration took steps to freeze people loyal to the administration or to its programs into the bureaucracy. The John-

son administration created programs, staffed them outside the civil service system, and then blanketed them into the civil service. Malek also alleged that the Johnson administration eliminated managerial positions vacant at the end of Johnson's term, filled up high-salary jobs (on which there were ceilings set by Congress and the Bureau of the Budget) with career employees who could not be demoted or have their pay cut according to civil service rules, and that Johnson was personally involved in the selection of higher-level career employees. See U.S. Congress 1973, 8908–9, 9006, 9014–16; Heclo 1977, 70–76; Henry 1969; U.S. House 1976a, 281; Weko 1995.

5. For a good journalistic review of politicization under Nixon, see Sherrill, Robert, "The Hatchetman and the Hatchetmyth," *Washington Post*, February 6, 1972, O11.

6. U.S. Congress 1973, 8903–9050. There is some disagreement as to whether Malek or his former aide, Alan May, is the actual author of the document but it is widely referred to under Malek's name.

7. The Civil Service Reform Act (CSRA) created the Senior Executive Service (SES), gave presidents the ability to appoint 10 percent of these managers from outside the civil service, and granted presidents new power to remove and select career managers for executive-branch management positions. For details on increases in appointees, see Goldenberg 1984, Rosen 1983. See also Causey, Mike, "Reagan's Plum Book Plumper than Carter's," *Washington Post*, May 11, 1984, C2. The number of Schedule C appointees actually began increasing dramatically in the Carter administration.

8. Hoffman, David, and Ann Devroy, "Bush's First Week: Plans and Pitfalls," *Washington Post*, January 29, 1989, A1; Causey, Mike, "Great Expectations," *Washington Post*, January 30, 1989, D2.

9. For details on the partisan and ideological composition of employees in these agencies, see Aberbach and Rockman 1976.

10. Schlesinger 1965, 680.

11. Moe 1985; Rudalevige 2002; Rudalevige and Lewis 2005.

12. Moe 1985, 245.

13. Heclo 1975.

14. Ibid., 81.

15. Ibid., 82.

16. Light 1995.

17. Since the 1939 creation of the Executive Office of the President (EOP), the president has been served by a continuing body of professional personnel that are employed across administrations. These professionals help presidents perform their constitutional and statutorily delegated responsibilities. Principal among these are those employed in the president's budget agency, who through transition materials to incoming presidents, memos, and budget and policy roles have communicated to the president what is in the president's institutional interest. Historically, the Bureau of the Budget (BOB) was not only a budgetary agency. It was also a full-service management agency, using a variety of tools to improve compliance with presidential directives and enhance efficiency. It had a significant management apparatus that performed organizational studies, made recommendations to the president, and kept track of federal personnel policy.

Through transition materials, memos during the president's term, budgetary and legislative recommendations, and executive management activities the agency articulated, communicated, and publicized the president's institutional interests in the executive branch. Topics covered in transition memos, for example, included basic information on the civil service system and federal organization, but also a number of presidency-specific issues, such as which agencies were not subject to effective presidential control, how Congress was encroaching on executive powers, and the state of knowledge on how presidents should organize both the institutional apparatus of the presidency and the executive branch as a whole for maximum administrative influence. The information on the federal personnel system described the different federal civilian personnel and benefits systems. It also provided background on attempts to centralize personnel control, providing history, different proposals, and analysis. Over time, competitors for the budget agency's powers have arisen and BOB/OMB's role in budget making has increased in importance; these two factors have lessened the importance of OMB as the institutional memory and protector of the presidency.

18. Whittington 1999.

19. See Moe and Wilson 1994.

20. For a review of literature on the economy and presidential elections, see Campbell 2000, 126. See, however, Bartels 2007.

21. Labaton, Stephen, "S.E.C.'s Embattled Chief Resigns In Wake of Latest Political Storm," *New York Times*, November 6, 2002, A1.

22. *A Discussion with Gerald R. Ford: The American Presidency* (Washington, D.C.: American Enterprise Institute, 1977), 11.

23. I talk explicitly about the president's incentives, but these incentives apply equally to the president's subordinates. The Secretary of Defense views the politicization decision in the same way as the president does, although he or she is only concerned about the Department of Defense. This is important because many politicization decisions are most proximately the choice of the president's appointees rather than the president directly.

24. More specifically, presidents not only prefer that on average (mean) the policy outcomes end up right where the agency intended for them to end up, but also that the mistakes, particularly extreme mistakes from the president's perspective, are minimized. In other words, presidents are risk-averse. I assume that the mistakes are uniformly distributed around the mean. If they are asymmetric, so that failures happen in the president's favor, presidents will prefer more politicization than otherwise.

25. That is, the agency's induced ideal point is a weighted average of the agency's inherent ideal point and the president's ideal point, and the weighting is a function of the percentage of an agency's employees that are political appointees.

26. 29 U.S.C. 651.

27. For example, in 1987 several Democratic members of Congress accused the Reagan administration of "packing" the top ranks of government with appointees, to the detriment of the federal service. Backed by a General Accounting Office (GAO) report tracking appointments, these members denounced an increase in SES appointees, particularly in the agencies that manage the govern-

ment, such as OPM (personnel), the GSA (facilities), and OMB (finances). See Havemann, Judith, "Top Federal Jobs 'Politicized,' " *Washington Post*, August 6, 1987, A1.

28. See Epstein and O'Halloran 1999; Huber and Shipan 2002; Lewis 2003; McCubbins, Noll, and Weingast 1987, 1989; McCubbins and Schwartz 1984; and Moe 1989.

29. This effect is bounded by the president's ideal policy. Congress will not ask for more appointees than are necessary to change agency policy to the president's ideal policy. Adding more presidential appointees beyond this point will make it no more likely that the agency will reflect Congress's preferences.

30. Indeed, one Republican personnel official volunteered that an EPA full of free-market environmentalists would be preferred to a low-competence EPA except to the extent that they would all leave at the end of the administration. Personal interview, fall 2006, Washington, D.C.

31. See Bilmes and Neal 2003; Bok 2003.

32. Whereas the United States employs over 3,000 presidential appointees, other developed countries have between 100 and 200. See Raadschelders and Lee 2005.

33. Fred Malek put the number of Congressional musts at a dozen a month during the Nixon administration; National Academy of Public Administration 1984, 21; telephone interview with Rep. Marion Berry (D-AR), December 8, 2006; telephone interview with Rep. Henry Waxman (D-CA), December 11, 2006.

34. Telephone interview with Mark Hunker, September 26, 2006.

35. Telephone interview, fall 2006.

36. This is from a memo called "Lessons for the Eleven Weeks," August 13, 1992, republished in Jones 2000, 125. See also Patterson and Pfiffner 2001, 430.

37. 39 Stat. 169.

38. "Army Bill Joker Aims to Rob Wood of Honor Medal," *New York Times*, May 20, 1916, A1.

39. "Postmasters to Continue as Political Appointees" (UPI), *Washington Post*, June 19, 1952, 1. This article details how "local people can hold their local representative to account" by maintaining the patronage system for regional appointments.

40. See Maranto 2004 for a discussion of how policy disagreement between presidents and agencies and between appointees and careerists is greatest after party changes in the White House.

41. Nixon 1978, 352, as quoted in Milkis and Nelson 2003.

42. This was stated nicely by former Reagan Defense Department appointee Lawrence Korb. In 1993 he wrote, "Clinton must realize that because of his draft record, he will never be popular with the military, and that neither he nor any politician is fully qualified to be commander-in-chief. Ronald Reagan was never popular with workers at places like the Department of Housing and Urban Development or the Department of Education, nor did he care" (Korb, Lawrence J., "The President and the Military at Odds," *Brookings Review* 11 [Summer 1993], 5).

43. Personal communication with Donald J. Devine, September 13, 2006.

44. Some other factors arguably include agency size or culture. Some large agencies have enough slack to assume a large number of appointees without noticeable large effects on performance. Others have learned to cope over time. One agency official described to me how a cabinet department in the Clinton administration accepted 17 Schedule C appointees under duress from the White House and responded by placing them in offices segregated from the rest of the department and literally giving them nothing to do. These agencies can accommodate more appointees than others without concerns for performance, but there are more general characteristics across agencies that influence how easily they can accommodate appointees.

45. "Andrew Jackson's First Message to Congress (1829)," In Nelson, Michael, ed., *The Evolving Presidency* (Washington, D.C.: CQ Press), 76.

46. Some agencies are also better able to attract and retain employees through special hiring authorities. These agencies can offer higher salaries, relieve college debt, cut out paperwork, and relax restrictions on outside work. In these cases, agency capacity should be higher and politicization should also be an attractive strategy for control. Of course, as I describe below, agencies that receive special salary authorities often have extremely difficult tasks that require highly qualified employees.

47. Rourke 1997 has an excellent discussion of this within his larger study of professionalism and politicization.

48. Henry 1960, 655; Kenworthy, E. W., "Eisenhower Seeks Cut in Career Men," *New York Times*, March 1, 1957, 1.

49. Huddleston and Boyer 1996, 37.

50. Henry 1960, 655–57. See also Kenworthy, E. W., "President's Order Opens New Jobs for Party Men," *New York Times*, March 3, 1957, 174. This article notes that over half of all incumbents had been retained and an additional 20 percent of positions had been filled from the career ranks.

51. Telephone interview with James B. King, September 22, 2006.

52. Nathan 1975, 1983; Rudalevige 2002. The latest evidence suggests that centralization and politicization are substitutes. Centralization often occurs when politicization is difficult, such as at the beginning of presidential terms, when a new administration is first filling out its agency teams, or at the end of terms, when the administration is having a difficult time holding the team together. See Rudalevige and Lewis 2005.

53. Pear, Robert. 2007, "Bush Directive Increases Sway on Regulation," *New York Times*, January 30, 2007, A1.

54. Indeed, if presidents employ these other strategies apart from politicization, this should make it less likely that the patterns described above are necessary or will emerge in data analysis.

55. As recently as 2001, one report labeled the department's handling of federal grant money as "gross mismanagement," and the GAO noted that the department had only partly met one out of six goals listed as part of its Government Performance and Results Act submissions to Congress. Part of the problem was that its performance report was incomplete and shoddy. It did not include information about the agency's goals, did not explain why they were not met, and did not indicate how they would be met. The GAO's reports particularly targeted

NOTES TO CHAPTER FOUR

fraud, lax oversight, and performance inadequacies in financial management, the disbursement of grants, and purchasing. See Ballard, Tanya, "Education Department Gets Low Marks on Performance Report," *Government Executive*, August 16, 2001; Lunney, Kellie, "Report Raps Education for 'Gross Mismanagement' of Grants Program," *Government Executive*, February 5, 2001.

56. See U.S. Office of Management and Budget, *Budget of the United States Government FY 2004: Performance Management and Assessments* (Washington, D.C.: U.S. Government Printing Office, 2005).

57. Portions of this appendix were previously published in Lewis 2005c.

Chapter Four
The Pattern of Politicization: A Quantitative Overview

1. As I explain below, there are three difficulties. First, the types of political appointments (for example, Schedule C, NEA, noncareer SES) change over time and this makes analyses over time problematic. Second, the necessary data for testing the key propositions, such as the number of managers and professionals in an agency, agency ideology, and career-manager wages, are not available for the majority of Plum Book data. Third, the quadrennial nature of the Plum Book data makes evaluating the rhythms of politicization within administrations impossible. These factors do not eliminate the usefulness of the Plum Book data for testing the theory and evaluating common views, but they do limit the ways in which it can be used.

2. As explained in chapter 2, I do not include presidential appointments without Senate confirmation (PA) because they are composed almost exclusively of White House personnel or advisory-commission members.

3. Morris, John D., "New Battle Ahead on Reorganizing," *New York Times*, June 5, 1952, 36; idem, "Senate Unit Acts to Kill 3 Reorganization Plans," *New York Times*, June 11, 1952, 19.

4. The OMB was formerly the Bureau of the Budget. The politicization of both OMB and OPM are documented in chapter 2, above. See also Heclo 1975, 1977.

5. Administrative assistant secretaries have historically controlled the departmental offices associated with government resources like personnel, financial management, procurement, and general services (for example, information technology [IT], space, vehicles). The two major executive-branch study commissions in the Truman and Eisenhower years both recommended that administrative assistant secretary positions be filled by career employees to ensure continuity and good management in the departments. Reorganization plans passed in 1950 made these positions career positions in the departments of Commerce, Justice, Labor, and Treasury, and they were career positions by informal norm in the other departments. The norm and the formal rule both began to be violated starting in the Kennedy administration. In practice it was hard to separate policy from departmental management decisions about personnel, finances, and procurement; and by the Nixon administration, outsiders appointed to these posts were routinely given career status by the CSC despite the commission's own objections. Hugh Heclo concludes that "in 1977 almost all the career ASAs [assis-

tant secretaries for administration] had been replaced by men with little or no government experience, and the experiment in top-level administrative continuity was, for all practical purposes, a dead letter" (1977, 76). See "The Federal Political Personnel Manual," 8913, and Heclo 1977, 76–78. See also Causey, Mike, "The Federal Diary: Top Personnel Jobs Are Going Political," *Washington Post*, May 15, 1979, C2.

6. See Maranto 2004 for a discussion about how policy disagreement between presidents and agencies and between appointees and careerists is greatest after party changes in the White House.

7. See Herman, Ken, "White House Jobs: Tough Sell?" *Cox News Service*, April 30, 2006.

8. Some statutes, rather than specifying the details of PAS positions in great detail, authorize a fixed number of PAS positions that presidents can allocate throughout a department at their discretion. For example, the law creating the DHS allows the president "not more than 12" assistant secretaries but does not specify where those assistant secretaries are to be placed within the organization chart of the department. Interestingly, the statute also apparently provides the president with the ability to fill some assistant secretary slots without requiring Senate confirmation. See Hogue 2004.

9. Jehl, Douglas, "New C.I.A. Chief Chooses 4 Top Aides From House," *New York Times*, October 1, 2004; Pincus, Walter, and Dana Priest, "Goss Brings 4 Staffers From Hill to CIA," *Washington Post*, October 1, 2004, A4.

10. Priest, Dana, and Walter Pincus, "Deputy Chief Resigns from CIA," *Washington Post*, November 13, 2004, A1; Priest, Dana, "Shake Up at CIA Headquarters Continues," *Washington Post*, November 15, 2004; Pincus, Walter, "Changing of the Guard at the CIA," *Washington Post*, January 6, 2005, A3.

11. Jehl, Douglas, "New C.I.A. Chief Tells Workers to Back Administration Policies," *New York Times*, November 17, 2004.

12. Pincus, "Changing of the Guard at the CIA."

13. See, for example, Glassman, James K., "Gossify the Whole Bureaucracy," *Scripps Howard News Service*, November 22, 2004; Pincus, Walter, "McCain Backs CIA Shake-Up," *Washington Post*, November 15, 2004, A2; Priest, Dana, and Walter Pincus, "CIA Chief Seeks to Reassure Employees," *Washington Post*, November 16, 2004, A1.

14. Jehl, Douglas, "C.I.A. Churning Continues as 2 Top Officials Resign," *New York Times*, November 16, 2004.

15. Duffy, Michael, and Mitch Frank, "In Your Face at the CIA." *Time* 164 (November 29, 2004): 24.

16. "CIA Director Goss Resigns." *Associated Press*, May 5, 2006; "Goss: CIA resignation 'one of those mysteries.' " *CNN*, May 6, 2006.

17. These cases included the case of Donald Sweeney, an Army Corps of Engineers economist, whose revelations led to dramatic changes in the way the Corps planned projects, and the case of two border patrol agents who disclosed security weaknesses along the U.S.-Canada border. Friel, Brian, "Top Two Whistleblower Protectors Resign," *Government Executive*, May 12, 2003.

18. Ibid.

19. Gruber, Amelia, "Whistleblower Agency Attacks Case Backlog," *Government Executive*, April 8, 2004.

20. It is hard to tell exactly when the increase in the number of appointees occurred, but Bloch's appointee team included 1 appointed SES deputy director and 5 Schedule C appointees in 2004. His predecessor served with 1 appointed SES deputy director and 3 Schedule C employees, according to the 2000 edition of the Plum Book. U.S. Senate 2000; U.S. House 2004.

21. Kauffman, Tim, "Employees File Complaint Against Special Counsel," *Federal Times*, March 7, 2005.

22. U.S. Government Accountability Office 2004b.

23. Some also complained that the reorganization placed the Hatch Act unit (which prevents political and electioneering activity by federal employees) under a political appointee, although previously the unit had reported to a career employee. Letter from Carol A. Bonosaro, President of the Senior Executives Association, to Scott J. Bloch, Special Counsel, January 28, 2005 (see the Senior Executives Association website, available at www.seniorexecs.org).

24. Lee, Christopher, "Head of Worker Protection Office is Accused of Retaliatory Transfers," *Washington Post*, January 11, 2005, A13.

25. Lee, Christopher, "Dispute at Whistleblower Office," *Washington Post*, February 24, 2005, A19; Pulliam, Daniel, "OSC Chief Defends Management of Agency," *Government Executive*, May 24, 2005.

26. Kauffman, "Employees File Complaint Against Special Counsel."

27. Barr, Stephen, "Agency's Reorganization Results in Accusations, Employees Leaving," *Washington Post*, March 18, 2005, B2.

28. Gruber, Amelia, "Special Counsel Report Counters Complaints From Watchdog Groups," *Government Executive*, May 18, 2005.

29. Duffy and Frank, "In Your Face at the CIA," 24.

30. They document that President Kennedy had 286 positions at the rank of secretary, deputy secretary, undersecretary, assistant secretary, or administrator. At the end of the Clinton administration there were 914 such positions.

31. Similarly, some growth in PAS positions is to be expected with the addition of seven new cabinet departments between 1953 and 2005. If the addition of new government agencies explains the growth in appointments, this also means something different than the politicization of the existing bureaucracy. The departments created during this period include HUD, HHS, the VA, DHS, as well as the Departments of Transportation, Energy, and Education.

32. One difficulty with analyzing the Plum Book is that its contents have changed some over time. Specifically, between 1984 and 1988 the Plum Book stopped listing a number of positions that, while technically filled by political appointment, rarely turned over (for example, the chaplaincy of West Point). The Plum Book has also irregularly listed the positions filled by Senior Foreign Service officers subject to political appointment in the State Department. The change in the Plum Book format between 1984 and 1988 could cause problems for inference if the numbers of consequential appointees actually *increased* after 1984, but this increase is missed because the compilers of the Plum Book changed their rules as to what would be listed. While I may be undercounting the number of appointees after 1984 relative to the pre-1984 period, it is highly

unlikely that the number of appointees is higher after 1984 than it was in 1980. First, the effect of the change in the Plum Book between 1984 and 1988 is minimized in my data since I exclude all nonsalaried and part-time appointed positions—the types of positions that are among the most likely to be excluded in 1988 but not in 1984. Second, other reliable counts from OPM confirm that both noncareer SES and Schedule C appointments declined between 1984 and 1988. According to OPM, the number of appointed SES members decreased between 1984 and 1988 from 665 to 659, and the number of Schedule C positions decreased by 2. See United States Office of Personnel Management 1997. See also Havemann, Judith, "Pruned 'Plum Book' to Hit Shelves," *Washington Post*, November 8, 1988, A17. Finally, if we examine only the number of appointees between 1988 and 2004, ignoring any potential change in the Plum Book between 1984 and 1988, there has still been a decline of about 30 appointees. The difference between 1988 and 2000 is over 350 appointed positions. It should also be noted that the patterns shown in tables 4.1 and 4.2 still exist whether the Department of State is included or excluded. Figures are robust to the exclusion of the 1988 data. In fact, the differences between party change and no–party change and between unified and divided government are more pronounced without the 1988 data.

33. Prior to the creation of the SES there were 479 noncareer executives. After the Civil Service Reform Act there were 828. There was also a significant increase of 600 Schedule C positions between 1976 and 1980.

34. For a discussion of the contracting workforce, see Light 1999.

35. Telephone interview with Donald J. Devine, September 13, 2006.

36. Specifically, Schedule C appointees underwent a significant change during this time period and a new type of appointed position, the noncareer executive assignment, came and went.

37. For example, one of the concepts that is difficult to measure properly with the Plum Book data is politicization itself. Measuring politicization as the number of appointees in a given agency is inappropriate since larger agencies naturally will have greater numbers than smaller agencies. Measuring politicization as the percentage of appointees in an agency is also inappropriate since the percentage appointed in any given agency is very small. Large changes to the percentage can occur because of changes in agency employment that have nothing to do with politicization. This makes drawing inferences about politicization increases or decreases difficult. A more appropriate measure of politicization is the percentage of appointees relative to the number of managers but data on the number of managers is available only back to the end of the second Reagan administration.

38. It is possible to estimate models on Plum Book data from 1988 forward but to do so would require connecting OPM data to Plum Book data for each of the five Plum Books (that is, 1988, 1992, 1996, 2000, and 2004). To date, no one has done this. Doing so is difficult because of the labor involved and because the organizational units reported by the Plum Book do not always match up with the units for which OPM collects data. Fortunately, the OPM itself collects the same data as the Plum Book data, plus significantly more, dating back to 1988. The OPM data is superior to the Plum Book data since it is yearly and allows analysis at the bureau level, the appropriate level for analysis of politicization. The disad-

vantage to using the OPM data is that it counts persons rather than positions, making it difficult to disentangle increases or decreases in PAS positions from vacancies.

Chapter Five
The Pattern of Politicization: A Closer Quantitative Analysis

1. Executive Order 13422, January 18, 2007 (72 FR 2763, January 23, 2007). Under the previous order, Executive Order 12866, the regulatory policy officer was designated by the Secretary and was to be involved at every stage of the rule-making process. Now the regulatory policy officer must be an appointee and sign off on decisions rather than be involved throughout. See Katzen, Sally, "Katzen House Subcommittee Testimony on OMB and Regulatory Oversight," House Committee on Science and Technology, Subcommittee on Investigations and Oversight, February 13, 2007 (available online at www.law.umich.edu/newsandinfo/katzen.htm).

2. Pear, Robert, "Bush Directive Increases Sway on Regulation," *New York Times*, January 30, 2007; Skrzycki, Cindy, "Bush Order Limits Agencies' 'Guidance,' " *Washington Post*, January 30, 2007, D1.

3. Eggen, Dan, "Justice Department Fires 8th U.S. Attorney," *Washington Post*, February 24, 2007, A2; Goldstein, Amy, and Dan Eggen, "Number of Fired Prosecutors Grows," *Washington Post*, May 10, 2007, A1.

4. The number of managers is defined in the most generous way possible. The definition includes personnel with supervisory responsibilities, which can be anyone from a group- or team-leader to an agency supervisor or executive. Between 1988 and 2005 OPM used different codes to indicate supervisory status. These codes vary from 2 to 8. If an employee is coded with a 2, this means "position requires the exercise of supervisory or managerial responsibilities that meet, at least, the minimum requirements for application of the General Schedule Supervisory Guide or similar standards of minimum supervisory responsibility specified by position classification standards or other directives of the applicable pay schedule or system." This is the highest managerial classification. Prior to 1993 code 2 was subdivided into two separate codes, 1 and 3. After 1993 codes 1 and 3 were merged into code 2 and were phased out. Unfortunately, data is only available for code 3 prior to 1993. For most agencies the transition to code 2 from 1993 to 1995 led to a dramatic increase in the number of employees counted as managers. To measure managers I subtracted the number of employees that did not fall in a managerial category (coded with an 8) from the total number of employees. The median percentage of an agency's employees that were managers under this definition was 18 percent, and 98 percent of the cases fall within 5 percent and 66 percent. The highest percentage of managers was 86 percent, in the Office of Energy within the U.S. Department of Agriculture. There were 17 instances (out of 3,666 cases) where agencies had no managers. These occurred where there were vacancies in the appointed positions.

5. See Lewis 2005c for details.

6. See Lewis 2003.

7. We may be inclined to want to count the number of appointed positions. This is a misnomer, however, since only PAS personnel fill appointee *positions*. For the other types of appointees it makes little sense to talk of "appointed positions." There is no such thing as a vacant SES-appointee position or a vacant Schedule C position. Once appointees leave posts, the appointee-nature of the posts leaves with them. If an appointee vacates an SES job, it can be filled by a careerist member of the SES or an appointee. This is true for all general SES jobs, both those currently held by appointees and those held by careerists. If a Schedule C appointee leaves their position, the appointment authority is revoked and the appointed position no longer exists. If the administration wants to have an appointee in a role similar to that of the departing appointee, they must go through the process of creating a new Schedule C position. The best we can do to get a measure of politicization for Schedule C and appointed members of the SES is to count the number of appointees in an agency at a given time.

8. Eilperin, Juliet, "The Interior Department's 'Relief Pitcher,' " *Washington Post*, June 1, 2006, A17 (via Lexis-Nexis).

9. White 1954, 347–57.

10. See Maranto 2004; Patterson and Pfiffner 2001. See also Devroy, Ann, and Al Kamen, "At Changeover, Democrats Will Be Sparse in Many Agencies," *Washington Post*, January 20, 1993, A14 (via Lexis-Nexis); Kamen, Al, "This Time, More Company at the Top," *Washington Post*, November 25, 1997, A17 (via Lexis-Nexis).

11. Aberbach and Rockman 2000, 104; Maranto 2004.

12. For evidence that these agencies are filled with large numbers of patronage appointees, see "Growing Commerce Department Deemed 'Dumping Ground,' " *The Pantagraph* (Bloomington, Indiana), December 27, 1996, A2 (via Knight-Ridder/Tribune–Lexis-Nexis); Munroe, Tony, "Saiki Was Riding and SBA Wave Out of the Political Backwaters," *Washington Times*, December 30, 1992, C1 (via Lexis-Nexis); and Pasternak, Judy, "White House Appoints Loyalists to Education Department Posts," *Los Angeles Times*, October 3, 1999, B10.

13. For a good discussion of ideal-point estimates, see McCarty, Poole, and Rosenthal 2006, chap. 1. I use Poole's 1998 common-space scores. Higher values indicate a more conservative president and the scores for Ronald Reagan, George H. W. Bush, Bill Clinton, and George W. Bush are 0.581, 0.528, -0.432, and 0.47, respectively.

14. Specifically, we contacted thirty political scientists specializing in American or bureaucratic politics, three journalists writing on topics related to the bureaucracy, two persons working in various think tanks with expertise on bureaucracy and administration, and two employees of nonpartisan government agencies.

15. See Clinton and Lewis 2007 for details. In cases where it was feasible, models were estimated using estimates of agency liberalism-conservatism directly. In cases where this was not feasible, models include indicators for traditionally liberal (0,1; 25 percent) and conservative (0,1; 40 percent) agencies. Agencies were coded as "liberal" or "conservative" if they were statistically distinguishable from the mean agency rating. The agency ratings themselves vary from .02 to 4.49 with a mean of 2.27 and standard deviation of 1.07.

16. See White 1954, 349

17. See Lewis 2005c.

18. According to OPM, professional occupations are those white-collar occupations that "require knowledge in a field of science or learning characteristically acquired through education or training equivalent to a bachelor's or higher degree with major study in or pertinent to the specialized field, as distinguished from general education. The work of a professional occupation requires . . . the application of an organized body of knowledge that is constantly studied to make new discoveries and interpretations, and to improve the data, materials, and methods" (U.S. Office of Personnel Management 2006).

19. The percentage of each agency's employees that are professionals varies from 0 to 86 percent. The average is 25 percent, with a standard deviation of 19 percent.

20. According to OPM, technical occupations are white-collar jobs "that involve work typically associated with and supportive of a professional or administrative field, that is *nonroutine in nature*; that involves *extensive practical knowledge*, gained through *on-job experience* and/or specific training less than that represented by college graduation. Work in these occupations may involve substantial elements of the work of the professional or administrative field, but requires less than full competence in the field involved [emphasis added]" (U.S. Office of Personnel Management 2006).

21. The percentage of each agency's employees that are employed in technical occupations varies from 0 to 94 percent. The average is 12.5 percent, with a standard deviation of 11 percent.

22. I examine weekly average SES wages (weekly average earnings for the 99th percentile of workers) in 1982 dollars. The minimum value is -1.83; the maximum is .075. The mean is −.55, with a standard deviation of .61. The average SES salary was higher than the earnings of all percentiles lower than the 99th. Salaries for the SES prior to 1994 come from U.S. Office of Personnel Management, *Salary Table* (Washington, D.C.: U.S. Government Printing Office), 79–93. The exception is 1992 for the SES wages. I got this figure from Linda Oppenheimer in the Social Science Reference Center at Princeton University's Firestone Library. She got the figure from an OPM publication called, "The Status of the Senior Executive Service, 1992–1993." The rest of the salary information comes form OPM's website, available at www.opm.gov/oca/06tables/index.asp. Information on private-sector earnings comes from Jordan 2007.

23. I use the absolute value of the difference in the ideal-point estimates of the House median and the president. This value varies from .24 to .67 with a mean of .48 and a standard deviation of .17.

24. The CPDF data provides 3,666 observations on the 256 agencies. The median number of observations per agency is 18 observations. This dataset includes all agencies in existence between 1988 and 2005, except that it excludes advisory, multilateral, and educational and research institutions. To access datasets, codebooks, instructions for use of the data, and commands used to estimate the models, see www.princeton.edu/~delewis/data.htm.

25. They control for ideology by either including an indicator for whether or not the president is a Republican (0,1; 56 percent of cases) or the president's ideal-point estimate. The trend is a variable that takes on values from 0 (1988) to 17 (2005).

26. I have also estimated models with year-of-term indicators. These produce similar results but have the disadvantage of reducing degrees of freedom. They correlate with other key variables, such as party change, unified government, Republican presidents, and wage differences.

27. The log of agency employment varies from 0 to 12.81; the mean value is 6.90 and the standard deviation is 2.20 SD.

28. All commissions are coded with a 1 and other agencies 0 (19 percent).

29. Agencies in the Executive Office of the President (EOP) are coded with a 1 and all other agencies are 0 (4 percent). I have also estimated models excluding agencies in the EOP and the results are substantively similar.

30. All agencies with no larger agency infrastructure above them are coded with a 1; all other agencies are coded with a 0 (37 percent).

31. All unaffiliated parts of larger departments are also coded with a 1; all other bureaus and agencies are coded with a 0 (5 percent). In models without the unaffiliated parts of larger departments, the results are similar with one exception. The interaction of presidential and agency preferences in the model of PAS appointees is smaller and significant at the .10 level rather than the .05 level.

32. I have also estimated models with controls for the size of the White House staff. This is a count of the number of White House employees from the *United States Government Manual.* I am grateful to Matt Dickinson for providing this data. I exclude this control from the main specifications because it is correlated with other covariates that vary only by time. The results are similar except for one key variable in models of PAS appointees. Preference divergence between the president and Congress in these models is estimated to increase politicization in the short run rather than decrease it in the long run, as indicated in table 5.7. Increasing White House staff is significantly correlated with long-term decreases in PAS appointees but short-term increases in appointed SES and Schedule C appointments.

33. It should be noted that 4 percent of cases are from agencies with their own personnel system and 8 percent of cases are from agencies whose personnel systems do not include SES employees. In models where SES appointees are the dependent variable, agencies whose personnel systems do not include SES employees are excluded. In models estimated excluding agencies with their own personnel systems, the results are similar with one exception. The interaction of presidential and agency preferences in the model of PAS appointees is smaller and significant at the .10 level rather than the .05 level.

34. The dataset includes politicization data from 1988, the last year of the Reagan presidency. Since this is only one year of the Reagan presidency and analyses of changes in politicization make it impossible to draw inferences about 1988, this chapter can only discuss the three presidencies listed. According to OPM, the CPDF codes changed during this period, but many agencies did not adjust their self-reporting behavior consistent with the code changes; hence, there may be miscounting. As an employee in the Office of Federal Civilian Workforce Statistics explained to me, "For any data submitted by agencies in 1988, there would probably be some discrepancy. Because the coding changed in the CPDF as of 1986, some agencies may not have changed their coding" (email

correspondence with British Morrison, Office of Federal Civilian Workforce Statistics, August 4, 2004).

35. The log of agency managers varies from 0 to 10.95 and has a mean of 5.27 with a standard deviation of 2.02 SD.

36. When models are estimated using the cases remaining after taking logs without adding 1 to $y_{i,t}$ and $m_{i,t}$, the results are substantively similar although the coefficients are estimated less precisely. This is to be expected since the number of cases is 1,606 (146 agencies), 1,614 (172), and 1,878 (171), respectively, for PAS appointees, SES appointees, and Schedule C appointees. The substantive changes are as follows: Increasing policy disagreement between the president and Congress is estimated to lead to a short-term increase in PAS appointees. PAS appointees are also estimated to increase in the short run for traditionally conservative agencies. The interaction of presidential and agency preferences in the model of PAS appointees is larger but estimated less precisely. The p-value is $p < 0.18$ rather than $p < 0.05$. In models of the SES, an increase in the percentage of employees that are professionals is estimated to lead to a short-term increase in SES appointees, although increases in technical employees are estimated to lead to both short- and long-term decreases in appointees.

37. For a good review of dynamic specifications, see Beck 1991.

38. λ is estimated to be .11 in model 4 of table 5.5, below.

39. Beck and Katz 1995 show via simulation that panel-corrected standard errors are successful in accounting for contemporaneous and panel heteroskedastic standard errors. Specifically, these models are estimated using the xtpcse command in Stata 9.0. I have also estimated models of the different types of appointees jointly through seemingly unrelated regression and the results are similar.

40. All simulations based upon estimates from model 4 in table 5.5 unless stated otherwise. They hold other variables at their means or reasonable values and simulate changes only in the independent variable of interest. So, for example, simulations of the effects of a party change in the White House on politicization do not take into account the influence of a trend or year of the president's term.

41. Telephone interview with Mark Hunker, September 26. 2006.

42. *Federal Yellow Book* (New York: Leadership Directories, Spring 2006), 98–100.

43. See, for example, Zremski, Jerry, "White House Seeks Shake-up of Seaway Administration," *Buffalo News*, May 8, 1997, 1E (via Lexis-Nexis).

44. See McCarty and Razaghian 1999.

45. These agencies start with numbers of PAS appointees in the 90th–95th percentile.

46. Some care should be taken in interpreting the models including wage differentials. This measure does not vary by agency. It only varies over time. It is highly correlated with several variables, their differences, and their lags. For example, it is correlated at .52 with the lag of presidential ideology and −.49 with the difference of presidential ideology. Its lag was correlated at −.55 with the (first) George W. Bush administration. It is similarly correlated with the difference and lag of indicators for Republican presidents. In my judgment it was best to estimate simpler, stripped-down models, and draw inferences from these mod-

els rather than more complicated specifications where a number of highly correlated covariates are included. In some of the more complicated models, the signs
on the wage difference switch to suggest that higher outside wages increase
rather than decrease politicization. Scholars interested in these models are encouraged to get the data and batch files from the author.

47. Krugman, Paul, 2007, "Overblown Personnel Matters," *New York Times*,
March 12, 2007, A23.

48. For details on confirmations, see McCarty and Razaghian 1999.

49. For a review of the controversy over the NEA and the George W. Bush
administration's tenure of the agency, see Rauber, Marilyn, "NEA Has
Undergone Artful Makeover," *Richmond Times Dispatch*, April 24, 2005, A16 (via
Lexis-Nexis).

50. U.S. Senate 2000, 267–68.

51. U.S. House 2004, 181.

52. Rauber, "NEA Has Undergone Artful Makeover."

53. Munroe, "Saiki Was Riding and SBA Wave Out of the Political Backwaters."

54. U.S. Senate 2000, 291–94; U.S. House 2004, 195–97; *Federal Yellow Book*,
Spring 2006, 1134–41.

55. I have examined differences among agencies related to the prevalence of
Schedule A positions, as well. Some agencies, such as the Department of Justice,
employ personnel (for instance, attorneys) under Schedule A since it is not practical to hold examinations for these positions. These employees do not enjoy the
same protections as civil servants, and the prevalence of such positions arguably
gives executives more personnel control. Agencies with high percentages of
Schedule A positions include the National Security Council (NSC), the Office of
Thrift Supervision, and the Board of Veterans Appeals. Models estimated with
controls for the number of Schedule A employees do not change the general
results of the models and indicate that agencies with high numbers of Schedule
A employees maintain higher numbers of appointees than other agencies.
Whether or not an agency has its own personnel system or a high number of
Schedule A employees could be caused by the same factors that explain politicization. If this is the case, it is hard to determine the unique influence of the personnel system or the number of Schedule A employees on politicization. If exceptions
to Title 5 civil service requirements are motivated by the desire for more political
control over personnel, as in the case of the DHS, the presence of a unique personnel system could substitute for a larger number of appointees. If agency-specific
personnel systems are given to agencies with distinctive hiring needs, the separate
personnel system could substitute for a fewer number of appointees because agencies with unique hiring needs are arguably most sensitive to politicization.

Chapter Six
Politicization and Performance: The Case of the
Federal Emergency Management Agency

1. Adams, Rebecca, "FEMA Failure a Perfect Storm of Bureaucracy," *CQ Weekly*,
September 12, 2005, 2378; U.S. Senate 2006, 14–1.

2. See, for example, Bok 2003; Maranto 1998, 2001; Moe 1985.

3. See National Commission on the Public Service 1989 but also Crewson 1995. For a good review of performance-related pay and public-sector work, see Burgess and Ratto 2003.

4. Bilmes and Neal 2003. Of course, by this logic those who leave the private sector to come back to government work as appointees are arguably the least successful in the private sector.

5. Kaufman 1965; Simon et al. 1950 [1991].

6. See, for example, Cohen 1998; Heclo 1975, 1977; Kaufman 1965; National Commission on the Public Service 1989, 2003; Suleiman 2003.

7. For good reviews, see Allison 1979; Moore 1995.

8. Moore 1995.

9. Bok 2003; Krause, Lewis, and Douglas 2006; Suleiman 2003.

10. For a good review of federal pay relative to private-sector pay, see Lewis 1991.

11. Burgess and Ratto 2003; Crewson 1995; Rainey and Steinbauer 1999.

12. The quotation refers to appointees burrowing in and taking career jobs at the end of an administration. See Clark, Timothy B., and Marjorie Wachtel, "The Quiet Crisis Goes Public," *Government Executive*, June 1988, 28.

13. Spiers, Ronald I., "Two Bush Mistakes," *Washington Post*, July 23, 1989, D1.

14. For an excellent treatment of the way that merit protections can create incentives for the development of site-specific expertise, see Gailmard and Patty 2007.

15. Chang et al. 2003; Lucier et al. 2003.

16. Boylan 2004; Heclo 1977; Mann 1965; Stanley, Mann, and Doig 1967.

17. Clark and Wachtel, "The Quiet Crisis Goes Public," 28.

18. As quoted in Pfiffner 1996, 65.

19. See Bilmes and Neal 2003; Bok 2003.

20. Krause, Lewis, and Douglas 2006.

21. Whereas the United States employs over 3,000 presidential appointees, other developed countries have between 100 and 200; see Raadschelders and Lee 2005.

22. From the New Deal through the early 1980s, when the Supreme Court invalidated the legislative veto, Congress regularly delegated to the president reorganization authority. Under this authority presidents would submit reorganization plans to Congress that would go into effect after a specified date unless Congress explicitly acted to reject the plans. See Lewis 2003, 80. For FEMA, see Reorganization Plan 3 of 1978, 92 *STAT.* 3788; Executive Order 12127, 44 *FR* 19367, April 3, 1979; Executive Order 12148, 44 FR 43239, July 20, 1979. For a concise legal history of federal disaster relief since the 1950s, see Hogue and Bea 2006.

23. See National Academy of Public Administration 1993; Roberts 2006; Ward et al. 2000.

24. Roberts 2006, 61.

25. Carter 1979.

26. These included a new director and deputy director that would oversee no more than 4 new associate directors. The plan also provided for the transfer of 2 appointees from the National Fire Prevention and Control Administration; see Reorganization Plan 3 of 1978, 92 *STAT.* 3788.

27. The SES appointees primarily filled regional-director roles while the Schedule C appointees filled staff and public relations roles.

28. Daniels and Clark-Daniels 2000, 10; National Academy of Public Administration 1993, 48; Wamsley et al. 1996, 273.

29. Carter 1979.

30. Cooper and Block 2006; National Academy of Public Administration 1993, 53; Ward et al. 2000.

31. See Ward et al. 2000, 1025.

32. Daniels and Clark-Daniels 2000, 24; Roberts 2006, 61.

33. National Academy of Public Administration 1993, 53.

34. Ibid., 16.

35. Franklin, Daniel. 1995, "The FEMA Phoenix," *Washington Monthly* (July–August 1995).

36. National Academy of Public Administration 1993, 42–43; see also Ellig 2000, 8.

37. National Academy of Public Administration 1993, 69–70; Wamsley et al. 1996, 271–72.

38. National Academy of Public Administration 1993, 70.

39. Ibid., 73.

40. Telephone interview with Jan Naylor Cope, October 30, 2006; Simendinger, Alexis, "Executive Branch Courts Hill Staffers Left Jobless After Elections," *Government Executive*, December 19, 2006.

41. "Mr. Bush Inherits the Wind," *New York Times*, September 2, 1992, A18.; Earley, Pete, "Smith Accuses FEMA of Grab for Power," *Washington Post*, September 3, 1984, A19.

42. Earley, "Smith Accuses FEMA of Grab for Power."

43. "Head of Disaster Relief Agency, Targeted in Inquiries, Resigns," *Los Angeles Times*, July 25, 1985, A8; Kurtz, Howard, "FEMA Chief, 6 Aides Defy Hill Subpoena," *Washington Post*, December 13, 1984, A1.

44. Winess, Michael, "U.S. Relief Agency Seeks Relief from Criticism," *New York Times*, October 25, 1989, A29.

45. U.S. House 1992; Lippman, Thomas W., "Wounded Agency Hopes to Heal Itself by Helping Hurricane Victims," *Washington Post*, August 28, 1992, A21.

46. National Academy of Public Administration 1993, 50.

47. Claiborne, William., "Panel Backs Nominee for Disaster Agency; Clinton Pledges Better Days at FEMA," *Washington Post*, April 1, 1993, A21.

48. U.S. House 1992, 536.

49. None of the ten largest national disasters handled by FEMA occurred during the agency's first ten years, meaning none of the events it was forced to confront were so demanding that they exceeded FEMA's limited capabilities. See Daniels and Clark-Daniels 2000, 24, and Hollis 2005, 2.

50. Havemann, Judith, "Finding More Fault at FEMA," *Washington Post*, October 26, 1989, A29.

51. Franklin, "The FEMA Phoenix," 39.

52. "Waiting for FEMA? Take a Number," *Washington Post*, October 1, 1989, A4; McAllister, Bill, "FEMA Officials Admit Response to Hugo Was Slow," *Washington Post*, October 6, 1989, A29; Roberts 2006, 64–65.

53. Daniels and Clark-Daniels 2000, 12.

54. Claiborne, "Panel Backs Nominee for Disaster Agency"; Claiborne, William, "At FEMA, Allbaugh's New Order; Ex-Bush Campaign Head Brings Hands-On Managerial Style," *Washington Post*, June 4, 2001, A17.

55. Mathews, Jay, "Quake Leaves Frustration in Bay Area," *Washington Post*, April 17, 1990, A4.

56. Ward et al. 2000, 1025.

57. Franklin,"The FEMA Phoenix," 39; Mathews, "Quake Leaves Frustration in Bay Area."

58. Franklin,"The FEMA Phoenix," 40.

59. Roberts 2006, 65.

60. Davis, Bob, "Brewing Storm: Federal Relief Agency is Slowed by Infighting, Patronage, Regulations," *Wall Street Journal*, August 31, 1992, A1; Lippman, Thomas W., "Hurricane May Have Exposed Flaws in New Disaster Relief Plan," *Washington Post*, September 3, 1992, A21.

61. Bovard, James, "FEMA Money! Come and Get It!" *American Spectator* 29 (September): 24–31.

62. Lochhead, Carolyn, "Pete Stark Withdraws House Bill to End FEMA," *San Francisco Chronicle*, September 16, 1993, A8.

63. Claiborne, William, " 'Culture' Being Clubbed; Mikulski, Witt Intend to Shake Up FEMA," *Washington Post*, May 20, 1993, A21; U.S. House 1992, 541.

64. Sylves 1994; Lochhead, "Pete Stark Withdraws House Bill to End FEMA"; Murray, Mark, "FEMA Administrator Wins Management Kudos," *Government Executive*, January 16, 2001.

65. See Sylves 1994 for a review.

66. National Academy of Public Administration 1993, 72.

67. Claiborne, " 'Culture' Being Clubbed; Mikulski, Witt Intend to Shake Up FEMA"; Veron, Ilyse J., "High Marks for FEMA—for Now," *CQ Weekly*, July 17, 1993, 1862.

68. As quoted in Roberts 2006, 70.

69. Ibid.

70. Wamsley et al. 1996, 272.

71. Daniels and Clark-Daniels 2000, 13.

72. Telephone interview with Bob Nash, January 8, 2007.

73. For an insightful review, see Cooper and Block 2006, chap. 2.

74. Daniels and Clark-Daniels 2000, 16.

75. Roberts 2006, 69.

76. "FEMA's Far-Reaching Public Affairs Efforts Mitigate Flood of Concerns," *PR News* 53 (May 5, 1997): 1; Lilleston, Randy, "Earthquake Aid, Politics Keep FEMA Chief on Go," *Arkansas Democrat-Gazette*, February 6, 1994, A1; Daniels and Clark-Daniels 2000.

77. Roberts 2006, 69.

78. Ibid., 71; Bovard, "FEMA Money! Come and Get It!"

79. Schneider, Keith, "In this Emergency, Agency Wins Praise for Its Response," *New York Times*, July 20, 1993, A12.

80. For details of FEMA's response, see Claiborne, "At FEMA, Allbaugh's New Order; Ex-Bush Campaign Head Brings Hands-On Managerial Style"; for discussion of Witt's contacting members of Congress, see Roberts 2006, 69.

81. Veron, "High Marks for FEMA—for Now."

82. Schneider, "In this Emergency, Agency Wins Praise for its Response."

83. Veron, "High Marks for FEMA—for Now"; Franklin, "The FEMA Phoenix," 42.

84. Cooper and Block 2006, 63.

85. Lilleston, "Earthquake Aid, Politics Keep FEMA Chief on Go"; Zuckman, Jill, "Federal Response; Embattled Agency Rebuilds Its Image," *Boston Globe*, January 19, 1994, A10.

86. Lilleston, "Earthquake Aid, Politics Keep FEMA Chief on Go."

87. Ibid.

88. Franklin, "The FEMA Phoenix," 42.

89. See "Calif. Fire Response Saves FEMA Image," *Charleston* [West Virginia] *Gazette*, January 3, 1994, B9; Franklin, "The FEMA Phoenix," 42; Schneider 1998, 50–52.

90. Franklin, "The FEMA Phoenix"; Daniels and Clark-Daniels 2000; Schneider 1998; Hogue and Bea 2006.

91. Roberts 2006, 57.

92. Ibid.

93. Anrig 2007, 8; Ellig 2000.

94. Murray, "FEMA Administrator Wins Management Kudos."

95. Klinenberg, Eric, and Thomas Frank, "Looting Homeland Security," *Rolling Stone*, December 15, 2005 (online edition, available at www.rollingstone.com/politics/story/ 8952492/looting_homeland_security/).

96. As quoted in Roberts 2006, 72.

97. Ibid., 73.

98. Ibid., 75; Claiborne, William, "Disaster Management Cuts Raise Concerns," *Washington Post*, May 8, 2001, A21.

99. Anrig 2007, 9.

100. Claiborne, "At FEMA, Allbaugh's New Order; Ex-Bush Campaign Head Brings Hands-On Managerial Style."

101. Four of these were staff positions in the Director's office.

102. Source: U.S. Office of Personnel Management, Central Personnel Data File (available online at www.fedscope.opm.gov).

103. Grunwald, Michael, and Susan B. Glasser, "Brown's Turf Wars Sapped FEMA's Strength," *Washington Post*, December 23, 2005, A1.

104. He then worked briefly as White House liaison in the Commerce Department before appointment as the Associate Administrator of the Small Business Administration (SBA); see Claiborne, "At FEMA, Allbaugh's New Order; Ex-Bush Campaign Head Brings Hands-On Managerial Style."

105. Craig was also lobbyist for the National Rural Electric Cooperative Association, and a campaign advisor and fundraiser; see Silverstein, Ken, "Katrina's Aftermath: Top FEMA Jobs—No Experience Required," *Los Angeles Times*, September 9, 2005, A10.

106. U.S. Senate 2006, 14–5.

107. U.S. Senate 2006, 14–4. For an example, see Carter, Mike, and Susan Kelleher, "Local FEMA Chief Had Little Disaster Experience," *Seattle Times*, September 10, 2005, A1.

108. U.S. Senate 2006, 14–4.

109. Anrig 2007, chap. 1.

110. Claiborne,"Disaster Management Cuts Raise Concerns"; Roberts 2006, 75; Harris, Shane, "What FEMA May Have Gotten Right," *National Journal*, September 17, 2005, 2842.

111. Lunney, Kellie, "FEMA Was Prepared for Terrorist Acts, Agency Chief Says," *Government Executive*, October 16, 2001; Schimmel 2006, 32.

112. Chen, David W., "FEMA Criticized for Its Handling of 9/11 Claims," *New York Times*, January 8, 2003, A5; Henriques, Diana B., "Senate Seeks Inquiry Into FEMA 9/11 Role," *New York Times*, May 4, 2002, B4; Wald, Matthew L., "With Hurricane Charley, a Federal Agency Gets a New Chance to Prove Itself," *New York Times*, August 26, 2004, 16.

113. Henriques, "Senate Seeks Inquiry Into FEMA 9/11 Role."

114. Wald, "With Hurricane Charley, a Federal Agency Gets a New Chance to Prove Itself."

115. Hollis 2005, 7; Schimmel 2006, 31–34; Roberts 2006, 76.

116. The appointee number comes from OPM's Fedscope website (available online at www.fedscope.opm.gov). Information on Allbaugh's location comes from Cooper and Block 2006.

117. Daniels and Clark-Daniels 2000, 8.

118. U.S. Senate 2006, 14–5.

119. Ibid.

120. The authors of the 2002 act intended for FEMA to absorb the Office of Domestic Preparedness (ODP), a Justice Department office that gave out terrorism-preparedness grants. In January 2004, however, the Department's first Secretary, Tom Ridge, instead moved ODP to the DHS Secretary's office and began transferring FEMA preparedness grants and personnel to ODP. Part of Ridge's decision to wrest preparedness out of FEMA's control stemmed from congressional support for ODP and his personal conflicts with Brown. DHS officials viewed Brown as a vigorous turf warrior rather than a team player insofar as Brown was aggressively trying to protect FEMA's role in the department. After a 2005 review of the new department's organization and structure, new DHS Secretary Michael Chertoff completed the process begun by Ridge. He replaced FEMA (called the Emergency Preparedness and Response Directorate) with two new directorates. The first was called the Preparedness Directorate and was created from an elevated ODP and what remained of FEMA's grant-making personnel and budgets. The second new directorate was named the Emergency Management Directorate and comprised what remained of FEMA. See Grunwald and Glasser, "Brown's Turf Wars Sapped FEMA's Strength"; U.S. Senate 2006, 14–3.

121. Roberts 2006, 78.

122. Grunwald and Glasser, "Brown's Turf Wars Sapped FEMA's Strength."

123. U.S. Senate 2006, 14–7, 8–9.

124. Barr, Stephen, "Morale Among FEMA Workers, on the Decline for Years, Hits Nadir," *Washington Post*, September 14, 2005, B2. The survey referred to in the article was conducted in the fall of 2002, before FEMA's move into DHS.

125. Mann 2004.

126. Sullivan 2006.

127. Hsu, Spencer S., "Leaders Lacking Disaster Experience," *Washington Post*, September 9, 2005, A1.

128. U.S. Senate 2006, 14–7.

129. Glasser, Susan B., and Josh White, "Storm Exposed Disarray at the Top," *Washington Post*, September 4, 2005, A1; U.S. Senate 2006, 15.

130. While some criticized the agency for being too slow in 2004, the primary criticism leveled against the agency was that it had been both too lax and too generous in its recovery efforts; see Schimmel 2006, 66.

131. Adams, "FEMA Failure a Perfect Storm of Bureaucracy"; U.S. Senate 2006, 14–1.

132. U.S. Government Accounting Office 2006; U.S. Senate 2006.

133. DHS Inspector General's report, November 2005, as quoted in U.S. Senate 2006, 15; U.S. Government Accounting Office 2006, 14; Strohm, Chris, "Exercise Months Before Katrina Showed Gaps in Response," *Government Executive*, December 15, 2005.

134. For a good review, see U.S. Government Accounting Office 2006, 5–9; Cooper and Block 2006.

135. U.S. House 2006, 2.

136. U.S. Senate 2006, 15.

137. On September 1, as New Orleans was under water, DHS contractors received drafts of documents describing the "national preparedness goal," described as the "rules of engagement" for catastrophic events. The documents, over four hundred pages of material, were not supposed to be released until October. See Glasser and White, "Storm Exposed Disarray at the Top."

138. A Disturbing View from Inside FEMA," *CNN Online*, September 17, 2005 (available at www.cnn.com/2005/US/09/17/katrina.response/index.html.

139. U.S. Senate 2006, 9.

140. Ibid.

141. Roberts 2006, 78.

142. U.S. Senate 2006, 7.

143. Grunwald and Glasser, "Brown's Turf Wars Sapped FEMA's Strength."

144. U.S. Senate 2006, 14–8, 14–11.

145. U.S. Senate 2006, 4.

146. Adams, "FEMA Failure a Perfect Storm of Bureaucracy."

147. Hsu, Spencer S., "Chertoff Vows to 'Re-engineer' Preparedness," *Washington Post*, October 20, 2005, A2.

148. U.S. Senate 2006, 10.

149. " 'Can I Quit Now?' FEMA Chief Wrote as Katrina Raged," *CNN Online*, November 3, 2005 (available at http://www.cnn.com/2005/US/11/03/brown.fema.emails/).

150. Silverstein, "Katrina's Aftermath."

Chapter Seven
Politicization and Performance: The Larger Pattern

1. For an excellent review, see Boyne 2003. See also Brewer and Selden 2000.

2. For examples, see Clark, Timothy B., and Marjorie Wachtel, "The Quiet Crisis Goes Public," *Government Executive*, June 1988, 28.

3. For a general discussion of difficulties managing career employees, see Kettl and Fesler 2005, 178–79.

4. Brewer and Selden 2000.

5. This research finds that state-level forecasting agencies with either appointed directors and careerist employees or careerist directors and at-will employees produce the most accurate forecasts; see Krause, Lewis, and Douglas 2006. At the federal level, the evidence suggests no difference in current-year forecast performance among agencies, based on differences in agency design. Krause and Douglas 2005 examine current-year forecasts by the Council of Economic Advisers, the Office of Management and Budget (OMB), the Congressional Budget Office (CBO), and the Federal Reserve. Krause and Douglas 2006 show no difference in the current-year fiscal projections for the CBO and the OMB. Some studies, however, indicate that the more-politicized OMB is systematically more optimistic in some of its future-year forecasts than the less-politicized Social Security Administration (SSA), although the optimism appears unrelated to changing politicization levels within each agency over time. See Krause and Corder 2007.

6. There was a 51 percent response rate in 2002 and a 54 percent response rate in 2004. For full details, see www.fhcs2004.opm.gov. The Office of Personnel Management (OPM) made the data available in different levels of aggregation in order to protect the identity of survey respondents. Individual-level data is only available at the highest level of aggregation. So, for example, we might know that Respondent 1 works in the Department of Justice but we do not know whether he or she works in the Civil Rights Division or the Tax Division. Agency-level data is available at lower levels of aggregation, so that we know, for example, what percentages answered "Yes" to question 11 in 2004 in each division. I use the agency-level data to maximize the variation on the degree of agency political penetration. OPM made the aggregate data on survey responses available to the Partnership for Public Service, a nonprofit agency whose mission is to encourage public service as a career. I obtained the data from the partnership subject to certain limitations on its use. The size of the samples drawn from the different agencies varies depending, in part, on the size of the agency. The smallest sample was drawn from the Office of the Inspector General in HUD (3) and the largest was drawn from the Army Corps of Engineers (6,295). The average sample size is 594 persons (s.d. 638).

7. Portions of the PART research have previously appeared in Lewis 2007.

8. The instrument is adjusted for the type of program under consideration (regulatory, block-grant, research-and-development, and so forth); see U.S. Office of Management and Budget 2002, 2003.

9. Disagreements between the OMB and agencies are resolved by appeals up the OMB hierarchy. Appeals first go to the OMB branch chief and then to the division director and program associate director, if necessary.

10. U.S. Office of Management and Budget 2002, 2003.

11. The George W. Bush administration claims a loosely stratified sampling scheme was used to select the first cohort. When asked to describe the initial sampling scheme, the OMB's Program Associate Director Marcus Peacock called the approach a "stratified sampling scheme." He said OMB tried to get a diverse group of programs, large and small, programs with a history of good management and bad management, and programs with different missions and functions. Comments made at *Program Performance and the FY 2004 Budget Process* conference, June 13, 2003, 2247 Rayburn House Office Building, Washington, D.C.

12. Anecdotal evidence from interviews with the OMB and agency officials involved in the PART process indicates that both the bureau chiefs being evaluated and budget examiners doing the evaluating believe that the scores measure variance in true management quality. See Gilmour 2006.

13. For a review of problems with the implementation of PART, see U.S. Government Accountability Office 2004a, 2005a. For a discussion of the usefulness of the PART grades for comparing management quality across programs, see Gilmour and Lewis 2006c.

14. Of course, if appointees were selected to run only the hardest programs or if appointees wanted programs to fail, this would make this data difficult to interpret. I deal with each of these possibilities in more detail below and in appendix 7A.

15. *Federal Yellow Book* (New York: Leadership Directories, various years); U.S. Senate 2000; U.S. House 2004.

16. Of the 242 bureau chiefs, 2 had atypical appointment authorities—that is, Schedule C, presidential appointee without Senate confirmation (PA).

17. I have replicated the succeeding analysis with program categorical grades. Appointees get lower average program grades, as well. In general, categorical grades provide less information than numerical scores and are more prone to political manipulation, so I focus on PART scores rather than on the categorical grades. Subsequent analyses using PART scores have been replicated with program grades, but the estimates for program grades are generally estimated less precisely. They are available upon request from the author.

18. The figure 7.2 equation is PART Score = $64.47 - 0.49 *\%$ Managers appointed ($N=407$, $R2. = 0.09$). I exclude outliers, namely, all agencies where the percentage appointed is in the 99th percentile or higher (greater than 80 percent of managers are appointees), which are clear outliers in the data. When I graph the relationship with these cases included, the regression line also slopes downward noticeably, but the majority of the cases are bunched up closer to the y-axis. Throughout the analysis that follows I exclude the extreme values. I have estimated models with the extreme values and reached similar results. To do so, however, requires the inclusion of a squared term to model nonlinearity. The results consistently indicate that increasing the percentage of appointed managers decreases PART scores significantly. Not surprisingly, given the functional form, the effects are largest to start and then peak at about 100 percent ap-

pointed. Substantively, increasing politicization 0–10 percent is estimated to decrease total PART scores by 6 points, 10–25 percent by 5.5 points, and so forth.

19. The percentages do not sum to 100 due to rounding.

20. Source: U.S. Office of Management and Budget 2005. In the analysis to come I include indicators for program function and I control for the natural log of the program budget.

21. Moe 1989.

22. Source: Office of Personnel Management, Central Personnel Data File. Agency employment (3,027, median; 12,419, mean; min., 10; max., 230,238). Agency managers (426, median; 1,378, mean; min., 2; max., 23,832. Agency programs (4.6, mean; min., 1; max., 13). I have also estimated models that include the number of managers/number of employees as a measure of thickness. The results are the same and in these models thickness is positively correlated to PART scores.

23. Source: U.S. Senate 2000; U.S. House 2004. These indicators are one way of measuring the degree of presidential influence over a bureau. I have also estimated models using an ordinal measure of presidential influence where agencies in the Executive Office of the President (EOP) are coded with a 0, agencies in the cabinet a 1, independent administrations a 2, independent commissions a 3, and other agencies (including the District of Columbia, government corporations, and joint federal-state agencies) a 4. I have interacted this measure with the appointee indicator to see whether the influence of appointees on management differs depending on the degree of insulation. These models confirm what is reported here: that appointee-run programs get systematically lower management grades. I could not reject the null hypothesis that the coefficients on the insulation indicator and the interaction were 0.

24. I use agency liberalism-conservatism estimates from Clinton and Lewis 2007, which are described in more detail in chapter 5, above.

25. Modeling the selection of appointees and careerists directly does not influence the estimates of appointments on PART scores, which suggests that appointees do have a distinct influence on performance. It is not that appointees are selected to administer the most difficult programs. I leave the technical details of the analysis to the notes here and present a more extended discussion in appendix 7A.

26. These results are available upon request from the author. For a full discussion of the possibility that Republican appointees want programs to fail and this is the reason appointee-run programs get lower PART scores, see Appendix 7A.

27. I have also estimated models that examine the interaction between appointee management and the composition of the agency's managers overall. In these models careerist managers are always estimated to have higher PART scores than appointees, and increasing percentages of appointees in the management team reduce PART scores. There is some evidence that agencies managed by careerists get slightly higher PART scores when appointees are added to the management team, but the coefficients are not significant and these estimates are based on only a handful of cases. In most cases careerist-run agencies have very few, if any, appointees on the management team. I have also examined the influence of appointees on agencies that have agency-specific personnel systems. The

models indicate that programs administered by agencies with their own personnel systems get higher PART scores than other programs, provided the agencies
are administered by career managers. The best estimated performance is from
careerist-run programs in agencies with their own personnel systems, followed
by careerist-run programs where employees are drawn from the civil service. Appointee-run programs with civil service managers are the third-best performers,
and the poorest-performing bureaus are those with appointee-management and
agency-specific personnel systems. Some caution should be applied here, however, since only two programs (both in the Nuclear Regulatory Commission
[NRC]) are run by careerist managers in agencies with their own personnel system. These estimates are mostly consistent with the findings of Krause, Lewis,
and Douglas (2006), who find the highest performance in agencies that mix at-
will and merit-based staffing.

28. Mackenzie 1987.

29. One difficulty here is that tenure could be endogenous. If a program is
very difficult to manage, this could influence both how long a manager serves
and its PART score. I deal with this issue fully in appendix 7A.

30. Results for previous bureau experience and tenure weaken in models controlling for the percentage of managers appointed. Specifically, while the coefficient is the same size and direction, the standard error on the coefficient for
previous bureau experience is larger in these models: that is, it is significant at
only the .10 level in a two-tailed test. The coefficient on tenure and tenure
squared is still in the expected direction, but it is smaller and no longer significant. It is unclear whether the weakening of the results is due to a decrease in
the number of cases (549, 459 versus 334) or whether the coefficient on tenure
was picking up the effects of politicization of the work environment. These results
are available from the author upon request.

31. While there were other questions arguably related to performance in each
of these areas, I tried to balance concerns for rigor with the need for parsimony.
I, therefore, focus only on those questions most directly related to performance.
Interested readers can find the other questions addressed in U.S. Office of Personnel Management 2002, appendix A; U.S. Office of Personnel Management
2004, appendix B.

32. In two of the seven questions, the question wording was slightly different
in 2002 than in 2004. Specifically, one question says, *I hold my organization's leaders
in high regard* in 2002 but *I have a high level of respect for my organization's senior leaders*
in 2004. Another says, *Managers promote communication among different work units
(for example, about projects, goals, needed resources)* in 2002 but simply *Managers promote
communication among different work units* in 2004. This can lead to problems in inference if differences in question wording are correlated with key variables of interest. To ensure the comparability of the questions, I (1) compared the distributions
of the responses in 2002 with the responses in 2004 in these two cases and (2)
correlated responses in 2002 and 2004 with a related variable where there was no
difference in question wording. If the distributions looked similar and correla-
tions looked similar, I concluded that variables with different question wordings
could be considered the same. In the first case the means were 44 and 50, with
standard deviations of 7.4 and 8.6 for 2002 and 2004, respectively. Each was corre-

lated with the question about whether senior leaders created motivation and commitment in the workforce at 0.91. In the second case, the means were 50 and 53, with standard deviations of 6.5 and 7.4, respectively. They were correlated at the 0.63 and 0.67 level with the question about whether managers reviewed the organization's progress toward long-term goals. I also estimated models with split samples and the results confirm what is reported here with one exception. In the model of *I hold my organization's leaders in high regard* in 2002 the coefficient on percentage of managers appointed is estimated less precisely (p < .32) than what is reported in the text. These results are available from the author upon request.

33. Appointee percentage varied from 0 to 53, with a standard deviation of 7.

34. There are notable outliers in politicization. Specifically, there are four agencies with management teams including over 38 percent (99th percentile) appointees. These include the Office of the Secretary of Defense (2002, 2004), OMB (2002), the Office of the United States Trade Representative (2002), and the Office of Elementary and Secondary Education (2002). Excluding outlier cases using different thresholds has very little influence on the outcomes (for example, 90th, 95th, 99th percentile).

35. The influence of appointee percentage is nonlinear. As the percentage of appointees increases, its influence lessens. The influence of appointees is estimated to be increasingly negative until about two standard deviations away from the mean level of appointees. The nonlinear nature of the appointee percentage implies that the influence of appointees would be positive in several of the models if the appointee percentage exceeded 30 percent. There are five agencies with appointee percentages above 30 percent, two agencies in the EOP, two Offices of the Secretary (Defense), and the Office of Elementary and Secondary Education. It is questionable whether the experience of personnel in these agencies is generalizable to other employees.

36. Mackenzie 1987.

37. Blumenthal, Sidney, "A Vanguard for the Right," *Washington Post*, September 22, 1985, A1; idem, "Quest for Lasting Power," *Washington Post*, September 25, 1985, A1; Roberts, Steven V., "Preserving Reagan's Legacy," *New York Times*, May 7, 1987, B14; telephone interview with Donald J. Devine, September 13, 2006.

38. For most of these models, the relevant coefficients are larger and estimated more precisely than the models included in the text. The exceptions to this general pattern are fully specified models of manager background. These models are estimated on fewer cases since there is missing data in some of the control variables. In these models the coefficients are slightly smaller and estimated less precisely so that they are no longer significant.

39. In order for the models to be identified one must include exogenous regressors that predict whether a bureau chief is a careerist or an appointee but not PART score directly. I include several exogenous regressors in the instrumental variables specifications. To begin, consider that whether a bureau chief is an appointee or a careerist has a lot to do with the politics at the time a program is created in addition to the choices of the current administration (Epstein and O'Halloran 1999; Lewis 2003, 2005c; McCarty 2004; Moe 1989; Zegart 1999). As such, with the help of a colleague, I found the date each program was created

and coded each program according to political factors at the time it was created. Many aspects of the political environment at the time the program was created should help predict whether the program is administered by an appointee or a careerist. First, presidents add more appointees in their first terms and in certain years within those terms. I include indicator variables both for second term and years within a term. I include an indicator for whether an agency is created at the start of a new administration (0,1). I also include an indicator for whether the program was created during a war (0,1). During times of war, presidents are given more control over the bureaucracy. To account for the choices of the current administration, I include indicators for when the program was evaluated by the George W. Bush administration. The probability that a program is administered by an appointee should vary depending on when it is evaluated. There are more appointees in the administration in the second year, for example, than in the third or fourth years. First-stage estimates suggest that the year of the current president's term and the newness of the administration are significantly related to whether or not a program is administered by an appointee. War, second terms, and periods of divided government are close to significance. After model estimation I used two methods to determine whether an instrumental variables approach was necessary. The first was a simple Hausman test. I could not reject the null hypothesis that the coefficients were equal. For the second test, I regressed whether or not the bureau chief was a careerist (0,1) on the exogenous regressors. I then obtained predicted values and inserted those into the original OLS regression. I could not reject the null hypothesis that the coefficient on these fitted values was equal to 0.

40. It is possible that the instruments I chose are not completely independent of the PART score. For example, if people learn during the PART scoring process how to better fill out the worksheet, the PART score may be correlated with the year of evaluation. If the instruments are not exogenous, then the estimates of the instrumental variables specifications are questionable, and thus some caution should be used when interpreting the coefficient estimates on tenure.

41. I use the scores from Clinton and Lewis 2007, described in greater detail in chapter 5, above. "Conservative" agencies are those whose liberalism-conservatism estimates were statistically greater than 0.

42. I have estimated models interacting appointee management with agency-specific personnel systems and the results suggest that agency-specific personnel systems are correlated with better performance in cases where the agencies are managed by career civil servants. In cases where appointees manage agencies with agency-specific personnel systems, the effect of the agency-specific personnel system disappears.

43. I code all agencies in the Department of Defense with a 1 and all other agencies with a 0 for the defense indicator. To code regulatory agencies I use Dudley and Warren 2003. This regular publication of the Weidenbaum Center tracks regulatory spending over time on an agency-by-agency basis and is a useful tool for identifying which federal agencies engage in regulatory behavior (the information is available online at http://wc.wustl.edu). To code science agencies I use a list of the most important science positions produced by the National Academy of Sciences; see National Academy of Sciences 1992, 2000, 2004.

44. Specifically, in the models including fixed effects the coefficients on appointee management are similar except that the coefficients are sometimes smaller and estimated less precisely. In the split samples the coefficient estimates are very similar.

45. I have performed standard regression diagnostics on the models and they indicate a few problems. In the models on (1) whether or not managers provide the job-relevant knowledge and skills and (2) whether or not managers promote communication, I could reject the null of homoskedasticity in models without the adjustment on the standard errors. Models estimated with generic robust standard errors produced similar conclusions. The diagnostics also revealed outliers in the percentage of managers appointed and the ratio of managers to employees. The outlier cases on percentage of managers appointed are discussed in the text. Models estimated without these cases produce estimates consistent with expectations. Specifically, the effects become more linear and remain negative, indicating that increases in appointees are correlated with lower evaluations. The three outlier cases on ratio of managers to employees are Pacific Air Forces, HQ Air Intelligence Agency, and the Office of the Inspector General in HUD. Each has 100 percent managers. Excluding these cases from the analyses produces no substantive change in the estimates.

46. Since theoretically politicians could choose career civil servants, military officers, or political appointees to run an agency, the first stage predicts whether an appointee runs the agency relative to a careerist. I exclude defense agencies where military officers were also a possibility. It should be noted, however, that the estimates were estimated imprecisely. I therefore conclude that some caution should be used in interpreting these results.

Chapter Eight
Learning the Lessons of Politicization

1. Interview with Mickey Edwards (R-OK), Princeton, New Jersey, October 18, 2006.

2. Telephone interview with Arnie Miller, October 18, 2006.

3. As quoted in Weko 1995, 46.

4. Eggen, Dan, "6 of 7 Dismissed U.S. Attorneys Had Positive Job Evaluations," *Washington Post*, February 18, 2007, A11; Eggen, Dan, and Paul Kane, "Justice Department Would Have Kept 'Loyal' Prosecutors," *Washington Post*, March 16, 2007, A2.

5. Eggen, Dan, "Justice Department Expands Probe to Include Hiring Practices," *Washington Post*, May 31, 2007, A4.

6. I estimate the same model for the FHCS data as in chapter 7, using responses to survey questions 47–49 as the dependent variable. The coefficients on appointee leadership (0,1) or appointee percentage (mean 2.88; s.d. 7.01) are large and significant ($p < .05$). Agencies headed by appointees are estimated to have 4–6 percent fewer respondents agreeing with statements suggesting that politicizing-type activity is not present. Increasing the appointee percentage from the median to the 75th percentile decreases the average agreeing with these statements by 1.5 to 2.5 percentage points.

7. See, generally, Derlien 1996 and Suleiman 2003. But see also Derlien 1985 (Germany); Dunn 1997 (Australia); Fry 1984, Mascarenhas 1993, and Ridley 1985 (Britain); Merikoski 1969 and Stahlberg 1987 (Finland). Concerns about politicization in Germany go back at least as far as the Weimar Republic, when right-wing parties accused the government of furthering a "party book administration"; see Derlien 1985, 3.

8. Dunn 1997, 10.

9. Rhodes 2000; Suleiman 2003, 254–55.

10. Derlien 1985 describes these patterns particularly after party turnover in Germany in 1969 and 1982.

11. Telephone interview with James B. King, September 22, 2006.

12. Suleiman 2003.

13. Evans and Rauch 1999; Rauch and Evans 2000.

14. Telephone interview with James B. King, September 22, 2006.

15. This is not to mention PA appointees located primarily in the White House.

16. Rapoport and Stone 2005.

17. Hogue 2003.

18. Revkin, Andrew C., "A Young Bush Appointee Resigns His Post at NASA," *New York Times*, February 8, 2006.

19. Richard Clarke, "Against All Enemies: Inside America's War on Terror," speech delivered at the Woodrow Wilson School of Public and International Affairs, Princeton University, November 10, 2004.

20. Hsu, Spencer S., "Bush Balks at Criteria for FEMA Director," *Washington Post*, October 7, 2006, A2.

21. The bill, H.R. 3925, was introduced September 27, 2005, in the 109th Congress, 2d Session; details are available online at www.oversight.house.gov/ story.asp?ID=930.

22. Lipton, Eric, "FEMA Calls, but Top Job is Tough Sell," *New York Times*, April 2, 2006, A1.

23. Ban and Marzotto 1984.

List of Interviews

Presidential Personnel Office

Biggins, J. Veronica
Cope, Jan Naylor
Dunlop, Becky Norton
Horner, Constance
Hunker, Mark
James, Pendleton
Johnson, Clay
King, James B.

Malek, Fred
Miller, Arnie
Moy, Ed
Nash, Bob
Patterson, Bradley H.
Sheketoff, Emily
Untermeyer, Charles

Office of Personnel Management

Brook, Douglas
Cohen, Steve
Devine, Donald J.
Everett, Delores
Flynn, Ed
Hausser, Doris
Horner, Constance

Hunker, Mark
James, Kay Coles
King, James B.
Lachance, Janice
Okin, Carol J.
Shein, Leigh
Sheketoff, Emily

Other Public Officials

Adamske, Steven
Berry, Marion (D-AR)
Borbely-Batis, Anne-Marie
Edwards, Mickey (R-OK)
Finkel, Adam

Neel, Roy
Schnapp, Robert
Volcker, Paul
Waxman, Henry (D-CA)
Wilkerson, Lawrence

References

A Discussion with Gerald R. Ford: The American Presidency. 1977. Washington, D.C.: American Enterprise Institute.

Aberbach, Joel D., and Bert A. Rockman. 1976. "Clashing Beliefs Within the Executive Branch: The Nixon Administration Bureaucracy." *American Political Science Review* 70 (2):456–68.

———. 1990. "From Nixon's Problem to Reagan's Achievement: The Federal Executive Reexamined." In *Looking Back on the Reagan Presidency*, ed. L. Berman. Baltimore, Md.: The Johns Hopkins University Press.

———. 2000. *In the Web of Politics: Three Decades of the U.S. Federal Executive.* Washington, D.C.: Brookings Institution Press.

Allison, Graham T. 1979. "Public and Private Management: Are They Alike in All Unimportant Respects?" Paper presented at Public Management Research Conference, Washington, D.C.

Anrig, Greg. 2007. *The Conservatives Have No Clothes: Why Right-Wing Ideas Keep Failing.* New York: John Wiley and Sons.

Arnold, Peri E. 1998. *Making the Managerial Presidency: Comprehensive Reorganization Planning, 1905–1996.* 2nd rev. ed. Lawrence: University Press of Kansas.

Arnold, R. Douglas. 1979. *Congress and the Bureaucracy: A Theory of Influence.* New Haven: Yale University Press.

Balla, Steven J. 1998. "Administrative Procedures and Political Control of the Bureaucracy." *American Political Science Review* 92 (3):663–73.

Ban, Carolyn. 1984. "Implementing Civil Service Reform: Structure and Strategy." In Patricia W. Ingraham and Carolyn Ban, eds. *Legislating Bureaucratic Change: The Civil Service Reform Act of 1984.* Albany, N.Y.: State University of New York Press.

Ban, Carolyn, and Patricia W. Ingraham. 1984. "Introduction." In Patricia W. Ingraham and Carolyn Ban, eds. *Legislating Bureaucratic Change: The Civil Service Reform Act of 1984.* Albany, N.Y.: State University of New York Press.

Ban, Carolyn, and Toni Marzotto. 1984. "Delegations of Examining: Objectives and Implementation." In Patricia W. Ingraham and Carolyn Ban, eds. *Legislating Bureaucratic Change: The Civil Service Reform Act of 1984.* Albany, N.Y.: State University of New York Press.

Bardach, Eugene. 1977. *The Implementation Game.* Boston, Mass.: MIT Press.

Bartels, Larry. 2007. *Unequal Democracy: The Political Economy of the New Gilded Age.* Unpublished manuscript, Princeton University.

Beck, Nathaniel, and Jonathan N. Katz. 1991. "Comparing Dynamic Specifications: The Case of Presidential Approval." *Political Analysis* 3:51–87.

———. 1995. "What to Do (and Not to Do) with Time-Series Cross-Section Data." *American Political Science Review* 89 (3):634–47.

Bilmes, Linda J., and Jeffrey R. Neal. 2003. "The People Factor: Human Resources Reform in Government." In *For the People: Can We Fix Public Service?* ed. J. D. Donahue and J. S. Nye. Washington, D.C.: Brookings Institution Press.

Bok, Derek. 2003. "Government Personnel Policy in Comparative Perspective." In *For the People: Can We Fix the Public Service?* ed. J. D. Donahue and J. S. Nye. Washington, D.C.: Brookings Institution Press.

Boylan, Richard T. 2004. "Salaries, Turnover, and Performance in the Federal Criminal Justice System." *Journal of Law and Economics* 47:75–92.

Boyne, George A. 2003. "Sources of Public Service Improvement: A Critical Review and Research Agenda." *Journal of Public Administration Research and Theory* 13 (3):367–94.

Brauer, Carl. 1987. "Tenure, Turnover, and Postgovernment Employment Trends of Presidential Appointees." In *The In-and-Outers: Presidential Appointees and Transient Government in Washington,* ed. G. C. Mackenzie. Baltimore, Md.: The Johns Hopkins University Press.

Brewer, Gene A., and Sally Coleman Selden. 2000. "Why Elephants Gallop: Assessing and Predicting Organizational Performance in Federal Agencies." *Journal of Public Administration Research and Theory* 10 (4):685–711.

Brown, Roger G. 1982. "Party and Bureaucracy: From Kennedy to Reagan." *Political Science Quarterly* 97:279–94.

Burgess, Simon, and Marisa Ratto. 2003. "The Role of Incentives in the Public Sector: Issues and Evidence." *Oxford Review of Economic Policy* 19 (2):285–300.

Burke, John P. 2000. *Presidential Transitions: From Politics to Practice.* Boulder, Colo.: Lynne Rienner.

———. 2004. *Becoming President: The Bush Transition, 2000–2003.* Boulder, Colo.: Lynne Rienner.

Campbell, James E. 2000. *The American Campaign.* College Station, Tex.: Texas A&M University Press.

Carpenter, Daniel P. 2001. *The Forging of Bureaucratic Autonomy: Reputations, Networks, and Policy Innovation in Executive Agencies, 1862–1928.* Princeton, N.J.: Princeton University Press.

———. 2005. "The Evolution of the National Bureaucracy in the United States." In *The Executive Branch,* ed. J. D. Aberbach and M. A. Peterson. New York: Oxford University Press.

Carter, James Earl. 1978. *Message of the President Accompanying Submission of Reorganization Plan No. 3 of 1978.* Washington, D.C.: Government Printing Office.

Chang, Kelly, Stuart V. Jordan, David E. Lewis, and Nolan M. McCarty. 2003. "The Tenure of Political Appointees." Paper presented at Annual Meeting of the Midwest Political Science Association, Chicago, Ill.

Chang, Kelly, David E. Lewis, and Nolan M. McCarty. 2000. "Turnover Among Political Appointees." Paper presented at Annual Meeting of the American Political Science Association, Washington, D.C.

Clayton, Cornell. 1992. *The Politics of Justice: The Attorney General and the Making of Legal Policy.* Armonk, N.Y.: M. E. Sharpe.

Clinton, Joshua D., and David E. Lewis. 2007. "Expert Opinion, Agency Characteristics, and Agency Preferences." *Political Analysis,* Forthcoming.

Cohen, David M. 1998. "Amateur Government." *Journal of Public Administration Research and Theory* 8:450–97.

Cook, Daniel M., and Andrew J. Polsky. 2005. "Political Time Reconsidered: Unbuilding and Rebuilding the State Under the Reagan Administration." *American Politics Research* 33 (4):577–605.

Cooper, Christopher, and Robert Block. 2006. *Disaster: Hurricane Katrina and the Failure of Homeland Security.* New York: Times Books.

Corwin, Edward S. 1939. "The President as Administrative Chief." *Journal of Politics* 1(2):17–61.

Crewson, Philip E. 1995. "A Comparative Analysis of Public and Private Sector Entrant Quality." *American Journal of Political Science* 39 (3):628–39.

Daalder, Ivo H., I. M. Destler, James M. Lindsay, Paul C. Light, Robert E. Litan, Michael E. O'Hanlon, Peter R. Orszag, and James B. Steinberg. 2002. *Assessing the Department of Homeland Security.* Washington, D.C.: Brookings Institution Press.

Daniels, R. Steven, and Carolyn L. Clark-Daniels. 2000. *Transforming Government: The Renewal and Revitalization of the Federal Emergency Management Agency.* Report for PriceWaterhouseCoopers Endowment for the Business of Government, April 2000.

David, Paul T., and Ross Pollock. 1957. *Executives for Government: Central Issues of Federal Personnel Administration.* Washington, D.C.: Brookings Institution Press.

Davies, J. Clarence. 1984. "Environmental Institutions and the Reagan Administration." In *Environmental Policy in the 1980s*, ed. N. Vig and M. Kraft. Washington, D.C.: CQ Press.

de Tocqueville, Alexis. 1966 [1835]. *Democracy in America.* Ed. J. P. Mayer and M. Lerner. New York: Harper and Row.

Derlien, Hans-Ulrich. 1985. "Politicization of the Civil Service in the Federal Republic of Germany—Facts and Fables." In *The Politicization of Public Administration*, ed. F. Meyers. Brussels: International Institute of Administrative Sciences, 3–38.

———. 1996. "The Politicization of Bureaucracies in Historical Perspective." In *Agenda for Excellence 2: Administering the State*, ed. B. G. Peters and B. A. Rockman. Chatham, N.J.: Chatham House.

Devine, Donald J. 1987. "Political Administration: The Right Way." In *Steering the Elephant: How Washington Works*, ed. R. Rector and M. Sanera. New York: Universe Books.

Dickinson, Matthew J. 1997. *Bitter Harvest: FDR, Presidential Power and the Growth of the Presidential Branch.* New York: Cambridge University Press.

———. 2005. "Who Counts? Measuring White House Staff Size, 1947–2004." Paper presented at the annual meeting of the American Political Science Association, Washington, D.C.

Dresang, Dennis L. 2002. *Public Personnel Management and Public Policy.* 4th ed. New York: Longman.

Dudley, Susan, and Melinda Warren. 2003. *Regulatory Spending Soars: An Analysis of the U.S. Budget for Fiscal Years 2003 and 2004.* St. Louis: Weidenbaum Center, Washington University.

Dunn, Delmer D. 1997. *Politics and Administration at the Top: Lessons from Down Under.* Pittsburgh: University of Pittsburgh Press.

Durant, Robert F. 1992. *The Administrative Presidency Revisited: Public Lands, the BLM, and the Reagan Revolution.* Albany: State University of New York Press.

Dutt, Sagarika. 1995. *The Politicization of the United Nations Specialized Agencies: A Case Study of UNESCO.* Lewiston, N.Y.: Edwin Mellen Press.

Edwards, George C., III. 2001. "Why Not the Best? The Loyalty-Competence Trade-Off in Presidential Appointments." *Brookings Review* 19 (2):12–16.

Ellig, Jerry. 2000. *Learning from the Leaders: Results-based Management at the Federal Emergency Management Administration.* Washington, D.C.: Mercatus Center, George Washington University.

Epstein, David, and Sharyn O'Halloran. 1999. *Delegating Powers.* New York: Cambridge University Press.

Evans, Peter, and James E. Rauch. 1999. "Bureaucracy and Growth: A Cross-National Analysis of the Effects of 'Weberian' State Structures on Economic Growth." *American Sociological Review* 64:748–65.

Fry, Geoffrey K. 1984. "The Development of the Thatcher Government's 'Grand Strategy' for the Civil Service: A Public Policy Perspective." *Public Administration Review* 62:322–35.

Gailmard, Sean, and John W. Patty. 2007. "Slackers and Zealots: Civil Service, Policy Discretion, and Bureaucratic Expertise." *American Journal of Political Science*, 51(4):873–89.

George, Alexander L. 1980. *Presidential Decisionmaking in Foreign Policy: The Effective Use of Information and Advice.* Boulder Colo.: Westview.

Gilmour, John. 2006. "Implementing OMB's Program Assessment Rating Tool (PART): Meeting the Challenges of Integrating Budget and Performance." Report, IBM Center for the Business of Government. Available online at businessofgovernment.org/pdfs/GilmourReport.pdf.

Gilmour, John, and David E. Lewis. 2006a. "Assessing Performance Budgeting at OMB: The Influence of Politics, Performance, and Program Size in FY 2005." *Journal of Public Administration Research and Theory* 16 (2):169–86.

———. 2006b. "Does Performance Budgeting Work? An Examination of OMB's PART Scores." *Public Administration Review* 66(5):742–52.

———. 2006c. "Political Appointees and the Competence of Federal Program Management." *American Politics Research* 34 (1):22–50.

Golden, Marissa Martino. 2000. *What Motivates Bureaucrats? Politics and Administration During the Reagan Years.* New York: Columbia University Press.

Goldenberg, Edie N. 1984. "The Permanent Government in an Era of Retrenchment and Redirection." In *The Reagan Presidency and the Governing of America,* ed. L. M. Salamon and M. S. Lund. Washington, D.C.: Urban Institute Press.

———. 1985. "The Grace Commission and Civil Service Reform: Seeking a Common Understanding." In *The Unfinished Agenda for Civil Service Reform,* ed. C. H. Levine. Washington, D.C.: Brookings Institution Press.

Gore, Al. 1993. *From Red Tape to Results: Creating a Government that Works Better and Costs Less.* New York: Basic.

Halberstam, David. 1969. *The Best and the Brightest.* New York: Random House.

Heclo, Hugh. 1975. "OMB and the Presidency—The Problem of 'Neutral Competence.' " *The Public Interest* 38 (Winter):80–98.

———. 1977. *A Government of Strangers: Executive Politics in Washington.* Washington, D.C.: Brookings Institution Press.

Henry, Laurin L. 1958. "Transferring the Presidency." Paper presented at Annual Meeting of the American Political Science Association, St. Louis, Mo.

———. 1960. *Presidential Transitions.* Washington, D.C.: Brookings Institution Press.

———. 1969. "The Presidency, Executive Staffing, and the Federal Bureaucracy." In *The Presidency,* ed. A. Wildavsky. Boston: Little, Brown, and Co.

Hess, Stephen, and James P. Pfiffner, eds. 2002. *Organizing the Presidency.* Washington, D.C.: Brookings Insitution Press.

Hogue, Henry. 2003. *Homeland Security: Components and Management Positions in the New Department, Congressional Research Service Report for Congress, RL 31492.* Washington, D.C.: Congressional Research Service.

———. 2004. *Filling Presidentially Appointed, Senate-Confirmed Positions in the Department of Homeland Security, Congressional Research Service Report for Congress, RL 31677.* Washington, D.C.: Congressional Research Service.

———. 2005. "Presidential Appointments Requiring the Advice and Consent of the Senate: Background and Current Issues." In *Science and Technology in the National Interest: Ensuring the Best Presidential and Federal Advisory Committee Science and Technology Appointments,* ed. National Academy of Sciences. Washington, D.C.: National Academy Press.

Hogue, Henry B., and Keith Bea. 2006. *Federal Emergency Management and Homeland Security Organization: Historical Development and Legislative Options, Congressional Research Service Report for Congress,* June 1, 2006.

Hollis, Amanda Lee. 2005. "A Tale of Two Federal Emergency Management Agencies." *Forum* 3(3):1–14.

Howell, William G. 2003. *Power Without Persuasion: A Theory of Presidential Action.* Princeton, N.J.: Princeton University Press.

Howell, William G., and David E. Lewis. 2002. "Agencies by Presidential Design." *Journal of Politics* 64 (4):1095–1114.

Huber, John D., and Nolan M. McCarty. 2004. "Bureaucratic Capacity, Delegation, and Political Reform." *American Political Science Review* 98 (3):481–94.

Huber, John D., and Charles R. Shipan. 2002. *Deliberate Discretion?* New York: Cambridge University Press.

Huddleston, Mark W., and William W. Boyer. 1996. *The Higher Civil Service in the United States: Quest for Reform.* Pittsburgh: University of Pittsburgh Press.

Imber, Mark F. 1989. *The USA, ILO, UNESCO, and IAEA: Politicization and Withdrawal in the Specialized Agencies.* Southhampton, U.K.: Macmillan.

Ingraham, Patricia W. 1984. "The Civil Service Reform Act of 1978: The Design and Legislative History." In Patricia W. Ingraham and Carolyn Ban, eds. *Legislating Bureaucratic Change: The Civil Service Reform Act of 1984.* Albany: State University of New York Press.

———. 1992. "The Reform Game." In *The Promise and Paradox of Civil Service Reform,* ed. Patricia W. Ingraham and D. H. Rosenbloom. Pittsburgh: University of Pittsburgh Press.

Johnson, Ronald N., and Gary D. Libecap. 1994. *The Federal Civil Service System and the Problem of Bureaucracy.* Chicago: University of Chicago Press.

Jones, Charles O. 2000. *Preparing to Be President: The Memos of Richard E. Neustadt.* Washington, D.C.: AEI Press.

Jordan, Stuart V. 2007. "OIRA Review and Presidential Control of Agencies." Working paper, University of Rochester.

Kaufman, Herbert. 1965. "The Growth of the Federal Personnel System." In *The Federal Government Service*, ed. W. S. Sayre. Englewood Cliffs, N.J.: Prentice-Hall.

———. 1976. *Are Government Organizations Immortal?* Washington, D.C.: Brookings Institution Press.

Kerwin, Cornelius M. 1999. *Rulemaking: How Government Agencies Write Law and Make Policy.* 2nd ed. Washington, D.C.: CQ Press.

Kettl, Donald F., and James W. Fesler. 2005. *The Politics of the Administrative Process.* 3rd ed. Washington, D.C.: CQ Press.

Krause, George A. 2002. "Signal Uncertainty, Organization of Political Institutions, and the Pursuit of Bureaucratic Responsiveness." Paper presented at Political Control of the Bureaucracy Conference, George H. W. Bush School of Government and Public Service, Texas A&M University, College Station, Tex.

Krause, George A., and J. Kevin Corder. 2007. "Explaining Bureaucratic Optimism: Theory and Evidence from U.S. Federal Executive Agency Macroeconomic Forecasts." *American Political Science Review* 101 (February):129–42.

Krause, George A., and James W. Douglas. 2005. "Institutional Design versus Reputational Effects on Bureaucratic Performance: Evidence from U.S. Government Macroeconomic and Fiscal Projections." *Journal of Public Administration Research and Theory* 15 (2):281–306.

———. 2006. "Does Agency Competition Improve the Quality of Policy Analysis? Evidence from OMB and CBO Current-Year Fiscal Projections." *Journal of Policy Analysis and Management* 25 (Winter):53–74.

Krause, George A., David E. Lewis, and James W. Douglas. 2006. "Political Appointments, Civil Service Systems, and Bureaucratic Competence: Organizational Balancing and Gubernatorial Revenue Forecasts in the American States." *American Journal of Political Science* 50 (3):770–87.

Lane, Larry M. 1988–89. "The Administration and Politics of Reform: The Office of Personnel Management." *Policy Studies Journal* 17(2):331–51.

———. 1992. "The Office of Personnel Management: Values, Policies, and Consequences." In *The Promise and Paradox of Civil Service Reform*, ed. Patricia W. Ingraham and D. H. Rosenbloom. Pittsburgh: University of Pittsburgh Press.

Levitan, David M. 1946. "The Responsibility of Administrative Officials in a Democratic Society." *Political Science Quarterly* 61 (4):562–98.

Lewis, David E. 2002. "The Politics of Agency Termination: Confronting the Myth of Agency Immortality." *The Journal of Politics* 64 (1):89–107.

———. 2003. *Presidents and the Politics of Agency Design: Political Insulation in the United States Government Bureaucracy, 1946–1997.* Stanford: Stanford University Press.

———. 2005a. "The Presidency and the Bureaucracy: Management Imperatives in a Separation of Powers System." In *The Presidency and the Political System*, ed. M. Nelson. Washington, D.C.: CQ Press.

———. 2005b. "Presidents and the Politicization of the United States Federal Government, 1988–2004." Paper presented at Annual Meeting of the Midwest Political Science Association, Chicago, Ill.

———. 2005c. "Staffing Alone: Unilateral Action and the Politicization of the Executive Office of the President, 1988–2004." *Presidential Studies Quarterly* 35 (3):496–514.

———. 2007. "Testing Pendleton's Premise: Do Political Appointees Make Worse Bureaucrats?" *Journal of Politics* 69 (4):1073–88.

Lewis, Gregory. 1991. "Turnover and the Quiet Crisis in the Federal Civil Service." *Public Administration Review* 51 (2):145–55.

Light, Paul. 1992. *Forging Legislation*. New York: W. W. Norton.

———. 1995. *Thickening Government: Federal Hierarchy and the Diffusion of Accountability*. Washington, D.C.: Brookings Institution Press.

———. 1999. *The True Size of Government*. Washington, D.C.: Brookings Institution Press.

Long, Norton E. 1949. "Power and Administration." *Public Administration Review* 9(4):257–64.

———. 1954. "Public Policy and Administration: The Goals of Rationality and Responsibility." *Public Administration Review* 14(1): 22–31.

Lucier, Chuck, Rob Schuyt, and Eric Spiegel. 2003. "Deliver or Depart: CEO Succession 2002." *strategy+business* 31 (Summer):32–45.

Mackenzie, G. Calvin, ed. 1987. *The In-and-Outers: Presidential Appointees and Transient Government in Washington*. Baltimore, Md.: The Johns Hopkins University Press.

Mann, Dean E. 1964. "The Selection of Federal Political Executives." *American Political Science Review* 58 (1):81–99.

———. 1965. *The Assistant Secretaries: Problems and Processes of Appointments*. Washington, D.C.: Brookings Institution Press.

Mann, Pleasant. 2004. Letter to Senator Hillary Rodham Clinton, June 21, 2004 *(available online at www.pogo.org/*m/cp/cp-2004-AFGE4060-FEMA.pdf*)*.

Maranto, Robert. 1998a. "Rethinking the Unthinkable: Reply to Durant, Goodsell, Knott, and Murray on 'A Case for Spoils' in Federal Personnel Management." *Administration and Society* 30 (1):3–12.

———. 1998b. "Thinking the Unthinkable in Public Administration: 'A Case for Spoils' in the Federal Bureaucracy." *Administration and Society* 29 (6):623–42.

———. 2001. "Why the President Should Ignore Calls to Reduce the Number of Political Appointees." *Heritage Foundation Backgrounder* (1413).

———. 2004. "Bureaus in Motion: Civil Servants Compare the Clinton, George H. W. Bush, and Reagan Presidential Transitions." *White House Studies* 4 (4):435–51.

Maranto, Robert, and Karen M. Hult. 2004. "Right Turn? Political Ideology in the Higher Civil Service, 1987–1994." *American Review of Public Administration* 34 (2):199–222.

Mascarenhas, R.C. 1993. "Building an Enterprise Culture in the Public Sector: Reform of the Public Sector in Australia, Britain, and New Zealand." *Public Administration Review* 53 (4):319–28.

McCarty, Nolan M., and Keith T. Poole. 1995. "Veto Power and Legislation: An Empirical Analysis of Executive and Legislative Bargaining from 1961 to 1986." *Journal of Law, Economics, and Organization* 11 (2):282–312.

McCarty, Nolan M., and Rose Razaghian. 1999. "Advice and Consent: Senate Responses to Executive Branch Nominations, 1885–1996." *American Journal of Political Science* 43 (3):1122–43.

McCarty, Nolan M., Keith T. Poole, and Howard Rosenthal. 2006. *Polarized America: The Dance of Ideology and Unequal Riches.* Boston, Mass.: MIT Press.

McCubbins, Mathew D., and Thomas Schwartz. 1984. "Congressional Oversight Overlooked: Police Patrols versus Fire Alarms." *American Journal of Political Science* 32 (1):165–77.

McCubbins, Mathew D., Roger Noll, and Barry Weingast. 1987. "Administrative Procedures as Instruments of Political Control." *Journal of Law, Economics, and Organization* 3:243–77.

———. 1989. "Structure and Process, Politics and Policy: Administrative Arrangements and the Political Control of Agencies." *Virginia Law Review* 75 (2):431–82.

McDonald, Forrest. 1994. *The American Presidency: An Intellectual History.* Lawrence: University Press of Kansas.

Meier, Kenneth J. 2000. *Politics and the Bureaucracy: Policymaking in the Fourth Branch of Government.* 4th ed. Orlando, Fla.: Harcourt.

Merikoski, Veli. 1969. *The Politicization of Public Administration.* Helsinki: Suomalainen Tiedeakatemia.

Moe, Terry M. 1982. "Regulatory Performance and Presidential Administration." *American Journal of Political Science* 26 (2):197–224.

———. 1985a. "Control and Feedback in Economic Regulation: The Case of the NLRB." *American Political Science Review* 79 (4):1094–1116.

———. 1985b. "The Politicized Presidency." In *The New Direction in American Politics,* ed. J. E. Chubb and P. E. Peterson. Washington, D.C.: Brookings Institution Press.

———. 1989. "The Politics of Bureaucratic Structure." In *Can the Government Govern?* ed. J. E. Chubb and P. E. Peterson. Washington, D.C.: Brookings Institution Press.

———. 2006. "Political Control and the Power of the Agent." *Journal of Law, Economics, and Organization* 22 (1):1–29.

Moe, Terry M., and Scott A. Wilson. 1994. "Presidents and the Politics of Structure." *Law and Contemporary Problems* 57 (2):1–44.

Moore, Mark H. 1995. *Creating Public Value.* Cambridge, Mass.: Harvard University Press.

Mosher, Frederick C. *Democracy and the Public Service.* New York: Oxford University Press.

Nathan, Richard P. 1975. *The Plot that Failed: Nixon and the Administrative Presidency.* New York: John Wiley and Sons.

———. 1983. *The Administrative Presidency.* New York: John Wiley and Sons.

National Academy of Public Administration. 1984. *Presidential Appointee Project: Conference of Former Presidential Personnel Assistants.* Washington, D.C.: National Academy of Public Administration.

———. 1993. *Coping with Catastrophe: Building an Emergency Management System that Meets People's Needs in Natural and Manmade Disasters.* Washington, D.C.: National Academy of Public Administration.

———. 2004. *Recommending Performance-Based Federal Pay.* Washington, D.C.: National Academy of Public Administration.

National Academy of Sciences. 1992. *Science and Technology Leadership in American Government: Ensuring the Best Presidential Appointments.* Washington, D.C.: National Academy Press.

———. 2000. *Science and Technology in the National Interest: The Presidential Appointment Process.* Washington, D.C.: National Academy Press.

———. 2004. *Science and Technology in the National Interest: Ensuring the Best Presidential and Federal Advisory Committee Science and Technology Appointments.* Washington, D.C.: National Academy Press.

National Commission on the Public Service. 1989. *Leadership for America: Rebuilding the Public Service.* Washington, D.C.: Brookings Institution Press.

———. 2003. *Urgent Business for America: Revitalizing the Federal Government for the 21st Century.* Washington, D.C.: Brookings Institution Press.

Nelson, Michael. 1982. "A Short, Ironic History of the American National Bureaucracy." *Journal of Politics* 44:747–78.

———, ed. 2004. *The Evolving Presidency.* 2nd ed. Washington, D.C.: CQ Press.

Neustadt, Richard E. 1990 [1960]. *Presidential Power and the Modern Presidents: The Politics of Leadership from Roosevelt to Reagan.* New York: Free Press.

———. 2000. "Neustadt Advises the Advisers." In *Preparing To Be President: The Memos of Richard E. Neustadt,* ed. C. O. Jones. Washington, D.C.: AEI Press.

Patterson, Bradley H., Jr. 2000. *The White House Staff: Inside the West Wing and Beyond.* Washington, D.C.: Brookings Institution Press.

Patterson, Bradley H., Jr., and James P. Pfiffner. 2001. "The White House Office of Presidential Personnel." *Presidential Studies Quarterly* 31(3):415–38.

———. 2003. "The Office of Presidential Personnel." In *The White House World,* ed. M. J. Kumar and T. Sullivan. College Station, Tex.: Texas A&M University Press.

Pfiffner, James P. 1996 [1988]. *The Strategic Presidency: Hitting the Ground Running.* Lawrence: University Press of Kansas.

Poole, Keith. 1998. "Estimating a Basic Space from a Set of Issue Scales." *American Journal of Political Science* 42 (July):954–93.

Pressman, Jeffrey L., and Aaron Wildavsky. 1973. *Implementation.* Berkeley: University of California Press.

Raadschelders, Jos C. N., and Kwang-Hoon Lee. 2005. "Between Amateur Government and Career Civil Service: The American Administrative Elite in Cross-Time and Comparative Perspective." *Jahrbuch Fur Europaische Verwaltungsgeschichte* 17:201–22.

Rainey, Hal G., and Paula Steinbauer. 1999. "Galloping Elephants: Developing Elements of a Theory of Effective Government Organizations." *Journal of Public Administration Research and Theory* 9 (1):1–32.

Randall, Ronald. 1979. "Presidential Powers versus Bureaucratic Intransigence: The Influence of the Nixon Administration on Welfare Policy." *American Political Science Review* 73 (3):795–810.

Rapoport, Ronald B., and Walter J. Stone. 2005. *Three's a Crowd: The Dynamic of Third Parties, Ross Perot, and Republican Resurgence.* Ann Arbor: University of Michigan Press.

Rauch, James E., and Peter Evans. 2000. "Bureaucratic Structure and Bureaucratic Performance in Less Developed Countries." *Journal of Public Economics* 75:49–71.

Rhodes, R.A.W. 2000. "New Labour's Civil Service: Summing-up Joining-up." *Political Quarterly* 71 (2):151–66.

Ridley, Frederick. 1985. "Politics and the Selection of Higher Civil Servants in Britain." In *The Politicization of Public Administration,* ed. F. Meyers. Brussels: International Institute of Administrative Sciences.

Roberts, Patrick S. 2006. "FEMA and the Prospects for Reputation-Based Autonomy." *Studies in American Political Development* 20 (Spring):57–87.

Rosen, Bernard. 1982–83. "A Disaster for Merit." *Bureaucrat* (Winter):8–18.

———. 1983. "Effective Continuity of U.S. Government Operations in Jeopardy." *Public Administration Review* 43 (5):383–92.

Rosenbloom, David H. 1979. "Civil Service Reform, 1978: Some Issues." *Midwest Review of Public Administration* 13 (September):171–75.

———. 1997. "The U.S. Constitutional Separation of Powers and Federal Administration." In *Modern Systems of Government: Exploring the Role of Bureaucrats and Politicians,* ed. A. Farazmand. Thousand Oaks, Calif.: Sage.

Rouban, Luc. 2003. "Politicization of the Civil Service." In *Handbook of Public Administration,* ed. B. G. Peters and J. Pierre. London: Sage.

Rourke, Francis E. 1992. "Responsiveness and Neutral Competence in American Bureaucracy." *Public Administration Review* 52 (6):539–46.

———. 1997. "Politics and Bureaucracy: Their Impact on Professionalism." In *Modern Systems of Government: Exploring the Role of Bureaucrats and Politicians,* ed. A. Farazmand. Thousand Oaks, Calif.: Sage.

Rudalevige, Andrew. 2002. *Managing the President's Program: Centralization and Legislative Policy Formulation, 1949–1996.* Princeton, N.J.: Princeton University Press.

Rudalevige, Andrew, and David E. Lewis. 2005. "Parsing the Politicized Presidency: Centralization, Politicization, and Presidential Strategies for Bureaucratic Control." Paper presented at Annual Meeting of the American Political Science Association, Washington, D.C.

Salamon, Lester M., and Alan J. Abramson. 1984. "Governance: The Politics of Retrenchment." In *The Reagan Record,* ed. J. L. Palmer and I. V. Sawhill. Cambridge, Mass.: Ballinger.

Schimmel, Rob. 2006. *Structure and Performance at the Federal Emergency Management Agency: The Lessons of History, DHS, and Katrina.* Undergraduate Senior Thesis, Princeton University.

Schlesinger, Arthur M., Jr. 1965. *A Thousand Days.* Boston, Mass.: Houghton Mifflin.

Schneider, Saundra K. 1998. "Reinventing Public Administration: A Case Study of the Federal Emergency Management Agency." *Public Administration Quarterly* 22(1):35–57.

Simon, Herbert A., Victor A. Thompson, and Donald W. Smithburg. 1991 [1950]. *Public Administration.* New Brunswick, N.J.: Transaction.

Skowronek, Stephen. 1982. *Building a New American State: The Expansion of National Administrative Capacities, 1877–1920.* New York: Cambridge University Press.

Somers, Herman Miles. 1965. "The President, Congress, and the Federal Government Service." In *The Federal Government Service,* ed. W. S. Sayre. Englewood Cliffs, N.J.: Prentice-Hall.

Stahlberg, Krister. 1987. "The Politicization of Public Administration: Notes on the Concept, Causes, and Consequences of Politicization." *International Review of Administrative Sciences* 53:363–82.

Stanley, David T., Dean E. Mann, and Jameson W. Doig. 1967. *Men Who Govern: A Biographical Profile of Federal Political Executives.* Washington, D.C.: Brookings Institution Press.

Stanley, Harold W., and Richard G. Niemi. 2006. *Vital Statistics on American Politics, 2005–2006.* Washington, D.C.: CQ Press.

Starobin, Paul. 1984. "Surviving at EPA." John F. Kennedy School of Government Case Program. Cambridge, Mass.: John F. Kennedy School of Government, Harvard University.

Stewart, Joseph, Jr., and Jane S. Cromartie. 1982. "Partisan Presidential Change and Regulatory Policy: The Case of the FTC and Deceptive Practices Enforcement, 1938–1974." *Presidential Studies Quarterly* 12 (4):568–73.

Stillman, Richard J. 2000. *Public Administration: Concepts and Cases.* 7th ed. Boston, Mass.: Houghton Mifflin.

Sugiyama, Shigeki. 1985. *Protecting the Integrity of the Merit System: A Legislative History of the Merit System Principles, Prohibited Personnel Practices, and the Office of Special Counsel.* Washington, D.C.: Office of the Special Counsel, Merit Systems Protection Board.

Suleiman, Ezra. 2003. *Dismantling Democratic States.* Princeton, N.J.: Princeton University Press.

Sullivan, Matthew D. 2006. *Structural Problems Hindering FEMA in the Aftermath of Hurricane Katrina.* Undergraduate Senior Thesis, Princeton University.

Sylves, Richard T. 1994. "Ferment at FEMA: Reforming Emergency Management." *Public Administration Review* 54(3):303–7.

Tendler, Judith. 1997. *Good Government in the Tropics.* Baltimore, Md.: The Johns Hopkins University Press.

Theriault, Sean M. 2003. "Patronage, the Pendleton Act, and the Power of the People." *Journal of Politics* 65 (1):50–68.

Thompson, James R. 2001. "The Civil Service Under Clinton: The Institutional Consequences of Disaggregation." *Review of Public Personnel Administration* 21 (2):87–113.

U.S. Civil Service Commission/Office of Personnel Management. Various Years. *Employment and Trends.* Washington, D.C.: Government Printing Office.

U.S. Commission on National Security/21st Century. 2001. *Road Map for National Security: Imperative for Change* (available online at www.nssg.gov).

U.S. Congressional Research Service. 1976. *History of the Civil Service Merit Systems of the United States and Selected Foreign Countries.* Washington, D.C.: Government Printing Office.

U.S. Congress. House Committee on Post Office and Civil Service. 1960. *Policy and Supporting Positions* 86th Cong., 2nd Sess.

U.S. Congress. House. Committee on Post Office and Civil Service. 1968. *Policy and Supporting Positions.* 92nd Cong., 2nd Sess.

U.S. Congress. House Committee on Post Office and Civil Service. 1976a. *History of the Civil Service Merit Systems of the United States and Selected Foreign Countries.* Washington, D.C.: Government Printing Office.

U.S. Congress. House. Committee on Post Office and Civil Service. 1976b. *Policy and Supporting Positions.* 96th Cong., 2nd Sess.

U.S. Congress. House. Committee on Post Office and Civil Service. 1984. *Policy and Supporting Positions.* 100th Cong., 2nd Sess.

U.S. Congress. House. Committee on Appropriations. 1992. *Report on the Federal Emergency Management Agency* (Point paper). 103rd Congress, 1st Sess. Reprinted in CQ Electronic Library, CQ Historic Documents Series Online Edition, hsdc92–0000090942 (available online at http://library.cqpress.com/historicdocuments/hsdc92–0000090942).

U.S. Congress. House. Committee on Post Office and Civil Service. 1996. *Policy and Supporting Positions.* 104th Cong., 2nd Sess.

U.S. Congress. House. Committee on Government Reform. 2004. *Policy and Supporting Positions*, 108th Cong., 2nd Sess.

U.S. Congress House. Committee on Government Reform. Minority Staff. 2006a. *The Growth of Political Appointees in the Bush Administration.* May 2006 (available online at http://oversight.house.gov/Documents/20060503160909–97328.pdf).

U.S. Congress. House Select Bipartisan Committee to Investigate the Preparation for and Response to Hurricane Katrina. 2006b. *A Failure of Initiative: The Final Report of the Select Bipartisan Committee to Investigate the Preparation for and Response to Hurricane Katrina.* 109th Congress, 2nd Sess. (available online at www.katrina.house.gov/full_katrina_report.html).

U.S. Congress. Senate. Committee on Post Office and Civil Service. 1964. *Policy and Supporting Positions.* 86th. Cong. 2nd Sess.

U.S. Congress. Senate. Committee on Post Office and Civil Service. 1973. *Policy and Supporting Positions.* 93rd Cong. 1st Sess.

U.S. Congress. Senate. Committee on Governmental Affairs. 1980. *Policy and Supporting Positions.* 98th Cong., 2nd Sess.

U.S. Congress. Senate. Committee on Governmental Affairs. 1988. *Policy and Supporting Positions.* 102nd Cong., 2nd Sess.

U.S. Congress. Senate. Committee on Governmental Affairs. 2000. *Policy and Supporting Positions.* 106th Cong., 2nd Sess.

U.S. Congress. Senate. Committee on Homeland Security and Government Affairs. 2006. *Hurricane Katrina: A Nation Still Unprepared.* 109th Cong., 2nd

Sess. (available online at www.hsgac.senate.gov/index.cfm?Fuseaction=Links .Katrina).

U.S. Congress. Select Committee on Presidential Campaign Activities. 1973. *Presidential Campaign Activities of 1972*, vol. 19: *Watergate and Related Activities, Use of Incumbency-Responsiveness Program.* 93rd Cong., 2nd Sess.

U.S. Department of Commerce. Bureau of the Census. *Historical Statistics of the United States: Colonial Times to 1970.* Washington, D.C.: Government Printing Office.

U.S. Department of Defense. Directorate for Information Operations and Reports. 2004. *Active Duty Military Personnel by Rank/Grade.* Washington, D.C.: U.S. Department of Defense.

U.S. General Accounting Office. 1987. *Federal Employees: Trends in Career and Noncareer Appointments in Selected Departments.* GAO/GGD-87–103FS. Washington, D.C.: General Accounting Office.

———. 1989. *Managing Human Resources: Greater OPM Leadership Needed to Address Critical Challenges.* GAO/GGD-89–19. Washington, D.C.: General Accounting Office.

———. 1992. *Political Appointees: Number of Noncareer SES and Schedule C Employees in Federal Agencies.* GAO/GGD-92–191FS. Washington, D.C.: General Accounting Office.

———. 1995a. *Civil Service Reform: Changing Times Demand New Approaches.* Washington, D.C.: General Accounting Office.

———. 1995b. *Personnel Practices: Selected Characteristics of Recent Ramspeck Act Appointments.* GAO/GGD-95–173. Washington, D.C.: General Accounting Office.

———. 1997a. *The Excepted Service: A Research Profile.* Washington, D.C.: United States General Accounting Office.

———. 1997b. *Personnel Practices: Career Appointments of Former Political and Congressional Employees.* GAO/GGD-97–165. Washington, D.C.: General Accounting Office.

———. 2000. *Personnel Practices: Career Appointments Granted Political Appointees From October 1998 Through June 2000.* GAO/GGD-00–205. Washington, D.C.: General Accounting Office.

U.S. Government Accountability Office. 2004a. *Performance Budgeting: Observations on the Use of OMB's Program Assessment Rating Tool for the Fiscal Year 2004 Budget.* GAO-04-174. Washington, D.C.: Government Accountability Office.

———. 2004b. *U.S. Office of Special Counsel: Strategy for Reducing Persistent Backlog of Cases Should Be Provided to Congress.* GAO-04-36. Washington, D.C.: Government Accountability Office.

———. 2005a. *Performance Budgeting: PART Focuses Attention on Program Performance, but More Can Be Done to Engage Congress.* GAO-O6–28. Washington, D.C.: Government Accountability Office.

———. 2005b. *U.S. Office of Special Counsel: Selected Contracting and Human Capital Issues.* GAO-06-16. Washington, D.C.: Government Accountability Office.

U.S. National Archives and Records Administration. Office of the Federal Register. Various Years. *United States Government Manual.* Washington, D.C.: Government Printing Office.

U.S. Office of Management and Budget. 2002. *Instructions for the Program Assessment Rating Tool.* Washington, D.C., July 12, 2002.

———. 2003. *Budget of the United States Government FY 2004: Performance Management and Assessments.* Washington, D.C.: Government Printing Office.

———. 2005. *Budget of the United States Government, FY2006: Program Assessment Rating Tool.* Washington, D.C.: Government Printing Office.

U.S. Office of Personnel Management. N.d. *Evolution of Federal White-Collar Pay* (available online at www.opm.gov/strategiccomp/HTML/HISTORY1.asp).

———. *Central Personnel Data File* (available online at www.http://fedscope .opm.gov).

———. 1997. *The Fact Book.* Washington, D.C.: Office of Personnel Management.

———. 2001. *Guide to the Senior Executive Service.* Washington, D.C.: Office of Personnel Management.

———. 2002. *What Do Federal Employees Say? Results from the 2002 Federal Human Capital Survey.* Washington, D.C.: Office of Personnel Management.

———. 2003a. *Biography of an Ideal: A History of the Federal Civil Service.* Washington, D.C.: Government Printing Office.

———. 2003b. *Federal Civilian Workforce Statistics, May 2003.* Washington, D.C.: Office of Personnel Management.

———. 2003c. *The Fact Book.* Washington, D.C.: Government Printing Office.

———. 2004. *What Do Federal Employees Say? Results from the 2004 Federal Human Capital Survey.* Appendix B. Washington, D.C.: Office of Personnel Management (available online at www.fhcs2004.opm.gov/FHCS_2004_Report.pdf).

———. 2006. *The Guide to Personnel Data Standards.* Washington, D.C.: Office of Personnel Management (available online at www.opm.gov/feddata/ guidance.htm).

Van Riper, Paul P. 1958. *History of the United States Civil Service.* Evanston, Ill.: Row, Peterson and Company.

Wamsley, Gary L., and Aaron D. Schroeder. 1996. "Escalating the Quagmire: The Changing Dynamics of the Emergency Management Policy Subsystem." *Public Administration Review* 56(3): 235–44.

Wamsley, Gary L., Aaron D. Schroeder, and Larry M. Lane. 1996. "To Politicize is Not to Control: The Pathologies of Control in the Federal Emergency Management Agency." *American Review of Public Administration* 26(3):263–85.

Ward, Robert, Gary Wamsley, Aaron Schroeder, and David B. Robins. 2000. "Network Organizational Development in the Public Sector: A Case Study of the Federal Emergency Management Administration (FEMA)." *Journal of the American Society for Informational Science* 51(11):1018–32.

Weber, Max. 1946a. "Bureaucracy." In H. H. Gerth and C. Wright Mills, eds. *From Max Weber: Essays in Sociology.* New York: Oxford University Press.

———. 1946b. "Politics as a Vocation." In H. H. Gerth and C. Wright Mills, eds. *From Max Weber: Essays in Sociology.* New York: Oxford University Press.

Weko, Thomas J. 1995. *The Politicizing Presidency: The White House Personnel Office, 1948–1994.* Lawrence: University Press of Kansas.

West, Martin. 2006. "Bargaining with Authority: The Political Origins of Public-Sector Collective Bargaining." Unpublished Manuscript, Brown University.

White, Leonard D. 1954. *The Jacksonians: A Study in Administrative History, 1829–1861.* New York: Macmillan.

———. 1958. *The Republican Era, 1869–1901.* New York: Macmillan.

Whittington, Keith. 1999. *Constitutional Construction: Divided Powers and Constitutional Meaning.* Cambridge, Mass.: Harvard University Press.

Whittington, Keith, and Daniel P. Carpenter. 2003. "Executive Power in American Institutional Development." *Perspectives on Politics* 1 (3):495–513.

Wilson, James Q. 1989. *Bureaucracy.* New York: Basic.

Wilson, Woodrow. 1887. "The Study of Administration." *Political Science Quarterly* 2 (June):197–222.

Wood, B. Dan. 1990. "Does Politics Make a Difference at the EEOC?" *American Journal of Political Science* 34 (2):503–30.

Wood, B. Dan, and James E. Anderson. 1993. "The Politics of U.S. Antitrust Regulation." *American Journal of Political Science* 37 (1):1–39.

Wood, B. Dan, and Richard W. Waterman. 1991. "The Dynamics of Political Control of the Bureaucracy." *American Political Science Review* 85 (3):801–28.

———. 1994. *Bureaucratic Dynamics: The Role of Bureaucracy in a Democracy, Transforming American Politics.* Boulder, Colo.: Westview.

Zegart, Amy B. 1999. *Flawed by Design.* Stanford: Stanford University Press.

Zuck, Alfred M. 1989. "The Future Role of OPM." *Bureaucrat* 18 (Spring):20–22.

Index